EXPERIENCING PUBLIC RELATIONS

Experiencing Public Relations examines the everyday experiences of PR practitioners in order to better understand how public relations is perceived by those both outside and within the field. The book aims to provoke debate around the nature of public relations by looking at how it is defined at a theoretical level, compared to how it is lived and represented in the real world.

Chapters feature work from some of the world's leading public relations scholars. They cover a diverse range of subjects, such as representations of PR in fiction and film, terrorist use of public relations, the impact of social media on this medium and a study of 'dirty work' within the PR industry. The book also explores international PR practices, presenting analysis from contributors based in Argentina, Australia, Brazil, Colombia, El Salvador, Germany, India, Mexico, New Zealand, Norway, Poland, Russia, Slovenia, South Africa, Spain, Sweden, Taiwan, UAE, UK, USA and Venezuela.

Experiencing Public Relations goes beyond the 'frontstage' scholarship of public relations to bring together stories of public relations in daily life, revealing how influential theories work out in practice and translate into different cultural and social contexts. This book will provide researchers, professionals and students with a vital perspective on the inner workings of public relations today.

Elizabeth Bridgen is Principal Lecturer in Public Relations at Sheffield Hallam University, UK. Her research explores the lives of public relations practitioners with a particular focus on gender, diversity, and the impact of technology on working lives.

Dejan Verčič is a professor and Head of the Department of Communication at University of Ljubljana, Slovenia. His research focuses on globalization and strategic communication. He is a member of the European Communication Monitor (www.communicationmonitor.eu) research team, and since 1994 he has organized BledCom (www.bledcom.com).

EXPERIENCING PUBLIC RELATIONS

International Voices

*Edited by Elizabeth Bridgen
and Dejan Verčič*

LONDON AND NEW YORK

First published 2018
by Routledge
2 Park Square, Milton Park, Abingdon, Oxon OX14 4RN

and by Routledge
711 Third Avenue, New York, NY 10017

Routledge is an imprint of the Taylor & Francis Group, an informa business

© 2018 selection and editorial matter, Elizabeth Bridgen and Dejan Verčič; individual chapters, the contributors

The right of Elizabeth Bridgen and Dejan Verčič to be identified as the authors of the editorial material, and of the authors for their individual chapters, has been asserted in accordance with sections 77 and 78 of the Copyright, Designs and Patents Act 1988.

All rights reserved. No part of this book may be reprinted or reproduced or utilised in any form or by any electronic, mechanical, or other means, now known or hereafter invented, including photocopying and recording, or in any information storage or retrieval system, without permission in writing from the publishers.

Trademark notice: Product or corporate names may be trademarks or registered trademarks, and are used only for identification and explanation without intent to infringe.

British Library Cataloguing-in-Publication Data
A catalogue record for this book is available from the British Library

Library of Congress Cataloging-in-Publication Data
Names: Bridgen, Elizabeth, editor. | Verčič, Dejan, editor.
Title: Experiencing public relations: international voices / edited by Elizabeth Bridgen and Dr. Dejan Verčič.
Description: Abingdon, Oxon; New York, NY: Routledge, 2018. | Includes index.
Identifiers: LCCN 2017022111 | ISBN 9781138632431 (hardback: alk. paper) | ISBN 9781138632448 (pbk.: alk. paper) | ISBN 9781315208251 (ebook)
Subjects: LCSH: Public relations–Cross-cultural studies. | Intercultural communication.
Classification: LCC HM1221 .E964 2018 | DDC 659.2–dc23
LC record available at https://lccn.loc.gov/2017022111

ISBN: 978-1-138-63243-1 (hbk)
ISBN: 978-1-138-63244-8 (pbk)
ISBN: 978-1-315-20825-1 (ebk)

Typeset in Bembo
by Deanta Global Publishing Services, Chennai, India

CONTENTS

List of figures	*vii*
List of tables	*viii*
List of contributors	*ix*

1 Introduction: experiencing public relations   1
Elizabeth Bridgen and Dejan Verčič

2 Experiencing public relations as an academic discipline:
What do scholarly views and published research tell us?   6
Alenka Jelen-Sanchez

3 Dealing in facts   26
Howard Nothhaft

4 Confessions of a public relations practitioner:
hidden life in the open plan office   39
Paul Willis

5 Personality in practice   51
Sarah Williams

6 Public relations as 'dirty work'   66
Elizabeth Bridgen

7 The anatomy of a spokesperson in South Africa: sometimes a
lie is kinder than a truth (African proverb)   81
Ronél Rensburg

vi Contents

8 'Can you see me?' Images of public relations in *Babylon*   95
Kate Fitch

9 Public relations in fiction   105
Philip Young

10 Social media and the rise of visual rhetoric: implications for
public relations theory and practice   123
Ganga S. Dhanesh

11 From propaganda to public diplomacy: the Chinese context   137
Chun-Ju Flora Hung-Baesecke and Minghua Xu

12 Influences of postcolonialism over the understanding and
evolution of public relations in Latin America   152
*Juan-Carlos Molleda, Ana María Suárez Monsalve, Andréia Silveira
Athaydes, Gabriel Sadi, Elim Hernández and Ricardo Valencia*

13 Fanning the flames of discontent: public relations as a
radical activity   165
Øyvind Ihlen

14 Subversion practices: from coercion to attraction   174
Sergei A. Samoilenko

15 Analysing terrorist use of public relations:
ISIS and Al Qaeda   194
Greg Simons

16 Epilogue: How people experience public relations:
applying Martin Buber's phenomenology to 'PR tree'   209
Jordi Xifra

Index   217

FIGURES

2.1 Pie chart showing orientation of the studies 17
2.2 Graph showing research approaches in public relations research 18
2.3 Graph showing research approaches in public relations journals 19
2.4 Graph showing the use of different research methods
in different periods 20

TABLES

2.1	Table showing sample size and number of articles published in selected journals 2006–2015	13
2.2	Table showing ten most prominent theories according to the number of the articles in which they are mentioned	15
3.1	Table showing Enlightenment ideals versus reality	30
6.1	Table showing examples of moral and emotional taint	70

CONTRIBUTORS

Andréia Silveira Athaydes has a PhD in Organizational Communication from the University of Málaga, Spain and a Masters in Administration and Marketing from the University of Business and Social Sciences, Argentina. She is a Professor Researcher and Advisor of International Relations at the Lutheran University of Brazil. She is a member of the Latin American Communication Monitor for Brazil.

Elizabeth Bridgen is Principal Lecturer in Public Relations at Sheffield Hallam University, UK and teaches on both postgraduate and undergraduate PR programmes. She previously lectured at De Montfort University, Leicester, UK and the University of Akureyri, Iceland. Her research explores the lived experience of people working in public relations and the impact that technology has on their lives, with a particular focus on gender and diversity. Her work has been published in *Journal of Media Practice* and *PRism* and she has written on practice issues for numerous online publications including *Comms2Point0* and *Vuelio.com*. She has also contributed to a number of practice-based books such as *How to Get a Job in PR* (2013) and *PRStack2* (2015).

Ganga S. Dhanesh PhD, (National University of Singapore) is Assistant Professor at the College of Communication and Media Sciences, Zayed University, United Arab Emirates. She has had experience in corporate and non-profit organisations and has published in the areas of corporate social responsibility and internal relations in books and journals such as *Journal of Communication Management, Journal of Public Relations Research, Management Communication Quarterly, Public Relations Review* and *Public Relations Inquiry*.

x Contributors

Kate Fitch PhD is a senior lecturer at Monash University in Melbourne, Australia; she previously lectured at Murdoch University. An award-winning teacher, she received an Australian Learning and Teaching Council Citation for Outstanding Contribution to Student Learning in 2011. Dr. Fitch has published on diverse public relations topics, including gender, history, social responsibility, pedagogy and popular culture. Her work has been published in *Public Relations Review, Public Relations Inquiry, Media International Australia, Ethical Space: International Journal of Communication Ethics* and *PRism.*

Elim Hernández is currently a second-year PhD student in Media Studies at the University of Oregon, US. He holds a Master of Art in Communication from the University of Texas Rio Grande Valley and a Bachelor of Art in Communication Sciences from the National Autonomous University of Mexico (UNAM). His research interests lie primarily in the area of strategic communication (advertising).

Chun-Ju Flora Hung-Baesecke teaches at Massey University in Albany, New Zealand. She is the 2015–2016, 2016–2017 Arthur W. Page Legacy Scholar and, in 2014, she was appointed as Educator Fellow by the Plank Center for Leadership in Public Relations, sponsored by Edelman Public Relations. She presents her research at international conferences and publishes in various international refereed public relations and communication journals, such as *Journal of Public Relations Research, Journal of Communication, Journalism & Mass Communication Quarterly* and *Public Relations Review.*

Øyvind Ihlen PhD is a professor at the Department of Media and Communication, University of Oslo and co-director of POLKOM - Centre for the Study of Political Communication. He has published over seventy journal articles and book chapters, and has produced nine books (in the capacity of either writer or editor), including *Public Relations and Social Theory: Key Figures and Concepts* (2009) and the award-winning *Handbook of Communication and Corporate Social Responsibility* (2011). His research focuses on strategic communication/public relations using theories of rhetoric and sociology.

Alenka Jelen-Sanchez PhD is a lecturer in Public Relations at the University of Stirling and teaches postgraduate modules on public relations and public communication theories, public affairs and advocacy, and research methods. Her research focuses on public relations as an academic discipline; relationships between media and politics; gender in media and public relations; and public communication of loss and mortality. Her research has been published in international academic journals *Public Relations Inquiry, British Politics* and *Public Relations Review.* She has edited books and professional public relations publications and regularly presents at academic conferences.

Contributors **xi**

Juan-Carlos Molleda PhD is Professor and Edwin L. Artzt Dean of the School of Journalism and Communication at the University of Oregon, US. He is also Academic Trustee of the Institute for Public Relations, Board Member of The LAGRANT Foundation and Co-Director of the Latin American Communication Monitor.

Howard Nothhaft PhD is Assistant Professor in Strategic Communication at the Department of Strategic Communication, Lund University, Campus Helsingborg, Sweden. He attained his PhD from Leipzig University with a dissertation based on a shadowing study of communication managers. His research interests lie in the area of communication strategy and the implications of strategic communication for democracy.

Ronél Rensburg (D Litt et Phil, CPRP, FPRISA) is the Head of the Division of Communication Management in the Faculty of Economic and Management Sciences at the University of Pretoria. Her areas of specialisation are communication and reputation management in corporate ethics, strategic communication in corporate governance, government communication and public relations. She is currently editing two textbooks in the areas of corporate communication and reputation management and revising a book on grassroots public relations in South Africa.

Gabriel Sadi is currently a PhD candidate (Communication) at Universidad Austral. In the academic field, in which he has been working the last thirteen years, he performs as Professor, Researcher and Director of the public relations programme at Universidad Abierta Interamericana, while carrying out duties as a Lecturer in Corporate Communication at the undergraduate and graduate level at Universidad de Belgrano. His main areas of interest are public relations epistemology and the social implications of the practice. He has over fifteen years' experience in public relations consultancy, mainly for non-profit organizations and governmental institutions.

Sergei A. Samoilenko is a public relations instructor in the Department of Communication at George Mason University, Fairfax, Virginia. His research focuses on issues in crisis communication and reputation management. Samoilenko is a founding member of CARP, the Research Lab for Character Assassination and Reputation Politics, based at George Mason University, Virginia (http://communication.gmu.edu/research-and-centers/carp). He is one of the editors of the forthcoming *Routledge Handbook for Character Assassination and Reputation Management*.

Greg Simons is currently a researcher at the Centre for Russian and Eurasian Studies (UCRS) at Uppsala University and a lecturer at the Department of Communication Science at Turiba University in Riga, Latvia. He teaches a course on Mass Media and Contemporary Armed Conflict at Uppsala University. He is

xii Contributors

on the Senior Editorial Board of the Journal for Political Marketing. His research interests include: changing political dynamics and relationships, mass media, public diplomacy, political marketing, crisis management communications, media and armed conflict and the Russian Orthodox Church. He also researches the relationships and connections between information, politics and armed conflict more broadly, such as the GWOT and Arab Spring.

Ana María Suárez Monsalve is a candidate for a PhD in Latin American Studies at the University of Chile, Magister in Education at Pontifical Javeriana University, Colombia and Associate Professor at the University of Medellín, Colombia. She is a member of the research groups Communication Organization and Politics (COP) and GRECO at the University of Medellín, a member of Colombian Communications Research Association, Latin American Communication Research, and the International Mass Communications Research Association. She is a member of the researcher team of the Latin American Communication Monitor.

Ricardo Valencia is a PhD candidate in Media Studies at the University of Oregon. He received an MA in Media Studies from the University of Hamburg and Aarhus University (Denmark). Between 2010 and 2014, he worked as a diplomat at the embassy of El Salvador in the United States where he lead the strategic communications of the diplomatic mission. His research interests are at the intersection of public relations, critical theory, public diplomacy and transnational activism.

Dejan Verčič PhD (London School of Economics) is Professor and Head of the Department of Communication at the Faculty of Social Sciences, University of Ljubljana, Slovenia. He has published fourteen books and written more than 300 articles, book chapters, monographs, reviews and conference papers. In both 2000 and 2010 he received special awards from the Public Relations Society of Slovenia (of which he is a founding member); in 2001 he was awarded the Alan Campbell-Johnson Medal for outstanding service to international public relations by the UK Chartered Institute of Public Relations (of which he is a Fellow); and in 2016, he received the Pathfinder Award, the highest academic honour bestowed by the Institute for Public Relations (IPR) in New York.

Sarah Williams is Principal Lecturer in Marketing at University of Wolverhampton, UK. Her research focuses on the lived experience of public relations practitioners including the enactment of professionalism and the impact of digital technologies on PR practice and identity. Sarah's published work includes a chapter on 'Marketing in Operations Management in the Travel Industry' and 'Always On: Managing Online Communities in a 24/7 Society', a chapter in Promotional Strategies and New Service Opportunities in Emerging Economies, as well as peer-reviewed articles in the *Asia Pacific Public Relations Journal* and a number of refereed conference proceedings.

Contributors **xiii**

Paul Willis PhD is Professor of Corporate Communication at the University of Huddersfield. Paul works with senior professional communicators in government, NGOs and the private sector. He teaches on the Government Communication Service *Inspire* programme and delivers a range of other innovative co-created executive education programmes at Masters-level. Paul is an active researcher and his work can be found in leading academic journals and textbooks in his field. He is the co-author of *Strategic Public Relations Leadership* (2013) which explores the key facets of leadership for communication professionals.

Jordi Xifra is Professor at the Universitat Pompeu Fabra, Barcelona, Spain, where he teaches history of propaganda and public relations, and strategic planning of public relations. He is the Director of the Degree in Advertising and Public Relations at the same university. His research focuses on public relations history (intellectual history included), public relations sociology, public affairs and public relations film discourse. He has published more than fifteen books on public relations and public affairs in Spain and South America, a number of chapters in international books, and his articles have been accepted for publication in *Public Relations Review, Journal of Public Relations Research* and *American Behavioral Scientist*, among others.

Minghua Xu is an associate professor at the School of Journalism and Information Communication, Huazhong University of Science and Technology. Her current research focuses on international communication, cross-cultural communication, media sociology and the application of new media technology. Minghua Xu is the author of several SSCI and SCI articles, papers and monographs on her teaching and research interests.

Philip Young is a senior lecturer in Public Relations at Birmingham City University, UK, having previously worked at Lund University, Sweden, and the University of Sunderland, UK.

1

INTRODUCTION

Experiencing public relations

Elizabeth Bridgen and Dejan Verčič

Public relations defines itself as a strategic management function – that is how it wants to perceive itself and how it wants others to see it. Public relations managers are generally knowledgeable and experienced; they understand how communication fits into broader leadership behaviour and, for that reason, they belong to the dominant coalition in their organization – in other words, they are among those people at the top who make the real decisions. This is the picture students get from their public relations textbooks, this is how practitioners tell their 'war stories' at conventions and how they grade their best cases for public relations awards and competitions. But this is, in the words of the sociologist Erving Goffman, the public relations *frontstage*.

In his book *Presentation of Self in Everyday Life* (1959), Goffman developed a metaphor of theatrical production to describe social behaviour. We all live in a duality of frontstage and backstage behaviour:[1] we wear comfortable clothes at home, and dress up when we leave the house. We have parts of our houses which are presentable to our guests (and usually tidy) and we have rooms which are generally messier and into which we usually don't invite guests (unless we are or we want to get intimate with them). We talk, behave and interact differently in backstage than in frontstage. Frontstage is a public place, backstage is private.

The difference between frontstage and backstage is the foundation of impression management processes at the level of individuals, and of reputation management at the level of organizations. Goffman describes these actions as the creation of 'working consensus' – with social actors deciding how to present themselves among each other and to the world at large. By the same token, there are public images of public relations as an aspirational profession, and there are privately experienced practices of public relations. The vast majority of public relations practitioners are not strategists; they don't hold managerial positions and they don't belong to the dominant coalition.

2 Elizabeth Bridgen and Dejan Verčič

It is part of growing up to understand these differences, and recognize the nuances between what is shown and thus seen, and what is absent or hidden. In traditional crafts and professions, there is a process of apprenticeship and specialization on which trainees and students spend years, not only to complement their knowledge with practical skills, but also to see 'how things are done' in 'the real world', often meaning that there are dirty details to every big endeavour. It takes time, experience and inculturation to fully appreciate the importance of backstage in any theatrical production, public relations included.

At the 2015 EUPRERA (European Public Relations Education and Research Association) autumn congress in Oslo, where the concept for this book was conceived, a quick and unscientific count of the papers presented revealed that over 80 per cent of them focussed on the frontstage of public relations – the theory, practice and benefits of public relations. At the conference academics and postgraduate students presented new business models and theories exploring management behaviour. They discussed the strategic development of major corporations, critiqued business school curricula and presented their analysis of what organizations said and did. The focus was on 'big events' (such as crises or change) or the work carried out by senior management (or by anonymous junior staff on their behalf). All this scholarship, while often thorough and well-intentioned, only discussed public relations or communications as a 'thing' or in the abstract; its worth or value was taken for granted. The lives and experiences of those carrying out the work of public relations, the negative or problematic side of public relations, the obscure and the unusual (from a Western perspective) and the everyday work of the practitioner was hardly discussed.

So after listening to, writing about and contributing to articles, journals, conferences and books about the frontstage of public relations, we decided to ask our colleagues to write about the backstage of public relations. This would not only be at the individual level (for instance, what work looks like at the bottom of a hierarchical pyramid), but also on an organizational and institutional level and from both a national and international perspective. We were interested in finding out about some of the practices that are constitutive parts of public relations and that are usually unseen or (even purposefully) hidden.

Falconi (2006) estimates that between 2.3 and 4.5 million people work in public relations worldwide, with 83,000 in the UK (Public Relations Consultants' Association, 2016) and 400,000 in the United States (Falconi, ibid.). All these individual practitioners experience public relations in different ways and carry different understandings of the work they do. They also have their own strategies and models – not the grand models of academic papers but models and strategies which give them a way of surviving the workplace or carrying out the work they are tasked to do (something which both Williams and Willis discuss in their chapters).

The stories of these people remain largely untold in favour of the 'big theories' or the frontstage of public relations. However, these are the people who try to bring these 'big theories' – and the everyday plans and campaigns that accompany them – to life. They are also the people who are told to carry out the *unpleasant* side of

Introduction **3**

public relations or who carry out the everyday, the trivial or irrelevant within the industry.

If you, as a reader, want proof that the backstage is rarely discussed in scholarly work, as an experiment, we ask you to look at the programme for a public relations conference or the table of contents of a public relations textbook. Essentially, everyday life in public relations is largely ignored in favour of the scholarship that attempts to position public relations as a 'serious' discipline. There will be many chapters and papers on public relations strategy and crisis communications but few on 'stunts', consumer public relations or everyday office life. Furthermore, you are unlikely to hear a non-judgemental paper or read a neutral chapter on unethical public relations or public relations for a controversial organisation. But there are junior and senior public relations practitioners carrying out communications roles within these 'unethical' companies, often trying to do the best job that they can. Why do we never think to write about their lives?

The 'turn' towards a more critical style of public relations scholarship over the last two decades has increased the number of articles, papers and book chapters exploring the experience of individuals in public relations (this has often been from a feminist perspective – e.g. Tsetsura, 2012; Fröhlich and Peters, 2007) but as Jelen-Sanchez observes in Chapter 2, quantitative research dominates in key public relations journals and therefore overlooks individual experience or that which cannot be explained in numerical form.

As lecturers in public relations, we were aware that students entering the field still had little idea what to expect from a public relations workplace. Essentially, they knew what they were meant to do but not how they were meant to 'act' or how their colleagues would behave. Who prepared them for the brainstorming sessions described by Willis which were routed in anarchy and 'inappropriate' behaviour? How did they navigate the demands of their employers and the need to act as a 'professional' when the tasks they were asked to do were impossible? How would the ethical models they learnt by rote for exams help them when faced with an ethical dilemma? And what can we learn from the fictional accounts of public relations life described by Young and Fitch in their chapters? Potentially, these are the only representations of 'backstage' public relations that practitioners (or their family) will ever see. The problem is that when these representations are inaccurate, we believe that this affects how people view public relations practice. But what we need to ask ourselves is this: Are such fictional representations really inaccurate or do they simply show the part of public relations life that we don't want anyone to see?

But everyday life in public relations goes beyond the lived experience of practitioners. The less-than-palatable side of public relations (which is also rarely discussed in public relations writing) forms a major part of the lives of some employees. Public relations practitioners carry out the work that is 'dirty'; they work for unpalatable organizations and on dubious campaigns and they use language to manipulate, which is something Bridgen discusses in her chapter. The fact that this puts the new and rather fragile business of public relations in an unfavourable light doesn't mean that this aspect shouldn't be discussed. Is the 'unpleasant' side of public relations and

4 Elizabeth Bridgen and Dejan Verčič

the communication devices described by Dhanesh and Simons too horrid to write about? Or does it simply not tally with the 'professional project' of public relations? While public relations scholarship has moved on, making radical public relations writing more acceptable (as described by Ihlen in his chapter), radical *subjects* are having a tougher time breaking through.

Communication, and thus public relations, constitutes organizations and societies. Similar to lecturers and writers, practitioners select what to show to each other and to the world at large as 'proper public relations' (frontstage). Organizational and societal observers are generally blind to the essential functions performed by public relations in organizations and societies worldwide; we are illiterate when it comes to understanding what public relations means to, and in, our contemporary media and networked environments. Spokespeople, as Rensburg discusses in her chapter, talk to us for and instead of organizational leaders, often creating parallel communicative realities to those we experience in everyday life. Post-truth and post-factual worlds can only exist in communication, and no matter how much professional societies try to dissociate the practice from these neologisms, the fact is that the practices they denote are more often than not produced by active engagement of public relations people. Movements from literal to visual, from rational to emotional communication are driven by research showing that – it works!

The totality of world politics, from terrorism to the rise of China, is incomprehensible if we don't recognize the role of public relations in these processes and that is why the chapters by Molleda, Suárez, Athaydes, Sadi, Hernandez and Valencia, and by Hung-Baesecke and Xu, are so valuable as they discuss public relations in particular countries from an 'insider's' point of view, rather than relying on an 'outsider' to give their perspective. No wonder public relations has entered fiction and popular culture, giving public relations practitioner characters the leading roles and their own movies and TV series (e.g. *Absolutely Fabulous, Scandal, Sex and the City, Thank You for Smoking, The Candidate, The Queen, The West Wing* and *Wag the Dog*) – although many commentators from within public relations protest that these cultural artefacts falsify the reality of the 'profession' and give it a bad 'image'. Public relations is all this and much more. With Facebook and Google developing technology for augmented reality, we as practitioners, academics and students are prepared to be that public relations community that will be one of the first to exploit new opportunities to mould human lives.

In developing this book and inviting authors to contribute, we were not trying to be 'objective' and present a totality of experiences in public relations; something like that would be impossible anyway. We were looking for colleagues who are interested in the hidden and overlooked parts of the practice. We envisioned that this edited volume would be interesting to graduate students in public relations, corporate communications, marketing and strategic communication, and related disciplines like organizational behaviour and management. It could also help inexperienced as well as seasoned practitioners make sense of their personal feelings about their jobs and what they see at work. We were, therefore, working towards a complementary reading to the mainstream public relations literature which is predominantly about the good side of public relations; we find it to be a sign of the maturity of a practice that it can also confess and articulate its darker and muddier sides. Humans and our actions are not perfect, and telling people that they can expect only the best in their lives may make them miserable later down the road. So, to be clear: public relations, like any human endeavour, is also a bullshit job, business function and social practice.

But as lecturers and teachers, we are meliorist by definition: we believe that by empirical and theoretical investigation we can better understand and interact with the world around us. By digging into the dirt, you can obtain valuable insights into how things operate. This knowledge is useful for orientation in the universe, not only in its physical landscape, but also within our heads. Students and practitioners alike will be better off being familiar with the different features of public relations, and it is by admitting the not-so-palatable ones that we can aspire to improve them. It is areas such as this – truth, post-truth and information warfare (subversion included) – which are discussed by Nothhaft and Samoilenko.

Life is what happens to you while you're busy making other plans (sang John Lennon in *Beautiful Boy*). This book is about the public relations that happens while managers are busy making their strategic plans.

Note

1   Goffman also talks about 'off-stage', but we can forget about that for the purpose of this introduction.

Bibliography

Falconi, T.M. (2006) 'How big is public relations (and why does it matter)?' http://www.instituteforpr.org/wp-content/uploads/Falconi_Nov06.pdf [Accessed 25 February 2017].

Fröhlich, R. and Peters, S. (2007) 'PR "bunnies" caught in the agency ghetto? Gender stereotypes, organizational factors, agencies and women's careers in PR'. *Journal of Public Relations Research*, 19(3), pp. 229–254.

Goffman, E. (1959) *Presentation of Self in Everyday Life*. New York: Doubleday.

Public Relations Consultants Association (2016) 'PR census reveals that the PR industry is worth £129bn', http://news.prca.org.uk/pr-census-2016-reveals-that-the-pr-industry-is-worth-129bn [Accessed 1 February 2017].

Tsetsura, K. (2012) 'A struggle for legitimacy: Russian women secure their professional identities in public relations in a hyper-sexualized patriarchal workplace', *Public Relations Journal*, 6(1), pp. 1–21.

2

EXPERIENCING PUBLIC RELATIONS AS AN ACADEMIC DISCIPLINE

What do scholarly views and published research tell us?

Alenka Jelen-Sanchez

Introduction

Public relations has matured as a discipline with a distinct literature and multi-paradigmatic approaches (Curtin, 2012; Pasadeos *et al.*, 2010), yet still struggles with credibility and recognition in academia, practice and society. While this is common for newer, vocationally oriented disciplines (Fitch and Third, 2010), it is also partly due to trends in public relations scholarly research. My previous study (Jelen, 2008) investigating the nature of the scholarly endeavours concluded that public relations is characterized by insularity; there is a concentration of topics on professional practice studied from a functional/management perspective anchored in Western scholarship and mostly instrumental, descriptive scientific research dominated by quantitative methods. This focus resulted in reproduction rather than production of knowledge.

In line with other early reviews of public relations scholarly work (Holtzhausen, 2000; Karlberg, 1996; McElreath and Blamphin, 1994; McKie, 2001; Pasadeos and Renfro, 1992; Pasadeos *et al.*, 1999; Sallot *et al.*, 2003), the study called for expansion and diversification of topical and methodological horizons, multicultural diversity, and better integration with neighbouring disciplines. These, besides the discipline's youth, were perceived as the major causes for public relations' lack of prestige and respect. Building on this study, the chapter aims to investigate academic endeavours and evaluate the progress of the discipline, particularly in terms of theoretical perspectives, topics and methodological approaches ten years later.

Recent literature suggests that public relations has developed immensely over the past decade, addressing several of the calls above. An increase in the numbers of academics, publications, conferences, students and university programmes has brought a healthy diversity to the field (Dühring, 2015; Ihlen and Verhoeven, 2012; Pasadeos *et al.*, 2010). The critique of historically dominant excellence study,

Experiencing public relations academically **7**

functional/normative approach and post-positivist orientation has accelerated rapidly. Alternative perspectives, including critical, cultural, social, postmodern, rhetorical and feminist have moved from the fringes to the core of the discipline in what Edwards and Hodges (2011) call a socio-cultural turn. They started expanding the horizons of public relations research with a wealth of new topics, theories and methodologies (Coombs and Holladay, 2012; Ihlen and Verhoeven, 2012). Within the variety of approaches, scholars have also been increasingly integrating insights from other established disciplines into public relations. McKie *et al.* (2012) describe public relations as in productive flux, a state in which the once-dominant paradigm still has points to make, while giving way to socio-cultural shift.

The vibrant maturation of the field has not been without challenges, disagreements, confusions, transitions and transformations. Scholars have been struggling with accepting multi-paradigmatic diversity (Curtin, 2012), which re-opened several 'old' concerns, from theory-building to the discipline's identity, definition, purpose and boundaries (Bardhan and Weaver, 2010; Edwards, 2012; Ihlen and Verhoeven, 2012). These concerns, combined with excessive pluralism, fragmentation, eclecticism and failure to accomplish a theoretical core that would have an impact beyond our boundaries, are perhaps the reasons why public relations has still not received academic prestige and due recognition in other disciplines and in society (Dühring, 2015; Fitch and Third, 2010).

Chapter overview

The chapter begins with an overview of the status of the discipline of public relations and its critiques, particularly from socio-cultural and critical schools of thought. After the review, the chapter outlines the methods used in this study, consisting of content analysis of public relations journals and interviews with public relations scholars. While content analysis is common in introspective studies, the use of interviews offering insights into trends and processes behind published scholarship represents a rather unique approach. Based on the results of the study, the chapter presents academic experiences, views, perceptions, evaluations and opinions of the discipline of public relations in combination with the theoretical, topical and methodological landscape manifested in journal articles to determine trends and gaps. The chapter concludes by comparing the findings to those of ten years ago, offering a reflection on scholarly efforts and their implications for the progress of the discipline, and identifying directions for the future.

Status and critiques of the discipline of public relations

That public relations is a dynamic and vibrant discipline is clearly reflected in introspective studies analysing citation networks, theoretical development, topics and methodological approaches. These not only increased in frequency, but also in scope, addressing several specialist areas, including crisis communication (Ha and Boynton, 2013), digital communication and new media (Duhé, 2015; Verčič *et al.*,

8 Alenka Jelen-Sanchez

2015; Ye and Ki, 2012), organization public relations (Huang and Zhang, 2013; Ki and Shin, 2006), international public relations (Jain *et al.*, 2014) and history (Watson, 2014), to name a few. With a handful of exceptions (e.g. Hatherell and Bartlett, 2006; Míguez-González *et al.*, 2014; Weaver, 2013; Xifra, 2009; Xue and Yu, 2009), the studies remain focused on the US scholarship with *Public Relations Review* and *Journal of Public Relations Research*, the leading journals in the field, featuring in virtually every study employing content analysis (the present study is no exception while also adding European journals to the enquiry). This growing literature suggests that there are lively discussions on the status of public relations as an academic discipline, but also that the field is in the process of diversification and fragmentation with strong ethnocentric tendencies.

From the dominance of excellence to the multi-paradigmatic discipline

Public relations started as an instrumental and functional discipline, primarily concerned with organizational communication, public relations professionalism and how it can be of benefit to organizations (Edwards, 2016). This was the focus of the excellence study, a comprehensive, general theory of public relations based on the proposition that public relations contributes to the effectiveness of organizations when it helps them build long-term relationships with strategic publics (Pasadeos *et al.*, 2010). The study and its extensions (e.g. models, roles, relationship management theory) were central to establishing public relations as an independent discipline and have had a strong agenda-setting, even hegemonic, effect on public relations academia and practice across the world (Hatherell and Bartlett, 2006; Ihlen and van Ruler, 2009; Macnamara, 2012; Pasadeos *et al.*, 2010; Roper, 2005). This is, to an extent, not surprising as, according to its founders (Grunig *et al.*, 2006), excellence 'has provided a comprehensive paradigm that has integrated and expanded public relations research' and 'served as a focal point for debate and criticism – a focus that Kuhn (1970) believed is a necessary condition for a science to be mature' (p.24). This is an assumption that has been recently contested.

If a decade ago a growing sentiment of the field was to establish an overarching, unified paradigm (Botan and Hazleton, 2006), the entry of socio-cultural and critical scholarship into mainstream public relations at the beginning of the new millennium sparkled paradigm struggles. Countering the normative/functional assumptions that society exists around equilibrium, symmetry and consensus, the socio-cultural turn introduced wider questions of power, diversity, activism and the role of public relations in increasingly technological, global and multicultural societies (Bardhan and Weaver, 2010; Edwards and Hodges, 2011; Ihlen and van Ruler, 2009; Valentini *et al.*, 2012). This turn also started eroding the dominance of excellence and advocated for new ways of paradigmatic thinking (Coombs and Holladay, 2012). Curtin (2012), counter-arguing Grunig *et al.* (2006) and claiming that Kuhn (2012) saw social sciences as inherently multi-paradigmatic, welcomes this development and states that 'creating an environment within public relations scholarship that is inclusive of and values all paradigmatic approaches would form a critical stage in the maturation of the field' (p.43). She identifies four different paradigms in public relations: the dominant *post-positivist* paradigm with the *critical/ cultural*, the *constructivist* and the *postmodern* paradigm representing marginal perspectives, yet gaining their importance and critical mass around the globe. Several others are mentioned in public relations literature, from management, symmetrical, reflective, rhetorical and strategic management to feminist paradigms (Aldoory, 2005; Edwards, 2012; Pasadeos *et al.*, 2010). Public relations scholars seem to be uneasy about this diversity and hesitant to adopt a dialectical approach to paradigms, which would enable us to engage in multiple ways of conducting research and see the possible connections between paradigms, as well as hold contradictory ideas simultaneously (Bardhan and Weaver, 2010).

At the same time, public relations discipline is still woefully lacking in non-Western paradigmatic approaches, including in Eastern thought and other cultural and global perspectives (Bardhan and Weaver, 2010; Curtin, 2012). Despite the recent rise in non-US scholarship and the very encouraging advancement of culturally situated public relations research in Europe, Australasia and Latin America, 'the public relations body of knowledge has developed and continues to develop ethnocentrically' (Sriramesh, 2012, p.10).

Theoretical development and theory building

While a decade ago scholars were concerned with searching for a grand, unified theory of public relations within a single paradigm framework, there is a recent realization that given the cultural and societal diversity of public relations, such a search would be the 'pursuit of the wrong goal' (Curtin, 2012, p.34). The discipline seems to have gone to the other extreme with a plethora of theories in public relations academia, mostly imported from elsewhere, but with very limited theory building. Dühring (2015) observes that '[h]ardly any other field among the social sciences is so prone to theory importation while, on the other hand, providing no substantial theory building of its own, especially none that is of interest to other disciplines' (p.17). If there was a lot of optimism surrounding theory development in the early 2000s (Pasadeos *et al.*, 2010; Sallot *et al.*, 2003), the progress in the last decade has, at best, plateaued (Meadows and Meadows, 2014; Sisco *et al.*, 2011).

In spite of increased theoretical diversity and interdisciplinarity, several scholars observe that the most used and influential theories in the field still tend to gravitate towards the body of Grunig's work with role theory, excellence theory/ models, relationship theories and the situational theory of publics on the list of most frequently used theories (Pasadeos *et al.*, 2010; Sisco *et al.*, 2011). Contingency theory, crisis/risk communication, feminist theory and cultural theories also feature prominently (Sisco *et al.*, 2011). Meadows and Meadows (2014), on the other hand, show that public relations scholars most frequently cast their net in communication studies, with agenda-setting theory, the situational theory of publics, critical theory/critical discourse analysis and framing as the most commonly used theoretical approaches in leading public relations journals. However, the views of public relations academics and practitioners differ somewhat from published scholarship as they see stakeholder theory, agenda building, the situational theory of publics, complexity theory, postmodern theory and the power control perspective as the most relevant theories, while also expressing the need for public relations research to be more sociologically fundamental (Wehmeier, 2009). This coincides with Heath's (2006) proposal to develop 'fully functioning society theory' as an all-inclusive framework to describe the role of public relations in society. Development of such 'home-grown' theories would be much needed, considering that we have made little progress towards a coherent theoretical building, and have had hardly any impact beyond our discipline (Broom, 2006; Sisco et al., 2011; Wehmeier, 2009).

Topics on the public relations research agenda

In one of their earlier citation studies, Pasadeos et al. (1999) noted that – unlike other disciplines – public relations is suffering from topical concentration on roles, corporate management, issues management and models, resulting in reproduction rather than production of knowledge. Their follow-up study (Pasadeos et al., 2010) indicated that new, more diverse research topics have emerged in the discipline, notably: international public relations, new technologies (one of the fastest growing areas with increasing emphasis on social media (see Ye and Ki, 2012)), crisis communication and gender. Meadows and Meadows (2014) added professional standards, ethics and social responsibility, and image/reputation management as most frequently studied topics, while Sisco et al. (2011) additionally listed public relationships, organizational studies and diversity and minority studies. The latter topics indicate the emergence of the socio-cultural turn, which with several areas of interest, including power, race, culture, colonialism and inequality, still does not receive the same attention as topics traditionally linked to functionalist and managerial perspectives (Edwards, 2016).

Several calls were made in the 1990s claiming that if public relations is to mature as a discipline and establish credibility in the scientific arena, it will need to consciously uncouple the intellectual agenda from practice (Dozier and Lauzen, 2000) and address public relations' wider social implications and its role in contemporary society (Karlberg, 1996). Scholars interviewed in my previous research were slightly sceptical of this view as they tended to align with the argument that the basis of every scientific discipline is to help advance and be responsive to practice (Cheng and de Gregorio, 2008; Morton and Lin, 1995), otherwise we might lose our disciplinary focus or even disappear. Indeed, one of the central criticisms of critical and socio-cultural scholarship is that, while it identifies socio-cultural concerns, it falls short of providing solutions to these problems for public relations practice (Bardhan and Weaver, 2010).

Despite such concerns, there has been a shift towards studying public relations as a social force (Ihlen and van Ruler, 2009) and future recommendations for public relations research do seem to steer away from organization-centric topics. Ihlen and Verhoeven (2012) state that research should be concerned with questions of power, equality, social change, identity-building, behaviour, ethics, responsibility and language; topics increasingly relevant to communication and public relations scholars in contemporary society. Another area that has also received scarce attention are publics who 'not only receive communications from organizations but who are able today to rapidly communicate and interact with organizations and other publics' (Pasadeos *et al.*, 2010, p.153). Their perceptions of organizational communication, its effects and impacts on the recipients and their relationships, remains to a large extent unexplored.

Methodological approaches and methods in public relations research

Both epistemologies, positivist and interpretative, currently co-exist in public relations literature (DiStaso and Stacks, 2010; Pasadeos *et al.*, 2011) with epistemological walls that are 'easily hurdled', yet the post-positivism and quantitative methods dominate the discipline (Curtin, 2012; Ye and Ki, 2012). Quantitative research is perceived as a 'formal' approach allowing for greater objectivity in scientific observations, which presumably helps the discipline to be taken more seriously (Curtin, 2012; Holtzhausen, 2000). In my previous research, scholars identified the excessive use of quantitative methods as problematic and symptomatic of the fact that public relations has not entirely got to grips with the interpretivistic paradigmatic shift that occurred in other social sciences. Instead, qualitative research still tends to be perceived as 'informal' and 'very subjective', thus struggling to be accepted as valid, stand-alone research for discovering meaningful patterns (Pompper, 2006). If we are to create more robust, ethical and sound research to advance public relations discipline and practice, both methodological traditions need to be recognized as valid and co-existing on an equal footing (Daymon and Holloway, 2011).

The majority of introspective studies indeed show that quantitative research dominates public relations scholarship[1] (Pasadeos *et al.*, 2011). DiStaso and Stacks (2010) conclude that quantitative methods are twice as common as qualitative methods, with surveys and content analysis employed most often (McKie, 2001; Meadows and Meadows, 2014). These were followed by interviews; rhetorical, historical and critical research; case studies; and, to a marginal degree, experiments and focus groups. The researchers also observed that the use of quantitative research has been increasing since 2004 with the sharpest increase of content analysis (see also Meadows and Meadows, 2014). In terms of qualitative methods, the use of interviews and focus groups is steadily growing over time, while the usage of case studies has decreased. Albeit still marginally present, multiple/mixed methods and triangulation research designs have been slightly increasing, most often in interview-survey combination (Pasadeos *et al.*, 2011).

Looking at the methods above, it becomes clear that public relations is not particularly adventurous in adopting innovative methodological applications that

12 Alenka Jelen-Sanchez

are well established in other disciplines, including ethnography, action research and social network analysis, which all have significant potential to contribute to a greater understanding of complex public relations phenomena and provide a more solid empirical ground for theory development. Ethnography particularly stands out as a method that is long overdue to be incorporated and is surprisingly rarely present given the nature of phenomena studied by public relations and its potential contribution to both theory and practice (Everett and Johnston, 2012; L'Etang, 2010, 2011). This approach, together with other in-depth qualitative methods (e.g. discourse analysis, storytelling, narrative and semiotic analysis) designed to tackle 'messiness and complexity' in public relations, has been advocated by socio-cultural and critical scholarship with promising potential for greater methodological diversity and generation of new knowledge that would push the discipline forward (Edwards and Hodges, 2011).

Academic and structural pressures on public relations scholars

Discussions on the state of the field very often attribute responsibility to scholars and their endeavours with hardly any consideration of the wider academic system and structural and institutional pressures within which they operate. These should not be pushed into the background as they represent crucial drivers of scientific research. Curtin (2012) emphasizes that choosing a paradigm and research methods is a political decision; 'what gets published, funded and recognized is, in large part, dependent on whether the researcher's paradigmatic perspective is congruent with that of editorial boards, granting agencies, or promotion and tenure committees' (p.39). Very often, scholars find themselves under time and publication pressures, leading to 'regurgitation and application of inadequately explicated concepts and models already published in public relations literature' (Broom, 2006, p.148) and 'blitzkrieg' research approaches (L'Etang, 2010). As elaborated by one of the participants in my previous research:

> There is much pressure on [...] scholars to produce a lot of knowledge as they are trying to get promoted within the universities, so that leads people to do a lot of research quickly and not reflectively enough [...] A lot of researchers currently seem to just "jump around," do one thing in one area and move to another one, meaning there is not a lot of research that builds on itself.
>
> *(Jelen, 2008, p.53)*

Additionally, scarce funding and an inability to attract competitive research grants were identified as one of the core reasons for the field's insularity (Fitch and Third, 2010; Hatherell and Bartlett, 2006). Greater investment in research would, at least in principle, encourage expansion of topical and methodological horizons, facilitate theory building, increase relevance of public relations to other disciplines and society, grant scholars greater respect and credibility, and, in turn, attract more funding and investment into the field.

Methods of the study

With the purpose of investigating the progress and status of scholarly endeavours in the discipline of public relations, particularly in the last decade, this study conducted content analysis of articles published in four leading (two US and two European) public relations journals from 2006 to 2015 and interviews with 15 public relations scholars to explore scholarly perceptions of, and experience with, the discipline of public relations and its developments while identifying trends in theoretical perspectives, topics and methodological approaches.

As in my previous study (Jelen, 2008), *Journal of Communication Management* (JCM), *Journal of Public Relations Research* (JPRR) and *Public Relations Review* (PRR) were included in the sample with the addition of *Public Relations Inquiry* (PRI) (established in 2011) as it is particularly focused on socio-cultural and critical scholarship (L'Etang *et al.*, 2012). The research examined a representative sample[2] of 573 randomly selected articles (see Table 2.1), which were coded according to authors' institutional affiliation; the type of the article; up to two topics; focus; theories; the context of the study; the methodological approach; and methods as described by the authors, with particular attention to title, abstract and keywords. In cases where abstracts were ambiguous on any of these elements, the rest of the article was consulted. The data was analysed with SPSS.

In-depth semi-structured interviews offering insights into scholarly experience, opinions and views behind the published scholarship were conducted between March and September 2016. The sampling strategy, aiming at symbolic representation of public relations academics, combined purposive and snowball sampling with a special consideration of participants' expertise in the disciplinary development of public relations (e.g. publications, positions) as well as their affiliation, scholarly and cultural background. The data were analysed with NVivo using concept-driven coding of emerging themes. The use of interviews represents a unique approach in introspective studies, which, with the exception of Wehmeier's (2009) Delphi study, do not use 'live' participants and mostly rely on analyses of published scholarly works.

Table 2.1 Sample size and number of articles published in selected journals 2006–2015

Journal	Sample size (n) ($\gamma = 95\%$; $\alpha = \pm 5\%$)	Total number of articles (N)
Journal of Communication Management (JCM)	146	235
Journal of Public Relations Research (JPRR)	138	214
Public Relations Inquiry (PRI)	57	67
Public Relations Review (PRR)	232	587
Total	573	1.103

14 Alenka Jelen-Sanchez

Results: Scholars' experience and published research

Scholarly views on the development and status of the discipline

Scholarly views on the discipline and its developments were overall not particularly positive. All of them acknowledged a remarkable growth in the number of researchers and professorial positions, conferences, publications, study programmes and students as well as increased richness, variety, diversity and openness of the discipline. This growth and expansion is reflected in the 'branching out' of the discipline into several specialisms (e.g. history, ethics, public affairs, public diplomacy, internal communication), with their specialist conferences and literature. There is also a notable move from instrumental and descriptive to more critical and sophisticated scholarship but, although we are moving in the right direction, the academics believe that we have not harnessed this potential for growth to the extent that we should have. This is evident in the rather slow progress of the discipline, which can no longer be considered as young, yet remains immature in some aspects of its development and struggle for recognition.

Critical and socio-cultural shift was identified as a key development that has importantly transformed the landscape of our discipline. It has expanded and diversified topics, theoretical approaches, methodologies, scope and understanding of public relations and, importantly, has challenged the prevalence of the excellence paradigm. Such development was in general welcomed, but not without concerns. Scholars emphasised that we are witnessing disintegration of the dominant paradigm, which, according to Kuhn (2012), typically results in complexity and chaos over defining and identifying the discipline. If a few decades ago the discipline had a very clear core functional/management orientation and understanding with an organizational focus, we are nowadays not only faced with confusions, ambiguities and diverging approaches and ideas, but also struggle to come to terms with them (see Curtin, 2012; Edwards, 2012; Ihlen and Verhoeven, 2012). Instead of creating an inclusive environment, in which scholars would 'disagree with deep respect and engage in [a dialogue with] curiosity in our own differences', as stated by one of the participants, a strong cultural division emerged between Grunigian/functionalist and critical/socio-cultural scholars, who, with different ideological and philosophical positions, either ignore or criticize each other (occasionally with passion and very often to show that their approach is better). Interview results indicate that the two groups, while agreeing on the core of the problem, disagree on how to resolve the current state and achieve greater recognition and maturity. While the former emphasize that we need greater clarity in the discipline and a stronger sense of who we are, the latter advocate that the strength of our diversity is in the adaptability and agility that makes us important players in both an organizational and a social context.

Despite greater diversity in the discipline, research published in mainstream public relations journals still demonstrates strong ethnocentric[3] tendencies. Half of the articles included in this research were written by scholars based in the US (with over one third of them studying the US context), followed by significantly lower representation of Australian (6.3%) and UK-based scholars (6.1%), while representation of 42 other countries was lower than 3%. Taken altogether, albeit not to dismiss cultural diversity within these contexts, European scholarship comes second in dominance (28.2% authorship; 19.2% context), followed by a significantly lower presence of Asian (11.3% authorship; 11.0% context) and Australasian studies (10.7% authorship; 4.7% context), while Africa and Latin America remain marginally visible.

Considering the presumed growth of international public relations (Pasadeos *et al.*, 2010), it is somewhat disappointing that only 9.9% of articles were co-authored by scholars based in different countries and only 12.0% focussed on studying international and/or global contexts. This strong American presence, also noted in the interviews, has important imperialistic implications for the conceptual and epistemological underpinnings of the discipline, which is still short of true global inclusiveness (Bardhan and Weaver, 2010; Verčič *et al.*, 2001).

Theoretical diversity in the light of poor theoretical development

The theoretical landscape of our discipline appears to be somewhat more diverse, yet poorly developed and characterized as particularly immature and unsophisticated. The participants expressed concerns over theoretical fragmentation of the discipline, a 'parasitic' attitude in adopting theories from other areas and a lack of accumulation of knowledge. This situation has worsened with the erosion of excellence as a fundamental theory and, while socio-cultural and critical approaches are bringing very interesting new theoretical ideas and insights, there is little building on this knowledge. As one of the participants illustratively stated, with various social and cultural theoretical approaches introduced into the field 'it is like opening a door and nobody goes ahead'.

These assumptions were confirmed in the content analysis. Over 480 different theories appeared in the articles, 331 of them being referred to in only one article. Most articles (53.4%) mentioned between one and three theories with an average of 2.41 theories per article. Apart from a few 'home-grown' public relations theories, scholars borrowed from a variety of disciplines, from communication, media,

Table 2.2 Ten most prominent theories according to the number of articles.

	Theories	Articles (n)	Articles (%)
1	Public relations theory	127	22.1
2	Relationship (management) theory, OPR, relational theory	111	19.3
3	Excellence/symmetry theory	65	11.3
4	SCCT/crisis communication theory	60	10.4
5	Communication theory	26	4.5
6	Grounded theory; systems theory	24	4.2
7	Situational theory of publics	23	4.0
8	Contingency theory; critical theory; stakeholder (management) theory	22	3.8
9	Social theory, image restoration theory	21	3.7
10	Attribution theory	20	3.5

16 Alenka Jelen-Sanchez

political, cultural, management and organizational studies, to sociology, psychology and natural sciences. However, as documented in previous studies (Pasadeos *et al.*, 2010; Sisco *et al.*, 2011) and also noted in the interviews, the majority of theoretical approaches still gravitate towards excellence-related theories[4] (with the exception of role theory, which has, according to one of the participants, 'run its course'), crisis communication and relationship theories (see Table 2.2), with a visible yet marginal entry of critical and social theories advocated by socio-cultural tradition.

Several participants emphasized that a significant proportion of scholarly research remains atheoretical. Indeed, one quarter of the articles did not make a reference to any theory. In addition, only 15.7% claimed to be theoretically driven with half of the articles concerned exclusively with practical contributions and one third claiming contribution to both. This shows a relatively strong vocational orientation of the discipline, which to an extent hinders theoretical development. As emphasized by one of the participants:

> Our general modus operandi is to run after practice, so we see something is of increasing interest in practice, it is being done, it is discussed in management discourse [...] then we jump into it and make our contributions somehow. And that's fine to a degree. But there has to be more than that. At the very core, there has to be genuine attempt to understand what is it that we are doing, what are the principles underlying [public relations, otherwise] the really interesting [theoretical] stuff that actually explains how does it work may be done somewhere else.

Another participant concurred with this risk that other areas, e.g. cognitive science or management disciplines, will 'take over' theoretical development that should be in the public relations domain. The participants expressed a need for greater and more robust theorization on two levels: in terms of theoretical and conceptual depth, and in the development of our own original theories, either in terms of expanding the existing ones or proposing new ones. In line with Wehmeier's (2009) recommendation, there is urgency in developing an extensive, sociology-level theory, which would serve as an integrative framework of middle-ranged theories and explain the role of public relations in society (Heath's (2006) fully functioning society theory was mentioned as one of the possibilities). Such development is needed for the field to progress and mature as well as to bring relevance to other academic and social arenas.

Topics and research agenda in public relations

The interviews indicated that public relations scholars have been expanding their horizons and are studying diverse topics with several new areas, yet there is still a strong emphasis on crisis communication, relationships, social media and corporate social responsibility (CSR). The content analysis again to a large extent confirms these perceptions. Drawing on existing introspective studies (Meadows and Meadows, 2014; Pasadeos *et al.*, 2010; Pasadeos *et al.*, 1999; Sallot *et al.*, 2003; Sisco *et al.*, 2011), the study identified over 40 topics in journal articles. The most often studied topic is crisis and risk communication (16.4% of the articles), which most participants do not find justifiable considering how rare crises are in practice. This is followed by digital, social and mobile (DSM) media (14.5%), public relations practice/occupation (13.1%), relationships (10.5%), strategic communication and communication management (10.3%) and media and media relations (10.3%). Topics inherent in the socio-cultural and critical tradition, including race, minorities, gender, LGBT (lesbian, gay, bisexual and transgender), diversity, culture, activism, society and power still have a rather marginal presence in the mainstream journals, confirming Edwards' (2016) claim, also echoed in the interviews, that they still do not receive the same attention as topics traditionally linked to functionalist and managerial perspectives. However, the data indicates that the studies concerned with these phenomena are increasing, while previously prominent research on models, roles, image and reputation, as well as research in social psychology, seems to be stagnating. Both interviews and content analysis demonstrated an increased scholarly interest in history, engagement, dialogue, advocacy, activism and public diplomacy.

When asked which topics are lacking in public relations research, the participants identified global public relations, ethics, philosophy and epistemology of public relations. Even more pressing was the lack of engagement with 'big themes' and current developments in society, including migration, political shifts, populism, capitalism, democracy, power, public relations and development, big data, terrorism and conflict, racism, persuasion, religion, health, cognition and sense-making. This was partially attributed to the lack of scholarly confidence, but also a scarcity of bigger projects and interdisciplinary collaborations required to tackle these areas. The problem is not only that public relations scholars do not study these areas, but also that we seem to be invisible in public debates surrounding them, which does not help us in advancing

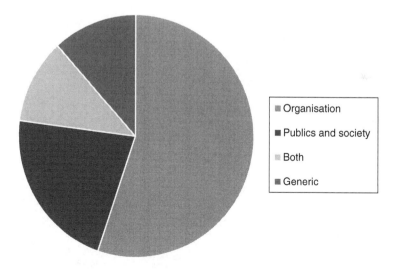

FIGURE 2.1 Orientation of the studies

our societal relevance and visibility (Dimitrov, 2015). If a decade ago scholars were sceptical of the societal approach and researching the societal implications of public relations, now there is a general agreement that we need to overcome the organization-centric fixation and be valuable not just for practitioners, but also for society. Despite this consensus, published research remains strongly organization-focused with only one fifth of the articles studying public relations phenomena exclusively from a publics/stakeholders or society perspective (see Figure 2.1). This, combined with a limited set of research methods (discussed in the next section), contributes to a still problematic reproduction of knowledge in the discipline.

Methods and methodologies

While the participants observe a wider range of research methods used to study public relations phenomena, the range of methods remains rather limited. With qualitative research gaining its legitimacy, they in principle agree that both positivist and interpretivist epistemologies are accepted in the field, yet quantitative research still holds a 'wild card' in terms of preferential treatment and frequency.

The results of the content analysis confirm the quantitative orientation of public relations research, which is not as strong as suggested by previous studies (e.g. DiStaso and Stacks, 2010). Excluding one quarter of discussion articles, half of the empirical articles adopted a quantitative approach (48.9%) with qualitative research at 38.7%, but gradually increasing through time (see Figure 2.2). If we look at specific journals, JPRR is by far most quantitatively oriented, followed by PRR, while qualitative approaches take the lead in JCM and even more so in PRI, which is in line with its purpose being almost exclusively qualitatively oriented (see Figure 2.3). Strong preferential orientation of the journals, albeit important in offering space

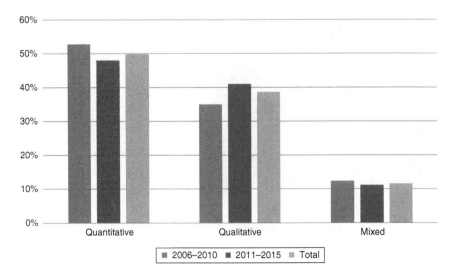

FIGURE 2.2 Research approaches in public relations research

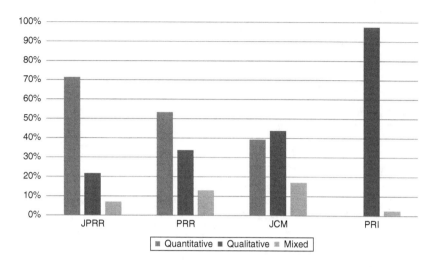

FIGURE 2.3 Research approaches in public relations journals

for specific types of research, might have damaging side-effects as they are likely to result in insularity and limited progress. One of the participants also mentioned that this might further encourage 'global imbalance' in terms of the dominance of post-positivism in North America and qualitative, critical, interpretive work in Europe.

The mixed and multiple methods approaches remain scarce. A vast majority of articles relied on one research method (79.1%), 14.8% of articles combined two methods and the rest combined three to five methods. The researchers most often mixed methods from the quantitative and qualitative tradition, particularly in survey-interview combination, followed by triangulations within the qualitative tradition, mostly within case studies and ethnographic approaches, while using more than one method represents uncommon practice in quantitative research.

The most often used method remains survey (36.9%), followed by interview research (28.6%), which in comparison with previous studies (e.g. DiStaso and Stacks, 2010; Meadows and Meadows, 2014) overtook content analysis (23.7%) (see Figure 2.4). These methods were also identified by the participants as in 'plentiful supply' (with this research just as much to blame). Somewhat less commonly present were case studies, experiments[5] and ethnography, which in comparison with previous studies represents a new entry among the most often used methods, and focus groups. Other methods, each present in less than 4% of the articles, included textual, document, discourse, historical, rhetorical, framing, semiotic, conversation and network analysis, action research, Delphi study, expert audit, event study method, critical incident technique, systematic review, team feedback and group talks, abductive method, qualitative dyads, and propaganda analysis. Some of these together with content analysis (particularly qualitative) and focus groups do seem to be gaining their importance at the expense of other dominant methods.

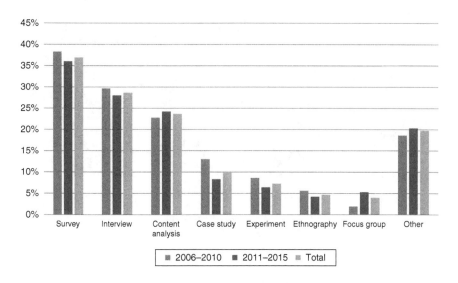

FIGURE 2.4 The use of different research methods in different periods

Most of the participants expressed an opinion that the rather narrow scope of methods is out of date and not particularly well suited for creative research, progress and innovations. The results indicate that methods designed to tackle the 'messiness and complexity' associated with socio-cultural approaches are particularly weakly represented in the discipline; according to one of the participants, this 'translation of radical theories into research methodology is not happening so much yet.' Scholars would in general like to see more ethnography, but also action research, critical discourse analysis, semiotic analysis and Delphi studies (these were used in >2% of the articles). Other recommended methods include big data analysis (in qualitative and quantitative terms), visual methodologies and secondary analysis or re-analysis of existing sets of data, which would allow us to explore wider social and cultural trends. In general, we are not embracing the new methodological trends and possibilities offered by new technologies or employed in other disciplines, which, according to one of the participants, demonstrates our disconnectedness from broader developments in methodology and research methods.

Systemic obstacles and directions for the future

The participants were overall (perhaps too) critical of the current state in the discipline of public relations. Even though they recognized that the standards have improved, they emphasized the problematic of volatile theoretical frameworks and simplistic, convenient and descriptive research methods, often failing the 'so what?' question. This is particularly true for small-scale, isolated, 'do it yourself' research projects with several limitations, ingrained in public relations academic culture. Research that is done too quickly and not reflectively enough still commonly lands on editors' desks. The blame for this is not necessarily attributed to scholars, but the university systems exerting publication and teaching pressures. As emphasized by one of the participants, 'we no longer have the luxury of time and in order to produce at the rate that we have to produce we are doing it at the expense of quality.' This problematic, albeit not specific to public relations, hurts our discipline in the long run as it means that we are not developing our research at the highest possible standard, nor are we gaining recognition and respect outside of our boundaries.

This is also partially related to the problematic of funding and a lack of resources to do major research studies in our area. Even though in some countries the participants testified to successful funding applications and partnerships with practice, most of them emphasized that it is nearly impossible to get public funding for public relations research. Pejorative connotations and a lack of recognition of our discipline do not help and scholars often find their way around this by avoiding the term 'public relations' in their applications or forming larger interdisciplinary projects with colleagues from more established disciplines. Several participants emphasized that this is also the direction in which we will see our field developing: becoming more interconnected, open-minded and addressing public relations phenomena from a more complex, societal perspective. The essence of our future lies in developing relationship and dialogue, in the first instance within our discipline, but also with other disciplines, practice and relevant stakeholders. We are in an exciting field, and if the scholars are bleak about the present, they are far more positive about our future.

Conclusion

Public relations is a vibrant field that is still searching for its centre and substance and 'strives to be thoughtful, innovative, important, relevant, and useful' in the process (Heath, 2010, p.xi), but with limited success. Encouraging growth, expansion and diversification of the discipline in the last decade has not produced significant change in the dominant theoretical, topical, methodological and ethnocentric trends, justifying scholarly frustrations with unsatisfactory progress. Simultaneously, eroding the pervasiveness of excellence and the impetus of the socio-cultural turn have brought the discipline to a critical point in its development, at which we are experiencing a disintegration of the dominant paradigm. In this state of confusion and complexity, academics struggle to embrace multi-paradigmatic diversity and to work across different traditions to address the challenges that the discipline is facing, particularly scarce theoretical development, limited societal impact, blurred identity and low external recognition. Despite different backgrounds, there was a consensus among scholars regarding these core problems and the question is whether we can work together to address them. Building relationships and establishing dialogue within our discipline and beyond was indeed identified as one of the key areas for future development.

Interviewees in general agreed that functional/management tradition, while still having contributions to make, is giving way to the socio-cultural turn pushing

22 Alenka Jelen-Sanchez

the focus of scholarship from functionalist, post-positivist and organization-centric models to more socially, critically and culturally orientated approaches. Such a turn, however, has not yet significantly materialized in mainstream public relations journals. It has had some visible impact in terms of theoretical diversity, but only marginally in terms of topics and methodological approaches. Most of the published work still evolves around 'traditional' topics with a strong excellence footprint on the theoretical landscape and the supremacy of quantitative research. This indicates that functional/management and critical/socio-cultural scholarship are not yet on a par. However, we must be careful when making such conclusions due to sampling bias in journal selection. As indicated by one of the critical scholars, they tend to publish outside of mainstream public relations journals, which means that the critical and socio-cultural work might have a stronger presence elsewhere.

There is still a notable lack of creativity and innovation in our scholarly endeavours, particularly when compared to intellectual currents in neighbouring disciplines. We do seem to have made stronger connections with them; however, while we extensively borrow and adopt theories and concepts from them, we have failed to provide a substantial theory and knowledge development of our own, particularly one that would be of relevance beyond our boundaries (Dühring, 2015). This, together with an organization-centric research agenda, methodological insularity, ethnocentricity of the discipline and 'do it yourself' research, too often resulting in reproduction of knowledge, hinders public relations' scientific progress and academic reputation. Lack of resources in the field, struggles to obtain funding and systemic pressures on scholars further obstruct our development. In the future, public relations scholars will need to engage in solid theoretical development, global and paradigmatic inclusiveness, interdisciplinary collaborations, researching socio-cultural implications of public relations and addressing 'big themes' to progress, mature and establish greater legitimacy, credibility and respectability of our discipline in academia, practice and society.

Notes

1   Some studies (e.g. Meadows and Meadows, 2014; Pompper, 2006) observe that qualitative research takes a marginal lead in public relations journals, but it is worth noting that these studies counted critical analysis/critique/essay as a qualitative method, which is not classified as empirical research in this study. Only articles using research methods are classified as such.
2   Editorials, introductions to special issues, call for papers, book reviews and research in brief were excluded in the sample.
3   This result might have been different had we considered public relations journals based in other countries and published in other languages.
4   'Public relations theory', which was most commonly mentioned in journal articles, according to one of the participants usually refers to excellence and related concepts and ideas.
5   A clear majority of experiment research was conducted using students as participants (26 out of 31 experimental studies or 83.9%). The only other method, in which students were used as respondents, was survey research, but to a significantly lesser extent (13 out of 157 or 8.3%). The interview participants were in general critical of such practices.

Bibliography

Aldoory, L. (2005) 'A (re)conceived feminist paradigm for public relations: A case for substantial improvement', *Journal of Communication*, 55(4), pp.668–684.

Bardhan, N. and Weaver, C.K. (2010) 'Introduction: public relations in global cultural contexts', in Bardhan, N. andWeaver, C.K. (eds.), *Public Relations in Global Cultural Contexts: Multi-Paradigmatic Perspectives* (pp.1–22). London: Routledge.

Botan, C. and Hazleton,V. (2006) 'Public relations in new age', in Botan, C.H. and Hazleton, V. (eds.), *Public Relations Theory II* (pp.1–18). Mahwah, NJ, London: LEA.

Broom, G.M. (2006) 'An open-system approach to building theory in public relations', *Journal of Public Relations Research*, 18(2), pp.141–150.

Cheng, I.-H. and de Gregorio, F. (2008) 'Does (linking with) practice make perfect? A survey of public relations scholars' perspectives', *Journal of Public Relations Research*, 20(4), pp.377–402.

Coombs,W.T. and Holladay, S.J. (2012) 'Fringe public relations: How activism moves critical PR toward the mainstream', *Public Relations Review*, 38(5), pp.880–887.

Curtin, P. A. (2012) 'Public relations and philosophy: Parsing paradigms', *Public Relations Inquiry*, 1(1), pp.31–47.

Daymon, C. and Holloway, I. (2011) *Qualitative Research Methods in Public Relations and Marketing Communications*, 2nd ed. London: Routledge.

Dimitrov, R. (2015) 'Silence and invisibility in public relations', *Public Relations Review*, 41, pp.636–651.

DiStaso, M.W. and Stacks, D.W. (2010) 'The use of research in public relations', in Heath, R.L. (ed.), *The SAGE Handbook of Public Relations*, 2nd ed. (pp.325–337). Los Angeles, London, New Delhi, Singapore,Washington DC: Sage.

Dozier, D.M. and Lauzen, M.M. (2000) 'Liberating the intellectual domain from the practice: Public relations, activism, and the role of the scholar', *Journal of Public Relations Research*, 12(1), pp.3–22.

Duhé, S. (2015) 'An overview of new media research in public relations journals from 1981 to 2014', *Public Relations Review*, 41(2), pp.153–169.

Dühring, L. (2015) 'Lost in translation? On the disciplinary status of public relations', *Public Relations Inquiry*, 4(1), pp.5–23.

Edwards, L. (2012) 'Defining the 'object' of public relations research: A new starting point', *Public Relations Inquiry*, 1(1), pp.7–30.

Edwards, L. (2016) 'An historical overview of the emergence of critical thinking in PR', in L'Etang, J., McKie, D., Snow, N. and Xifra, J. (eds.), *The Routledge Handbook of Critical Public Relations* (pp.16–27). London: Routledge.

Edwards, L. and Hodges, C. E. M. (2011) Introduction: Implications of a (radical) socio–cultural 'turn' in public relations scholarship, in Edwards, L. and Hodges, C. E. M. (eds), *Public Relations, Society and Culture* (pp.1–14). London, New York: Routledge.

Everett, J.L. and Johnston, K.A. (2012) 'Toward an ethnographic imperative in public relations research', *Public Relations Review*, 38(4), pp.522–528.

Fitch, K. and Third, A. (2010) 'Working girls: Revisiting the gendering of public relations', *PRism*, 7(4), pp.1–13.

Grunig, J.E., Grunig, L.A. and Dozier, D.M. (2006) 'The Excellence Theory', in Botan, C.H. and Hazleton,V. (eds.), *Public Relations Theory*. (pp.21–62) Mahwah, NJ, London: LEA.

Ha, J.H. and Boynton, L. (2013) 'Has crisis communication been studied using an interdisciplinary approach? A 20-year content analysis of communication journals', *International Journal of Strategic Communication*, 8(1), pp.29–44.

24 Alenka Jelen-Sanchez

Hatherell, W. and Bartlett, J. (2006) 'Positioning public relations as an academic discipline in Australia', *Asia Pacific Public Relations Journal*, 6(2), pp.1–13.

Heath, R.L. (2006) 'Onward into more fog: Thoughts on public relations' research directions', *Journal of Public Relations Research*, 18(2), pp.93–114.

Heath, R.L. (2010) 'Preface', in Heath, R.L. (ed.), *The SAGE Handbook of Public Relations*, 2nd ed. (pp.xi–xv). Los Angeles, London, New Delhi, Singapore, Washington DC: Sage.

Holtzhausen, D.R. (2000) 'Postmodern values in public relations'. *Journal of Public Relations Research*, 12(1), pp.93–114.

Huang, Y.-H.C. and Zhang, Y. (2013) 'Revisiting organization-public relations research over the past decade: Theoretical concepts, measures, methodologies and challenges', *Public Relations Review*, 39(1), pp.85–87.

Ihlen, Ø. and van Ruler, B. (2009) 'Introduction: Applying social theory to public relations', in Ihlen, Ø., Fredrikson, M. and van Ruler, B. (eds.), *Public Relations and Social Theory Key Figures and Concepts* (p.viii, p.376). London: Routledge.

Ihlen, Ø. and Verhoeven, P. (2012) 'A public relations identity for the 2010s', *Public Relations Inquiry*, 1(2), pp.159–176.

Jain, R., De Moya, M. and Molleda, J.-C. (2014) 'State of international public relations research: Narrowing the knowledge gap about the practice across borders', *Public Relations Review*, 40(3), pp.595–597.

Jelen, A. (2008) 'The nature of scholarly endeavors in public relations', in van Ruler, B., Tkalac Verčič, A. and Verčič, D. (eds.), *Public Relations Metrics: Research and Evaluation* (pp.36–59). New York: Routledge.

Karlberg, M. (1996) 'Remembering the public in public relations research: From theoretical to operational symmetry', *Journal of Public Relations Research*, 8(4), pp.263–278.

Ki, E.-J. and Shin, J.-H. (2006) 'Status of organization–public relationship research from an analysis of published articles, 1985–2004', *Public Relations Review*, 32(2), pp.194–195.

Kuhn, T.S. (1970) *The Structure of Scientific Revolultions*, 2nd ed. Chicago, IL: University of Chicago Press.

Kuhn, T.S. (2012) *The Structure of Scientific Revolutions*, 4th ed. Chicago, IL: University of Chicago Press.

L'Etang, J. (2010) '"Making it real": Anthropological reflections on public relations, diplomacy and rhetoric', in Heath, R.L. (ed.), *The SAGE Handbook of Public Relations*, 2nd ed. (pp.145–162) Los Angeles, London, New Delhi, Singapore, Washington DC: Sage.

L'Etang, J. (2011) 'Imagining public relations anthropology', in Edwards, L. and Hodges, C.E.M. (eds.) *Public Relations, Society and Culture. Theoretical and Empirical Exploration* (pp.15–32). London, New York: Routledge.

L'Etang, J., Xifra, J. and Coombs, T. (2012) 'Breaking boundaries', *Public Relations Inquiry*, 1(1), pp.3–6.

McElreath, M.P. and Blamphin, J.M. (1994) 'Partial answers to priority research questions— and gaps—found in the Public Relations Society of America's body of knowledge'. *Journal of Public Relations Research*, 6(2), pp.69–103.

McKie, D. (2001) 'Updating public relations: "New science," research paradigms and uneven developments', in Heath, R.L. (ed.), *Handbook of Public Relations*. Thousand Oaks, CA: London; New Delhi: Sage, pp.75–91.

McKie, D., Gregory, A. and Ingenhoff, D. (2012) 'Overview of the "state of the field"', *Public Relations Review*, 38(5), pp.807–809.

Macnamara, J. (2012) 'The global shadow of functionalism and Excellence Theory: An analysis of Australasian PR', *Public Relations Inquiry*, 1(3), pp.367–402.

Meadows, C. and Meadows, C.W. (2014) 'The history of academic research in public relations: Tracking research trends over nearly four decades', *Public Relations Review*, 40(5), pp.871–873.

Míguez-González, M.I., Baamonde-Silva, X.M. and Corbacho-Valencia, J.M. (2014) 'A bibliographic study of public relations in Spanish media and communication journals, 2000–2012', *Public Relations Review*, 40(5), pp.818–828.

Morton, L.P. and Lin, L.Y. (1995) 'Content and citation analyses of Public Relations Review', *Public Relations Review*, 21(4), pp.337–349.

Pasadeos, Y., Berger, B. and Renfro, R.B. (2010) 'Public relations as a maturing discipline: An update on research networks', *Journal of Public Relations Research*, 22(2), pp.136–158.

Pasadeos, Y., Lamme, M.O., Gower, K. and Tian, S. (2011) 'A methodological evaluation of public relations research', *Public Relations Review*, 37(2), pp.163–165.

Pasadeos, Y. and Renfro, B. (1992) 'A bibliometric analysis of public relations research', *Journal of Public Relations Research*, 4(3), pp.167–187.

Pasadeos, Y., Renfro, R.B. and Hanily, M.L. (1999) 'Influential authors and works of the public relations scholarly literature: A network of recent research', *Journal of Public Relations Research*, 11(1), pp.29–55.

Pompper, D. (2006) '30 years of public relations scholarship: A census of our research methods', *International Communication Association*, pp.1–34.

Roper, J. (2005) 'Symmetrical communication: Excellent public relations or a strategy for hegemony?', *Journal of Public Relations Research*, 17(1), pp.69–86.

Sallot, L.M., Lyon, L.J., Acosta-Alzuru, C. and Ogata Jones, K. (2003) 'From aardvark to zebra: A new millennium analysis of theory development in public relations academic journals', *Journal of Public Relations Research*, 15(1), pp.27–90.

Sisco, H.F., Collins, E.L. and Zoch, L.M. (2011) 'Breadth or depth? A content analysis of the use of public relations theory', *Public Relations Review*, 37(2), pp.145–150.

Sriramesh, K. (2012) 'Culture and public relations: Formulating the relationships and its relevance to the practice', in Verčič, D. and Sriramesh, K. (eds.), *Culture and Public Relations: Links and Implications* (pp.9–24) New York, London: Routledge.

Valentini, C., Kruckeberg, D. and Starck, K. (2012) 'Public relations and community: A persistent covenant', *Public Relations Review*, 38(5), pp.873–879.

Verčič, D., van Ruler, B., Bütschi, G. and Flodin, B. (2001) 'On the definition of public relations: A European view', *Public Relations Review*, 2007(4), pp.373–387.

Verčič, D., Verčič, A.T. and Sriramesh, K. (2015) 'Looking for digital in public relations', *Public Relations Review*, 41(2), pp.142–152.

Watson, T. (2014) 'Let's get dangerous – A review of current scholarship in public relations history. *Public Relations Review*, 40(5), pp.874–877.

Weaver, C.K. (2013) 'A history of public relations scholarship in Aotearoa New Zealand: From working on the margins to setting disciplinary agendas', *PRism*, 10(1), pp.1–15.

Wehmeier, S. (2009) 'Out of the fog and into the future: Directions of public relations, theory building, research, and practice', *Canadian Journal of Communication*, 34(2), pp.265–282.

Xifra, J. (2009) 'Recent Mediterranean literature on public relations: France, Italy, and Spain', *Journal of Communication Management*, 13(2), pp.191–196.

Xue, K. and Yu, M. (2009) 'A content analysis of public relations literatures from 1999 to 2008 in China', *Public Relations Review*, 35(3), pp.171–180.

Ye, L. and Ki, E.-J. (2012) 'The status of online public relations research: an analysis of published articles in 1992–2009', *Journal of Public Relations Research*, 24(5), pp.409–434.

3

DEALING IN FACTS

Howard Nothhaft

In a Masters-level public relations class, a group of students had prepared a crisis case for their fellow students. At its core, the fictitious scenario involved the king of a European country crashing his luxury sports car in the inner city in the early hours of the morning under the influence of alcohol. Except for the slightly bruised driver and the vehicle, which was a wreck to be towed away in public view, there were no casualties. The real damage, however, threatened to be constitutional. Since the king had lately suffered through a series of minor but embarrassing scandals, the monarchy hung on a thin thread in parliament; its abolition was a real option.

For most students, who were to take the role of the royal house's public relations counsels, the case was clear. Their recommendation was that the king abdicate in favour of the crown princess, who was far more popular anyway and would invigorate the waning enthusiasm for the monarchy. The discussions revolved mainly around questions of angle and wording. Should the king apologize? Should he admit to being an alcoholic? Should he, tears in his eyes, pledge to undergo therapy?

One group developed a different defence. They were prepared to admit that the king had crashed and recommended that the monarch abdicate in favour of the crown princess, at least in the foreseeable future. What they were concerned about was the impact of a reigning monarch 'hounded out of office' because of drunk driving. That, they feared, would gravely damage the monarchy, maybe beyond repair. The group proposed not to address any involvement of alcohol and to deny it if questioned. Instead, the story would be that the king had worryingly suffered something like a seizure while driving. He was currently under medical examination at the renowned Royal Institute of Medicine, a world-class facility. In the coming days, it would emerge that the monarch suffered from a hitherto undiagnosed neurological condition. Sadly, this condition would very probably force him to hand over the burdensome crown to his daughter.

The other students objected, some vehemently. That would be tantamount to lying, they argued (some pointed out, shrewdly, that it was lying). The teacher, to his own mild surprise, challenged them. Why, exactly, would it be lying, he asked? The students found the question bewildering. Obviously, because the abdication was not due to a medical condition. The king abdicated because he was caught drunk driving, because he crashed a car, because his irresponsible behaviour was irreconcilable with his role as head of state; he could have killed somebody. The story the other group suggested was a lie because it disagreed with the facts.

The teacher pointed out that the critics were assuming a perspective of Olympic omniscience. They knew that the king had imbibed alcohol because it said so in the case description. In reality (a fictitious reality in our hypothetical case), the question of whether the king had been under the influence and to what degree was a matter for the authorities to establish. In this case, no sample of royal blood had been taken and His Royal Highness would definitely not appear before a court, since the monarch, under the constitution of the country, could not be prosecuted. As for the medical condition, it was a matter for medical professionals to establish. And wasn't it highly probable that the doctors would find something wrong with a 68-year-old man? In any case, it was a certainty that the medical case establishing the king's vulnerable condition, prepared by the court physicians, would be beyond questioning; with seals and signatures and everything. And if the king did resign, the political case to question the Royal Institute's verdict, i.e. to inquire into a private person's health, was much reduced anyway.

A dealer in facts?

The teacher was the author, of course. To this day, I remain ambivalent about the case of the car-crashing king. Admittedly, whether the suggestion of the group could have worked depends on many other factors that were not addressed. What did the king do before he got in his car? Was he partying and visibly drunk in plain view of numerous witnesses? Was he undeniably intoxicated when the police arrived or could he have been merely concussed? But the intriguing thing was that the debate in class did not take the shape of a discussion about ethics or social constructionist epistemology. We talked strategy. The hypothetical nature of the case steered students away from the question of what really happened and towards the question of what a fact is. It ended with a student trying to sum up: one should not lie, she suggested, except, maybe, when one was in control of the apparatuses that produced facts, such as police taking alcohol tests or medical institutes arriving at diagnoses. Perhaps she could have formulated it more elegantly as follows: don't lie unless you can prove that you aren't. But the point that stuck with me, and of course resonated with sociological theory from Giddens (expert systems) to Latour (centres of calculation), was the image of 'fact-producing apparatuses' (see Schölzel and Nothhaft, 2016).

28 Howard Nothhaft

Is public relations dealing in facts or at least with facts, or is it about something else? Does a public relations practitioner have the mandate to lie if she can prove, by means of fact-producing apparatuses, that she didn't? I do not intend to answer these questions, but I want to explore the relationship between the concept of fact on one side and public relations in theory and practice on the other. The idea that guided my exploration (full disclosure here) is the suspicion that public relations practice is not about dealing in facts, at least not plainly, but that theory tends to treat the relationship in an obscure manner. Academic theory and practitioner discourse effectively suggest, by avoiding the question, that the matter is trivial, that public relations is a plain dealer in fact and that fact is an uncomplicated concept. The thorny issue of the 'big lie', as in the case of the car-crashing king, is avoided altogether or 'othered' as propaganda. Whether that is a deliberate joint strategy or part of a collective self-deception, as some authors claim (Seiffert and Thummes, 2017), is up for debate. The net result, in any case, is a highly ambivalent experience for students and practitioners as well as theorists, because the suggestion is neither plausible nor taken seriously by anyone outside the industry. The current debate about post-truth politics, post-factual societies, together with the slightly older debate about post-democracy, is highly interesting in this context, because the moral panic triggered by it reveals that society is apparently unaware, or pretends to be unaware, of public relation's modus operandi and the role of fact-producing apparatuses. Thus, my exploration happens in three steps: First, by examining modern public relations' conceptual DNA; second by discussing this conceptual DNA against the backdrop of the current discussions about post-truth politics and related ideas; third, by taking a cursory look at how Anglo-American public relations textbooks deal with the concept of fact.

Fact in public relations' DNA

Where and when public relations first emerged as a 'species', either bearing the name or not, is a matter of debate. What cannot be doubted, however, is that the strand of Anglo-American DNA in public relations' genes is strong, maybe even dominant. It is interesting, therefore, that US historiographers of public relations normally identify Edward Bernays and Ivy Lee as founding fathers of the profession. Bernays, in that context, is often credited with bringing his uncle Sigmund Freud's deep understanding of the human psyche to the counselling of industrialists. Lee's achievement, on the other hand, is identified as laying down the principles of proper press and media work. While earlier press-agentry often meant coaxing or pressuring journalists (Miller Russell and Bishop, 2009), Lee's approach, formulated in his famous Declaration of Principles, committed to fact and verifiability of fact:

> This is not a secret press bureau. All our work is done in the open. We aim to supply news. This is not an advertising agency; if you think any of our matter ought properly to go to your business office, do not use it. Our matter is

Dealing in facts **29**

accurate. Further details on any subject treated will be supplied promptly, and any editor will be assisted most cheerfully in verifying directly any statement of fact.[1]

Although scholars have become warier of Lee over the years, Hallahan, after a multi-faceted investigation of the Colorado Coal Strike, still supports the industry's narrative, at least in principle: 'Clearly, the ideals that he [Lee] espoused in his famous Declaration of Principles of 1906 signalled a move away from pure press-agentry. He helped forge a model of public relations based on the dissemination of factual and timely information given gladly to the press and public' (2002, p.298). It is of course true that Lee: (a) did not always live up to that ideal; (b) argued later that corporations should not only provide facts but advocate their own case; and (c) advised business leaders to seek appeal not only with facts, but via emotion or imagination (see Miller Russell and Bishop, 2009, p.98, for a concise overview). For the present context, however, the most important insight is the conception of public relations as a complementary function to journalism, mainly concerned with providing the facts.

Whether that model worked depended of course on whether journalism ever lived up to the ideal of 'simply' reporting the facts, or at least ever believed in it. It is interesting, therefore, that Lloyd and Toogood (2015), in their attempt to understand journalism and public relations today, in the digital age, trace the influence of Walter Lippmann. Lippmann, they argue, already understood in the 1920s that public relations was not naively providing the facts, because journalism was not, and never had been, about naively reporting them. What journalism produced, in Lippmann's words, was a 'stylized' version of the facts arranged in 'narrative shape'. As Lippmann put it, '[t]he development of the publicity man is a clear sign that the facts of modern life do not spontaneously take a shape in which they can be known. They must be given a shape by somebody, and since in the daily routine reporters cannot give a shape to facts, and since there is little disinterested organization of intelligence, the need for some formulation is being met by the interested parties.' (2004, p.187/11922). Lloyd and Toogood (2015, p.6) summarize: 'If journalism is the "first draft of history", then public relations is the first draft's first draft.'

One can argue, of course, that Lee's Declaration laid the groundwork for one type of public relations only – press and media relations – and that the subsequent experience of two world wars, with their massive propaganda efforts, must have left its mark on any naïve belief about factuality. However, another document that is sometimes considered constitutive of public relations, the Code of Athens, authored by Lucien Matrat and published first in 1965, then amended in both 1968 and 2009, clearly commits to Lee's model. The Code of Athens (IPRA, n.d.) advises public relations practitioners to refrain from many things, but amongst them are 'Subordinating the truth to other requirements' (Art. 11) and 'Circulating information which is not based on established and ascertainable facts' (Art. 12). Although recent scholarship has suggested that Matrat's code never amounted to more than a publicity tool (Watson, 2014), these strangely worded injunctions are still held in

30 Howard Nothhaft

high regard as a criterion that differentiates modern Western public relations from the propaganda of fascist and communist regimes.

Post-truth, post-fact, post-democracy

If journalism is the first draft of history, its factuality is no small matter. Yet in the wake of Donald Trump's election as 45th president of the United States, observers on both sides of the spectrum are suggesting that the pundits of the respective other side have left facts and truth by the roadside, that a shocking new era of fake news is nigh: the era of post-truth.

As Oxford Dictionaries declared 'post-truth' its 'word of the year' in 2016 (Flood, 2016), there is no point in pretending to originality in dealing with this topic, but it might be worthwhile to ask what, apart from the moral panic, is substantially new. In order to bring some perspective to the discussion, I begin by outlining the idea of post-truth, then bring it into contact with two older but related ideas: post-democracy and post-factual society.

The term 'post-truth politics' is commonly ascribed to blogger David Roberts, who used it in 2010 to describe 'a political culture in which politics (public opinion and media narratives) have become almost entirely disconnected from policy (the substance of legislation)' (Roberts, 2010). The core of Roberts' argument was that people do not gather facts, build knowledge and then carefully weigh the pros and cons in order to arrive at reasoned political standpoints. Instead, they employ heuristics, i.e. mental shortcuts, with the majority opinion and their 'tribal affiliation' being two of the most important: what reasonable, decent folks like myself and my favourite politicians (or my favourite conspiracy website) believe cannot be too wrong. Thus, while the Enlightenment ideal of democracy theory assumed that voters, at least in principle, follow a deliberate, rational procedure, Roberts pointed out that the reality amounts to almost exactly the opposite, as Table 3.1 shows.

Another term that is vaguely associated with post-truth is post-factuality, as in, for example, 'Welcome to a post-factual era' (Sirota, 2007), 'Living in a post-factual world' (Monty, 2016) and 'Welcome to the post-truth presidency' (Marcus, 2016). The precise meaning of post-factuality remains vague, but there is a common motif:

TABLE 3.1 Enlightenment ideals versus reality

Enlightenment ideal	Reality
1 Gather facts	1 Choose a tribe or party based on value affiliations
2 Draw conclusions from the facts	2 Adopt the issue positions of the tribe
3 Form issue positions based on the conclusions	3 Develop arguments that support those issue positions
4 Choose a political party that shares those issue positions	4 Choose facts to bolster those arguments

Source: Based on Roberts (2010).

Dealing in facts **31**

the diagnosis that facts, even when established beyond doubt, do not matter any longer in political discourse. Political actors continue to hammer home their message even if the message has been proven, or at least 'declared' factually wrong, by, for example, authorities or scientists. Fake news is cropping up everywhere; emotion and gut feeling have become not only more important than truth, but have replaced it (ironically, many of the diagnoses of a post-factual condition on the web appear to be rants fuelled by emotion and underpinned by gut feeling; as such, they do not rise above post-factuality themselves, which is perhaps pleasing).

Post-democracy is a term associated with the work of political scientist Colin Crouch, who mainly wrote in reaction to Tony Blair's New Labour government. In Crouch's own words, '[a] post-democratic society is one that continues to have and to use all the institutions of democracy, but in which they increasingly become a formal shell' (Carrigan, 2013). In the original publication, Crouch elaborates:

> Under this model, while elections certainly exist and can change governments, public electoral debate is a tightly controlled spectacle, managed by rival teams of professional experts in the techniques of persuasion [...] The mass of citizens plays a passive, quiescent, even apathetic part [...] Behind this spectacle of the electoral game, politics is really shaped in private by interaction between elected governments and elites that overwhelmingly represent business interests.
>
> *(Crouch, 2004, p. 4)*

Post-truth, post-fact and post-democracy come together in a diagnosis that makes one worry about the patient, our democracies. The good news is that there are reasons to believe that the patient has been living with this condition for quite a while. Arguably, there is very little happening today that would have shocked Walter Lippmann or Edward Bernays. Nor should contemporary pundits be too shocked, since Roberts' insights about voter behaviour are well-known and apply to humans in many other contexts, as psychologists like Daniel Kahneman or Jonathan Haidt have pointed out. Even humanist intellectuals, who normally avoid cognitive science, should not be too shocked. Lippmann's argumentation in *The Phantom Public* (1925) is not too far away from Colin Crouch, despite its elitism. Daniel Boorstin, it may be remembered, wrote similar things in *The Image: A Guide to Pseudo-Events in America*, and that was in 1961. Guy Debord's *Society of Spectacle*, published in 1967, in a way belongs to the same genre. Around 2005, comedian Stephen Colbert attracted worldwide attention for using the word 'truthiness' ('veritasiness'), the quality of something 'feeling true', to satirize the administration of George W. Bush. In 2009, Pulitzer prize-winning journalist Chris Hedges wrote a passionate pamphlet titled 'Empire of illusion: The end of literacy and the triumph of spectacle', which basically makes the very same point: illusion and spectacle have supplanted reality and authenticity to an unprecedented degree. Postmodernists should not be shocked at all, of course, since an ironic stance towards factuality is their preferred habitus anyway.

Facts and fact-construction in public relations textbooks

The third step in my exploration of the relationship between public relations and fact is to take a look at how public relations textbooks present the issue. 'Take a look' is deliberately colloquial, because I applied a convenience sample (Saumure and Given, 2008) and a very simple research strategy: the stressed student test. What I did was to approach the textbooks lining my bookshelves in the way a stressed student in anticipation of being examined on the PR-and-fact-issue might have sought enlightenment. Thus, the first move was to check whether the term 'fact' appears in the register. The second was to look at the table of contents in order to see whether there was a chapter or sub-chapter that addressed the terms 'fact' or related concepts such as truth, objectivity, veracity etc. The third move, in absence of any findings so far, was to read more or less unsystematically into sections which typically address issues of factuality, i.e. chapters on ethics and sections about content creation and message formulation.

The validity (Miller, 2008) of my very simple approach rests on the assumption that textbooks, as opposed to journal articles and thematic anthologies, convey the dominant or mainstream view in a given field. Other scholars have made the same assumption before, for example Hoy, Raaz and Wehmeier (2007) who, in their quest to trace the dominant story of public relations history, chose to analyse textbook chapters, not journal articles. It is textbooks, in this view, that lay the foundations for the students' general understanding. In my approach, I assumed moreover that textbooks are pedagogically structured so that concepts of central importance are marked by being treated in dedicated chapters or at least sub-chapters, even if they do not make it into the register for some reason. The question I ask, it must be remembered, is not whether factuality is problematized at all, but whether it is problematized as a central question of public relations practice.

As for the results, the registers of public relations textbooks, it is safe to say, tend not to list the term 'fact'. None of the 14 textbooks I looked at, in the wider or narrower sense, contained an entry. My sample, strictly a convenience sample based on the bookshelf strategy, included: Jarol B. Manheim's *Strategy in Information and Influence Campaigns* (2011); Danny Moss and Barbara DeSanto's *Public Relations: A Managerial Perspective* (2011); Keith Butterick's *Introducing Public Relations* (2011), Trevor Morris and Simon Goldsworthy's *PR Today* (2012); Glen Broom's *Effective Public Relations* (2009, 10th edition); Ralph Tench and Liz Yeomans' *Exploring Public Relations* (2009, 2nd edition); Joep Cornelissen's *Corporate Communication* (2014, 4th edition); John Doorley and Helio Fred Garcia's *Reputation Management* (2015, 3rd edition); W. Timothy Coombs and Sherry Holladay's *It's not just PR* (2014, 2nd edition); W. Timothy Coombs and Sherry Holladay's *PR: Strategy and Application* (2010); Derina Holtzhausen's *Public Relations as Activism* (2012); Paul Argenti's *Corporate Communications* (2009). Only in two cases were there closely related entries. Ronald D. Smith's *Strategic Planning for Public Relations* (2013, 4th edition) contained an entry about 'factual propositions' (p.191), which dealt with facets of a messaging strategy based on logos the appeal to reason. Anthony Davis' *Mastering*

Dealing in facts **33**

Public Relations contained an entry about 'filleting the facts' (p.133), which dealt with the internal censorship some practitioners seem to experience.

It is of course impossible to judge what the conspicuous absence of the term 'fact' in the registers of public relations textbooks means. Admittedly, many registers tended to rather contain names and technical terms, not abstract concepts: Fabiani, Mark; Facebook; Fair-Housing-Act, Fax machine, etc. Another limitation might be that 'fact' is just too big a concept to address properly in a beginner's book. But then again, 'transparency' is abstract and big as well, and it did make its way into most registers; 'truth', however, rarely did.

Even with due caution, then, it is hard to avoid the impression that textbook authors are treating the question of factuality like a can of worms. Not one of the textbooks contained a dedicated chapter or sub-chapter that treats the question of what a fact is in a systematic, non-trivial way: in other words, I did not come across a chapter or sub-chapter that would have systematically shed light on the problem of the car-crashing king. Most textbooks contained a chapter on ethics, of course, and most of the chapters addressed issues like veracity or truthfulness in some way or another. But chapters or at least sub-chapters that take the question of what a fact is and go beyond everyday knowledge – and specifically address the issue of the 'big lie' involving fact-producing apparatuses, for example – are in general, to my knowledge, not on offer (however, several textbooks discuss front groups or networks of influence).

There were passages and sections which treated the topic of factuality, but they tended to be buried in the body of the text. Interestingly, many illuminating passages about factuality and truth were provided in the context of legal issues and especially tort law. In Danny Moss and Barbara DeSanto's *Managing Public Relations*, as well as in Cutlip's *Effective Public Relations*, there are chapters about public relations and the law, for example, and both chapters address the problem of portraying someone in a 'false light'.

Passages and sections in other chapters were sometimes little more than snippets, but they nevertheless remind the reader that factuality is not a trivial matter. Anthony Davis begins *Mastering Public Relations* (2007) by interrogating the concept of spin, for example. While admitting that there is spin and that the term is associated with public relations in the collective imagination, he suggests that the popular term has become 'a handy tool for the lazy journalist and broadcaster, the ready means to insinuate in substitution for reporting fact' (2007, p.3). Doorley and Garcia, in *Reputation Management*, make an interesting choice of words that indicates that zones of moral ambiguity cannot always be navigated safely: 'The ethical challenge of professional public relations is dealing with truth, falsity, and ambiguity, and managing through the muddle with integrity' (2015, p.48).

In addition to the occasional snippet, there are sub-sections that do not address factuality explicitly, but problematize the complex implicitly. Cornelissen, in *Corporate Communication*, devotes a long discussion of his chapter on Media Relations to framing theory, for example, and in essence argues that media relations is not about the facts *per se*, but about their framing (2014, pp.145-160). In Jarol B.

34 Howard Nothhaft

Manheim's *Strategy in Information and Influence Campaigns*, the author severely questions the conventional stance that argumentation based on fact is the key to successful campaigns: 'While rhetoricians, democratic theorists, philosophical purists and others may object to the characterization, for the strategist substantive argumentation is often tangential and actual content peripheral to the truly essential decisions regarding the persuasion of individuals' (2011, p.65). Manheim, who goes on to discuss the theories of cognitive dissonance and elaboration-likelihood, continues: 'Argumentation and content, then, are often best understood not as the essence of persuasion, but as the pre-screened and carefully structured packaging that draws targeted individuals to engage with the campaign ...' (2011, p.65).

Trevor Morris and Simon Goldsworthy (2012), who begin their chapter on ethics in *PR Today* by noting that some textbooks 'treat public relations as a branch of moral philosophy' (p.41), pinpoint the real reason for the special status of facts, namely that their accuracy might be verifiable:

> If it comes to be known that a PR person is not a source of reliable information then journalists and others will look elsewhere for facts and comments. Therefore, lying about specific facts and figures is usually a bad idea, and in some contexts may be illegal. But beyond that social attitudes to lying vary.
>
> *(Morris and Goldsworthy, 2012, p.41)*

One of the strongest and most illuminating passages comes from Anne Gregory, a globally acknowledged public relations academic with a background in practice. In *Exploring Public Relations*, Gregory treats public relations as planned communication. She gives the example of an organization that is determined to improve its rusty image as an old-fashioned employer. The procedure of message creation and content production is described as follows:

> Identify realistic elements of persuasion. Work on the basis of fact. For example, the organization may have introduced a crèche and family-friendly work practices [...] All these facts demonstrate that the organization is not an old-fashioned employer, and should form the platform for programme content. However, facts are rarely enough. People are not just rational beings, so it is important to add human emotion to these facts. People associate more readily with other people and their experiences rather than with purely factual information. .
>
> *(Gregory, 2009b, p. 187)*

Another interesting passage by Gregory is to be found in the chapter on ethics. The author asks students to consider what the difference is between the acceptable practice of 'putting a gloss' on something and unacceptable 'spinning'. In her answer, the author explains that the key issue was the 'intention to deceive'. She writes: 'A good gloss should provide the recipients of the information with a fair and truthful representation of a company, even if it's a positive representation. If other information is

Dealing in facts **35**

obtained, the recipient of the "good gloss" should still recognize the representation as reflecting the facts' (2009a, p.287).

It is important to note that I only stumbled upon these and other, similar passages by reading 'suspicious' sections about, for example, message formulation. I was not guided to these passages because they were under the headline fact versus spin or fact versus emotion. Since my reading into the textbooks was guided by the register and the table of contents, I am sure it remains incomplete. There are probably many other similar passages buried in the text in some context or another, but I do not feel obliged to identify isolated sections by reading cover to cover. As I said, it is to be expected that a textbook is pedagogically structured, so what is systematically important should be under its own headline or sub-headline, or at least make it into the register. My claim was weak: simply that public relations theory treats factuality in an obscure way. Going through the textbooks has strengthened my belief that this is the case, by and large, although I admit that I was pleasantly surprised by straightforward sections like Gregory's, and Morris and Goldsworthy's.

Conclusion

Is the idea of public relations, as it developed historically and as it is practised today, to deal plainly in fact? Lee's Declaration and the Code of Athens suggest it, but textbooks, by and large, do not systematically elaborate. Can it be that they do not do so because the public relations' factuality is so obvious and the concept of fact so unproblematic? Given the many scandals over the years, the heated debates and the prominence given to the question of ethics, that is unlikely. No one doubts that there are practitioners who do not deal plainly, like my group of students in class. But are they rogue cases or the ones who 'got it'? May it be that public relations is about a good story, about narration, emotion, even fiction – based in fact, but not restricted to fact – like the story of a king with a debilitating neurological disease (sad), but a young daughter ready to take over (beautiful)? So, what about the role of fact-producing apparatuses – what Latour terms 'centres of calculation' (Latour 1987, pp.215–257)? What if there is no case description, no omniscient narrator, but a clinical diagnosis of a neurological condition, as opposed to zero legally relevant evidence of alcohol? People here and now can believe what they want, of course, but is not the real question what can be the basis of political action in parliament and, ultimately, what is enshrined in the history of the country? Aren't those members of parliament who vote against the king, because they 'feel' the story doesn't add up, despite medical and legal evidence to the contrary, the real post-truthers?

My exploration of public relations' relationship with facts has strengthened my conviction that public relations certainly deals with facts – but not plainly. The logics of public relations and journalism as 'first drafts of history', strictly to be written in a way appealing to the tribe, played and continues to play a great part in the post-truth/post-fact/post-democracy nexus. Take the passage by Anne Gregory: to advise that 'facts are rarely enough' sounds wise enough and to me there is nothing controversial nor ethically problematic in it. But view it against the backdrop of the post-truth debate and many of the elements apparently causing such moral panic are in place: work on the basis of facts, but do not stick to the facts; humans are not rational, so make sure to appeal to emotions; at the end of the day it's about people (i.e. your tribe) not information.

In earlier work done together with colleagues (Nothhaft, von Platen, Young, and Nothhaft, 2014), we argued that public relations' logical structure is gamesmanship, defined as 'the attempt to win one game by playing another' (Howe 2004). The game played is winning favour for one's good and rational arguments in public 'debate', it seems, but practitioners attempt to win it by influencing what is debated how, in which emotional context, in which affective frame:

> The professional judgement of PR practitioners ultimately is a judgement about what one can get away with in public and media. What is believed and what is not. How empty can a glass be for it to be declared, accurately and truthfully, half-full? Where does providing only relevant information – to cut out the irrelevant information is in the public interest, surely – deteriorate into suppressing information unfavourable to the client? In which contexts is it legitimate for the public interest to shift away the emphasis from facts to narrations, to fictions?
>
> *(Nothhaft et al., 2014, p.4)*

Academics, with a few exceptions, are still loath to admit to this dynamic clearly and openly. But it explains what many other theories of the plain dealer variety do not explain: that public relations, or corporate communication or strategic communication, has become a global industry, not only with low-paid jobs, but with highly paid experts and advisers who give 'strategic advice', and who would not exist if public relations were the service of organizing the dissemination and circulation of simple facts. Lippmann saw this in the 1920s, when he wrote: 'Were reporting the simple recovery of obvious facts, the press agent would be little more than a clerk' (Lippmann 2004/11922, p.). Thus, public relations theory will not make sense, and public relations' identity crisis will not be solved, until the complexities of the concept of fact – and its corollaries truth, truthfulness, accuracy, honesty, veracity, etc – are coherently integrated into a non-trivial theoretical framework.

But what about the practitioners who deal plainly and simply in fact every day? Are they deceiving themselves, as Seiffert and Thummes (2017) suggest? Some probably do. For others, it is probably fairer to say that they are being deceived, not necessarily by persons, but by the assemblage of things. Put very simply, one could say that there is a minor league and a major league of public relations. While the former is about selection, interpretation and circulation of facts, the latter is about creation of facts via control of fact-producing apparatuses: networks of research institutes, think tanks, intellectuals, etc. The minor league game is played and understood by many nowadays. The major league game is played by elites, the privileged. For one moment, however, in a hypothetical scenario, the dividing line ran right through my classroom.

Notes

1   The text quoted here, which can be found in virtually every public relations textbook, is taken from Miller Russell and Bishop (2009, p.91). The authors give the following source: Morse, S. (1906, September). 'An awakening in Wall Street'. *The American Magazine,* 62, pp.457–463. According to Morse's article, which was about large corporations breaking their silence towards the public, Lee's declaration was sent to city editors at the time of the 1905 strike.

Bibliography

Argenti, P., 2009. *Corporate Communication,* 5th edition. Boston, MA: McGraw-Hill.

Broom, G.M., 2009. *Cutlip & Center's Effective Public Relations,* 10th edition. Upper Saddle River, NJ: Pearson Prentice Hall.

Butterick, K., 2011. *Introducing Public Relations: Theory and Practice.* London: Sage.

Carrigan, M., 2013. 'British politics and policy: Five minutes with Colin Crouch'. [Online] Available at: http://blogs.lse.ac.uk/politicsandpolicy/five-minutes-with-colin-crouch/ [Accessed 21 February 2017].

Coombs, W.T. and Holladay, S., 2010. *PR. Strategy and Application.* Chichester, UK: Wiley-Blackwell.

Coombs, W.T. and Holladay, S., 2014. *It's not just PR. Public Relations in Society.* Chichester, UK: Blackwell.

Cornelissen, J., 2014. *Corporate Communication: A Guide to Theory & Practice.* London: Sage.

Crouch, C., 2004. *Post-Democracy.* Cambridge, UK: Polity.

Davis, A., 2007. *Mastering Public Relations.* Basingstoke, UK: Palgrave.

Doorley, J. and Garcia, H.F., 2015. *Reputation Management.* Abingdon, UK: Routledge.

Flood, A., 2016. '"Post-truth" named word of the year by Oxford Dictionaries'. *The Guardian,* 15 November.

Gregory, A., 2009a. 'Ethics and professionalism in public relations'. In: *Exploring Public Relations.* Harlow, UK: Pearson, pp.273–289.

Gregory, A., 2009b. 'Public relations as planned communication'. In: *Exploring Public Relations.* Harlow, UK: Pearson, pp.174–197.

Hallahan, K., 2002. 'Ivy Lee and the Rockefellers' Response to the 1913–1914' Colorado Coal Strike. *Journal of Public Relations Research,* 14(4), pp.265–315.

Holtzhausen, D., 2012. *Public Relations as Activism.* New York: Routledge.

Howe, L., 2004. 'Gamesmanship'. *Journal of the Philosophy of Sport,* 31(2), pp.212–225.

Hoy, P., Raaz, O. and Wehmeier, S., 2007. 'From facts to stories or from stories to facts? Analyzing public relations history in public relations textbooks'. *Public Relations Review,* 33(2), pp.191–200.

IPRA, n.d. *Code of Athens.* [Online] Available at: https://www.ipra.org/static/media/uploads/pdfs/ipra_code_of_athens.pdf [Accessed 20 February 2017].

Latour, B., 1987. *Science in Action: How to Follow Scientists and Engineers through Society.* Cambridge, MA: Harvard University Press.

Lippmann, W., 2004. *Public Opinion.* Kindle Edition. Mineola, NY: Dover.

Lloyd, J. and Toogood, L., 2015. *Journalism and PR. News Media and Public Relations in the Digital Age.* London, New York: Reuters.

Manheim, J.B., 2011. *Strategy in Information and Influence Campaigns.* New York: Taylor & Francis.

Marcus, R. 2016. 'Welcome to the post-truth presidency'. *Washingtonpost.com.* Available at: https://www.washingtonpost.com/opinions/welcome-to-the-post-truth-presidency/2016/12/02/baaf630a-b8cd-11e6-b994-f45a208f7a73_story.html?utm_term=.f517d8b7a511 [Accessed 2 December 2016].

Miller Russell, K. and Bishop, C.O., 2009. 'Understanding Ivy Lee's declaration of principles: U.S. newspaper and magazine coverage of publicity and press agentry, 1865–1904'. *Public Relations Review*, 35(2), pp.91–101.

Miller, S., 2008. 'Validity'. In: *The SAGE Encyclopedia of Qualitative Research Methods*. Thousand Oaks, CA: Sage.

Monty, S. 2016. 'Living in a Post-Factual World'. *ScottMonty.com*. Available at: http://www.scottmonty.com/2016/11/living-in-post-factual-world.html [Accessed 16 November 2016].

Morris, T. and Goldsworthy, S., 2012. *PR Today. The authoritative guide to public relations*. New York, Basingstoke, UK: Palgrave Macmillan.

Moss, D. and DeSanto, B., 2011. *Public Relations. A Managerial Perspective*. London: Sage.

Nothhaft, H., von Platen, S., Young, P. and Nothhaft, C., 2014. *Public Relations: Rules, Gamesmanship and the Professional Project*. Lund, unpublished manuscript.

Roberts, D., 2010. 'Grist Politics' [Online] Available at: http://grist.org/article/2010-03-30-post-truth-politics/ [Accessed 20 February 2017].

Saumure, K. and Given, L.M., 2008. 'Convenience Sample'. In: *The SAGE Encyclopedia of Qualitative Research Methods* (p.125). Thousand Oaks, CA: Sage.

Schölzel, H. and Nothhaft, H., 2016. 'The establishment of facts in public discourse: Actor-Network-Theory as a methodological approach in public relations research'. *Public Relations Inquiry*, 5(1), pp.53–69.

Seiffert, J. and Thummes, K., 2017. 'Self-deception in public relations. A psychological and sociological approach to the challenge of conflicting expectations'. *Public Relations Review*, 43(1), pp.133–144.

Sirota, D. 2007. 'Welcome to the Post-Factual Era' *Huffington Post*. Available at: http://www.huffingtonpost.com/david-sirota/welcome-to-the-postfactua_b_42527.html [Accessed 3 March 2007].

Smith, R.D., 2013. *Strategic Planning for Public Relations*. Abingdon, UK: Routledge.

Tench, R. and Yeomans, L., 2009. *Exploring Public Relations, 2nd edition*. Harlow, UK: Pearson.

Watson, T., 2014. 'IPRA Code of Athens—The first international code of public relations ethics: Its development and implementation since 1965'. *Public Relations Review*, 40(4), pp.707–714.

4

CONFESSIONS OF A PUBLIC RELATIONS PRACTITIONER

Hidden life in the open plan office

Paul Willis

Introduction

This chapter explores the periphery of public relations practice. It is concerned with neglected aspects of organizational life which, although understated and underestimated, can have a significant impact on how people work together effectively. The chapter makes no claims towards objectivity or impartiality. It instead draws upon my own experiences as a practitioner to promote alternative ways of understanding how things get done in public relations teams. The chapter's peripheral and candid personal orientation is designed as a counterpoint to more mainstream narratives of public relations practice. For example, the sector is awash with illustrations of best practice as leading figures from the industry talk about the factors which underpin their success. According to many award-winning campaigns (such as those featured by the public relations trade publication *PR Week* or showcased at the annual Cannes Lions International Festival of Creativity), as well as the accounts of senior professionals at high-profile events like the World Public Relations Forum, effectiveness tends to be governed by rational decision-making, clarity of purpose, strategic certainty and seamless campaign implementation. The reality portrayed is one of linear cause and effect in which public relations leaders consciously create the conditions in which their teams can flourish in support of specified organizational objectives.

While this advice and guidance can generate useful insights, it should also carry a health warning. The communication is usually promotional in nature and designed to showcase the practitioner's organization, as well as themselves. *Ex post facto* accounts of events designed to enhance individual and/or collective reputation is one reason why scholars have long warned against the dangers of relying on great man and great woman versions of history. Nevertheless, much of what we are told about the mechanics of public relations practice is informed by what can be framed

40 Paul Willis

as 'great practitioner history'. A consequence of the promotional bias inherent in these narratives is that they tend to paint pictures of working environments unsullied by poor decisions, irrationality, conflict, misunderstandings and unintended consequences. Anyone with even the briefest experience of working in an organization would suggest this is a fantasy. While the public relations industry is replete with women and men doing great work in challenging circumstances, focussing on these grand narratives of practice leads to an inaccurate, sanitized and arid understanding of how public relations teams actually function. The reality is messier and, quite frankly, more interesting.

To support this claim, the chapter engages in a process of experiential learning and develops insights generated by observations relating to different episodes from my career as a public relations practitioner in the United Kingdom. By reflecting on these incidents, the intention is to initiate a learning cycle and move from being someone who 'experienced an experience' to an observer engaged in a process of analytical detachment (Kolb, 1984). The purpose of this process is to 'create a new form of experience on which to reflect and conceptualise' which can then lead to some form of action or improved action (Moon, 2004, p.25). The intention is to then use this method of learning to unearth practical and theoretical insights of value to both public relations professionals and scholars.

The chapter's next section begins with relevant details from my career. This short biographical overview is important as it provides the background to the study, particularly the practical experiences and preoccupations which influence the chapter's orientation. For example, the biographical discussion sets the scene for why particular perspectives from complexity science are used as a conceptual lens through which to view my life as a public relations practitioner. In making sense of this experience, Chia's work (2011, 2013) on the efficacy of the oblique is especially highlighted. His theorizing is used to explain how traditional accounts of practice underestimate the importance of seemingly peripheral and insignificant factors. Chia argues these can be more influential than those that are designed to make a difference. To illustrate the point and contextualize this thinking for our field, the chapter explores the use of humour in a public relations team. It is noted that while there has been a great deal of research in organizational studies which explores the role of humour in workplace teams, it remains an under-explored area in public relations. Fusing these different interdisciplinary perspectives with a critique of my own leadership practice highlights a range of insights linked to the limitations of planned leadership interventions. These include the role humour can play as a form of 'necessary subversion' by team members to check an unhelpful leadership intervention, as well as the importance of passivity and non-action. The chapter ends by drawing together key themes to help guide future practice and research.

A portrait of the author as a PR man

Providing a brief professional autobiography is important given the chapter's interest in experiential learning. This overview also supports a more general call for public relations scholars to explicitly embrace the personal when it comes to their own research. For example, McKie and Munshi (2007) note how 'the life stories of authors are often suppressed' in academic work, 'yet the history of every scholar's personal development ... impacts on their research' (p.5). Instead of succumbing to the temptation of what Fairclough (1989) categorizes as 'spurious neutrality' (p.5), this discussion follows McKie and Munshi's (2007) rallying cry by not only providing a career overview, but also kickstarting a process of reflection on the professional experiences shaping my orientation to the issues under discussion. These reflections have a confessional element given they highlight some of the biases and challenges impacting on my development as both a practitioner and researcher.

Before becoming an academic in 2008, I spent twenty years working as a public relations practitioner in agencies in London and the north of England, as well as a period working for a large, private sector in-house department in the capital city. The last ten years of my professional public relations career was spent as an Executive Board Director of an independently owned consultancy. My final role prior to leaving the company for a new career in academia was Deputy Managing Director. This job involved contributing to the leadership and management of a business with an annual turnover of £4 million and a staff of more than 50 people. The agency's income was generated principally through a range of consultancy interventions including strategic counsel, general advisory work, as well as campaign implementation in areas such as marketing communication, corporate social responsibility, public affairs and social marketing. Retained fee-paying clients included BMW, Diageo, Nestlé, Virgin, ASDA/Wal-mart, Vauxhall, the NHS, Department of Environment and Rural Affairs and The Football Association. The agency won many prestigious industry awards during my time there, including *PR Week*'s Consultancy of the Year Award.

Leading a team of people in this context was a challenge for which I received no training or any other form of formalized development support. The training I did receive earlier in my career tended to be concerned with functional public relations skills rather than the specific demands of leadership. The exception to this was a couple of training sessions on basic accounting skills designed to help with the financial aspects of my role when I was first promoted to the board. Otherwise, my learning was strictly 'on the job' as I tried to reflect on what worked and what did not work when overseeing a team of account handlers, administrators, financial professionals and other directors. I was fortunate that in my career I had worked with both good and bad leaders so was able to construct my own 'mental map' of what good practice looked like against which I benchmarked my performance. It would be inappropriate though to make any grand claims for this approach as, for the most part, what I was doing can be best characterized as 'making it up as I went along' in what was a demanding (and sometimes stressful) environment.

Some cold comfort was at hand, however, in my conversations with colleagues and others in the industry wrestling with the demands of similar roles. These discussions revealed that my situation was typical rather than atypical. Most of my peers had no formal leadership or, indeed, business training and seemed to have been

42 Paul Willis

promoted to their current positions on the basis of being good public relations practitioners rather than good leaders. This was a trend I detected in large as well as small consultancy operations. As the Chief Executive Officer (CEO) of a global public relations network later put it to me during an interview, 'in a people business I think you get promoted to lead people by being good at what you do, whether a lawyer or a public relations professional, but nobody ever teaches you to be a people leader or a business leader.'

Uncertainty rules

Leaving the consultancy and joining a university gave me the time and opportunity to engage more extensively with academic research. The most motivating aspect about becoming a researcher was the chance to consider perspectives that would have been helpful to me whilst working as a practitioner. Teaching public relations professionals on different postgraduate programmes and other courses also confirmed the earlier conclusions I had drawn when in consultancy practice. That is, the senior public relations practitioners that I encountered as a tutor tended not to have engaged systematically with any sort of communication or leadership theory, nor sought to apply such insights in practice. This conclusion began to suggest that if my research focussed on, and contextualized, particular aspects of leadership scholarship for public relations it could have a direct and beneficial impact on practice.

Given the scope and scale of research in the wider academy a key question for me as a researcher was where to start? In an attempt to answer this point I went back to my experiences as a leader in practice. The impression that has always stayed with me was that my colleagues and I operated in what we framed as a frantic, fast moving, turbulent and uncertain context. For example, we could not predict and were regularly surprised by the actions of the stakeholders we worked with whether clients, the media, campaign partners, politicians, activist groups or target audiences. At the same time, our stock-in-trade was the delivery of mediated campaigns wholly reliant on third party communication. A consequence of this was that we could never be certain our programmes would achieve the desired outcomes we set for them. Another headache, particularly towards the end of my time in practice, was trying to second-guess and respond to the impact and rapid dissemination of new communication technology on our practice.

Against this turbulent functional backdrop as leaders in the consultancy we also faced an unpredictable resource planning environment. Although most of our clients did pay a fixed monthly fee, making accurate financial projections to manage the company's overheads was problematic and an art rather than a science. As a small business working for an array of large and powerful organizations, our operating margins were also squeezed constantly by professional procurement teams. This sense of fiscal unease was further compounded by previous experience that told us that during times of economic downturn, public relations budgets were usually one of the first areas of corporate expenditure to be cut. Being able to navigate around these financial problems was important given an ongoing imperative to invest in

Confessions of a PR practitioner **43**

people, systems, technology, buildings and our own marketing, as well as keeping money aside for the unexpected.

Reflecting on this context as a researcher, the retrospective conclusion I drew was that my biggest challenge as a public relations leader was coping with uncertainty. How do you lead people and make decisions when you do not know what the future will be? From my perspective, this insight could be applied to both the biggest and smallest issues I confronted as a leader during my working week, whether linked to the functional challenges of public relations practice or the issues associated with running a business. This context can be framed as the times in my working life when I occupied vulnerable, 'not knowing' or 'not knowing with much confidence' spaces.

From the complex to the banal

These experiences drew me towards leadership perspectives that address directly the challenge of uncertainty, most notably those informed by complexity science (Uhl-Bien, Marion and McKelvey, 2007; Goldstein, Hazy and Lichtenstein, 2010; Stacey, 2012). I was also heartened by the two decades of discussion in public relations on the sciences of complexity initiated by scholars such as Murphy (1996;2007) and McKie (2001). A key lesson drawn from this literature is that the practices required to deal with uncertainty cannot be micro-managed or designed by leaders. Instead, complex contexts require leaders to enable rather than design so conditions can emerge which are characterized by adaptability, learning and creativity. Chia (2011) notes how this response to complexity runs counter to the inherent heroism that pervades Western management thought and which influences explanations of corporate success. According to this dominant model of management, it is the bold decisions and often high-profile planned actions taken by significant individuals that account for organizational effectiveness. Rational action and direct intervention in the pursuit of intended outcomes are the hallmarks of this narrative. Chia warns, though, that by viewing practice through this lens it is easy for us to become seduced by our own representations of reality, such as written public relations strategies and campaign plans. Confusing these abstract constructions with reality is an affliction which Whitehead (1985) calls misplaced concreteness.

The tendency to over-value individual agency, focus on the importance of direct intervention and create order through abstractions are all attempts to make sense of the world of work in more dramatic and tightly linked causal terms than may actually be the case. Chia (2013), in contrast, prefers to look elsewhere for what Weick (1976) describes as more loosely coupled explanations in which seemingly inconsequential and understated actions, gestures or responses can emerge as primary causal agents in their own right. He also suggests that greater attention should be given to the notion of passive non-action as a factor for success, in other words, the importance of leaders and others in the organization 'just allowing things to happen.' Considering the role of non-action further highlights the importance of the banal and humdrum in explaining how things get done in organizations.

Considering the role of humour

Engaging with the work of Chia and other complexity scholars can help to cast new light on our understanding of public relations practice. When reflecting on my own experiences as a public relations practitioner, the impact of seemingly peripheral influences on team performance becomes apparent. A good example of this is the role played by humour. In addition to complementing complexity perspectives, considering its influence intersects with a rich body of scholarship in organizational studies that investigates humour in the workplace. The breadth of this research is readily on show in edited volumes (Westwood and Rhodes, 2007), as well as in journal special issues devoted to the subject (Butler, Hoedemaekers and Russell, 2013). Connecting with this stream of research adds particular value to our field given that humour is a neglected subject of inquiry in public relations. Before discussing a particular experience from my own career involving humour in the workplace it is first necessary to issue a caveat. That is, the example outlined is unlikely to be amusing in the context of this chapter. In the words of the failed storyteller 'believe me, you really had to be there' to fully appreciate its comedic impact. The important point to remember, however, is that the incidents described were funny at the time and are put forward for illustrative purposes.

My story begins with a popular comedy series called *I'm Alan Partridge*, which was first broadcast in the UK by the BBC in 1997. Alan Partridge is a fictional television and radio host played by the British comedy actor Steve Coogan. During the television series the character exhibits a wide repertoire of boorish, offensive and indiscreet behaviour. The programme is a satire of, among other things, celebrity culture and the English class system. In one episode, which triggers the start of Partridge's downfall as a media personality, he pitches a number of ridiculous programme ideas over lunch to a disinterested television executive. As he becomes more desperate to impress, Partridge's suggestions become increasingly outlandish and he ends by putting forward the idea of 'monkey tennis'. This episode of *I'm Alan Partridge* became a cult classic and was popular with many of the people who worked in my last public relations consultancy. Furthermore, the phrase 'monkey tennis' became a humorous stimulus during the consultancy's group brainstorming sessions for what is positioned in this chapter as a form of 'necessary subversion' by team members.

In line with every other public relations business in the UK, our consultancy attached great importance to its capacity to generate creative campaign ideas in support of client objectives. In response to a new project brief, a member of the team would usually send out an email asking colleagues to attend a brainstorming session. At these meetings a brief explanation would be provided of the particular communication challenge that needed to be addressed and then ideas would be requested from those present. Most of these creative sessions took on the character of a lively and irreverent conversation at which ideas would be suggested at random and then recorded by the meeting's sponsor. Given the importance of effective creative process to the consultancy's success this method of working caused me some concern. I felt that creative sessions needed to be facilitated more professionally and to make use of a wider variety of creative techniques. To support these objectives we commissioned a creativity expert to train consultants in new ways of working to generate ideas.

This strategy to reconfigure how the consultancy approached the creative process failed. While some account teams made use of new creative techniques, the old way of running brainstorms still predominated when particular members of the team came together. A couple of times I attended sessions in which colleagues tried to enact the new methods we had been keen to promote as a board of directors. However, proceedings eventually slipped back to the original, anarchic way of generating ideas. The trigger for this reversion to the status quo usually involved the phrase 'monkey tennis'. For instance, in response to a question such as 'how might we do this', a member of the team would say something like 'how about we sponsor a monkey tennis tournament?' Mention of 'monkey tennis' would then act as a trigger for the rest of the group, encouraging other members of the team to call out a series of equally absurd, impractical and unsuitable (albeit funny) suggestions. After a burst of further Alan-Partridge-style campaign ideas and laughter, those participating would then go back to randomly calling out more practical suggestions in line with the client's brief. In doing so, there was no return to the more formal structure and techniques with which the session had begun.

What lies beneath?

At the time of these events I found the unwillingness of colleagues to adopt our new creativity practices frustrating. As a leadership team we had invested time and money in trying to improve a process that was crucial to our business. Given the uncertain operating environment which impacted on our campaigns, this learning and development strategy represented my attempt as a leader to create some order through rational action and direct intervention. I now recognize that, in doing so, I was encroaching on an aspect of the consultancy's operations that was best left alone and it is this conclusion that leads to the framing of the team's use of humour as a form of 'necessary subversion'. In their study of humour and subversion in the workplace Taylor and Bain (2007) describe how two groups of employees consciously use humour as a way of constructing an effective opposition to management. In these case studies humour is used by employees as a way of teasing and satirising individual members of the management team, often in quite vicious terms. In the experiences described in this chapter the effects of the humour were more subtle and benign, in effect, a 'low calorie' form of resistance. Rather than being used to ridicule individuals, its application instead complements Collinson's (1988) research which suggests that humour is applied to reinforce and reflect a shared sense of group identity. The joking triggered by the utterance of the phrase 'monkey tennis' created an environment which led to the brainstorms proceeding in a way which was in sharp contrast to the intentions of the leadership team. Members of the team were creating a counterculture in which a set of alternative

46 Paul Willis

behaviours could flourish: instead of participating in a more managed creative process, they wanted to have fun.

This form of subversion was justified for two reasons. First, the brainstorming sessions were principally concerned with generating 'bright ideas' to be used in client campaigns. The content of the discussion was therefore principally about tactics and implementation. Those in the session, other than members of the leadership team, would be responsible for ensuring the ideas that were selected came to fruition. While the leadership team might set the strategy and oversee the campaign, the rest of the group largely had the task of delivering specific outputs such as media relations activity and events. The content of the brainstorming sessions were therefore about the team's day-to-day work and the subversion which took place could be seen as a way of wresting control of these meetings back from the leadership team. This conclusion about establishing control is reinforced when thinking back to aspects of my own practice. For example, I was (and still am) a planning enthusiast. While not fond of administration, I do like process when it comes to problem solving and strategizing. Therefore, if a client or colleague required a detailed written communication or brand strategy then I was happy to do it. I found the process enjoyable, it played to my strengths and (I believed) added value to the consultancy. While consulting with colleagues during the creation of a strategic plan, I did have a tendency to develop a fixed view on how a particular communication challenge should be addressed. Therefore, while I may have had 'control' of the strategic aspects of a plan, the brainstorming sessions provided an opportunity for the team to shape its tactical direction.

My intervention also failed to recognize another important role fulfilled by the brainstorming sessions, which further supports the role humour can play in creating and sustaining a counter culture. For example, Noon and Blyton (1997) highlight its importance as a survival or coping strategy. In this context its purpose is to make the working day more tolerable and interesting, providing a form of respite from the stresses and strains generated by the execution of routine tasks. The consultancy's brainstorming sessions helped to fulfil this purpose as they took colleagues away from their desks into a more social, informal and funny environment. For members of the team the brainstorming sessions may have been as much a form of stress management as they were vehicles for generating ideas. Introducing further layers of process into these sessions only served to make them more like the rest of the working day. Rather than the consultancy's leaders promoting what Butler *et al.* (2011) call a contemporary culture of fun, it was left to the team to engage in the 'necessary subversion' that served to protect a light-hearted and enjoyable activity that could relieve tension and maintain motivation.

Re-applying a complexity lens

The experiences recounted in this chapter suggest that humour can be regarded as an important intangible asset in public relations teams. Its influence goes beyond ideas for humorous campaign execution designed to capture the attention of different audiences, or the creation of cultures of fun within organizations. In my case, humour was used as a form of 'necessary subversion' to undermine an unnecessary leadership intervention. Crucially, in the example given the influence of this humour was officially hidden from view. The anarchic nature of the consultancy's brainstorming sessions, sustained through the use of humorous subversion, was not something that would be shared with clients or other external stakeholders. Yet, these sessions played an important role in helping a talented team of consultants to deliver effective campaigns day after day, week after week.

The role of humour in this context serves to illustrate Chia's (2011) claim for the efficacy of the oblique and its indirect influence, while unrecognized at the time, should not mask the importance of its impact. In the case discussed in this chapter, humour was used as a way for the team to construct an effective opposition to the senior leadership team of which I was a member. Wresting control at appropriate times from an organization's formal leadership hierarchy is important and supports the distrust shown by complexity scholars for the heroic conceptualizations of leadership that focus on the brilliance of individuals. Complexity perspectives instead champion a more systematic perspective whereby leadership is conceived of as a collective, social process emerging through the interactions of many different people (Uhl-Bien, 2006). Viewed in this way leadership is best seen as a group activity and a dispersed resource that works through and within relationships. The use of humour by members of the consultancy's team ensured the control and leadership of the brainstorming sessions remained with them.

Reflecting on these experiences further supports Chia's insights on passive non-action. While Chia notes that just allowing things to happen should be considered as an alternative way of explaining why events turn out as they do, my experience underlines the positive role such passivity has as a conscious leadership strategy. Not interfering in how the brainstorms were run would have saved time, money and energy. My direct action also jeopardized a way of working that served a number of important functions within the consultancy. Considering my practice through Chia's lens of obliquity heightens appreciation for the mundane and humdrum in accounting for success at work, as opposed to more spectacular interventions. As Chia (2013) notes, a lot can be gained from considering 'the silent efficacy of indirect, passive and understated ways of responding'. This appreciation of the anti-heroic builds on Bourdieu's (1990) idea that self-restraint in organizational life can enable the development of ways of operating that help the organization to orientate for the future. Instead of the gloss of rationality and heroism, the focus is on modesty of action, patience in allowing things to happen and timeliness of intervention.

Directions for future research

These insights suggest interesting avenues for future research to better understand the world of public relations. For example, as a research community we lack a rounded appreciation of the organizational environments in which public relations practice takes place. Developing this type of understanding has yet to be

48 Paul Willis

a significant driver of research in the field and arrests our development towards becoming a fully functioning academic community. Scholars have either largely been concerned with what public relations can and should do as a function, or critically considered its impact on society. However, greater focus should be given to helping public relations practitioners acquire a particular form of contextual intelligence. While there is plenty of discussion in the literature about public relations professionals developing a heightened form of contextual intelligence with regard to the stakeholder environment, less focus is given to enhancing appreciation for the organizational environments they work in and which impact on their practice as functional experts and leaders.

This form of intelligence requires a heightened appreciation for the type of environmental uncertainty identified by complexity scholars. Working with public relations practitioners to better understand how to cope with these complex contexts becomes a priority and, as shown by this study, presents an opportunity for inter-disciplinary excursions in fields such as organizational studies. If this suggestion is then considered at a more micro level, a specific research priority illustrated by this chapter is the need to not only help public relations leaders equip themselves with a repertoire of coping strategies, but also an understanding of when and where different approaches should be deployed. For example, non-action and passivity have their place as leadership approaches, as do rational intervention and direct action. Research that can inform decision-making in this area therefore has the potential to support practitioners navigating their way around complex organizational environments.

The case discussed in the chapter additionally highlights the need in public relations for more 'history from below', a phrase popularized more than fifty years ago by the English historian E.P. Thompson (1966). According to Hitchcock (2013), 'history from below' seeks to bring to the fore the marginalized stories and experiences of people who did not have the opportunity to recount their version of events. A similar commitment to capturing these peripheral voices should be a priority in public relations. Regardless of whether my recollections are accurate or inaccurate, what is revealed in the specific episodes detailed in this chapter are not only the limits of my control and influence as a leader, but also my lack of understanding about the situation and the events as they unfolded. Furthermore, leaders might talk to their colleagues about what they are doing, how they are doing it or whether different approaches worked or did not work, but are they just getting a sanitized version of events and being told what people think they want to hear? Yet, if we go back to the idea of 'great practitioner history', it is usually those in senior positions who are invited to talk on conference platforms, present to students, or are interviewed by researchers to discuss the secrets of success. This situation brings to mind the aphorism that history is something that never happened, told by someone who was not there. It is these limitations that highlight why researchers need to engage with a variety of voices from within public relations practice, as further evidenced by Sarah Williams' insightful chapter in this volume (Williams, 2018). What goes on (or doesn't go on) in the open plan office is just as fascinating and important as what happens in the board room when it comes to understanding the factors that shape the successful practice of public relations.

Summary

This chapter reflects on episodes from my own career as a public relations professional. As a personal piece of research there are obvious limitations to my analysis. The discussion engages in an appraisal of my own actions, while at the same time seeking to interpret the behaviour and motivation of others. What appears is my version of events and the possibility clearly exists that in looking back on these episodes I have misunderstood what was going on around me. However, the potential for misunderstanding and/or misinterpretation only serves to reinforce a point made at the beginning of the chapter that the world of public relations practice is a messier and more complex place than is often portrayed. By recounting a small episode from my career, the discussion seeks to shine a light on those aspects of practice that are usually not spoken of. As an exploration of public relations periphery, the chapter looks sideways and considers what can happen at the margins of working life. The aim in doing so is to encourage a heightened appreciation for the oblique and understated. This orientation does not, though, discount the need or utility for more obvious and direct interventions in organizations. Rather, it should instead promote a sense of humility amongst practitioners when reflecting on their impact, as well as stimulating a wider curiosity about the dynamics and influences at play in organizations.

Acknowledgement: I would like to thank the organizers of the BCN PR Meeting. This international public relations conference is hosted every year in Barcelona and provides a wonderful environment for researchers to test and share ideas. This chapter is based upon a paper first presented at the conference.

Bibliography

Bourdien, P. (1990). *The Logic of Practice*. Cambridge, UK: Polity Press.

Butler, N., Hoedemaekers, C., and Russell, D.S. (2013). 'The comic organization'. *Ephemera*, 15(3): pp.497–512.

Butler, N., Olaison, L., Sliwa, M., Sorenson, B.M., and Spoelstra, S. (2011). 'Work, play and boredom'. *Ephemera*, 11(4): pp.329–335.

Chia, R. (2011). 'Complex thinking: Towards an oblique strategy for dealing with the complex'. In P. Allen, S. Maguire and B. McKelvey (eds.), *The SAGE Handbook of Complexity and Management* (pp.182–198). London: Sage.

Chia, R. (2013). 'In praise of strategic indirection: An essay on the efficacy of the oblique ways of responding'. *M@n@gement*, 5(16): pp.667–679.

Collinson, D. (1988). 'Engineering humour: Masculinity, joking and conflict in shop floor relations'. *Organization Studies*, 9(2): pp.181–99.

Fairclough, N. (1989). *Language and Power*. London: Longman.

Goldstein, J., Hazy, J., and Lichtenstein, B. (2010). *Complexity and the Nexus of Leadership: Leveraging Non-Linear Science to Create Ecologies of Innovation*. Englewood Cliffs, NJ: Palgrave Macmillan.

Hitchcock, D. (2013). 'Why history from below matters more than ever'. In M. Hailwood and B. Waddell (eds.), *The Future of History From Below: An Online Symposium*. Available at: https://manyheadedmonster.wordpress.com/history-from-below (Accessed on 11 April 2017).

Kolb, D.A. (1984). *Experiential Learning: Experience as the Source of Learning and Development*. Englewood Cliffs, NJ: Prentice Hall.

McKie, D. (2001). 'Updating public relations: New science, research paradigms, and uneven developments'. In R.L. Heath (ed.), *Handbook of Public Relations* (pp.75–91). Thousand Oaks, CA: Sage.

McKie, D., and Munshi, D. (2007). *Reconfiguring Public Relations: Ecology, Equity and Enterprise*. Abingdon, Oxon, UK: Routledge.

Murphy, P.J. (1996). 'Chaos theory as a model for managing issues and crises'. *Public Relations Review*, 22(2): pp.95–113.

Murphy, P.J. (2007). 'Coping with an uncertain world: The relationship between excellence and complexity theories'. In E.L. Toth (ed.), *The Future of Excellence in Public Relations and Communication Management* (pp. 119–134). Mahwah, NJ: Lawrence Erlbaum Associates.

Moon, J.A. (2004). *Reflection in Learning and Professional Development*. Abingdon, Oxon, UK: Routledge Falmer.

Noon, M. and Blyton, P. (1997). *The Realities of Work*. Basingstoke, UK: Macmillan.

Stacey, R. (2012). *Tools and Techniques of Leadership and Management: Meeting the Challenge of Complexity*. London: Routledge.

Taylor, P., and Bain, P. (2007). 'Humour and subversion in two call centres'. In S. Fleetwood and S. Ackroyd (eds.), *Critical Realist Applications in Organisation and Management Studies* (pp. 250–271). London: Routledge.

Thompson, E.P. (1966). 'History from below'. *The Times Literary Supplement*, 7 April, Issue 3, 345: p.279.

Uhl-Bien, M. (2006). 'Relational leadership theory: Exploring the social processes of leadership and organizing'. *The Leadership Quarterly*, 17(6): pp.654-676.

Uhl-Bien, M., Marion, R., and McKelvey, B. (2007). 'Complex leadership: Shifting leadership from the industrial age to the knowledge era'. *The Leadership Quarterly*, 18(4): pp.299–318.

Weick, K.E. (1976). 'Educational organizational systems as loosely coupled systems'. *Administrative Science Quarterly*, 21(1): pp.1–19.

Westwood, R., and Rhodes, C. (eds.) (2007). *Humour, Work and Organisation*. London: Routledge Falmer.

Williams, S. (2018) 'Personality in practice'. In E. Bridgen and D. Verčič (eds.), *Experiencing Public Relations: International Voices* (pp. 51–65). Oxford, UK: Routledge.

Whitehead, A.N. (1985). *Science and the Modern World*. London: Free Association Books.

5

PERSONALITY IN PRACTICE

Sarah Williams

Public relations scholars have argued that a body of knowledge, a code of ethics and a 'licence' to operate conferred by society are crucial for public relations to achieve professional status (Cutlip *et al.*, 2003, p.149). However, Svensson contends our understanding of professionalism should rather be contextual, considering 'practical know-how, experience and familiarity rather than theoretical and assertive knowledge' (2006, p.588). This relationship between education and tacit knowledge in public relations is complex. While authors such as Svensson advocate a measured, blended approach that layers informal, practical knowledge on top of formal, theoretical learning, public relations practitioners themselves are more suspicious of formal education and favour practical knowledge instead; as van Ruler notes, 'practitioners seem much more inclined to the emotional-intelligence perspectives, and maybe even to a large extent, to the personality model' (2005, p.16). This is supported by the fact that, in the UK, practitioners often complain that public relations education does not train people for practice; that it is more important that 'your face fits', than the fact that you have a public relations degree.

Van Ruler (2005) categorized theories of professionalism and professionalization into four models: knowledge, status, competition and personality. She argued that while scholars agree on a knowledge model as the basis for professionalism, practitioners appear to favour a personality model. In this chapter, I observe the 'lived experience' and actual practices of British public relations practitioners, exploring the role of personality in practice by observing the ways in which practitioners themselves define, interpret and enact the qualities or traits of a 'professional' worker; specifically I ask:

- In what ways do public relations practitioners define, interpret and enact professionalism?
- What is the role of 'personality' or emotional intelligence in the lived experience of public relations practitioners?

52 Sarah Williams

There is not a large body of work looking at professionalism in public relations, and those studies that do exist have largely adopted a qualitative stance: Asunta (2009) adopts a mixed methodology incorporating in-depth practitioner interviews, coupled with a pan-European quantitative survey, while Ashra (2008) employs an interesting diary strategy.

The interrelated concepts of professionalism, professionalization and being professional form the basis of the public discourse of the professional bodies in PR. However, while these terms are frequently, and often interchangeably, used, trade bodies and other occupational groups make no clear justification for employing them. Sociological definitions of professionalism and professionalization provide some means of analysing professional body policy in support of the professional project, in which the occupation has been engaged for a long time now. However the value of this work is limited as successive professional body policies have failed to result in professionalization of public relations; as L'Etang argued, 'the central story that emerges is that of the failure of the public relations occupation to professionalise' (2004, p.220). Indeed, L'Etang and Pieczka (in Heath, 2001, p.234) considered that, to date, professionalism in public relations discourse has featured 'as merely an historical process but that it should in fact be regarded as a more or less consciously used mechanism that is to deliver specific occupational goals.'

In this chapter, I reconsider what is meant by public relations professionalism by examining the way in which practitioners themselves define, interpret and enact the qualities or traits of a 'professional' worker. This, coupled with the sociological work on professionalism, suggests that an ethnographic study in the field of public relations, which observes the 'lived experience' and actual practices of British public relations practitioners, is a valuable approach.

Debates about professionalism are not new to public relations. Indeed, Hess (1948) formally articulated one of the aims of the newly formed Institute of Public Relations (IPR) as being 'to [raise] the status of those practising public relations to an agreed *professional* level' (in L'Etang, 2004, p.65, emphasis added), establishing the professional project as a key objective for the association from the outset. In common with many other professional bodies, the now Chartered Institute of Public Relations (CIPR) has largely failed in its bid to achieve what Kipping (2011, p.533) terms 'social closure' of the professional project when examined in light of key sociological debates on professionalism, yet the rhetoric of professionalism remains which suggests that there are alternative ways of conceptualizing it which may be more useful in examining professionalism in public relations.

The terms profession, professionalism and professionalization are often employed without consideration of their specific meanings, and while precise definitions may not be necessary for this work, it is nonetheless important to distinguish between these key concepts. The term 'profession' relates to an occupational field that is organized and structured in ways which will be discussed later and the process of professionalization, sometimes referred to as the professional project, is the means by which occupational groups and trade associations seek to become a profession. Professionalism is more complex a term to define, as this can relate to practitioner behaviours, as well as industry standards. Professionalism is contextual; it can be determined by occupational codes of conduct or by observing peer behaviour; it can be co-constructed or imposed. It is this imprecise nature of professionalism which makes it an interesting subject for ethnographic study as professional behaviours will be determined by each individual practitioner according to myriad variables.

The development of these themes in the literature over time highlights an evolution in the phenomenon of professionalism from an occupational to an organizational concern. Key sociological debates relating to professionalism highlight the role of the professional body in organizing actors in the field, whereas more recent academic developments point to professionalism as being embedded at an organizational level. However, neither of these approaches takes account of the role of the individual, nor of the myriad power plays at work in a consultancy environment.

Setting the scene: structural approaches to professionalism

Early work in the sociology of the professions examined structural approaches to professionalism and how the concept might be defined and managed. Millerson (1964) examined the concept of occupations using the creation of a professional body to secure professional status. He examined a variety of structural approaches to defining professionalism and concluded that there are six key characteristics:

i.   A profession involves a skill based on theoretical knowledge
ii. The skill requires training and education
iii. The professional must demonstrate competence by passing a test
iv. Integrity is maintained by adherence to a code of conduct
v.   The service is for the public good
vi. The profession is organised

(ibid., p. 4)

Although Millerson considered that professions needed this occupational structure, he did not believe that the creation of professional bodies necessarily provided this, 'the mere foundation of an organisation, to certificate members and control professional conduct, does not immediately entitle the occupation to be designated as a profession' (ibid. p.7), which suggests that there can be alternative means of managing professionalism and professional behaviour. The discourse of professionalism and the enactment of processes of professionalization are employed by trade bodies in an attempt to legitimize occupational groups for what Millerson (1964, p.10) termed a bid for 'occupational status'. Critiques of this discourse, including by Millerson himself (ibid. p.6), suggest that attempts to secure professionalization for occupational groups are idealistic and contrary to notions of individualization, which suggest that in our present 'risk society' there is pressure on the individual to take responsibility for themselves (Friedman and Phillips, 2002). Foucault's governmentality thesis (Faubion, 2000, pp.xxiii–xxix) also provides a useful lens through which to critique this 'ideal' of the professional, which could be said to be indicative of the subjugation of individual interests to those of the profession. This is bound up with Foucault's notion of the interrelatedness of power/knowledge implicit in discourses on professionalism; Macdonald considers that 'those who can develop and monopolise the language and concepts to be used in an area of social life do indeed have power rooted in knowledge' (1995, p.170). Colley and Guéry (2015, p.114) suggest that individuals play a central part in the professionalization of an occupation, 'this trend is driven partly by the claims of [...] practitioners themselves to assure the quality of the service they provide', and, while they relate the concept of professionalization to interpreters, there are clear parallels with public relations.

Expertise

Expertise is central to occupational approaches to professionalism. Friedman and Phillips (2004) suggest that any claim to professional status should be underpinned by higher education and identify that the early literature on the professions focussed on the learned nature of a professional occupation, on the insistence that a degree of education and training is required to underpin practice, that this body of knowledge should be ring-fenced to control entry to the professional and prevent imitation, and finally that a profession should conform to service ideals.

Mannheim (in Larson, 1977, p.xiv) considered education to be a leveller in professional terms as 'participation in a common educational heritage progressively tends to suppress differences of birth, status, profession and wealth, and to unite the individual educated people on the basis of the education they have received.' This hints at the role of education to create, what Larson (1977) termed, a 'professional class', once again relating the idea of status to notions of professionalism. However, these arguments assume an egalitarian society and do not take into account unequal access to education. For Bourdieu, education is in itself a form of cultural and social capital; he argued that 'academic qualifications are to cultural capital what money is to economic capital' (1977, p.187). In giving academic qualifications a fixed value, he argued, and relating those qualifications to a particular position, you devalue the individual experience; the individual is disposable, the qualification is all that matters.

However, Svensson (2006, p.585) contended that the opposite appears to be true in practice, 'according to the demand for a new professionalism, professional knowledge, competence and performance could be expected to be discursively defined more as an individual property and less related to a particular professional education and occupation – more as actual competence and less as formal education and licensing'. He further argued that 'knowledge, competence and skill are the most frequent cited synonyms for professionalism – sometimes in combination with other words and phrases' and that understanding of professionalism is contextual and 'emphasizes practical know-how, experience and familiarity rather than theoretical and assertive knowledge' (ibid., p.588). This relationship between education

Personality in practice **55**

and tacit knowledge in public relations is complex; while authors, such as Svensson, advocate a measured, blended approach which layers informal, practical knowledge on top of formal, theoretical learning, public relations practitioners themselves are more suspicious of formal education and favour practical knowledge instead.

For public relations, there is a tension between those elements of work that are highly routinized, and can therefore be formally taught, and those areas of the role which are subject to pressure and therefore may require the development of new knowledge, through experimentation in practice. The nature of knowledge in aspiring professions could also be considered to be different from that in established professions; occupations, including public relations, tend to rely on a combination of abstract and tacit knowledge, which cannot simply be abandoned in favour of a formal higher education base.

L'Etang claimed that public relations has yet to fully engage with this issue of providing a solid educational and theoretical knowledge base for practice. Charting the history of public relations' patchy and, at times, tumultuous relationship with education, L'Etang was sceptical of the legitimacy of calling public relations a profession, stating 'the history of public relations' engagement with education to date suggests that it is unlikely to achieve full professional status, at least in the foreseeable future' (2004, p.219). In other words, the largely practical nature of public relations work, and relatively low level of abstract knowledge, leaves the occupational group struggling with its jurisdiction, and therefore, its status. It is in the struggle to establish status that the discourse of professionalism emerges. The occupation employs the discourse of professionalism to secure status, but is hesitant, and sometimes even militant, in its rejection of the structures of professionalism.

Dynamic practice

But these structures of professionalism needn't be fixed or stagnant. Despite being almost fifty years old, Millerson's (1964) work on professionalization remains relevant because he focused on the idea that professionalism is not a static concept, but rather a dynamic concept which changes with time. Freidson (1994, p.14) also considered the notion of professionalism hard to define and argued that the problem of defining professionalism lies in its treatment as a fixed, generic concept, rather than what he termed 'a changing historic concept' (ibid., p.16). This echoes Millerson's notion that 'professional status is probably a dynamic quality' (1964, p.9). This suggests that the sociological concept of a profession is historically determined; therefore it follows that what it means to be a professional or to enact professional behaviours must also differ across time which leads to the re-conceptualization of professionalism not only as an occupational concern but also an individual and organizational one.

Organizational professionalism

While Millerson advocated an occupational approach to managing professionalism, his criticism of the role and value of some professional bodies highlighted a disparity

56 Sarah Williams

between sociological research on the professions and practice in the professions at that time. The gap between those early academic definitions of professionalism and how occupations organized and described themselves in practice has widened over time and more recent work defines professionalism as an organizational concern, thus, moving sociological debates from discussions about occupational professionalism to those centred on market professionalism.

Evetts described a shift to 'organizational' professionalism, as opposed to 'occupational' professionalism (2011, p.407), which she contended represented a move from Friedson's notions of occupational professionalism (which included trust, collegiality and autonomy) to more organizationally defined notions which are concerned with standardization, assessment and performance review and which reflect market concerns such as managerialism and commercialism. Of course, it could be argued that since public relations has never fully established itself as a profession, this shift may not be as easy to detect since occupational norms were never fully established.

Evetts (ibid.) made the distinction between professionalism imposed 'from above' and that imposed 'from within'. She argued that not only is the discourse different but the effects on the 'professional' practitioner differ wildly too, which suggests the value in research into the lived experience of practitioners. Another useful means of examining this change is offered by Faulconbridge and Muzio (2008) with their suggestion that notions of professionalism and organizational principles co-exist and mutually influence each other, thereby creating new hybrid arrangements. This notion of a blended method, of practitioners adopting both occupational and organizational approaches to professionalism, is interesting and, more importantly, practitioner-centred.

The role of the individual

It is clear, then, that individuals, as well as professional bodies, organizations and institutions, play a crucial role in the definition and understanding of professionalism. Svensson identified a need for a 'new' or 'modern' professionalism, which accentuates 'fewer traditional links and individuals' greater personal responsibility' (2006, p.509). His research identified professionalism as a 'phenomenon of the individual' (ibid.), but this concept of individualization could be a product of practitioners responding to organizational processes rather than occupational forces. So rather than practitioners adopting an individual approach, they are adopting an organizational one.

In his discussion on performance,[1] Goffman (1959, p.37) asserts that 'a given social front tends to become institutionalised in terms of the abstract stereotyped expectations to which it gives rise [...] The front becomes a "collective representation" and a fact in its own right.' Thus, the expectations of a particular role may be organizationally determined or established by the occupational field but the power of the individual to change or control that front is limited.

The term professionalism is now part of what Bourdieu termed 'the doxic experience'; the rhetoric of professionalism enables dominant actors to offer a distinct account of the world, which is then accepted as natural:

> The instruments of knowledge of the social world are in this case (objectively) political instruments which contribute to the reproduction of the social world by producing immediate adherence to the world, seen as self-evident and undisputed, of which they are the product and of which they reproduce the structures in a transformed form.
>
> *(Bourdieu, 1977, p.164)*

Therefore, professional traits, acts, thoughts and behaviours are seen to be predetermined according to the dominant ideology. However, in the case of public relations it is not clear what the dominant ideology is; sociological perspectives of professionalism do not fit, and in any case do not present a coherent account of what constitutes professional *behaviour*, while institutional accounts of professionalism in public relations focus on particular manifestations of professionalism (codes of conduct, continuous professional development etc.).

Personality matters

So while the idea and the rhetoric of professionalism is part of the doxic experience of public relations practitioners, the enactment of professionalism is subjective and determined by the individual practitioner and the institution and field they inhabit, with Svensson arguing 'professionalism seems to have always been perceived as a characteristic of individuals and professional practice, never on the organizational level, despite the interpretation in the sociology of professions that professionalism represents an ideology or culture on either the organizational or social level' (2006, p.588).

If the individual is central to the performance of professionalism, it follows that personality must also play a part in how that performance is enacted. The 'emotional-intelligence' or personality model offered by van Ruler (2005) is useful in understanding this role. It offers a view of professionalism that is client–centred and reflexive, privileging personal qualities such as creativity, flexibility and enthusiasm (van Ruler, 2005; Pieczka and L'Etang, 2006).

Far from being limited to describing a list of personal characteristics or personality traits, the personality model, or emotional-intelligence model, of professionalism explores the intersection of relationships between individuals, their co-workers and clients, and other professional relationships; it takes account of the 'everyday' circumstances in which these interactions take place, and the impact these interactions have on practitioners' own constructions of their identity.

There emerges in the literature a constructive overlap between the idea that professional behaviour operates at the level of the individual and the concept of actors being shaped by the habitus, field and capital that surround them, and in this

58 Sarah Williams

chapter I aim to uncover the doxic experience of public relations practitioners and explore the changed organizational locus of professionalism.

Observing the lived experience

Asunta (2009, p.330) identifies two approaches to the nature of public relations research: organizational and societal. In this chapter I explore a third, under-represented approach: that of the interplay between the individual and institutional levels. Much public relations research focuses on extrapolating technical, strategic and managerial aspects of the occupation; as Ashra affirms, 'existing research in public relations and corporate communication decontextualises aspects of roles, excellence and integration' (2008, p.210). In seeking to discover the 'lived experience' of practitioners, I attempt to locate professionalism in the context of practitioner behaviours and to enable individuals to articulate their understandings of the relationship between personality and professionalism.

Having spent over a decade working in public relations consultancies in the UK, I chose to explore the social world of public relations through immersion in a consultancy setting where all staff were public relations practitioners and therefore embedded in the field.

Ethnographic research seeks to understand the lived experience of participants and the context of their views and actions (Snape and Spencer, 2003). I chose an inductive and interpretive approach for the research design (Crotty, 1998), while my conceptual framework used an interpretive approach in which reality is made known through socially constructed meanings (Snape and Spencer, 2003). In interpretive research, meaning is disclosed, discovered and experienced; meanings are grounded in subjective, socially constructed contexts informed by the social worlds of the participants. Organizational ethnography acknowledges the contribution of anthropology and approaches common to exploring the social influences of how people construct meaning in natural settings (Neuman, 2003). The task for an ethnographer 'is not to determine the truth but to reveal the multiple truths apparent in others lives' (Emerson, Fretz and Shaw, 1995, p.3). Rather than assuming a subjectivist standpoint towards the research, which presupposes that social reality, i.e. professional behaviour, is constructed through the actions and decisions of individuals, instead I draw on the work of Bourdieu which, according to Ihlen (2009, p.65), attempts to make 'the opposition between subjectivism and objectivism obsolete.' In addition to observing the doxic experience of practitioners, my participant-observer stance enables these unopposed assumptions to be identified and challenged.

This approach offered insight into the meaning that individual practitioners ascribe to professionalism, including questions such as how practitioners define and enact 'professional' behaviours in the workplace, while at the same time using Bourdieu's (1977) framework to locate these actions in the wider structures of the field of public relations and explore the organizational and occupational cultural forces which influence the professional behaviours of public relations practitioners.

Critical ethnography has a political focus and involves the study of macro-social factors such as power while examining common sense assumptions and hidden agendas. Daymon and Holloway (2002, p.131) consider that this method allows theoretically informed descriptions to emerge from a combination of insider and outsider perspectives, a belief which allows me to draw on my own practitioner experiences.

I collected data from a small, UK-based public relations consultancy with 21 staff members over a period of several months, during which I engaged in numerous periods of observation of varying lengths. A range of observational data, including behaviour, appearance, performance and discourse were collected, in addition to which organizational artefacts pertaining to professionalism, such as reports, correspondence and plans, were also collected and organized thematically. For the purposes of this chapter I have changed the names of all the participants to protect their identities.

I was accepted as a participant-observer as I had been a former practitioner, and had worked alongside some of the staff at various points in my career. At first staff were at pains to demonstrate how professional they were and were constantly pointing out behaviours they considered to be professional; there was also a degree of nervousness and unease towards me from more junior members of the team, who were initially concerned that I might be a 'management spy'. Staff eventually became accustomed to my presence and I didn't get a sense that they were behaving any differently to normal.

My position as a previous practitioner meant that I was familiar with the habitus and while this was certainly advantageous in terms of gaining access to the field and helping the agency staff acclimatize to my presence, it was also problematic in that my experience blinded me, initially, to the breadth of potential encounters and incidents which could be recorded. My knowledge of the rituals and norms of practice meant that, initially, I didn't acknowledge certain behaviours as being worth mentioning. For instance, when a briefing meeting was used as an excuse for an extended lunchtime meeting in a local bar, I didn't initially note this down, acknowledging it as part of my personal experience of practising public relations and therefore not noteworthy. I soon realized that, far from being an objective observer, my experiences were central to my interpretation of how individuals were behaving; I was reflecting on my own experiences in interpreting those of other practitioners (Schön, 1987).

Playing the professional – observations

Style over substance

I encountered the need to not only be competent, but also to be seen to be competent. This manifested itself mainly during client encounters and seemed to reflect a lack of self-confidence and fear of the client. During a new staff induction, Alicia[2] outlined the procedure for answering the phones: 'Some clients expect

60 Sarah Williams

staff to know who they are and who they want to speak to.' There was some discussion about how this should be handled when answering the phones; one client had been irritated because a new staff member had not recognized her voice and put her through to the right person. Alicia explained that the correct course of action was that 'you should just put them through to an account director and pretend you know who they are. Part of our job is making the client feel important and you have to be seen to give them "special treatment".'

Putting on a front for the client is a recurring theme in the consultancy environment. The dress code changed when clients were due in the office, with all staff expected to 'look the part' for client meetings, not just those involved in the meeting itself. James, the managing director, explained to me that, 'the client expects to see a busy and professional office, not that we are not professional when they are not here but I like all staff to present a smart, professional image when they [the clients] come in.' This obsession with smart appearance reflecting competence and professionalism is accepted by staff: 'Everyone knows that you wear a suit when clients are coming in', affirms Sophie, 'we get an email letting us know when clients are coming in and you just know to dress differently.' This behaviour is commonplace and knowing the expected response to a client visit is part of the doxic environment in this public relations consultancy. So much so, that new starters are not explicitly told about it. I asked a new starter, Jane, how she had known to dress smartly when clients were due in given that she would not be in the meeting with them: 'At my last consultancy, client visits meant best behaviour and best image; everyone was expected to be smart and friendly and to look efficient.' It would appear, then, that this behaviour is common to the field of public relations, certainly in terms of consultancy environments, and that it forms part of the cultural norms of working in public relations such that it does not need to be explicitly stated to new staff. It is part of what Goffman (1959, p.37) describes as a front becoming a 'collective representation'; practitioner behaviour in front of and around clients is normalized in the field of public relations such that individual practitioners internalize the expectation and enact it without needing to be told to do so.

The theme of 'looking the part' and 'presenting an image' is accepted by staff as part of the job; the need to reflect a professional image or to play the role of a professional is accepted and acceptable to practitioners. When asked whether she thought it was ethical to behave differently in front of clients, Louise was certain that it was: 'Yes, I think it is ethical. I don't think we are hiding anything necessarily, just putting on a good show for the client. It's expected, like wearing your "Sunday best" to church. I'm sure they know that we don't dress like that every day anyway.' The idea that clients are complicit in the performance is redolent of a play, where both players and audience understand their role in the spectacle. In this way, the audience, or client, constructs, reconstructs and deconstructs the experience, making it part of their culture or doxic environment too.

The notion of impression management is closely related to ideas about public relations work but practitioners are themselves engaging with impression management when they select their 'front' for clients. Goffman (1959, p.6) disconnects

Personality in practice **61**

calculation from the purposes of individuals, opting instead for the situated conse-quences of an individual's expressive actions and thereby locating the meaning of actions in how others respond to them. Thus, when practitioners talk about 'look-ing the part' and 'dressing professionally' for their clients, this professional image may be interpreted differently by those same clients who may judge this as a sign of spin over substance, a form of professional deceit. Goffman (ibid.) asserts that individuals can only be confident of control over impressions given and introduces the notion of recipient advantage whereby the recipient is better placed to detect manipulative strategizing conduct than individuals are to enact it.

Backstage, beyond the sight of clients, practitioners are less formal and less restricted; staff share names of people who they don't want to take calls from and openly discuss their views of which clients they like and don't like. Office attire is more relaxed and so is the language; colourful language is used as punctuation and the façade of formal professionalism is dropped, particularly among more junior members of staff. This behaviour is tempered somewhat by the presence of senior members of staff, and at times the office can feel like a classroom when the pupils take advantage of the teacher being out of the room and are quieted by the return of the authority figure.

Creativity versus bureaucracy

In contrast to the days when clients are expected in to the office, much of the daily life is centred around bureaucracy. Here there was a discrepancy between how practitioners describe themselves and how they describe their work: 'I was drawn to working in public relations because I am a creative person', Jane told me, 'I always wanted to work in the creative industries.' When pressed to describe the more creative aspects of her work, however, Jane struggled: 'I suppose that writing press releases is a form of creative writing and I enjoy organizing client events.' She admitted that much of the day-to-day work focused on client reporting and audit trails, meetings and media relations, which didn't leave much time for creative writ-ing. 'It would be nice to do more of the creative side, but we have to justify our fee to the client and they expect results.' Again, this notion of client expectations drove the daily activities of public relations consultancies, leaving little time for practition-ers' creative ambitions to be realized. In practice, creativity was marginalized and much of the creative spirit, which was so fundamental to practitioners' self-concept, manifested itself in what they wore to the office rather than meaningful work. This seems to be redolent of Evetts' (2011, p.407) concept of 'organizational' profes-sionalism, a form where standardization and assessment take precedence over trust and autonomy, and where market concerns of return on investment and results take precedence over creativity and risk.

In fact, the nature of the work being undertaken, and the way in which that work was reported back to clients, seemed more focused on safe, tried and tested methods which were guaranteed to get results, rather than more creative and poten-tially riskier approaches.

System addict

Creeping managerialism and bureaucratic processes were given pithy titles to make creating audit trails more palatable. There was a perception that having clear management processes and forms, which could be audited and presented to the client, was indicative of professional behaviour; as Alicia explained, 'We need to have processes in place to better manage the workload. The company has grown rapidly and we don't really have enough systems in place to properly manage it.'

'Our clients want to work with a professional organization and, at the moment, our systems don't reflect that, so we need to address that', she added. In this way, managerial processes for the organization and management of work are conflated with being professional. This is at odds with sociological definitions of professionalism, which privilege ideas of autonomy and trust; in Alicia's view, professionalism is not about trust but rather about management and measurement, which is more in line with Evetts' (2011) 'organizational' professionalism than Friedson's (2001) 'occupational' professionalism.

Dogsbodies

Managing client expectations was considered to be a key aspect of professionalism by several members of staff and one which they mostly failed to pay attention to: 'We won't be truly professional until we can manage our clients better', argued Alicia. 'Many of our clients view us as 'dogsbodies', here to do their bidding rather than providing advice or consultancy and it's frustrating.' This is a common complaint, with staff explaining that some clients are quite abrupt, almost to the point of rudeness, with the consultancy staff, and this leaves them feeling that they are commoditized, rather than respected for their advice. There was still a focus on media relations work in the consultancy and, in particular, conducting 'ring rounds'[3] was a core activity for junior members of staff, despite more senior staff acknowledging that this activity may damage rather than enhance relationships with journalists. When questioned about this activity Jane explained, 'it is not ideal but it is what the client wants', indicating that a need to please the client superseded the need to be professional. This focus on professional pleasing seems to be self-destructive; practitioners know that it is damaging to the way in which they are viewed by clients but seem powerless to stop it. The belief that 'the client is always right' appears to undermine the self-confidence of practitioners, all of whom are experienced and highly educated, such that they focus more on process and technical craft, rather than autonomy, creativity and strategy.

The centrality of the notion of 'keeping the client happy' was evident in other areas too. Staff admitted that their writing style was often questioned or compromised by the client. Paul talked about, 'the dilemma of changing something just because a client has asked even though it may not add (and may even detract) from

Personality in practice **63**

the release itself'. This is at odds with the idealized view that public relations is a creative industry and that writing is a means of expressing practitioners' creativity.

Natalia also discussed the issue of clients not being forthcoming with information and not helping with providing information for campaigns and media enquiries. This kind of self-sabotage seems to be quite common with their small- to medium-sized[4] clients, who seem not to fully understand what the role of public relations consultancy is.

Most peculiar of all was that, despite this client focus, none of the team were able to say with any certainty that their clients were happy.

The play's the thing

What emerges is a picture of reality at odds with the desired position; a need to please and impress the client taking precedence over actual, sociologically defined professional behaviours. In this case, we see the performance of professionalism being considered as more important than professionalism itself; which is not to say that practitioners don't want to be professional, nor that they don't consider themselves to be professional, just that in putting client needs first and bowing to client pressures and expectations, professionalism is reduced to a set of performance criteria – dressing smartly, knowing the client's voice, having the right forms and systems – rather than a set of guiding principles.

The role of personality is also important here: a lack of professional self-confidence derived from the need to please the client means that practitioners' ideal identities as creative workers are in jeopardy; practitioner autonomy is seemingly undermined by a lack of trust in their abilities; and 'safe' activities are favoured over more creative or 'risky' activities.

A more considered understanding of the meanings that practitioners attach to the term 'professional' may provide the occupation with a means of robustly defending the use of the word, through the provision of an industry-specific definition, one which both reflects commonly accepted sociological definitions, while recognizing the 'lived experience' of practitioners who enact professionalism in their day-to-day activities. A practitioner-led understanding of what constitutes professionalism, however partial, should provide the starting point for further sociological and occupational research in public relations.

Notes

1 Goffman (1959) uses the term performance to refer to individual activity before a set of observers; he also relates the term 'front' to those situations in which the individual establishes the situation for the observer. Goffman (1959, p.38): 'Fronts tend to be selected, not created'.
2 All names have been changed to protect the participants.
3 A practice of calling journalists to see if they have received a press release and are likely to use it.
4 Based on staff headcount and turnover according to European Commission guidelines.

64 Sarah Williams

Bibliography

Ashra, N. (2008) *Inside Stories: Making Sense of the Daily Lives of Communications Practitioners*. Leeds, UK: University of Leeds.

Asunta, L. (2009) 'Perceptions of PR professionalism in 21st century Europe', in Rogojinaru, A. and Wolstenholme, S. (eds.), *Current Trends in International Public Relations* (pp.315–334). Bucharest, Romania: Tritonic.

Bourdieu, P. (1977) *Outline of a Theory of Practice*. Cambridge, UK: Cambridge University Press.

Colley, H. and Guéry, F. (2015) 'Understanding the new hybrid professions: Bourdieu, *illusion* and the case of public service interpreters'. *Cambridge Journal of Education*, 45 (1), pp. 113–131.

Cutlip, S.M., Center, A.H. and Broom, G.H. (2003) *Effective Public Relations*, 9th ed. London: Pearson.

Crotty, M. (1998) *The Foundations of Social Research: Meaning and Perspective in the Research Process*. London: Sage.

Daymon, C. and Holloway, I. (2002) *Qualitative Research Methods in Public Relations and Marketing Communications*. London: Routledge.

Emerson, R., Fretz, R. and Shaw, L. (1995) *Writing Ethnographic Fieldnotes*. Chicago, IL: University of Chicago Press.

Evetts, J. (2011) 'A new professionalism? Challenges and opportunities'. *Current Sociology*, 59, pp.406–422.

Faulconbridge, J. and Muzio, D. (2008) 'Organizational professionalism in globalizing law firms'. *Work, Employment and Society*, 22 (1), pp. 7–25.

Foucault, M. (2000) *Power: Essential Works of Foucault 1954–1984*, volume 3. London: Penguin (edited by James D. Faubion).

Freidson, E. (1994) *Professionalism Reborn: Theory, Prophecy and Policy*. Cambridge, UK: Polity Press.

Freidson, E. (2001) *Professionalism: The Third Logic*. Cambridge, UK: Polity Press.

Friedman, A. and Phillips, M. (2002) 'The role of mentoring in the CPD programmes of professional associations'. *International Journal of Lifelong Education*, 21(3), pp.269–284.

Friedman, A. and Phillips, M. (2004) 'Continuing professional development: developing a vision'. *Journal of Education and Work*, 17(3), pp.361–376.

Goffman, E. (1959) *The Presentation of Self in Everyday Life*. New York: Doubleday Anchor.

Heath, R. (2001) *Handbook of Public Relations*. Thousand Oaks, CA: Sage.

Hess, A. (1948) *IPR Annual Report*. London: Institute of Public Relations.

Ihlen, Ø., van Ruler, B. and Fredriksson, M. (2009) *Public Relations and Social Theory: Key Figures and Concepts*. Abingdon, UK: Routledge.

Kipping, M. (2011) 'Hollow from the start? Image professionalism in management consulting'. *Current Sociology*, 59 (4), pp. 530–550.

Larson, M.S. (1977) *The Rise of Professionalism: A Sociological Analysis*. Berkeley: University of California Press.

L'Etang, J. (2004) *Public Relations in Britain: A History of Professional Practice in the 20th Century*. Mahwah, NJ: Lawrence Erlbaum Associates.

Macdonald, K.M. (1995) *The Sociology of the Professions*. London: Sage.

Millerson, G. (1964) *The Qualifying Associations: A Study in Professionalization*. London: Kogan Page.

Neuman, W.L. (2003) *Social Research Methods: Qualitative and Quantitative Approaches*. London: Allyn & Bacon.

Piezcka, M. and L'Etang, J. (2006) 'Public relations and the question of professionalism', in L'Etang, J. and Pieczka, M. (eds.) *Public Relations: Critical Debates and Contemporary Practice*. London: Lawrence Erlbaum Associates, pp.265–278.

Schön, D.A. (1987) *Educating the Reflective Practitioner*. Aldershot, UK: Ashgate.

Snape, D. and Spencer, E. (2003) 'The foundations of qualitative research', in Ritchie, J. and Lewis, J. (eds.), *Qualitative Research Practice: A Guide for Social Science Students and Researchers*. London: Sage.

Svensson, L.G. (2006) 'New professionalism, trust and competence: Some conceptual remarks and empirical data', *Current Sociology*, 54(4), pp.579–593.

Van Ruler, B. (2005) 'Public relations: Professionals are from Venus, scholars are from Mars'. *Public Relations Review*, 31(2), pp.159–173.

Vollmer, H.M. and Mills, D.I. (eds.) (1966) *Professionalization*. Upper Saddle River, NJ: Prentice-Hall.

Willis, J.W. (2007) *Foundations of Qualitative Research: Interpretive and Critical Approaches*. Thousand Oaks, CA: Sage.

Winch, P. (1990) *The Idea of a Social Science and Its Relation to Philosophy*, 2nd ed. London: Routledge.

Winston, E. (2005) 'Designing a curriculum for American sign language/English interpreting educators', in Marschark, M. et al. (eds.), *Sign Language Interpreting and Interpreter Education*. New York: Oxford University Press.

Yeomans, L. (2014) 'Gendered performance and identity work in PR consulting relationships: a UK perspective', in Daymon, C. and Demetrious, K. (eds.), *Gender and Public Relations: Critical Perspectives on Voice, Image and Identity* (pp.87–107). London: Routledge.

6

PUBLIC RELATIONS AS 'DIRTY WORK'

Elizabeth Bridgen

Introduction

'Dirty work' refers to occupations which are likely to be perceived as dirty or degrading, of dubious virtue (Kreiner *et al.*, 2006), or using deceptive, intrusive or confrontational methods (Bove and Pervan, 2013). Jobs that academic literature has considered under the heading of 'dirty work' include career occupations such as gynaecological nursing (Bolton, 2005), policing (Dick, 2005), the work of funeral directors, and manual work such as gravedigging and refuse collecting (Ashforth and Kreiner, 1999). Hughes (1962) observed that in order to operate successfully, society delegates work to groups who act as agents on its behalf, thus effectively disowning and disavowing work it has mandated and relies upon. In essence, although society acknowledges that 'someone' has to do the dirty work, society also may ignore or judge those who do it.

This paper explores whether the practice or occupation of public relations could be analyzed through the prism of 'dirty work' via a critical discourse analysis of UK public relations trade magazine *PR Week*.

'Dirty work' is a 'social construction: it is not inherent in the work itself or the workers but is imputed by people, based on necessarily subjective standards of cleanliness and purity' (Ashforth and Kreiner, 1999, p.415). The area was originally divided into three categories (Hughes, 1958), although latterly a fourth has been added to take account of the shifting landscape of employment and the rise of service work. In the first category, 'dirty work' is seen as work that has a physical taint, and where workers deal directly with death, effluent and dirt. Such jobs include refuse collectors, dentists and butchers, and thus the 'taint' results from contact with different types of dirt or 'dirty' tasks. Secondly, dirty work is argued to be work that has a social taint. This is where workers deal with stigmatized or 'dirty' others – thus, this category can include prison guards, police officers and gynaecological nurses. Thirdly, the idea of moral taint has been applied to 'dirty work' (Ashforth *et al.*, 2007). This categorizes dirty work as being sinful, or of dubious virtue, or using deceptive, intrusive or confrontational methods. This category can include jobs as diverse as lap dancers, debt collectors, casino managers and police interrogators.

Finally, McMurray and Ward (2014) noted that emotion was lacking in the three dirty work categories defined above and suggested a fourth category of dirty work – emotional dirty work. This is work:

> which requires engagement with the expressed feelings of others (customers, clients, callers) that threaten the preferred order of a given individual or group. We have in mind emotions that are deemed out of place, contextually inappropriate, burdensome or taboo […] in the eye of the beholder rather than an objective state (Dick, 2005) […] Given the contextually relative and socially constructed nature of dirt it is likely that what constitutes 'emotional dirt' will vary across occupations. Whether and why anger, ecstasy, despair, joviality, desire or rage are deemed 'dirty' in the work of a particular occupational context will need to be elucidated in future research.
>
> *(p. 17)*

Such work includes occupations where the work and those who carry it out are 'spoiled, blemished, devalued, or flawed to various degrees' as a consequence of the stigma that arises from their work. McMurray and Ward positioned their study around volunteers working for Samaritans (a UK charity which provides confidential support to people in distress), but recognized that their definition was applicable to many other 'emotion laden' occupations including flight attendants, doctors' receptionists and erotic dancers (Mavin and Grandy, 2013). There is often the sense with emotional 'dirty work' that workers are required to perform emotional self-control where others would or could not and are doing the unpleasant jobs (such as, in the Samaritans case, talking non-judgementally to people who have committed activities that society condemns or, in the case of gynaecological nursing, dealing with death and bereavement) which others would rather not do. Essentially, emotional dirty work is work where people use and interact with their emotions in their dealings with aspects of life that society may not want to know about or would rather didn't exist.

The central point of this paper is to consider whether the practice of public relations could be understood through the prism of 'dirty work'. Hughes (1971) argued that 'dirty work may be an intimate part of the very activity which gives the occupation its charisma' (p.344), so viewing public relations through a prism of dirty work is not necessarily a negative way to view the occupation. It is more a way of understanding the impact of the self-view of the occupational brand of public relations, and through this gives us a fresh perspective on the aspects of public relations activities which the industry is embarrassed about or which need improving, and offering insight into why some of the industry's aims and ambitions (such as being seen as a profession and being viewed positively) are proving so difficult to achieve (Chartered Institute of Public Relations, 2015).

68 Elizabeth Bridgen

Defining the boundaries of the occupation of public relations is problematic as those definitions which exist are generalized in order to take into account the many different forms of public relations (e.g. Chartered Institute of Public Relations, 2017; Public Relations Society of America, 2012), are largely grouped around a generalized form of public relations as practised in a particular country and often focus on the outcome rather than the work itself (which is described below). Sometimes it is more helpful to see an occupation as a brand rather than a large set of tasks and outcomes and from this explore how workers form a collective identity around core activities and issues. If we take this perspective, we can start to understand that there is a significant difference between the external image and the internal identity of the occupational brand of public relations.

Public relations is not a synonym for 'media relations' (liaising with media outlets) but rather encompasses areas as diverse as event management, social media monitoring and activity, employee communication, strategic communication, activism, political lobbying, investor relations and relationship building. Furthermore, the nature and reach of the public relations function is constantly changing due to opportunities and pressures arising from globalization, media convergence and developments in communication technology.

This chapter focuses on aspects of public relations reported by industry magazine *PR Week*, which tends to present the job as a generalized, hierarchical, quasi-professional, white-collar role, the occupants of which have degree-level qualifications and/or take part in regular training – a view of public relations which may differ from actual workplace practices (McKie and Munshi, 2007).

An outline of past research on dirty work

Literature on dirty work does not just look at occupations that are considered socially, morally and/or physically tainted, but also at the employees who perform dirty work; such research also considers workers' attitudes towards their work (e.g. Shantz and Booth, 2014; Bolton, 2005) and the management of 'dirty workers' (e.g. Ashforth and Kreiner, 1999). People doing dirty work often possess a strong sense of self-esteem and pride despite society denying them any affirmation. This can be seen in many occupations (such as gynaecological nurses (Bolton, 2005) and funeral directors (Ashforth and Kreiner, 1999)), although the authors go on to say that some people who hold dirty occupations retain some ambivalence towards their role. Indeed, Ashforth and Kreiner (2002) note that there are many fluctuations in workers' identities and suggest that strong self and group identities can derive from a contradiction between employees' self-view and how they think others view their occupation. The authors note that such groups will normalize their work to such an extent that the extraordinary (in the eyes of society – the 'other') is viewed as ordinary.

Across many 'dirty' occupations, the positive meaning that workers construct from their role in the face of the stigmas attached to them can have several origins and outcomes. In some cases demographic clustering (i.e. when the majority

Public relations as 'dirty work' **69**

of workers fall into a similar demographic, as is the case with female hotel maids, young bouncers, minority farmhands – and, potentially, young, female, public relations practitioners) facilitates interaction (Ashforth and Kreiner, 1999). As a result, individuals come to socialize largely with co-workers and create their own meaning from their work (Trice, 1993, in Ashforth and Kreiner, 1999).

In addition, when the stigma of dirty work undermines the status of certain occupations in the eyes of society there is an argument that it simultaneously facilitates the development of strong occupation cultures. This allows people to take pride in their work (e.g. the gynaecological nurses discussed by Bolton (2005)) despite issues such as high turnover or reward structures that pit members against each other (Ashforth and Kreiner, 1999) and goes some way to suggesting why those carrying out dirty work can demonstrate great pride in their occupation as they feel united against a common enemy which may not understand or empathize with the work that they do.

Past papers on 'white collar' or 'professional' dirty work have inevitably focused on moral or social taint (e.g. Davis, 1984), since white collar workers tend not to get their hands or bodies dirty at work (although there are exceptions to this – e.g. dentists, some medical staff and funeral directors (Ashforth and Kreiner, 1999) with McMurray and Ward (2014) later adding emotional dirty work to the canon.

Society assigns meaning and values to roles that '[distinguish] the worthwhile, acceptable, clean, pure, orderly, unblemished and good: from the worthless, unacceptable, tainted, polluted, chaotic, stigmatized and bad' (Selmi, 2012, in McMurray and Ward, 2014 p.4), and as the dirty status of work is fluid and not something which can be measured quantitatively, an empirical measure of whether an aspect of public relations is, or is not, dirty work is not possible.

Methodology

This study takes the form of a critical discourse analysis which explores the way that the public relations industry magazine *PR Week* (a monthly title, despite its name) describes the activity of public relations. Focusing on a 13-month period from October 2013 to October 2014, the aim of the analysis was to discover whether the practice of public relations could be analyzed through the prism of 'dirty work' via the discussion of public relations in *PR Week* and what this tells us about the self-image of the industry. While a 'value-free' reading of *PR Week* is not possible (the author of this chapter used to work in public relations and is a public relations researcher and lecturer) it is also not desirable; a 'value-free' reading (if such a thing is possible) would not be advantageous when carrying out this work and would miss some of the contexts of issues discussed and perhaps not consider some of the more complex underlying tensions within the industry.

Since public relations workers rarely deal with stigmatized, or dirty, artefacts or others, this paper focuses on emotional and moral taint to explore whether we can analyze public relations via the prism of dirty work. Nine of the most common features of 'white collar' taint – emotional and moral taint (Table 6.1) – have been

70 Elizabeth Bridgen

TABLE 6.1 Examples of moral and emotional taint

Moral taint

1. Collectiveness in the face of opposition.
2. Proximity to notions of sin, dubious virtue or deception.
3. Having to do something that threatens the solidarity, self-conception or preferred orders of a given individual or community.
4. Use of deceptive, intrusive or confrontational methods.

Emotional taint

5. Having to exert emotional self-control.
6. Evidence of social prejudice or stigmatization by outsiders.
7. Demonstrating emotions about things they do not feel.
8. Requires engagement with the expressed feelings of others (customers, clients, callers) that threaten the preferred order of a given individual or group.
9. Using emotions when dealing with stigmatized others.

extracted from the work of Bolton (2005), Ashforth and Kreiner (1999, 2002), and McMurray and Ward (2014) and are used as identifiers to explore whether there is any resonance or connection with public relations work.

This study uses a critical discourse analysis which acknowledges the (assumed) power and position of privilege that those who write for *PR Week* hold and takes into account the level of control held by the publishers. Thus, this is an analysis of the views being popularized and presented by the industry, to the industry. As the only national printed magazine for public relations practitioners, and as part of the Brand Republic suite of titles held by the privately owned Haymarket Media Group (other media industry titles include: *Marketing*, *Campaign* and *Media Week*), the publication is able to command considerable equity in terms of the people it is able to interview and who contribute to it (the industry elite are frequently interviewed and asked to write 'thought pieces' for the publication, thus perpetuating a certain ideology of public relations as a white, middle class occupation). *PR Week* describes itself thus:

> *PR Week* is the world's leading PR and comms publication. In May 2014, it launched the first global PR destination combining the highly regarded US and UK sites and launching a brand new site in Asia [...] *PR Week* epitomises the modern business publishing brand [...] Breaking news, analysis, and opinion fuels PRWeek.com and is distributed through its website, bulletins, apps, magazines and via social media – Twitter and Facebook.
>
> *(PR Week, 2014: online)*

PR Week is presented as not just a magazine but a branded global product with international publications, online activities and events. However, it does not represent every type of public relations or every public relations practitioner, and it could be claimed that the UK edition has a London-centric corporate agency focus (as opposed to a regional focus or one that highlights the work of smaller public relations agencies or people working for not-for-profit, public sector or radical organizations).

PR Week changed from a weekly to monthly magazine in October 2013 with a new format and range of features. In the 13 months following the relaunch, the editor changed from Ruth Wyatt to Danny Rogers and a number of changes were made to the content of the magazine. For instance, regular features were launched, dropped or repositioned in different sections, making a month-on-month analysis of any 'regular' feature problematic. Hence, this analysis focuses on the Leader (where one of the two editors discusses a public-relations-related issue) and the news sections, which remained in the magazine over the 13 months of the study, although they did not always hold the same format or title.

During the time of the analysis the public relations industry was frequently making news in its own right due to the trial and subsequent conviction of both 'publicist' and 'PR guru' Max Clifford and Andy Coulson, the former British Prime Minister's former head of communications. These occurrences may have skewed the editorial towards an examination of the reputation of public relations (since these were high profile public relations practitioners whose activities were reported in mainstream media) but the magazine's near-obsession with these characters and the reason why they were presented within its pages as being to blame for the poor reputation of public relations is itself of interest.

Despite boldly announcing when the magazine was relaunched that 'news is going solely on our brand spanking new website' (October 2013), this was a fragile claim. A 'Global News' section was always present in the magazine along with details of people and agency movements in the industry, while a 'News Analysis' section was introduced in June 2014 and a 'News Roundup' section in the July/August 2014 edition. These news and editorial comment sections captured the mediated public relations issues of the month and allowed an insight into the worldview taken by the editorial team of *PR Week*.

This 13-month analysis of *PR Week* followed an earlier pilot study where articles were reviewed from the past decade of the magazine's online edition. This pilot demonstrated that *PR Week* reported the business and function of public relations relatively critically and while 'good news' was celebrated, this tended to be in terms of functional reporting (e.g. a person changing jobs, an organization increasing its spend on public relations, or a case study of a successful campaign). Interestingly, there was little written about the success of longer-term, strategic or 'below the radar' public relations activities and, where they were discussed, such reporting was ringfenced within a case study or within an interview with (or 'thought piece' by) a well-known figure in the public relations industry. This meant that longitudinal campaigns, or ongoing public relations work which could not be aligned to a well-known public relations institution, remained largely unreported.

The magazine provides its audience of public relations practitioners with news, information and gossip, and provides a forum for 'experts' to give their opinions on topics of their choosing, or which are current in the national or international

72 Elizabeth Bridgen

media. The magazine has something of a 'mission to explain' policy (possibly linked to the industry's quest to be seen as a 'profession', a move championed by the industry body the Chartered Institute of Public Relations) and thus advice and information is provided to help practitioners navigate the problems and issues of practice. Meanwhile, the lives and career trajectories of famous people in the industry are frequently celebrated and their advice is treated respectfully and uncritically. The analysis discussed below demonstrated that there is surprisingly little focus on the industry's more junior members, or on public relations as a regional activity, with the former frequently seen as the central focus of an 'issue' or 'problem'. In addition, 'amateur' public relations campaigns, however successful, are usually ignored even if they have caught the attention of mainstream media.

Studies of the reporting or news values of trade or professional media are few, so to start to understand why *PR Week* reports the industry so critically, we have to look at writing on news values and how journalists report on specialist areas. However, it is worth noting that Aldridge (1998) found that another media-related title, *Press Gazette*, also had a habit of criticizing and scrutinizing the occupation it reported on:

> As a crude measure I sampled the first five news stories plus the leading editorial in the *Press Gazette* for the first edition of each month from July 1995 to June 1996 (a total of about 70 items). News of acquisitions, mergers, shame-ups, job losses and resignations/sackings outnumbered those of launches of expansions by 27 to 16.
>
> *(1998, p. 117)*

Although this research was carried out during a time of flux in the newspaper industry, this suggests that a highly critical view of an occupational brand is not unique to *PR Week*.

Hansen (1994) observes that newspaper coverage of specialist areas such as science is governed and shaped by both macro-level factors such as ownership and cultural resonances, and by the more micro-level factors of journalistic practices, professional values and organizational arrangements. Thus, the reporting of public relations activities in *PR Week* is governed by a set of news values which reports 'bad news' while simultaneously promoting the interests of the public relations industry, such as improving the credibility of the 'profession' (something which the Chartered Institute of Public Relations and others, such as Coombs and Holladay (2013), reports the industry to be lacking).

Journalists who write for trade and professional publications, although usually experienced and qualified in journalism, may not necessarily have a background in the industry about which they write – which means that journalistic 'truths' (what Davies (2008) referred to as 'flat earth news') are repeated and understood to be true by those who write about them. Thus, the societal view of the public relations industry (that it is connected with spin and has a bad reputation) is potentially carried over into the industry publications. In addition, news organizations also rely heavily on each other for ideas. Gans (1979) argued that trade magazine editors read elite media such as *The New York Times* and *Washington Post* for story ideas, eliminating the need for independent judgement of newsworthiness (Weigold, 2001, p.167) – essentially, what the elite media say is true becomes the truth and is repeated in specialist publications. Thus, rather than looking at the news values which may be relevant to the public relations industry, *PR Week*'s news values derive from the mainstream media and its self-view echoes that of the dominant media rather than that of the industry itself.

A number of rhetorical devices were employed by *PR Week* in the articles under investigation, but in the main, two devices stood out – the journalist commentating as an 'expert' on the problems with the industry and the journalist 'speaking' for others and repeating 'societal' views on the public relations industry. These opinions of others were not verified but came directly from the journalist who thus appeared to be acting as a spokesperson for society and/or the public relations industry. Very rarely were quotes or statistics used to back up these opinions leading to a view of the public relations industry which was, in part, created or replicated by the industry journalists themselves.

Discussion: *PR Week* and dirty work

Through a critical discourse analysis of *PR Week* we can read certain articles and understand whether they are reporting the occupation of public relations through the lens of 'dirty work.'

Over the 13-month period of review there was a distinct switch in focus when the Leader writer changed from Brand Editor Ruth Wyatt to Editor-in-Chief Danny Rogers in May 2014 (these Leader writers took over editorship of the magazine at the same time). Wyatt's strident editorials focused on how outsiders saw the industry and the problems that existed within it. Her staccato style stressed urgency, for example: 'This month we look at how others see PR. And it's not pretty' (April 2014). Wyatt's editorials saw public relations as one united occupation and the different forms of public relations or individual issues experienced, as discussed above, were not considered. Rogers' editorials had a different focus in that they recognized that problems existed but that public relations practitioners, through hard work, good practice and education could move on from these – for instance, his bold claim that 'one hopes communications professionals will be able to move the agenda on from sordid "local stories like Max Clifford" to more important themes' (May 2014).

The repetition of an unfavourable societal view of public relations can serve a number of functions when viewed through the prism of dirty work. Firstly, it can allow practitioners to declare a moral distance from the problems of practice (Goffman, 1959), thus setting themselves free from negative associations. The distancing from 'brand public relations' is a common feature in the industry away from *PR Week* and there are a number of high profile public relations practitioners who have declared that public relations is 'dead' and that a new and more ethical form of

74 Elizabeth Bridgen

communications is needed (e.g. Pitcher, 2002; Phillips, 2014), while others style their practice as 'communications' rather than 'public relations'. Correspondingly, drawing on the work of Ashforth and Kreiner (1999), we can understand that the negative images of public relations published in *PR Week* and elsewhere can also allow practitioners to feel as though they are united in what – as has been discussed earlier – is a very disparate occupation. Thus, while journalists continue to repeat the worldview that public relations is viewed negatively (essentially, as a tainted brand) and is a practice with a large number of problems, they are not stopped by others in the industry and instead the industry rhetoric focuses on 'fighting back' and 'improving' public relations (e.g. Waddington, 2014). This is an interesting issue and this article proposes that this is because the 'dirty' side of public relations is one of the few aspects of the practice that practitioners have in common; it allows them to share experiences and feel a sense of solidarity. If we view this 'tainted' brand of public relations through the lens of Ashcraft (2007) we understand that this ongoing (and slightly one-sided) discussion produces and reproduces a particular occupational identity and lays down a specific discourse around the occupation of public relations.

The negativity towards public relations portrayed in the pages of *PR Week* can be seen as a potential explanation for public relations practitioners having a strong collective identity in the face of opposition (Ashforth and Kreiner, 1999). However, being part of an industry under attack also allows public relations practitioners to unite and differentiate themselves against those who do (what Exerson and Pollner (1976), writing on a community mental health team's encounters with clients, describe as) 'shit work'. In the context of public relations, this would be the immoral and corrupt aspects of the work (e.g. misrepresenting a company to the media, supressing unfavourable news or gaming search engine optimization (SEO) results), although this in itself is a shifting arena depending on the moral compass of the individual practitioner. So, while acknowledging that problems with practice do exit, they 'shift [...] the messy and stigmatizing [work] to others with less standing' (Shaw 2004, p.1,033) – such as jailed public relations practitioners like Clifford and Coulson.

This contradiction can be seen in the trial and subsequent conviction of publicist Max Clifford for sex offences in 2014. This both united and divided the public relations industry, with much of the debate centring on whether Clifford was, or was not, a public relations practitioner (*PR Week*, April 2014). The performance of 'distancing' the public relations industry from Clifford and his 'shit work' provided a springboard for *PR Week* to highlight the problems and issues that the occupation faced and discuss the men who had brought the industry into disrepute. This allowed a particular occupational perspective to dominate discussion:

> The public don't love PR either. The reports they read of PRs are rarely (ever?) favourable and recently have been dominated by the allegations made against Max Clifford [...] The papers he boasted of manipulating for decades have reported his trial [...] with ill-concealed glee.
>
> (*Ruth Wyatt, PR Week, April 2014*)

Public relations as 'dirty work' **75**

March has not been a good month for the public perception of PR with three PR men up before the beak at the same time. Max Clifford's trial for alleged indecent assault generated a great deal of coverage in its first few days. The trial of the PR's former director of communications Andy Coulson continues while Richard Hillgrove, best known for his aggressive defence of Charles Saatchi in his battle with Nigella Lawson, has appeared on tax evasion charges [...] In other industries the alleged aberrations of individuals would be treated as just that, but not PR which somehow seems to be tarred and feathered. We'll be looking at the reputation of PR in a future issue ...

(Ruth Wyatt, PR Week, March 2014)

Wyatt observes that 'In other industries the alleged aberrations of individuals would be treated as just that, but not PR which somehow seems to be tarred and feathered' while continuing to repeat the (her?) worldview that public relations is a problematic occupation. Indeed, the readiness of journalists to highlight the ways that the public relations industry was falling into sin and ill-repute was a common theme throughout the research period, and even relatively minor lapses by small public relations consultancies became national news:

The Drum Consultancy felt the wrath of freelance journalist Emma Lunn when it admitted lifting quotes from a story she had written and then attributing them to its clients [...] the Drum Consultancy chief Karen Hughes told Lunn that confusion among her staff as to what material was in the public domain as well as "an element of laziness" contributed to the error and offered to pay Lunn as a "goodwill" gesture.

(News Round Up, PR Week, September 2014)

Similarly, when John Lewis Director of Communications Peter Cross was suspended from his post (and reinstated without sanction) in July 2014, this too was headline news:

It was not clear why Cross was suspended or for how long and when *PR Week* contacted him, he declined to comment [...] A week later Cross was back in his post after John Lewis said it had completed an "investigation".

(News Round Up, PR Week, September 2014)

Both these pieces of news demonstrate the glee with which the journalists writing for *PR Week* seize on relatively minor transgressions and turn them into headline news (despite early claims that 'news' would be confined to the magazine's website). That is not to say that such news should not be reported, but their inclusion in the print edition of *PR Week* (rather than as online news) gives an indication that the journalists are eager to write about the accepted external image of public relations rather than consider what might be news (or useful) to a practitioner.

76 Elizabeth Bridgen

Public relations practitioners and the brand of public relations is occasionally attacked by prominent outsiders or industry commentators within the media. Wyatt, in her Leader of April 2014 (titled 'Are We Millwall?') considers this prejudice at length:

> Research commissioned by *PR Week* demonstrates the public's disdain for an activity they roundly reject as a profession [...] Their views are clearly at odds with a business that sees itself as being the corporate conscience. Low life versus moral high ground. It is curious that a business devoted to communicating positive messages, influencing belief and behaviour in favour of clients and disseminating complex ideas in an accessible manner should struggle so much with its own standing.
>
> *(Ruth Wyatt,* PR Week, *April 2014)*

Stauber and Rampton (1995) claim that public relations practice is synonymous with propaganda and its association with lies and manipulation. Thus, the critical view that 'public relations is deceptive' tallies with the journalistic 'truth' and is something that public relations practitioners are also told by organizations, such as the Chartered Institute of Public Relations, that they need to constantly defend themselves against. The defence of public relations is not carried out in the pages of *PR Week* but instead by professional associations such as the Public Relations Consultants' Association, the Chartered Institute of Public Relations and the blog posts of senior individuals within the industry. However, all this activity is on an ad hoc basis suggesting little appetite (or time) for a robust defence of the occupation.

The April 2014 issue of *PR Week* focused on and 'celebrated' this stigmatization, with a five-page feature focusing on 'PR's PR Problem', even showcasing fictional public relations people in popular culture who are part of this 'problem' – one of whom, Siobhan Sharpe (from the UK BBC TV series *Twenty Twelve* and *W1A*) featured on the front cover of that month's issue.

The survey on which 'PR's PR Problem' bases its evidence is made up of four leading questions asked to an unspecified sample of 1,000 people (PRs respond to fake survey accusations, April 2014). Mirroring the work of Emerson and Pollner some four decades earlier, 'negative statements … [came] … from the workers themselves' (1976, p.246). It is interesting that Emerson and Pollner found that workers were most likely to denigrate an aspect of their occupation where they had little or no control over what they did or were unable to use their technical skills. Thus, in this sense we can suggest that the public relations practitioners, unable to control the media frenzy surrounding the Max Clifford case, were happy to have their occupation denigrated in order that they could distance themselves from the 'shit work' it involved and position themselves as separate or better. Such denigration was not limited to the Max Clifford case, as a news report of the views of a BBC journalist recorded:

> Robert Peston, the BBC economics editor, left his handmark on the bruised cheek of the PR industry this month when he used the British Journalism

Review Charles Wheeler Lecture to attack what he said was its pernicious influence on modern media. "As a journalist I have never been in any doubt that PRs are the enemy".

(PR Week, July/August 2014)

Thus, public relations practitioners are seen as purveyors of half-truths and spin, both in their industry media and in mainstream media, associated with an industry which is working against and not with the 'responsible' media. Since the occupation is little understood outside the public relations industry, and badly explained by those within it, it is difficult for public relations practitioners – or the journalists who write for the sector – to defend themselves.

Conclusion

This analysis poses the hypothesis that public relations (or aspects of it) could be understood as dirty work with a moral taint. The findings from the critical discourse analysis of *PR Week* suggest that some aspects of public relations could be categorized as 'dirty work' and, while this in itself is not particularly noteworthy, it is valuable to explore how the marginalization of some types of public relations can lead to a stronger work group or culture, whether practitioners agree or disagree with the external image of their occupation. As Bolton (2005) observed, the discussion of the merits (or otherwise) of an occupation – in this case public relations – helps to unify public relations practitioners since 'the sense making is rarely diluted and, therefore, the community is continually strengthened as they only ever share their experiences with each other' (p.11).

In the case of a public relations executive, long hours; presenting an organization in the most favourable light (as opposed to objectively reporting facts as discussed by Notthaft (2018) in his chapter in this book); the accusations of being part of an occupation which disguises the source of the information' (Miller and Dinan, 2007, p.21); and the use of emotions at work to persuade clients, journalists, bloggers and suppliers to do things which will further the interests of an organization are valorized or simply normalized. Even being shouted at and abused by journalists is seen as part of the public relations role (as Shin and Cameron (2005) observe, 'tensions' between journalists and public relations practitioners are widely reported).

Thus, in concert with other dirty work occupations, the occupation of public relations, viewed through the pages of *PR Week*, can be seen as dirty work. It has – rather forced upon it by the journalists who report it – a proximity to notions of sin, dubious virtue or deception and it's through this, and social prejudice and stigmatization, that public relations practitioners demonstrate collectiveness. However, this is not in the form of rushing to protect their industry (this is left to professional associations and industry spokespeople) but in the form of discussing the problems with their occupation.

While in public relations literature (e.g. Theaker and Yaxley, 2012) there is evidence of the traits of emotional taint in terms of practitioners exerting emotional self-control and expressing feelings that they did not feel, this was not evident in the pages of *PR Week*, where the voice of the practitioner (as opposed to the industry) was absent. This suggests that further research in this area – perhaps through ethnography or in-depth interviews – would be valuable.

This chapter demonstrates an association of dirty work with public relations and where this is useful is that it demonstrates that seeing dirty work from the perspective of *PR Week* goes some way to explaining how being seen as dirty, as well as undermining the occupation, also helps to unify a group of disparate practitioners. As Emerson and Pollner (1976) point out, the 'embarrassment' that workers feel when they realize that performance is incompetent, actually helps to reaffirm proper 'standards of performance' (p.252) and could be seen as helping the drive by professional bodies to educate public relations practitioners.

This analysis only captured the views of practitioners mediated by journalists and did not explore their lived experience, which means that elements of emotional taint such as the demonstration of false emotions were not encountered by this particular methodological approach. However, the area of public relations and the frontstage/backstage (Goffman, 1959) emotions employed by practitioners has been discussed by Yeomans (2007) and Bridgen (2011) and the relationship between emotional labour, dirty work and public relations could and should be explored further.

Bibliography

Aldridge, M. (1998) 'The tentative hell-raisers: Identity and mythology in contemporary UK press journalism', *Media Culture Society*, 20(1), pp.109–127.

Ashcraft, K.L. (2007) 'Appreciating the 'work' of discourse: Occupational identity and difference as organizing mechanisms in the case of commercial airline pilots'. *Discourse & Communication*, 1(1), pp.9–36.

Ashforth, B. and Kreiner, G. (1999) '"How can you do it?" Dirty work and the challenge of constructing a positive identity', *Academy of Management Review*, 24(3), pp.413–434.

Ashforth, B. and Kreiner, G. (2002) 'Normalising emotion in organisations: Making the extraordinary seem ordinary', *Human Resource Management Review*, 12(2), pp.215–235.

Ashforth, B., Kreiner, G., Glark, M. A. and Fugate, M. (2007) 'Normalizing dirty work: Managerial tactics for countering occupational taint'. *Academy of Management Journal*, 50(1), pp. 149–174.

Bolton, S. C. (2005) 'Women's work, dirty work: The gynaecology nurse as "other"', *Gender, Work and Organization,* 12, pp.169–186.

Bove, L.L. and Pervan, S.J. (2013) 'Stigmatized labour: An overlooked service worker's stress', *Australasian Marketing Journal*, 21(4), pp.259–263.

Bridgen, L. (2011). 'Emotional labour and the pursuit of the personal brand: Public relations practitioners' use of social media'. *Journal of Media Practice*, 12(1), p.61–76.

Chartered Institute of Public Relations (2017) 'What is PR?'. Available at: https://www.cipr.co.uk/content/careers-advice/what-pr [Accessed on 4 March 2017].

Chartered Institute of Public Relations (2015) 'State of the Profession 2015'. Available at: http://www.cipr.co.uk/stateofpr [Accessed on 4 March 2017].

Coombs, W.T. and Holladay, S.J. (2013) *It's Not Just PR: Public Relations in Society*. Oxford, UK: Wiley Blackwell.

Davis, D.S. (1984), 'Good people doing dirty work: A study of social isolation', *Symbolic Interaction*, 7, pp.233–247.

Davies, N. (2008) *Flat Earth News*. London: Chatto and Windus.

Dick, P. (2005) 'Dirty work designations: How police officers account for their use of coercive force', *Human Relations*, 58(11), pp.1,363–1,390.

Emerson, R.M. and Pollner, M. (1976) 'Dirty work designations: Their features and consequences in a psychiatric setting', *Social Problems*, 23, pp.243–254.

Gans, H.J. (1979) *Deciding What's News: A Study of CBS Evening News, NBC Nightly News, Newsweek, and Time*. Evanston, IL: Northwestern University Press.

Goffman, E. (1959) *The Presentation of Self in Everyday Life*. New York: Doubleday Anchor.

Hansen, A. (1994) 'Journalistic practices and science reporting in the British press', *Public Understanding of Science*, 3, pp.111–134.

Goffman, E. (1959) *Presentation of Self in Everyday Life*. New York: Doubleday Anchor.

Hughes, E. (1962) 'Good people and dirty work', *Social Problems*, 10(1), pp.3–11.

Hughes, E. (1971) *The Sociological Eye: Selected Papers*. Chicago, IL: Aldine.

Kreiner, G.E., Blake E.A. and David M.S. (2006) 'Identity dynamics in occupational dirty work: Integrating social identity and system justification perspectives', *Organization Science*, 17(5), pp.619–636.

McKie, D. and Munshi, D. (2007) *Reconfiguring Public Relations: Ecology, Equity and Enterprise*. London: Routledge.

McMurray, R. and Ward, J. (2014) '"Why would you want to do that?": Defining emotional dirty work', *Human Relations*, 67(9), pp.1,123–1,143.

Mavin, S. and Grandy, G. (2013) 'Doing gender well and differently in dirty work: The case of exotic dancing', *Gender, Work & Organization*, 20(3), pp.232–251.

Miller, D. and Dinan, W. (2007) *A Century of Spin: How Public Relations Became the Cutting Edge of Corporate Power*. London: Pluto Press.

Nothhaft, H. (2018) 'Dealing in facts', in *Experiencing Public Relations: International Voices*. Oxon, UK: Routledge.

Phillips, R. (2014) 'Trust me PR is Dead'. Available at: http://unbound.co.uk/books/trust-me-pr-is-dead [Accessed on 18 November 2014].

Pitcher, G. (2002) *The Death of Spin*. London: Wiley.

Public Relations Society of America (2012) 'What is public relations? PRSA's widely accepted definition'. Available at: http://www.prsa.org/aboutprsa/publicrelationsdefined/#.VGtQl8mQnec [Accessed on 18 November 2014].

Selmi, G. (2012) 'Dirty talks and gender cleanliness: An account of identity management practices in phone sex work'. In Simpson, R., Slutskaya, N., Lewis, P. and Höpfl, H. (eds.), *Dirty Work: Concepts and Identities*. Basingstoke, UK: Palgrave Macmillan, pp.113–125.

Shantz, A. and Booth, J.E. (2014) 'Service employees and self-verification: The roles of occupational stigma consciousness and core self-evaluations', *Human Relations*, Available at: http://hum.sagepub.com/content/early/2014/04/07/0018726713519280.abstract [Accessed on 18 November 2014].

Shaw, I. (2004) 'Doctors, "dirty work" patients, and "revolving doors"', *Qualitative Health Research*, 14(8), pp.1,032–1,045.

Shin, J.H. and Cameron, G.T. (2005) 'Different sides of the same coin: Mixed views of public relations practitioners and journalists for strategic conflict management', *Journalism & Mass Communication Quarterly*, 82, pp.318–338.

Stauber, J. and Rampton, S. (1995) *Toxic Sludge Is Good for You*. Monroe, ME: Common Courage Press.

Theaker, A. and Yaxley, H. (2012) *The Public Relations Strategic Toolkit*. London: Routledge.

Trice, H.M. (1993) *Occupational Subcultures in the Workplace*. Ithaca, NY: ILR Press.

Waddington, S. (2014) 'Ten areas of change for public relations'. Available at: http://wadds.co.uk/2014/06/05/10-areas-change-public-relations/ [Accessed on 18 November 2014].

Weigold, M.F. (2001) 'Communicating science: A review of the literature', *Science Communication*, 23, pp.164–193.

Yeomans, L. (2007) 'Emotion in public relations: A neglected phenomenon'. *Journal of Communication Management*, 11(3), pp.212–221.

7

THE ANATOMY OF A SPOKESPERSON IN SOUTH AFRICA

Sometimes a lie is kinder than a truth (African proverb)

Ronél Rensburg

Introduction

This chapter is a reflection of my impressions as a researcher, speech-writer, and spokesperson coach on occasion. It is a depiction of the gruelling manoeuvres of spokespersons in a multifarious, post-apartheid South Africa. Examples and postulations in the chapter stem from data gleaned from discourse analyses that have been documented since 2007.

The chapter demarcates the spokesperson remit, proposes a contextual definition of the term spokesperson and describes types and performance dimensions of spokespeople. The chapter further offers an appraisal of the distinct dilemmas of spokespeople in South Africa – of their retorts and defenses of issues and utterances by individual leaders in the country. This chapter mainly considers spokespeople speaking for leaders in the government sector. The activities of this sector are regular news and spokesperson successes and mishaps have been ascertained through the recorded discourse analyses.

The chapter concludes by offering promptings for the 'anatomy' of a spokesperson in South Africa. These offerings might offer insight to spokespeople when they have to communicate on multiple platforms with all of their audiences during the current surge of absurdity, fake news and post-truth in an age of illogic.

The spokesperson remit

There is an increasing reliance on skilled spokespeople in attempts to maintain and enhance the reputation and virtue of organizations and leaders. Private companies, governments, not-for-profit organizations and individuals recognize that representing themselves before their audiences requires a lot more than peripheral skills. Their spokespeople must not only think, speak and operate appropriately when

82 Ronél Rensburg

confronted, they must also keep pace with the dizzying amount of information derived from the Internet, social media conversations, the folly of audiences and global television news networks. From specific explanations of services, products or policies, to general opinions on business and government regulations, spokespeople are sought out for responses to bring clarity to audiences. Since all organizations and individual leaders face increasingly complex communication challenges in a digital and post-truth environment, the need for training (including public relations training) and continuous professional development for spokespeople to meet these challenges, becomes pivotal. Adding to this is the mainstream and social media's escalating scrutiny of business, governments and industry, as well as the buffing and mending of the reputations of individual leaders, which forces spokespeople to be able to communicate immediately and effectively.

Before demarcating the spokesperson in South Africa, this chapter offers a contextual description of the spokesperson concept in the concurring literature. Although researchers have globally written about effective government communicators and public relations in the fields of public affairs and government (National Commission on the Public Service, 1989; White and Dozier, 1992; Lee, 2008; Strömbäck and Kiousis, 2013; Seitel, 2014), research and literature on the concept of 'spokesperson' is sparse.

However, the act of speaking for others has been a feature of human societies since the advent of speech. The label *spokesperson* arrived more recently. The term *spokesman* (explained as an 'interpreter') appeared in the 1510s and in the 1530s was regarded as someone *who speaks for another or others*. The term *spokeswoman* derived from the 1650s; *spokesperson* from 1972; and *spokesmodel* is evidenced from 1990 (Harper, 2010).

Defining and contextualizing spokesperson

The term 'spokesperson' describes a set of occupations that have in common the duty of communicating information to and from the media, government and public on behalf of an individual, agency or organization. The term is typically used to describe an aspect of any of the following jobs: public information officer, lobbyist, press secretary, public relations specialist or media affairs specialist. They can be activists too. Other stations are occasionally required to perform spokesperson duties, for example specialists in particular fields or organizational leaders.

Spokespeople operate as brand ambassadors, during crises, political and corporate scandals, in getting the story out, conveying good news, delivering bad news, promoting individuals, products, organizations, causes and services, and at times act as armaments for the reputation of entities. Whoever these spokespeople are, however they are termed and whatever they do, universally they ought to be eloquent.

> Eloquence is so powerful that it embraces the origin and operations and developments of all things in the world, all the virtues, duties, and natural principles related to the manners, minds, and lives of mankind. Eloquence

also determines customs, laws, and rights, controls government, and expounds every kind of topic in a polished and refined manner.

(Cicero, De Oratore, 3.XX)

Within the ambit of this chapter, I employ the term *spokesperson* and frame it as a person who is designated to officially speak on behalf of an individual, a group, a cause or an organization (own depiction).

South Africa has eleven official languages and most spokespeople in the country are fluent in at least two of these. Translations for the term *spokesperson* in the more-frequently spoken languages are: *woodvoerder* (Afrikaans), *mmuelli* (Sesotho), *sebaleni* (Xhosa) and *okhulumela* (Zulu).

Types of spokesperson

Apart from large corporations in the private sector, spokespeople are appointed in the Presidency, various government departments, for political parties, regional and local government, municipalities and non-governmental organizations (NGOs). They have specialised and carefully defined job descriptions, mainly occupy senior roles, and are usually situated in the departments or directorates of corporate communication, public affairs/public relations or reputation management in the public sector. Spokespeople in the private and public sector environment in South Africa normally have obligatory degrees (or equivalent qualifications) in public relations and communication management, journalism, political science, development studies and public management or public affairs. There are individuals that are not exclusively appointed as spokespeople, but to act in this role is on the list of duties reflected in their job descriptions. Others are exclusively appointed as spokespeople. Political and cause-related activists, as well as seasoned journalists, are at times assigned to spokesperson positions.

The Department of Tourism in South Africa recently advertised a position for Chief Director: Communications. The duties stipulated included:

> …providing leadership and strategic direction to the Chief Directorate; […] Provide high-level media liaison support to the Minister, Deputy Minister, Director General and the Department in General; Ensure effective management of all internal and external communication initiatives of the Department, including the production of publications such as annual reports and internal newsletters; *Act as the spokesperson for the Department* [own emphasis].
>
> *(Masindi, 2017)*

The following types of spokesperson are active in South Africa (some of the categories are similar to those in most countries):

Local, national and international celebrities are well-known and respected individuals who habitually serve as advocates for a cause or product and, over time, become associated with the item advocated. Instant recognition attracts the attention of audiences and makes whatever they are promoting more visible (cf. Van der Waldt *et al.*, 2009). *Created spokespeople* may be appointed by specific organizations, associations or causes to act as spokespeople in a particular situation for a particular reason. Research on the effectiveness of celebrity versus created spokespeople for organizations found that created spokespeople were more effective (Toncar *et al.*, 2007; Van der Waldt *et al.*, 2009).

Employees in organizations can also perform as spokespeople. Stephens and Faranda (1993) investigated the effective use of employees as advertising spokespeople for a services company. *Created spokes-characters* – non-human characters used to promote products and brands – are at times employed (Garretson and Niedrich, 2004, p.25). *Specialists* with knowledge in their respective fields (natural scientists, medical practitioners, economists, etc.) are approached to act in the role when it is deemed necessary.

Victims of crises, corporate scandal outcomes, and political wrongdoing or natural disasters might be enticed to provide testimonials of their experiences and act as spokespeople in the further battle for the cause (Toncar *et al.,* 2007).

CEOs (Chief Executive Officers) are the most desirable spokespeople to speak on behalf of their organizations, especially during a crisis (Reidenbach and Pitts, 1986), as they are seen as the nexus of an organization. Technically, though, they might be risky, as they could lack necessary spokesperson skills, for example public speaking skills (see Barton in Rose, 2008). Reidenbach and Pitts (1986) deduce that CEOs do not constitute the most effective spokespeople. In order for CEOs to be effective spokespeople, they must appear to be knowledgeable about their business environment and the topic at hand and be seen as experts in their fields: 'There appears to be nothing inherent in the title of CEO which automatically bestows high levels of credibility on an individual' (Reidenbach and Pitts, 1986, p.5).

Social media interventions (SMIs) are becoming powerful self-elected and difficult 'spokespeople' to handle. SMIs represent a new type of independent third party endorser that shapes audience attitudes through blogs, tweets and the use of other social media. Literature has identified characteristics of effective spokespeople, but relatively little is known about audience perceptions of the SMIs (Freberg *et al.*, 2011). In 2016, South Africa witnessed how SMIs can immediately mobilize and engage large groups of people during the 'FeesMustFall' student protests (*#FeesMustFall*, 2016).

There are two types of professionals that work in public relations in the executive branches of government that act as spokespeople for the Presidency and the South African president. They are political appointees and civil servants. These categories are similar to those used in the United States (cf. Alaimo, 2016). *Political appointees* are individuals that are personally selected by, and serve at the pleasure of, a president or a leader of government departments and political parties. They are often branded as 'spin doctors' across the world. When Mac Maharaj was appointed as spokesperson for South Africa's current leader, President Jacob Zuma, in 2011, he told the *Mail & Guardian* newspaper that he had no choice when Zuma asked him to take the position (8 November 2011). *Civil servants* serve across governmental administrations and are part of the employment and legal remit of the civil service and labour laws in the specific country.

Questions can be raised as to which of these two categories of officials serves as a more effective advocate for their leaders in the media (Alaimo, 2016). There are authors who suggest that civil servants may be motivated by objectives other than those of the leader of a country (Weber, 1958, p.224; Heclo, 1977, p.226; Moe, 1999, p.148). Alaimo's (2016) research found that civil servants advanced the goals and views of the President in the media better than political appointees. While appointees enjoyed somewhat greater access to agency decision-makers and were slightly faster to respond to the media, their communication lacked the deep policy knowledge that civil servants had. Political appointees further lacked credibility with the media because journalists assumed that statements by these individuals were politically motivated, and therefore discounted their claims. The media applied less incredulity to the information disseminated by civil servants (Alaimo, 2016). These are similar to views in South Africa.

The performance dimensions of a spokesperson

There are universally identified *performance dimensions* that spokespeople should exhibit. They have to master technical, managerial, strategic and leadership skills in their daily performance. Troester and Warburton (2001) indicate that a spokesperson has to: (1) Understand the nature and kinds of 'publics' (audiences) in public relations and communication, including the multiplicity of diverse message recipients; (2) Recognize the respective attitudes of audiences; (3) Accept that emotion is a communication variable; (4) Respond to the differences across all media platforms; (5) Master the dynamic and fluid nature of the public relations process.

This chapter reasons that spokespeople in South Africa ought to have four crucial performance dimensions: *credibility, trustworthiness, knowledge*, and *responsiveness and promptitude.*

Credibility

According to Lee (2008) a government spokesperson must possess credibility, responsiveness and knowledge. If a public affairs official – for example – does not possess these qualities, 'reporters [will] quickly turn against him' (p.98).

For Reidenwbach and Pitts (1986) the following credibility items for spokespeople are important: being well-known (prominence), believable and likeable, displaying integrity, being knowledgeable, an expert, influential and powerful. Work by Chaiken and Maheswaran (1994) indicates that 'source credibility exert[s] a strong persuasive impact' (p.337) on public attitude when the message is ambiguous, independent of its level of importance.

It is critical for spokespeople to establish credibility with their audiences but also the media because if a source enjoys credibility, the messages that he or she promulgates are more believable (Wilcox *et al.*, 2015). The spokesperson's role is akin to how Seitel (2014, p.106) argues, 'the practice of public relations is all about earning credibility'. Credibility is the most important asset of a public relations practitioner when working with the press. Broom and Sha (cited in Broom, Sha, and Seshadrinathan, 2013) and Grunig and Grunig (1992) argue that one of the most important characteristics to measure in order to ascertain the quality of the relationships an organization enjoys with critical constituencies is credibility. This rings true for spokespeople as well.

Trustworthiness

In advertising, the level of perceived trustworthiness of a source of information has been found to affect audience evaluation of a product (Priester and Petty, 2003). Additionally, the level of perceived trustworthiness appears to affect attitudes towards a product. Studies examining source credibility have concluded that message recipients are more inclined to adopt, or be persuaded by, messages when the source is viewed as highly expert, trustworthy, likeable or attractive (Eagly and Chaiken, 1993). A spokesperson should be trusted by the media and audiences in general.

Knowledge

Research by Morgan (1986, p.63) on reporters' experiences of government public information officers (PIOs) found that 'PIOs are faulted [...] principally [on] lack of technical knowledge but also an unwillingness to seek out such knowledge for reporters'. When asked about the weaknesses of PIOs, the main complaint by reporters was their lack of technical knowledge. Hess (1984, p.20) found that 'the new spokesman usually knows less about the subject and operation of an agency than many of the reporters he is expected to inform'.

In addition to policy knowledge, spokespeople must also possess knowledge of the views and activities of their agency's leadership. For this reason, Lee (2008, p.99) argues that effective government public affairs officials ought to have access to key principals in order to gain knowledge and credibility. Hess (1984, p.18) found that 'reporters believe that what makes a good press secretary is access, the perceived closeness to the head of the agency.'

Responsiveness and promptitude

Spokespeople can easily miss opportunities to shape media coverage, given modern 24-hour news cycles and media competition. It is therefore critical for spokespeople to respond rapidly to all audiences who need information, as well as to the media that are working under deadline pressures. Hess (1984, p.33) and Lee (2008) emphasize that responsiveness is one of the key qualities that the media demand from government agency spokespeople.

Other essential performance dimensions are hospitality, openness, honesty and understanding, initiative, the capacity to mediate the relations between officials and

Anatomy of a spokesperson in South Africa **87**

the media, responsible communication leadership, the capacity to manufacture a concise, intelligible and appealing text, knowledge of all media platforms, charisma, patience and the capacity to organize and lead the public relations and communication team (Howard and Matthews, 1985). Spokespeople should not answer questions to which they do not have clear answers, but must take up the task of swiftly finding the information and putting it at the disposal of audiences and the media. 'No comment' is always a comment.

Distinct dilemmas of spokespeople in South Africa

The 1994 democratic elections saw the end of apartheid and heralded the birth of the new South Africa. The transition was peaceful, mainly due to the prophetic charisma of Nelson Mandela. However, in 2017 the country and its people are still contending with the challenges of inequality, xenophobia, socio-economic and educational tribulations and struggles surrounding racism and sexism. South Africa is a hybrid of the first and third worlds and remains the economic gateway to the rest of Africa, but the current business and government environments are facing disparagement due to corruption, numerous scandals and difficulties with leadership, and the country's status as a 'developmental state' is currently being interrogated. The issue of government leaders and their spokespeople in South Africa has been a paramount item on the communication and public relations agendas in recent times.

The post-truth era lingers on while many leaders in the world resort to populism and forsake the values of objectivity, integrity, human solidarity and sometimes decency.

Apart from the emergence of social media, the political and economic turmoil of the past few years and their aftermath for global society and individual experiences reflect elements of post-truth communication. In *The Society of the Spectacle*, Guy Debord (1967) foretells phenomena like the ascent of populist politicians.

Spokespeople often become social, political and cultural equalizers during political upheaval as the public hankers for sense-making information. In a series of tweets Helen Zille, who is Premier of the Western Cape (one of South Africa's nine provinces) and the former leader of the Democratic Alliance (DA), the official opposition party in South Africa, asserted that there are many positive aspects to colonialism. 'For those claiming that the legacy of colonialism was ONLY negative, think of our independent judiciary, transport infrastructure, piped water', she tweeted (Hoby, 2017).

Zille's tweets drew strong criticism from political opponents and those within her own party, as well as on social media. Mmusi Maimane, who took the reins of the DA from Zille in 2015 (in conjunction with the spokesperson for the DA, Phumzile van Damme) had to act against these tweets, but also defend the reputation of the DA. In a rebuttal, Maimane tweeted that 'colonialism, like apartheid, was a system of oppression and subjugation. It can never be justified'. Maimane told local media that Zille's tweets were 'completely unacceptable and indefensible' (Hoby, 2017). However, a Twitter-storm against Zille's words ensued and a disciplinary hearing followed, eventually forcing her to apologize publically, though she did not recant her tweet.

Spokespeople face various predicaments: speaking on behalf of a public office or any other entity as a spokesperson may cause a distinct dilemma between fulfilling a contractual duty on the one hand, and adhering to moral principles and professional obligation to tell the truth (or at least to present the facts) on the other. At times spokespeople have to offer apologies, which might affect the reputation of both spokesperson and organization. Verhoeven, Van Hoof, Ter Keurs and Van Vuuren (2012) studied the effects on spokesperson reputation when offering apologies (or no apologies) during a crisis situation. They found that the crisis had more impact on corporate reputation and trust than on the spokesperson's reputation and trust. This indicates that the crisis is seen as the collective responsibility of the organization, rather than the personal responsibility of the spokesperson.

There is a particular impasse in countries where governance is largely characterized by a lack of disclosure or where 'undefended' issues need to be defended. In an 'off-the-cuff' remark on democracy, President Jacob Zuma said during the President's Question Time, in the National Assembly (13 September 2012): 'Sorry, we have more rights here because we are a majority. You have fewer rights because you are a minority. Absolutely, that's how democracy works. So, it is a question of accepting the rules within democracy and you must operate in them'.

In terms of basic democratic doctrines, this utterance from President Zuma can be graded as ill-informed. The spokesperson for the president at the time, Mac Maharaj, released a statement in response to ample criticism of President Zuma's remark by declaring that the comments had been 'misconstrued' by the media and that 'nothing could be further from the truth than the suggestion the President was trying to elevate the majority above the minority, but rather that the President was stating a fundamental democratic principle' (14 September 2012). This retort did not address the concerns raised at the time.

Any government and its agents' public and personal tribulations will be widely publicized. South Africa's government mishaps are also scrutinized on a regular basis. Spokespeople responsible for government communication and public relations in government departments in this country often have insuperable tasks as leaders may, on certain occasions, make statements that are awkward to explain and defend.

In a speech on Heritage Day, President Zuma remarked: 'Same sex marriage is a disgrace to the nation and to God. When I was growing up, 'ungqingili' [homosexuals in Zulu] could not stand in front of me, I would knock him out' (26 September 2006). This was probably President Zuma's most notorious cultural solecism, and came across as intolerant. What followed was a denunciation from inside and outside South Africa's gay community. Human Rights Commission Chief Executive Tshidiso Thipanyane described the comments as both regrettable and inflammatory. The damage was too gigantic for any spokesperson to remedy and President Zuma himself was forced to offer an apology, arguing that he 'did not intend to have this interpreted as a condemnation of gays and lesbians' (cf. Van Onselen, 2016).

The pervasive and instantaneous media content translates risks and spokespeople need to be ever-mindful of the operations of mainstream and social media and how rapidly utterances by leaders can be relayed globally and cause diplomatic ramifications. In an address to the Gauteng ANC Manifesto Forum in Johannesburg, President Zuma made the following intervention about roads in Malawi: 'We thank all citizens who have registered for the e-tolls so that we can continue to improve roads and boost economic growth in Gauteng. Gauteng must develop. It can't stand in one place [...]. We can't think like Africans in Africa in general. We are in Johannesburg. This is Johannesburg. It is not some national road in Malawi' (October 2013).

This is now branded as President Zuma's 'I am not an African' speech and caused a diplomatic incident between South Africa and Malawi. The Malawi Foreign Affairs Minister, Ephrahim Mganda Chiume, declared that the people of Malawi had been deeply insulted by the comments. The spokesperson for the South African Presidency responded: 'The President's comments have been taken out of context. In the broader sense South Africa achieved more in the past 19 years of freedom and democracy'. Mac Maharaj also had to defend President Zuma's controversial comments: 'The words have regrettably been taken out of context and blown completely out of proportion' (Breed, 2015). The South African government officially apologized to Malawi.

In a multicultural environment, remarks by leaders might lead to cultural misunderstanding and upheaval. During a presentation in Impendle in the Midlands, the president uttered: 'When I was in Venda recently, I was so impressed to see how people there express respect for other people. A woman would clap her hands and even lie down to show her respect. I was so impressed, if I was not already married to my four wives, I would go to Venda to look for a woman' (December 2013). A representative of the uMgungundlovu District Municipality, Phumla Ndende, remarked that before President Zuma 'appreciated' a culture, he should first assess if that culture was not oppressing women. The President's spokesperson, Mac Maharaj, could not at the time be reached for comment. Maharaj retired as spokesperson and from active work at the end of April 2015 at the age of 80 (Breed, 2015).

Another distinct dilemma of spokespeople in South Africa is created when they move from positions of so-called government 'spin doctors' to work as journalists. Their work as journalists is often thereafter condemned as being biased and portraying double standards. Former *Sowetan* newspaper journalist Anna Majavu was mistrusted for perceived journalistic bias and harbouring 'a malicious agenda' against the DA by the former DA spokesperson, Gareth van Onselen (Mothapo, 2014). Majavu herself previously worked for the South African Municipal Workers Union (SAMWU). Another DA representative, Ross van Linde, remarked bluntly that Majavu was not a journalist: '[She] is a former South African Municipal Workers Union spin doctor, who has a particular political agenda' (Mothapo, 2014). Gareth van Onselen has since moved from DA spokesperson to take up the position of journalist at both the *Sunday Times* and *Business Day* newspapers and might himself face related denunciations of which Majavu had been accused.

The anatomy of a South African spokesperson

What, then, should the components of a South African spokesperson be? Particularly those that have to speak on behalf of leaders in public office and government? Marland, Lewis and Flanagan (2017) state that the proliferation of Internet connectivity, smartphones and digital media is revolutionary for society and governance. Political events and information can increasingly be viewed live from almost anywhere. Issues management personnel are branching out from worrying about tomorrow's headlines to dealing with the last five minutes' tweets and Instagram posts, and the world is on the cusp of real-time media and image management. 'Continual communications control is the new reality of governance' (p.125). The spokesperson in South Africa must make peace with the fact that their work will have to be performed under 'continual communication control'.

In my view, Bheki Khumalo, the spokesperson of former South African president Thabo Mbeki, has been an exemplary spokesperson. During his service, he displayed many of the following components that I have selected for constructing the anatomy of a South African spokesperson.

Frankness

This is the provision of actual information in the place of misleading statements. One of the most difficult decisions organizations face in emergency situations is what information to reveal, what information to withhold and what information to 'frame' so as to provide the preferred impression (see Sandman, 2002/2003). The spokesperson should attempt not to flat-out lie. The aim here is not to 'lie' to audiences, but to 'shape' or 'frame' (at times 'distort') the impression given to audiences and the media by selecting which facts to give, which facts to withhold and how best to present the facts that are given. This is a habit that South African spokespeople should learn from the start.

The spokesperson has to be multi-faced, a reflector with many frontages and with multi-layered responses because heterogeneous audiences must be serviced simultaneously. He/she has to have excellent verbal and non-verbal skills, be diplomatic and even-tempered. The spokesperson will have a multi-pronged tongue. An added advantage will be if the spokesperson can glibly master all eleven South African languages and can relay overt and covert messages and meanings to audiences.

Risk-readiness

The spokesperson in South Africa should not treat speculation as fact. The environment is too complex and the audiences nearly always obfuscated. The spokesperson could, however, confront the 'what if' possibilities and outcomes in a given situation. The very concept of risk is what might happen, the assessment of the probability and consequence of possible futures. Risk communication will be about those possible futures. That is, risk communication can be a kind of speculation (Sandman, 2002/2003). The spokesperson should be risk-ready.

Assertive tentativeness

Spokespeople will often be asked whether their business and government leaders know what they are doing. When the situation is chaotic and uncertainty is high, someone will have to indicate that the experts and authorities also feel like the audiences in those circumstances. Overconfidence will not be an asset, whereas displaying tentativeness and a declaration from spokespeople that they are also not sure about something can be advantageous.

Professional benevolence

Most professional spokespeople are overly preoccupied with being professional, and insufficiently preoccupied with being compassionate (Sandman, 2002). If the situation is dire, the audience and media will rarely think that the spokesperson is too emotional, too benevolent or too personal. According to Sandman (2002) it is quite common for audiences to perceive the spokesperson as too controlled and too calm and therefore uncaring. The South African spokesperson must be both benevolent and professional.

Remorsefulness

Spokespeople regularly have to explain mishaps by leaders and institutions. It is an advantage to acknowledge previous mistakes and be apologetic. Spokespeople in South Africa have too often bent under scrutiny because they have to be on the defensive most of the time. It is pivotal for the spokesperson to be colour-brave and gender-subtle. The spokesperson must display humility, must not be mortified by the fumbles of leaders or embarrassed for being politically correct *ad nauseam*. During repentance the spokesperson should often take a neutral stance, the place 'in the middle'.

Cohesive communicator and message simplifier

In a given event, key messages are agreed on by the authorities and thereafter government leaders, agency heads and spokespeople stick to them with soldierly discipline. It is an attempt to create order out of the chaos of clutter, the overwhelming tumult of the modern public sphere. Spokespeople in South Africa have to be team players even if they are mavericks or disagree with the message. The attention span of most audiences is notoriously short. Messages and responses must be kept undemanding, but notable. The spokesperson will display superior social media conversation skills and will have to be available 24 hours a day.

Convincing to all audiences

This spokesperson has plentiful charisma, but not so copious as to overshadow the political leaders or too overbearing for the media and other stakeholders. A spokesperson in South Africa must know the facts of an issue, but must tell a story cautiously and be able to 'spin' compellingly if the need arises. The spokesperson usually has the notoriety of being a professional liar in the eyes of the public. But this messenger matters if he/she is a convincing story-teller.

Conclusive remarks

Recent public communication by spokespeople on behalf of their leaders is evidence that the current job descriptions of spokespeople are rapidly transforming. In their effort and haste to 'get the message out', spokespeople frequently have to lie for their leaders or sanitize the facts to 'keep the peace'. They become the 'messengers that have to be killed'.

South African spokespeople have to live and work with the lies of others – the leaders for whom they speak – because they have discovered they have to adapt to the verity that lying is becoming a new type of diplomacy (Mearsheimer, 2013). A concluding offering for the South African spokesperson's way forward comes from ancient Africa itself: 'One falsehood spoils a thousand truths' (African proverb).

Bibliography

Alaimo, K. (2016) 'The US President's most effective spokespeople'. In *Journal of Communication Management*, 20(2), pp.118–132.

Breed, M. (2015) Interview with Mac Maharaj. @MarnusBreed.

Broom, G.M., Sha, B. and Seshadrinathan, S. (2013) *Cutlip and Center's Effective Public Relations*. 11 ed. Harlow, UK: Pearson Education.

Chaiken, S. and Maheswaran, D. (1994) 'Heuristic processing can bias systematic processing – effects of sources credibility, argument, ambiguity, and task importance on attitude judgment'. *Journal of Personality and Social Psychology*, 66(3), pp.460–473.

DeBord, G. (1967) *The Society of the Spectacle* (translated by Donald Nicholson-Smith). New York: Penguin Books.

Eagly, A.H. and Chaiken, S. (1993) *The Psychology of Attitudes*. New York: Harcourt Brace Jovanovich.

'Fees Must Fall' student protests, demonstrations and campaign in South Africa (2016) #FeesMustFall.

Freberg, K., Graham, K. and McGaughey, K. (2011) 'Who are the social media influencers? A study of public perceptions of personality'. *Public Relations Review*, 27(1), pp.90–92.

Garretson, J.A. and Niedrich, R.W. (2004) 'Spokes-characters: Creating character trust and positive brand attitudes'. *Journal of Advertising*, 33(2), Summer 2004, pp.25–36.

Grunig, J.E. and Grunig, L. (1992) 'Models of public relations and communication'. In J.E. Grunig (ed.), *Excellence in Public Relations*. Hillsdale, NJ: Lawrence Erlbaum Associates, pp.285–326.

Harper, D. (2010) Etymology Dictionary. Available at: http://www.etymonline.com [Accessed 25 January 2017].

Heclo, H. (1977) *A Government of Strangers: Executive Politics in Washington*. New York: Brookings Institution Press.

Hess, S. (1984) *The Government/Press Connection: Press Officers and Their Offices*. Washington, DC: Brookings Institution Press.

Howard, C. and Mathews, W. (1985) *On Deadline – Managing Media Relations*. Long Grove, IL: Waveland Press.

Hoby, H. (2017) www.theoldreader.com [Accessed 20 January 2017].

Interview with Mac Maharaj (17 August 2012). In *Mail & Guardian*. Available at: http://www.iol.co.za/news/politics/mail--guardian-censored-1181232 [Accessed 20 March 2017].

Lee, M. (2008) 'The effective agency spokesperson'. In M. Lee (ed.), *Government Public Relations: A Reader* (pp.95–106). Boca Raton, FL: CRC Press.

Maersheimer, J. (2013) *Why Leaders Lie*. London: Oxford University Press.

Marland, A., Lewis, J.P. and Flanagan, T. (2017) 'Governance in the age of digital media and branding'. *Governance*, 30(1), pp.125–141.

Masindi, E. (2017) Department of Tourism. Advertisement. Available at: https://www.tourism.gov.za [Accessed 26 April 2017].

Mothapo, M. (2014) 'From DA spin-doctor to journalist: An open letter to Gareth van Onselen'. In *The Daily Maverick*. Available at: https://www.dailymaverick.co.za/oponionista/2014-01-21-from-da-spin-doctor-to-journalist-an-open-letter-to-gareth-van-onselen/+&cd=1&hl=en&ct=clnl&gl=za [Accessed 1 April 2017].

Moe, T.M. (1999) 'The politicized presidency'. In J.P. Pfiffner (ed.), *The Managerial Presidency*. College Station, TX: Texas A & M University Press, pp.144–161.

Morgan, G. (1986) *Images of Organization*. Newbury Park, CA: Sage Publications.

Priester, J.R. and Petty, R. (2003) 'The influence of spokesperson trustworthiness on message elaboration, attitude strength, and advertising effectiveness'. *Journal of Consumer Psychology*, 13(4), pp.408–421.

Reidenbach, E. and Pitts, R.E. (1986) 'Not all CEOs are created equal as advertising spokespeople: Evaluating the effective CEO spokesperson'. *Journal of Advertising*, 15(1), pp.30–46.

Rose, M. (2008) 'CEO as crisis spokesperson? Think again'. *Public Relations Strategist*. Autumn 2016.

Sandman, P.M. (2002/2003) 'Dilemmas in emergency communication policy'. Originally published in: Emergency Risk Communication CDCynergy (CD-ROM), February 2003. Available at: www.psandman.com [Accessed 27 March 2017].

Seitel, F.P. (2014) *The Practice of Public Relations*. Upper Saddle River, NJ: Pearson.

Speech by President Jacob Zuma at the *Gauteng ANC Manifesto Forum*, October 2013.

Speech by President Jacob Zuma during Question Time in the National Assembly, 13 September 2012.

Speech by President Jacob Zuma on Heritage Day (Impendle, Midlands, organized by the uMgungundlovu District Municipality, the South Africa Social Security Agency and the Provincial Treasury), 26 September 2006.

Speeches by President Zuma reported in the press. Available at: www.sowetanlive.co.za – 2016-11-29] and www.timeslive.co.za – 2016-11-29; city-press.news24.com – 2016-04-03 [Accessed 27 February 2017].

Stephens, N. and Faranda, W. (1993) 'Using employees as advertising spokespeople'. *Journal of Services Marketing*, 7(2), pp.36–46.

Strömbäck, J. and Kiousis, S. (2013) 'Political public relations: old practice, new theory building'. *Public Relations Journal*, 7(4), pp.1–11.

Toncar, M., Reid, J.S. and Anderson, C.E. (2007) 'Effective spokespeople in a public service announcement. National, local celebrities and victims'. *Journal of Communication Management*, 11(3), pp.275–285.

Troester, R. and Warburton, T.I. (2001) 'The technical communicator as corporate spokesperson: A public relations primer'. *Journal of Technical Writing and Communication*, 31(3), pp.241–256.9.

94 Ronél Rensburg

Van der Waldt, D., Van Loggerenberg, M. and Wehmeyer, L. (2009) 'Celebrity endorsements versus created spokespersons in advertising: A survey among students'. *South African Journal of Economic and Management Sciences*, 12(1), April, pp.100–114.

Verhoeven, J.W.M., Van Hoof, J.J., Ter Keurs, H. and Van Vuuren, M. (2012) 'Effects of apologies and crisis responsibility on corporate and spokesperson reputation'. *Public Relations Review*, 38, pp.501–504.

Volcker, P.A. and National Commission on the Public Service (1989) *Leadership for America: Rebuilding the Public Service*. Lanham, MD: Lexington Books.

Weber, M. (1958) *From Max Weber: Essays in Sociology* (Trans. by H.H. Gerth and C.W. Mills). New York, NY: Oxford University Press [Google Scholar] [Accessed 25 February 2017].

White, J. and Dozier, D.M. (1992) 'Public relations and management decision making'. In Grunig, J.E. (ed.) (1992) *Excellence in Public Relations and Communication Management* (pp.91–108). New York: Routledge.

Wilcox, D.L., Cameron, G.T. and Reber, B.H. (2015) *Public Relations: Strategies and Tactics*. New York: Pearson.

8

'CAN YOU SEE ME?'

Images of public relations in *Babylon*

Kate Fitch

Introduction

This chapter explores the significance of the image to public relations. Drawing on cultural studies scholarship on the visual turn and the renewed focus on images in contemporary culture, it considers both visual representations of, and their significance for, public relations. Historically, public relations activity has long been associated with the visual, through, for example, the production of posters, graphic design, publications, photography and film production. Archival records of photographs and films from press conferences and events reveal the attention paid to scene-setting and even the creation of the media spectacle, or what Boorstin (1992) refers to as 'pseudo events'. Yet, there is an irony that a field pejoratively perceived as overly concerned with image management has perhaps failed to adequately theorize the significance of the visual. This issue is not exclusive to public relations scholars as images tend to be assigned low status within the academy (Campbell and Schneeder, 2011) and scholars in many disciplines lack visual scientific literacy (Pauwels, 2000).

However, technological shifts in the twenty-first century mean that the image has an increasingly privileged status in communication. It is therefore significant to consider the ways in which meanings around public relations – both in terms of practitioners and practices and, more broadly, the industry – are constructed and interpreted through visual texts. Analysing visual representations potentially offers important insights into the cultural and symbolic power of public relations. This chapter considers the visual in representations of public relations, expanding the discussion beyond popular culture representations in television and film to understand contemporary meaning making around 'public relations'.

I offer in this chapter a case study of *Babylon* (Channel 4, 2014), a UK television series about public relations and the police force. Although a fictional representation

96 Kate Fitch

of public relations activity, as I have argued elsewhere (see Fitch, 2015a, 2015b), I consider popular culture a valuable space for exploring discourses of and analysing the meaning making associated with, public relations. The depiction of public relations in *Babylon*, where public relations plays a central role in the narrative, illustrates the prominence and significance of visual imagery to contemporary practice. Further, it allows an analysis of meaning making through the visual representation of public relations practitioners. This chapter is structured in three sections: it first explores scholarship on the significance of the image in communication; it then introduces *Babylon* in order to discuss images in relation to public relations; finally, it analyses the significance of the visual for public relations in a world where communication is primarily mediated on screens.

Public relations and the visual

Since the late twentieth century, there has been a renewed focus on the primacy of the image within the academy and greater recognition of its role in communication (Campbell and Schneeder, 2011). However, there is a need for a more critical understanding of the visual text, beyond an unproblematic transmission of meaning. Rather the visual text should be studied in terms of 'how that image was produced and made meaningful by its viewers' (Pink, 2003, p.186). From a cultural studies perspective, visual meanings are determined by the processes of production and consumption. Yet, despite the centrality of visual imagery to communication, and to representation, meaning and culture (Campbell and Schneeder, 2011), there is limited public relations scholarship specifically on its significance. In contrast, media and communication scholars have researched extensively the power of visual imagery in, for example, propaganda (Welch, 2013), advertising (Berger, 1972), corporate communication (Marchand, 1998), and other forms of persuasive communication. Some scholars acknowledge the importance of graphic and visual elements to the historical development of public relations although they tend to remain peripheral to most studies of the field. L'Etang (2004), for example, identified a close relationship between graphic design and public relations in her history of professional practice in Britain and Anthony (2012) highlights the strong links between documentary filmmaking and public relations. In this volume, Dhanesh (2018) identifies the significance of the visual image for contemporary practice and calls for more research into visual rhetoric within the discipline. Overall, studies of public relations and visual texts remain limited, despite the advent of social media and increasingly mobile communication. To ignore the visual is to resolutely ignore both the impact of technology on every facet of public relations, and in particular, the success of primarily visual platforms such as Pinterest, Snapchat, Instagram and YouTube, and just how much the screen (rather than the printed page) dominates interaction between organizations and publics.

Although there is limited critical research into the role visual texts play in public relations, there is a small but growing body of work on fictional, and particularly screen, representations of public relations. These include post feminist studies on the representation of female practitioners in books, television and film (Fitch, 2015a; Johnston, 2010); reviews of representations of public relations in books, film and television (Miller, 1999; Saltzman, 2012; Tsetsura *et al.*, 2015; Young, 2018); representations in specific sectors such as celebrity and government public relations (Ames, 2011; Lee, 2001, 2009); and representations in particular films or television programmes including *True Blood* (Fitch, 2015a) and *The West Wing* (Kinsky, 2006). However, the focus of these studies tends not to be the visual representation of practices and practitioners except as one element that contributes to the narrative. Rather, they are often concerned with whether public relations is represented accurately or positively. Popular culture offers the potential for diverse and critical readings around public relations (Fitch, 2015a, 2015b) and demands the active construction of meanings rather than offering an over-simplistic, transmission model of representation (Fiske, 1989; McQuail, 2005). This chapter therefore focuses on visual representations of public relations in a fictional television series, and in doing so highlights the ways in which meaning both around, and through, public relations is produced.

Public relations in *Babylon*

Babylon is described by one reviewer as a 'complicated and darkly satirical comedy about policing' (Hale, 2015). It could just as easily be described as a dark satire about public relations. The creators of *Babylon*, Sam Bain and Jesse Armstrong, have written other television shows 'concerned with the primacy of image making' (Hale, 2015). Armstrong contributed as a writer to the first three television series of Armando Iannucci's *The Thick of It* (2005–2012), and Iannucci's film, *In the Loop* (2009), which introduced the world to the foul-mouthed government communication director, Malcolm Tucker. Tucker, played by Peter Capaldi, is renowned for his abusive manner and manipulation of truth, and was voted the favourite fictional public relations practitioner globally by senior industry leaders in 2015 (Harrington, 2015). Iannucci later created the award-winning television series satirizing US presidential campaigns, *Veep* (2012–), for which Armstrong wrote one episode. Bain also contributed to the first episode of *The Thick of It*. They therefore have a tradition of dark comedy writing about British government and public institutions, where public relations and spin are central to the narrative, frequently manipulative and overly concerned with reputation management at the expense of 'truth'.

Babylon is about public relations and the tensions that result from attempting to open up, communicatively speaking, the modern police force. As such, it focuses specifically on the workplace, in contrast, for example, to earlier television shows in the 1990s, such as *Sex and the City*, that are part of the public relations popular culture canon where, at least in post-feminist programmes, 'the world of work largely disappears from view' (Arthurs, 2003). As the opening scene in the pilot episode suggests, communication management underpins and drives *Babylon*'s narrative. One television reviewer described the pilot episode:

98 Kate Fitch

> Richard Miller, chief constable of the London police department … hires an American PR executive named Liz Garvey (Brit Marling) in a big-picture move to hone the message and control the force's image, which is being battered by the aggressive British media.
>
> *(Goodman, 2015)*

Babylon therefore offers rich material for exploring diverse discourses of public relations and the ways in which public relations activity produces meaning. In addition to exploring the representation of both public relations practitioners and practices, I discuss the primacy of the visual image in the public relations work that is performed in *Babylon*.

Representing public relations practitioners

The first episode opens with a casually dressed woman with long blonde hair being filmed on stage as she begins a TedX talk. She is identified through text on the screen as Liz Garvey (played by American actor Brit Marling), Head of Communications at Instagram. Attempting to establish some rapport with her audience, she acknowledges her nervousness: 'It's honest, it's transparent, it's good PR'. This commitment to more open and accountable communication drives the series. Garvey is recruited from Instagram to be the Director of Communications at the London-based police force in order to bring about significant cultural change within the organization. Garvey espouses values such as transparency and a communication model she calls 360-degree communication. 'The age of information control is over' says Garvey in her TedX talk. Her character on occasion struggles to put this philosophy into practice, particularly in relation to her personal interactions with colleagues.

Garvey's physical appearance conforms in many ways to stereotypical images of the female public relations practitioner. Miller (1999) found that fictional female practitioners tend to be portrayed as single and attractive, and that there was a lack of diversity among practitioners. Just over a decade later Johnston (2010), while noting growing numbers of female practitioners in television and film portrayals, concluded they were overwhelmingly 'white and middle class' (p.12). Such physical attributes are coded along race, class and gender lines. Described by one reviewer as a 'a shiny American PR boss' (Nicholson, 2014), Garvey is articulate, middle class, educated and comfortable with public speaking, cameras, press conferences and media performances. Recruited from Instagram, she is also familiar with the brave new world (at least for the police force) of social media. Her portrayal of a female public relations practitioner echoes those of other white, middle class, blonde women in post-feminist screen texts: Bridget Jones (played by Renée Zellweger in *Bridget Jones's Diary* (2001)); Helen Quilley (played by Gwyneth Paltrow in *Sliding Doors* (1998)); and Samantha Jones (played by Kim Cattrall in *Sex and the City* (1998–2004)). *Scandal's* (2012–) African-American practitioner Olivia Pope, played by Kerry Washington, is a notable exception. Certainly, Saltzman (2012) noted that fictional representations of female practitioners became more common in the twenty-first century.

As an American, Garvey is an outsider to British culture and therefore an outsider to the traditions and institutional culture of the British police force. This outsider status is emphasized, as she has to clarify the meaning of British slang ('scrote') when seeing the rushes of a documentary film on the police force. At Garvey's first meeting with senior police command, Charles Inglis (played by Paterson Joseph) asks how she is coping with the 'culture shock' of moving 'from working for a website to a job where lives are on the line'. After some pointed banter, Garvey responds, 'You are the tough guys. I am the messenger girl.' As a woman, she is also outside the patriarchal power structures of the police force; at one point she aligns herself with the most senior female officer in the force before switching sides. However, these factors, that is, being American and female, only serve to emphasize that as a recruit from a social media platform, Garvey is even more of an outsider. The visual focus of Instagram is significant too. To emphasize Garvey's quest for visibility, she plaintively and repeatedly expresses concern prior to her first address to staff, 'are the people at the back going to be able to see me', due to the lack of staging or platform.

Garvey is constantly threatened by her second in command, Finn (played by Bertie Carvel). In many ways, Finn is the archetypal male practitioner identified by Miller (1999), in that he is both cynical ('sarcastic, edgy, angry, contemptuous, and driven') and manipulative ('a shark or a snake who is ruthless, deceptive, and predatory. These practitioners lie.') (p.9). One television reviewer described Finn as 'deliciously repellent' (Hale, 2015); he is certainly crude and obnoxious to Garvey – who was appointed over him – and works hard to undermine her. Finn is a descendent of Malcolm Tucker for whom public relations is a game of leaks, undermining the opposition, and controlling the flow of information, and where possible, the story. In a successful attempt to get Garvey to reverse his dismissal for lying to her, Finn threatens to expose her high salary and bonuses to staff – a level of openness that Garvey is unwilling to embrace. As Finn says pointedly, 'Remember Liz. Open communication channels, transparency.'

Representing public relations practice

Public relations work in popular culture tends to be presented in line with particular tropes. For example, in her analysis of *The West Wing*, Kinsky (2006) found that typical fictional public relations activity included 'writing, editing, researching, and monitoring the media' (p.24). Other scholars have pointed to the predominance of more technical tasks, such as publicity and event management, in relation to female practitioners in earlier television and film depictions (Miller, 1999; Johnston, 2010). Saltzman (2012), writing specifically on 'police information officers', noted that they tend to be 'portrayed as hard-working, dedicated public officials trying to keep a good relationship with the news media while having their hands full with uncooperative police officials' (p.33). In contrast, *Babylon* emphasizes visual aspects of public relations practice. Media relations is prominent but such activity is often shown through press conferences, off-the-record briefings, and the release of footage. The nature of public relations work differs too: there is little evidence of the writing, research or planning identified by Kinsky (2006), although 'responding to crises' remains highly pertinent. Some scholars have noted significant intertextual references and narrative drivers through broadcast and online media in other fictional representations of public relations (see, for example, Fitch, 2015a) but the complexity of 24/7 communication creates an unprecedented demand for visual communication. Social media is therefore important too, and Garvey's dream is for the police force to establish its own news centre in order to bypass traditional media outlets.

Babylon also differs from other fictional representations of public relations work in that much of the action is mediated through cameras and screens that are shown in almost every frame: vision both obtained and watched through CCTV in streets, buildings and vehicles, iPhones, tablet devices, drones, documentary cameras, television broadcasts, night vision goggles and so on. Every office at police headquarters has television screens in the background, in addition to various mobile devices and desktop computers that are constantly used for viewing footage, skyping and watching breaking news. In one example, senior members of the police force watch an online stream of prison riots unfolding in three-minute delay, even as the private contractor in charge of the prison denies riots are occurring. The editing of that footage to intercut with the contractor's statements ('it's a disturbance, not a riot'), only serves to show how the vision exposes those lies and therefore appears to offer a more authentic truth. In another scene, Garvey views an early edit of a reality television documentary about the police force and requests changes, confirming that the documentary is essentially a public relations exercise rather than a fly-on-the-wall documentary or exposé. The editing of footage shot by the documentary cameraperson further highlights the construction or manufacturing of alternate 'truths' or perspectives.

The prominence of visual images in almost every frame points to major themes of visibility and seeing. These themes are reflected in dialogue too, as in the example discussed in the previous section where Garvey worries about her capacity to be seen. 'Can you see me?' asks the second in command on Skype during a crisis situation before the feed breaks up. The themes of visibility, openness and transparency underpin the spoken rhetoric around communication. But these ideals are constantly threatened with exposure, cover-ups and concealment. The power of the image on mobile and television screens, ranging from a reality television documentary (itself a public relations exercise) to leaked CCTV footage of an armed officer attacking a waste bin, offer alternative narratives and expose the constructedness of visual images that show the police in a good light. The chief constable's death, a suicide in response to the threat of exposure of his serial philandering, leaves Garvey in a weakened position. In response, Garvey decides to support Sharon as the next chief constable. However, as she tells Assistant Commissioner Sharon Franklin: 'You are the invisible woman' and creates opportunities for her greater 'visibility' in the media.

Being seen, however, relates not only to openness but also to surveillance. As Berger writes, 'soon after we can see, we are aware that we can also be seen' (1972, p.9). Garvey accuses Finn, asking him 'Are you spying on me?', suggesting that visibility involves both watching and being watched in ways that can be confronting and unwanted. This perspective is reinforced by the constant editing of camera feeds into the narrative. The police force is not immune to this surveillance. During an unfolding crisis, it is reported, 'a news portal has hacked the drone feed'. The first thing a woman does on returning home to find the police tasering her partner is to pull out her iPhone and photograph her husband before turning the camera on the police to interrogate them. One officer is surreptitiously filmed by the documentary cameraperson confessing to planting evidence. This 'watching' threatens to undermine the credibility of the police force: drone feeds and police communications are not secure; there is evidence of poor emotional control and anger management by individual officers; and of lying, cover-ups and even corruption right up to the highest level within the force. The existence of such visual imagery, as photographs, as footage, as social media posts, challenges Garvey's commitment to truth, openness and transparency, as I discuss below, and reveals a more 'authentic' or at least alternative 'truth' to the narrative produced or manufactured through public relations work.

Imaging/imagining public relations

The visual image – mediated on screen – is king in the public relations work in *Babylon*. Images, and particularly moving images, obtained through drones, CCTV/security cameras, night vision cameras, gun sights, documentary filmmakers and through both amateur and professional iPhone vision, and shared extensively online as well as through traditional broadcast news media, offer the opportunity to change the narrative about the modern police force. The decision made by the new police commissioner in the final scene to release damning footage exposing a miscarriage of justice at a press conference, knowing that the footage is likely to soon circulate online and/or be released by media outlets, supports Garvey's oft-stated belief in open and transparent communication.

Truth and trust underpin Garvey's understanding of 'the new game' of public relations as 'a 24/7 world requir[ing] 360 degrees of communication'. In the words of one reviewer, Garvey was 'appointed on a platform of honesty and transparency, but the old, opaque system creaks into life around her while she desperately scrabbles for a way of presenting the truth' (Nicholson, 2014). In every episode, Garvey reiterates this commitment to truth with statements such as: 'What we need to do is just tell them the truth.' and 'And is the truth ...? Is that true?' Garvey advocates speaking directly to the people and bypassing journalists and traditional news media structures – failing to recognize that any communication from the police force is also mediated, massaged and arguably no more authentic. Truth, then, is constructed and public relations work is intimately involved in its construction, a point that is particularly noteworthy in a post-truth world (for a longer discussion of facts, truth and public relations, see Nothhaft (2018) in this volume). As Boorstin states in his damning critique of American culture, in which he perceives public relations plays a key role in creating illusions, 'what seems important is not truth but verisimilitude' (1992, p.212). Truth, then, is both illusory and manufactured.

Garvey fully comprehends the power of the visual in changing the narrative. Images circulating online undermine attempts to present the modern police force as open, transparent and indeed accountable. During a crisis, Garvey pointed out to the police command, 'You can't take control. That is the reality.' In response to a request to disable a suspect's Twitter account, Garvey said that means 'he gets reposted in a million other places … or I can put out the facts, confirm the name and we become a trusted source.' The openness that allows a documentary team to shadow officers on the ground is circumscribed both by the editorial control offered to the public relations department and by the production company managers who attempt to control a rogue camera operator who has both filmed and edited damning footage, which he is attempting to sell. Worse, an individual police officer – the subject of that footage – raids and arrests the camera operator in an attempt to destroy all evidence of the footage. It is worth noting that it is the actions of his colleague – who retrieves the USB and delivers it to Garvey – that allows the commander to release the footage. There are therefore, and perhaps not surprisingly, contradictory aspects to the power of the visual image and the commitment to openness in communication. The themes identified in the analysis of representations of public relations in *Babylon* turn upon binaried oppositions between openness and concealment; visibility and invisibility; and watching and being watched.

Conclusion

Analysing visual representations in popular culture potentially offers important insights into the cultural and symbolic power of public relations. This chapter therefore considered the visual in representations of public relations in a television series and argued that popular culture offers an important space for exploring contemporary meaning making in, and of, public relations. The visual image is fundamental to understanding public relations in its fictional representation in *Babylon*. The central character, conforming along gender, class and race lines to the stereotypical female public relations practitioner, is introduced on-screen via a TedX talk. The making of a documentary television programme within a television series only serves to emphasize both the entertainment aspects of public relations and the mediatization of much public relations activity through screens. Evidence of writing, editing and researching is limited except in the production of media releases and press statements. Images, and particularly moving images, are more powerful in terms of constructing narratives and telling stories. However, they are equally powerful in undermining the carefully constructed narratives of public relations and spin and offering counter-narratives and -perspectives. That much of the representation of public relations activity revolves around watching images on screens; thinking about visual representation (for example, at press conferences and unfolding events); circulating images (and deciding whether to release footage or vision); creating opportunities for visibility; and even, in line with one of Garvey's proposals, the creation of a police media centre where they can create – and to some extent control – their own content without relying on external news media, only serves to underline the significance of the visual for contemporary public relations practice. But, as *Babylon* reveals, pictures lie. They are always mediated, constructed, edited, circulated and can only ever tell a partial truth and one that is constantly threatened by other visual images that tell another version of that truth. The power of the image – with regard to truth telling and not truth telling and constructing one kind of truth – points very much to the significant role of visual imagery in meaning making and therefore in public relations work.

Bibliography

Ames, C. (2011) 'Popular culture's image of the PR image consultant: The celebrity in crisis', *The IJPC Journal*, 3, pp.90–106.

Anthony, S. (2012) *Public Relations and the Making of Modern Britain: Stephen Tallents and the Birth of a Progressive Media Profession*. Manchester, UK: Manchester University Press.

Arthurs, J. (2003) '*Sex and the City* and consumer culture: Remediating postfeminist drama'. *Feminist Media Studies*, 3(1), pp.83–98.

Babylon. (2014) Channel 4.

Berger, J. (1972) *Ways of Seeing*. London/Harmondsworth, UK: BBC/Penguin.

Boorstin, D. (1992) *The Image: A Guide to Pseudo-Events in America*. Harmondsworth, UK: Penguin.

Campbell, N. and Schneeder, J.E. (2011) 'Visual culture' in *Encyclopaedia of Consumer Culture*. Southerton, D. (ed.), Thousand Oaks, CA: Sage.

Dhanesh, G.S. (2018) 'Social media and the rise of visual rhetoric: Implications for public relations theory and practice'. In E. Bridgen and D. Verčič (eds.), *Experiencing Public Relations: International Voices*. London: Routledge.

Fiske, J. (1989) *Understanding Popular Culture*. London: Routledge.

Fitch, K. (2015a) 'Promoting the Vampire Rights Amendment: Public relations, postfeminism and *True Blood*', *Public Relations Review*, 41, pp.607–614.

Fitch, K. (2015b) 'PR goes pop: How popular culture challenges the professionalism of public relations', *Communication Director*, 4, pp.52–55.

Goodman, T. (2015, August 1) '"Babylon": TV Review'. *Hollywood Reporter*. Available at: http://www.hollywoodreporter.com/review/babylon-tv-review-762134 [Accessed 2 March 2016].

Hale, M. (2015, January 7) 'Jarring reality, doused with humor "Babylon", a dark British comedy about policing'. *New York Times*. Available at: https://www.nytimes.com/2015/01/08/arts/television/babylon-a-dark-british-comedy-about-policing.html?_r=0 [Accessed 2 March 2017].

Harrington, J. (2015, June 26) 'Global power book: Malcolm Tucker and CJ Cregg named as top fictional PRs', *PR Week*. Available at: http://www.prweek.com/article/1351517/global-power-book-malcolm-tucker-cj-cregg-named-top-fictional-prs [Accessed 4 October 2016].

Johnston, J. (2010) 'Girls on screen: How film and television depict women in public relations', *PRism*, 7(4). http://www.prismjournal.org [Accessed 8 December 2010].

Kinsky, E. (2006) 'The portrayal of public relations practitioners in *The West Wing*'. Paper presented to the Public Relations Division at the Association for Education in Journalism and Mass Communication annual conference San Francisco. Available at https://www.ijpc.org/uploads/files/Kinsky%20Portrayl%20of%20PR%20Practitioners%20in%20West%20Wing.pdf [Accessed 17 March 2017].

Lee, M. (2001) 'The image of the government flack: Movie depictions of public relations in public administration', *Public Relations Review*, 27(3), pp.297–315.

Lee, M. (2009) 'Flicks of government flacks: The sequel', *Public Relations Review*, 35(2), pp.159–161.

L'Etang, J. (2004) *Public Relations in Britain: A History of Professional Practice in the 20th Century*. Mahwah, NJ: Lawrence Erlbaum.

McQuail, D. (2005) *Mass Communication Theory*. London: Sage.

Marchand, R. (1998) *Creating the Corporate Soul: The Rise of Public Relations and Corporate Imagery in American Big Business*. Berkeley, CA: University of California Press.

Miller, K. S. (1999) 'Public relations in film and fiction: 1930 to 1995', *Journal of Public Relations Research*, 11(1), pp.3–28. Available at https://www.theguardian.com/tv-and-radio/2014/feb/09/babylon-tv-review-danny-boyle [Accessed 17 March 2017].

Nicholson, R. (2014, February 10) 'Babylon – TV review'. *The Guardian*. Available at: [Accessed 2 March 2016].

Nothhaft, H. (2018) 'Dealing with facts'. In E. Bridgen and D. Verčič (eds.), *Experiencing Public Relations: International Voices*. London: Routledge.

Pauwels, L. (2000) 'Taking the visual turn in research and scholarly communication: Key issues in developing a more visually literate (social) science', *Visual Studies*, 15(1), pp.7–14.

Pink, S. (2003) 'Interdisciplinary agendas in visual research: Re-situating visual anthropology', *Visual Studies*, 18(2), pp.179–192.

Saltzman, J. (2012) 'The image of the public relations practitioner in movies and television, 1901–2011', *The IJPC Journal*, 3, pp.1–50.

Tsetsura, K., Bentley, J. and Newcomb, T. (2015) 'Idealistic and conflicted: New portrayals of public relations practitioners in film', *Public Relations Review*, 41(5), pp.652–661.

Welch, D. (ed.) (2013) *Propaganda, Power and Persuasion: From World War I to Wikileaks*. London: IB Tauris.

Young, P. (2018) 'Public relations in fiction'. In E. Bridgen and D. Verčič (eds.), *Experiencing Public Relations: International Voices*. London: Routledge.

9

PUBLIC RELATIONS IN FICTION

Philip Young

In the introduction to *Making Sense of Suburbia Through Popular Culture*, Rupa Huq (2013) struggles to nail down her object of study, concluding that, 'In the absence of any definitive definition of what we mean by suburbia, the concept has frequently formed in the popular imagination through representations of it in popular culture' (p.1). If this is true of suburbia it is even more so of public relations, not least because public relations is so central to the processes of promotional culture. Huq's comments resonated with me because, for the last ten years or so, I have been collecting quotes from, primarily, British fiction that touch on public relations. For the Barcelona PR Meeting #3 in 2013 (Young, 2013), I experimented with creating a 'how-to' style handbook, which would explain the practice of media relations purely through a collection of quotes from novels. That same year, I contributed a section on the dark side of public relations as disclosed by fiction to a paper presented with colleagues from Lund University at the BledCom conference (Nothhaft, C., *et al.*, 2013).

In effect, these presentations speculated on the impression someone might have of public relations if all they had to go on was works of fiction. What emerged was a fragmented but in many ways cohesive picture of an unusual, pervasive and occasionally sinister occupation. It described what public relations might be, how it is practised, who it is practised by and for what ends. Beyond being merely descriptive, the approach also seemed to offer a lens for exploring the murkier areas of communication ethics, and a view of practice that concentrated attention on human experience and emotion, spanning rage, joy, exploitation, savagery, jealousy, boredom and disillusionment.

So this chapter sets out to tell the story within the story. Broadly, it begins with an epistemological inquiry into the nature of public relations, followed by an analysis of process, an ethnography developed by observing the working and social lives of its practitioners, and concluding with insights into ethical concerns. It takes a constructivist view of the discipline, in effect arguing that public relations is what people think it is, and that what they think it is comes, in part, from their interactions with popular culture. In taking this view, it recognizes that public relations and promotional culture are inherent in the creation of popular culture. And, of course, to be part of the discourse of popular culture, those books that make reference to public relations need promotion, so the authors themselves are exposed to – and to a greater or lesser degree, are complicit in – the promotional activity that surrounds their books.

Here, the lens of fiction is used to reveal truths about the nature of public relations. On one level the approach is normative: it uses fictional portrayals to construct an image of public relations, both as a practice and as a social force, and unsurprisingly it brings into focus a discourse that is at odds with the 'professional project' espoused by practitioner organizations, such as the UK's Chartered Institute of Public Relations (CIPR). But fiction can also reveal less obvious and less accessible truths – academic and industry case studies tend to highlight success, and practitioners can be less than candid about failures, mistakes and unsound judgements. It is not easy to imagine a methodology that could accurately deliver the binary opposite of the Grunigian Excellence study (Grunig, 1992), a normative account of bad practice and poor execution; fiction, however, offers many, many accounts of disastrous campaigns.

For practical reasons alone, it concentrates mainly on novels by British writers, leavened by a few mentions of US and European authors, based on a selective reading approach. I scanned fiction review pages for any mention of public relations in characters or plots, I plundered the bibliographies of chapters and papers that touched on similar ground, and welcomed recommendations from colleagues who were aware of my interest.

Bearing in mind the problems inherent in trying to define public relations, I have chosen to include any depiction that uses the label 'public relations'. It is not claimed that the sample is in any way complete or even representative in any meaningful sense (but, despite voluminous omissions, it appears to be based on the most extensive bibliography available of exclusively British fiction that mentions public relations). Some of the books have sold in reasonable numbers, others have had rather less commercial success. From the outset, it should be noted that popularity and exposure have not been taken much into account in this analysis: many more people will have encountered characters in TV series such as *Scandal's* Olivia Pope or Patsy and Edina from *Absolutely Fabulous* than will have chanced upon the characters who inhabit most of the books mentioned, so presumably the impact of these TV characters on the popular conscience must be significantly greater.

The use of fiction as a lens for examining the realities of public relations activity is justified by the assertion that for a novel to feel 'realistic' it must conform (to some degree at least) with the reader's experience and expectations. Even when realism is not central, for example in comic or satirical writing, the narrative will normally maintain some connection with assumptions and framings. Caricature only works when the subject remains recognizable.

Unfortunately for those concerned with the image of public relations, a very large proportion of the slightly out of focus but definitely recognizable fictional accounts are far from flattering. In a section headed 'The Reputation and Image of PR' Morris and Goldsworthy (2008, pp.17–24) note that even students wanting to join a public relations course have only a vague understanding of its function: it is at once glamorous, desirable and anonymous. They note that complainers within public relations want their industry to be taken seriously and resent the way it is often satirized without realizing that successful satire must have some basis in reality. Fiction has no obligation to deal in fact – but it must convince, it must create characters and situations that resonate with expectations.

If it is indeed true that many people considering a career in public relations, for want of better sources, are influenced by fictional representations in popular culture, does it matter that the picture that emerges is distorted, both glamorous *and* disreputable? If a more positive image were to be projected (though it is hard to see how this might come about) would this lure yet more people into what is after all a popular profession? Put another way, does the whiff of triviality and skulduggery drive would-be recruits away from the discipline? Take a profession that regularly does appear in fiction: do people become police officers because they read thrillers? Maybe not. Nor, presumably, would they be dissuaded by reading about the experience of the many crime fiction heroes who are miserable, lonely or understandably insecure, and who work in a genre which has a tradition of favouring outsiders who are much better at detection than the 'professionals'.

One common criticism is that the term public relations is used very loosely by novelists. By and large, public relations is seen as promotion, publicity and media relations. Not much is written about public relations as a strategic management function or the formation of rhetorical communities, and very few framings coincide with those favoured by academics or industry bodies (though some, possibly tongue-in-cheek, fictional descriptions do echo the more colourful vision statements on agency websites which emphasize solutions, critical issues, engagement and cultural relations).

Likewise, many involved in media relations pride themselves on being able to keep stories out of the news. Suppression is notoriously hard to research as it would clearly be self-defeating for the masters of this dark art to reveal their achievements. Novelists, on the other hand, can have great fun in exploring such practices, whether based in reality or imagination.

Here are a few examples:

> [The chief executive] knew the plan had failed and he'd underestimated the man he had recruited to protect the councillor and the council. Gary was supposed to have tried but ultimately fail to keep the scandal out of the papers. But he succeeded in taking the press out of the picture and so the plan was in tatters because they'd underestimated his skill and didn't know all of their own shortcomings.

> (Cole, The Last Punter, *2015, Kindle location 1806)*

In *Boomsday* by Christopher Buckley, a key character explains, 'This is a public relations firm. We're in the business of [...] apply[ing] fig leaves. We spread calm where there is uncalm. If there is noise, we apply silence. We make things better. At the very least, we seek to make things seem better' (2012, Kindle location 1310).

In *The Swimmer* by Joakim Sander, we see George flipping through a document: 'It was a classic nondisclosure agreement between him and Digital Solutions [...] He couldn't even mention to anyone that he worked for Digital Solutions or was aware of their existence [...] Nothing out of the ordinary, really. Many clients were concerned about their anonymity and were not always willing to be associated with a public relations firm known for being as ruthless as Merchant & Taylor' (2014, Kindle location 338).

In *Bloodland* (2011) by Alan Glynn, we meet Bob Lessing, 'a guy in his late fifties wearing a grey suit and a bow tie who runs a PR firm' who specializes in 'strategic communications and risk analysis for large companies working overseas.' Lessing tells a journalist, 'I work on the opposite side of the fence from you, and a lot of what I do is actually keeping people like you at bay. Or subtly veering you in certain directions. Perception management' (Kindle location 4852).

Diversion is one tactic, another is attrition. Take this example from *An Agent of Deceit* by Chris Morgan Jones: 'The PR people, Lock supposed, would no doubt tell him that the trick now was to ensure that Hewson got bored and didn't try to write any more stories – a highly desirable trick, if they could pull it off' (2012, Kindle location 1576).

Indeed, distortion and deception is so much a stock-in-trade that when the opposite happens it becomes a plot device in itself. Many fictional journalists expect spin and deceit, as in this exchange from *Under the Sun* by Nick Edmunds:

> What do you mean, "why not?" said Rupert. "Do you want me to follow it up? I thought the whole point of PR agencies was to lie and spin to stop investigative stories being followed up?"
>
> *(2012, Kindle location 1642)*

Fiction is willing, eager even, to describe activities that are common in practice but are excluded from the 'official' discourse, ranging from offers of hospitality that are sufficiently generous to change a journalist's perception of an organization, to what Burt (2012) and others refers to as the 'dark side', a shadowy industry that generates global revenues of more than $10 billion annually.

Take this vignette, in which a car maker flew groups of journalists to Venice, a city not really suited to 'ride and drive' motoring tests.

> The visit was organised as a gallery tour, with new cars artfully displayed alongside more valuable works. In the hotel room of every reporter, the host company deposited a heavyweight art-book as a keepsake. Sadly, the card explaining the complimentary gift was misplaced in one room. Only at

check-out, with the journalist wheeling a large TV-set through reception, did the PR team realise their mistake.

(Burt, 2012, Kindle location 1030)

Amusing fiction? Something from the chick lit end of the market? Sophie Kinsella? Wendy Holden? Daisy Waugh? Actually, it is an unsourced anecdote in Burt's *Dark Art* (2012), mentioned above, which must be considered to be a serious factual account of the PR industry.

Fiction distorts. It is hard to imagine a practitioner from any profession who has never read something in a book or seen something on TV without shaking their head in disbelief. Like many other similar fictional characters, Stieg Larsson's super hacker Lisbeth Salander does things no IT person can take seriously. As Gary Clarke, head of communications at the fictional Thamesway Council in *The Last Punter* explains:

Neither are true to life. They are the worst stereotypes [...] Yet TV writers don't seem to have cottoned on to reality. And the trouble is people assume real life is similar. It's just bollocks.

(Cole, 2015, Kindle location 675)

Much the same can be said about representations of public relations. Bear in mind that in real life author Graham Cole worked on Kent local newspapers and is communications manager at Gravesham Borough Council (James, 2015). Cole told UK trade magazine *PR Week* that the protagonist was 'a character who could (almost) be me (but with a more interesting life)' (ibid.).

PRs take a variety of roles in fiction. Often they are minor players, serving a functional purpose, such as police press officers in crime fiction (usually unappreciated by both the press and the police) or as an in-house spokesperson for organizations (usually engaged in spinning and often concealing) and occasionally as central characters where their professional practice is revealed in some detail.

The tactics employed by fictional PRs can extend to threats, bullying, violence, even murder, and misinformation, smear and sabotage are well-represented. It is worth noting that several of the novelists behind some of the more cynical and unsavoury characters have a background in public relations themselves. David Michie, who created Mike Cullen in *Conflict of Interest* (Michie, 2000) also wrote the critical non-fiction title, *The Invisible Persuaders* (1998), and Michael Shea, author of *Spin Doctor* (1995), penned a practical handbook of public relations techniques: *Influence: How to Make the System Work for You – A Handbook for the Modern Machiavelli* (1988).

Fiction deals in emotions. Naturally, few practitioner handbooks are much concerned with disappointment, disillusion or failure. That said, case study analyses of 'PR disasters', which might use Coombs' work on Situational Crisis Communications Theory (Coombs, 2007), can be read as following logics that are familiar from the story arcs of fiction. Even good people make bad decisions, and some people are simply bad. The actions of an organization, its culture and approach, must to some extent reflect the personalities of its leading players. Some decisions are driven not by sound management but by base emotions, such as revenge, jealousy, prejudice and malice, all powerful drivers for fiction but with little place in professional discourse.

Fiction can focus on the mundane and boring, the trivial and even worthless activities that make up part of most working lives. In novels, it is not unusual to find characters who are just plain bored. And it is not good for your love life either, as Ellie's latest failed date in *Fame Fatale* illustrates: "'He's in PR. I'm in PR.' 'So?' 'So nothing. Apart from the fact that we spent the evening discussing ways of getting more publicity for the brand of verruca cream he represents. He told me that he wouldn't rest until he had made it the country's number one foot fungus treatment'" (Holden, 2002, p.140).

Sometimes the activities of a PR can be a driver for plotlines, but more often 'PR' is shorthand for either a social stereotype or devious behaviour (and often, both). As an example, in *The Stornoway Way* by Kevin MacNeil (2005), the narrator observes, 'If we lived in the kind of place where rich people lived, [Karen] would have married a moneyed arsehole by now and got some kind of work-free job in fashion or PR, the kind of job where she would organise parties and have expensive wine-fuelled affairs rather than actually do anything' (p.132).

What is public relations?

In Murray Sayle's 1961 Fleet Street tale *A Crooked Sixpence*, two *Sunday Sun* reporters visit Oliver Dawson Associates: "'What's your business exactly, Dawson?'' asked Knight. ''Well, it used to be called publicity,'' said Dawson, ''We've only recently reached the status of a profession, if you know what I mean. The proper term is public relations''' (Sayle, 2008, p.155).

The reporters discover that Dawson has a couple of hundred accounts, mainly in the 'medical and theatrical professions': "'We work creatively, not to plug our clients indiscriminately, but to mould and guide the attitude of the public, to influence, in a straightforward way, of course, the editors of the mass media.''' His role is to 'get customers to the point of sale' by pinning handwritten cards in shops informing passers-by that Miss Maria now gives relaxing treatment and Miss Raymonde offers corrective treatment (ibid., p.156).

Knight explains: "'He's convinced himself that this is public relations and you will never shake him off it. It probably is, at that. What the hell is public relations, anyway.'' O'Toole replies: ''It means getting stories into papers without paying for them''' (ibid., p.157).

O'Toole's apparently dismissive definition neatly captures the divide between those who see public relations as, at heart, media relations, and those who regard interaction with journalists as a tactical specialism within the broader and more worthy art of strategic communication.

Although this study concentrates on UK fiction, any examination of public relations in popular culture must mention Nick Naylor, the star operator in *Thank You For Smoking*. The film is based on a book by Christopher Buckley, who also wrote *Boomsday*, where we meet. Terry Tucker, 'our communications evil genius'. Tucker is powerful, very much part of the dominant coalition: 'His title was communications director, but everyone seemed to take orders from him, including the chief of staff'. His role is also strategic: '"Is the point of this expensive lunch to get rid of me?" Cass asked. "No," Terry said. "This was my idea [...] I want you to come work for me." "In PR?" "Public relations is beneath you?" "I didn't mean it that way." "Yeah, you did. For starters, we don't call it PR here. 'Strategic communications'"' (Buckley, 2012, Kindle location 1220).

Framing public relations as strategic communications was, in part, a way of moving senior practitioners up the corporate chain and into the dominant coalition. In fiction, it can mean the deceit is more sophisticated. Take this, from *A Dying Breed* (2016) by BBC journalist Peter Hanington:

> "There's a new British Army PR guy I need to see. Remora, I think he's called." Riley straightened. "I know the one. Captain Remora ... he doesn't like being called the PR guy. He prefers Head of Strategic Communications. You'll know him when you see him – very British, very up his own bony ass."
>
> *(Kindle location 914)*

Often, the tensions in the public relations–journalism relationship are expressed in a way that lessens the stature of the PR: '"Oh well," I said, "there's nothing very much to know. He's a PR man." "Public relations? Is that all?" He sounded disappointed' (Eric Ambler, *The Intercom Conspiracy*, 1969, Kindle location 1634).

What do they do?

As I argued at the Barcelona PR Conference #3 in 2013, it would be perfectly possible to construct a 'handbook' for PRs drawn entirely from quotes taken from popular fiction written by British authors. Yes, there would be gaps, and some would argue that it was too heavily engaged with the intricacies of media relations, and too light on strategic communications. Certainly there would be criticisms that some of the functions described were not public relations at all, but publicity, propaganda or advertising.

As Miller says: 'Because most sources do not provide explicit definitions of PR, audience members might deduce its meaning by watching what its practitioners do. The characters have an incredibly wide range of duties' (Miller, 1999, p.12). She is right. In Richard T. Kelly's Tyneside-set *Crusaders* (2008), an ambitious novel grounded in sharp observation and gritty realism, vicar John Gore meets his sister in a brasserie (of course). Susannah has moved into lobbying: '"Well, I was fucked off with PR. Having to worry about the size of bloody billboards all the time ..."'

112 Philip Young

(Kelly, 2008, p.93). For most in PR, buying billboard space would fall under the heading of advertising.

Fictional public relations practitioners have a remarkably wide range of duties, but broadly, they can be summarized as sending out press releases, holding press conferences, running campaigns and staging events. The novelist may use the press release as a literary device for carrying narrative information or to build a picture of working practices, but more often than not it is for concealing, spinning – or just for fun. In *Billy Liar on the Moon,* a council press office issues a news release which announces: 'Shepford shows the way, ta-ra! Exports up by eight point five percent on some figures we have just made up' (Waterhouse, 1976, p.14). Disingenuous, yes, but it happens: In *Confessions of a Shopaholic,* hapless journalist Becky Smallwood can be grateful for help with her job: '"Savers can benefit from instant access," I type directly from the press release in front of me' (Kinsella, 2009, p.17).

Not that journalists are always so appreciative. In *Fame Fatale* by Wendy Holden we look on as 'Belinda [...] stared unenthusiastically at the latest pile of press releases and invitations sent in daily by PRs hoping the actor/film/TV programme/book/brand of margarine they represented might prove suitable for a *Tea Break*. On top was a summons to the relaunch of a range of tofu and vegetarian terrines' (Holden, 2002, p.104). Or 'Belinda plunged reluctantly into the press releases. It was like diving into a freezing, slimy pond, but without the glamour and interest that implied' (ibid.).

Press releases are not always helpful. In *Fame Fatale* Grace is upset when Henry Moon, the author she represents, is dropped from a literary festival and therefore won't be able to plug his Himalayan travel book, *Sucking Stones*. Organizer Eustace explains:"I suppose we sort of assumed it would be about, um, well, groupies."

"But I sent you a press release about Henry," Grace countered. "The Real Indiana Jones," she quoted."The Millennium Hemingway [...]."

"Yes, well," Eustace interrupted,"Um, I suppose we sort of focused on the title – you know how busy things get, no-one has time to read a whole *release*" (Holden, 2002, p.40).

Naturally, fictional press officers leak information, as in *Billy Liar on the Moon*: '[Pisspot] retrieved a memo stamped CONFIDENTIAL from the torn lining of his jacket pocket and peered at it over his half-moon spectacles. "Prague, city of, Stepford Council piss up in, figures relating to," he announced."And it goes without saying this doesn't come from me"' (Waterhouse, 1976, p.68).

And they (try to) spin:

> "This Prague beano," [Coun Drummond said]. "Like it played down Press, if all possible." "Yes, I bet you would, you crafty old bugger." The habit of various councillors of swanning off to exotic places such as Prague, Dar es Salaam and Paris on freeloading trips had been getting them talked about in the Evening Mail.

"See what I can do," [Billy] muttered. How was I supposed to do that? "Oh, by the way, I shouldn't make too much of that visit to Prague if I were you. They'll be travelling economy class and taking packed lunches?"

(ibid., p. 60)

Very often fictional PRs interact with journalists although relationships with the media are seldom happy. Few fictional journalists will admit to being influenced by public relations activities. Fictional press officers often work on newspapers before defecting to the 'dark side' for better money and more social hours. Warren Bartholomew, a former reporter who becomes press officer for the UrboPark shopping mall in Martyn Bedford's *Exit, Orange and Red* (1998) 'was consummately adept at managing information to Mall Admin's best advantage without alerting reporters to the fact that he'd steered them away from a more fruitful line of inquiry' (1998, p.62).

In Jim Kelly's *The Water Clock* (2002), we meet a man in a steel-grey suit and fake tan: 'This was the water authority chief PR, Christopher Slater-Thompson, known without a trace of affection, as "Mr Flannel"' (2002, p.271).

The press conference provides a stage for acting out media relations, and imparting or withholding information, and can be the only time we see explicit public relations or communications activity (they feature regularly if often unrealistically in crime fiction, apparently informed by TV news coverage). Others are doubtless the result of an author attending such events as part of their working life as a reporter. Once a financial journalist herself, Sophie Kinsella presumably attended presentations where 'the journalists are knocking back champagne as though they have never seen it before; the PR girls are looking supercilious and sipping water' (Kinsella, 2009, p.24).

Kinsella's Becky Smallwood goes to a lot of them: 'As the press conference is about to start [...] I open my notebook, write Brandon Communications at the top of the page and start doodling swirly flowers down the side. Beside me, Elly's dialling her telephone horoscope on her mobile. I take a sip of champagne, lean back and start to relax. There's no point in listening at press conferences. The information's always in the press pack and you can work out what they were talking about later' (ibid., p.27).

It is a bit easier than Maggie White's *The Saint Who Loved Me* tampon campaign launch which requires 'a softly-softly approach, discreet mailouts, advertorials, and one-ones at a Claridge's launch party [...] It'll just be me and Celia behind the teapot and sandwich trays. She'll be serving and I'll be smiling and showing slides on the highpower laptop all day [...] I'll see fifty people, maybe fifty-five. I will have taken the important people aside earlier. It's softly-softly with impact [...] meant to get the concept of discretion into the heads of journalists' (Thebo, 2002, p.165).

The tension between PRs and journalists is a recurrent theme, and it is usual that the journalist has even less time for the PR than vice versa.

In *Agatha Raisin and the Quiche of Death* (1992), M.C. Beaton's Raisin describes journalists as vultures, and her sidekick Ray is no more impressed.

114 Philip Young

When instructed to promote baby food by taking any journalist who has a baby out for lunch, he remarks: 'They don't have babies [...]. They give birth to bile' (Kindle location 1866).

In *The Saint Who Loved Me,* Maggie White despairs at the challenge of a product briefing for journalists: 'There's so much to hammer home into [their] gerbil-like skulls' (Thebo, 2002, p.231).

Under the Sun (2013) by Nick Edmunds brings us Verity, aged 38, 'Pure Perception PR is my company' (Kindle location 808) and the hapless Rupert, also 38, cyclist, environmentalist and five years a journalist on *Your Digital Home.* Their uneasy but symbiotic relationship is based on mutual distrust. They play the roles of adversaries, and the battleground is often truth:

> "PR? You mean being paid to tell porkies." "That's a bit strong, Rupert."
> *(Kindle location 818)*

> Verity looked at Rupert. He was a sad case. She wanted to come back at him but this was business; Rupert was a journalist, an influencer. He had power. Readers believed editorial eight and a half times more than adverts. She needed him onside.
> *(Kindle location 844)*

> Rupert looked at her. She'd changed the subject, she was slippery, how could he have found her attractive?
> *(Kindle location 848)*

> She was a lying, amoral PR person who lived on a diet of deceit. You couldn't trust a word she said, and she lived off the proceeds of selling her soul.
> *(Kindle location 5790)*

Although Verity is married, there is only one way the narrative is going to go …

> Verity held him. "Rupert, there is no such thing as truth. There is no such thing as a fact. Everything has a context, a spin, a different view point. Believe me, even two plus two, doesn't always equal four."
> *(Kindle location 5991)*

Crossing the line

Several of the novelists mentioned, including Bedford, Holden, Kelly and Kinsella, encountered public relations from the perspective of journalism. Those with some experience of handling communications for clients include Michael Shea, who was the Queen's press secretary, Martin Sixsmith, who went from reporting for the BBC to become a government advisor, and former practitioner David Michie.

Interestingly all three created powerful males who use the dark arts of public relations in ways which don't figure prominently in 'professional project' textbooks.

In *Conflict of Interest* Michie made Lombard the epitome of paranoid public relations. The urbane Shea introduces the equally urbane Dr Mark Ivor, 'a professional strategist, a spin doctor, of whom it is said, the only views he has of life are those of his clients.' Ivor admits to 'manipulating people, situations, not for financial gain, but because I enjoy it. Altering future history: does that sound pompous?' (1995, p.122).

To an extent, eschewing ethics aids such characters. Using public relations as a code for distortion and lies has legitimacy in fictional realities. In *Shopaholic* reporters are presented with a graph that shows an investment fund 'has consistently outperformed the rest of the sector'. Journalist Becky tells a friend this is not exactly fiddling: '"They just compare themselves to whoever is worse than themselves then call themselves the winners." I point to the graph in the brochure. "Look. They haven't actually specified what this so-called sector is"' (Kinsella, 2009, p. 116).

Ivor acknowledges known facts, proven facts, indisputable facts, media facts and created facts: 'All I do is provide the link where none exists. Bingo. A Fact is created' (Shea, 1995, p.2).

Some created facts have more impact than others. Mimi Thebo's *The Saint Who Loved Me* (2002), in which modern-day practitioner Maggie White meets Saint Peter, who 'does the PR for Jesus', and helped fake one of the best 'PR stunts' ever – the Resurrection.

> "This too was my work," he said. "And very bad at it I was."
>
> "You're saying you were Jesus's PR man?"
>
> "Yes, Maggie."
>
> "You are saying you were crap?"
>
> "PR is unsubstantial, no doubt about it. You're playing with rumours and shadows, trying to create something out of nothing, weaving illusions of stability. Not a reasonable career for a fisherman, really."
>
> *(Thebo, 2002, p.51)*

Sometimes those rumours and shadows are more sinister. Terry Tucker of *Boomsday* has built the successful public relations firm, Tucker Strategic Communications "on the premise that those with a debatable claim to humanity will pay through the snout to appear even a little less deplorable" (Buckley, 2012, Kindle location 132).

> Terry had represented them all, from mink ranchers to toxic waste dumpers, dolphin netters, unzipped politicians, makers of obesity-inducing soft drinks, the odd mobster and pension fund skimmers. Terry had apprenticed under the legendary Nick Naylor, at the now defunct Tobacco Institute.
>
> *(Buckley, 2012, Kindle location 132)*

The client is morally dubious: 'This "war criminal," as you put it, is a client of Tucker Strategic Communications. Someday, if all the crap we learned in Sunday school is correct, he will answer to a higher authority. Higher even than a morally superior twenty-nine-year-old PR chick. In the meantime, our job as strategic communicators is to–' (Buckley, 2012, Kindle location 140). Likewise, the Brussels-based public relations agency with impressive offices featured in *The Swimmer*, Merchant & Taylor, is described as being without scruples: 'You pay, you play was the unofficial motto. Chemicals, weapons, tobacco. Go right ahead. Hadn't Appleby even represented North Korea for a while back in the early 1990s? Or was that just a rumour?' (Zander, Kindle location 274).

Who does public relations?

In *The Last Punter* we meet Janet Downs, '[t]he latest in a long line of public relations people hired by the developer during the last few years. She was easily the best – and why wouldn't she be – she had been Zara Kingsley's predecessor as Gary's deputy. He'd taught her most of the 'dark arts' and she had a keen mind. If she had a failing, and it was a big 'if', it was a tendency to overreact in a crisis. A knock at the door was followed by a slight, unfeasibly pretty and petite blonde preceded by a smile and a cheery: "Hello Tom, Guy … and Gary. I'm not late am I?"' (Cole, 2015, Kindle location 2861).

Note the reference to high turnover, suggesting a fraught client-agency relationship, then picture Janet. She is pretty and petite, prone to being too emotional, not as calm and clear-headed as the man who had taught her the dark arts. As Miller (1999), in her groundbreaking article *Public Relations in Film and Fiction: 1930 to 1995* illustrates, public relations roles in fiction are heavily gendered. The men are either powerful and glamorous or they are clapped out hacks spiralling into despair, and the women are either bossy and driven, or scatter-brained and a little disillusioned. At a technician level, practitioners are often presented as being bored with their work and prone to questioning its value.

Miller looks at the demographics of actors playing public relations roles in film and fiction and identifies a high proportion of men, little diversity and the suggestion of glamour. Morris and Goldsworthy (2008) suggest that popular culture sees the public relations world in two principal and contrasting ways. Firstly, as overwhelmingly female (through the US television series *Sex and the City*, or the BBC comedy *AbFab*) where 'the work may seem trivial but it is also varied and fun' (2008, p.20) and secondly, in an overwhelmingly male framing, a world of spin doctors working for political parties, governments, large companies or powerful commercial interests: 'Today any political or corporate-based drama would seem incomplete without a – often sinister – spin doctor"' (ibid., p.21). Miller attempts a textured, typological approach, Morris and Goldsworthy flesh out the 'allure' of PR by grouping examples under various claims, including 'PR epitomizes self-assured modern womanhood' (ibid., p.7).

Either way, it is very hard for the observer not to approach the analysis without baggage. As Morris and Goldsworthy suggest, an obvious example is assumptions surrounding gender balance – that there are many more women at entry levels but the higher echelons are the preserve of men in suits. The 2017 Chartered Institute of Public Relations *State of the Profession* survey found that 61 per cent of UK practitioners were women, but they earned in raw terms £12,316 less (£5,784 less after regression analysis) (2017, p.22), and more than twice as many men than women earned over £100,000 a year (2017, p.6). Nine out of ten UK practitioners identify as white (2017, p.5). Daisy Waugh puts it rather more pointedly, describing the workforce of Top Spin agency in *The New You Survival Kit* as: 'Thirty-seven slim women and two fat ones, one West Indian post boy and three lean and well-dressed white men' (Waugh, 2002, p.8).

The hierarchy defined by gender and power can be reflected in the workplace. In Keith Waterhouse's 1976 comedy *Billy Liar on the Moon*, the press team is starkly of its time, when men did the thinking and drinking, and women the admin: '"Where are those bloody girls? They should have typed it up days ago" "Powdering their arses," said Hattersley. "Give them a chance, it's only ten to eleven."' (Waterhouse, 1976, p.41).

Certainly there are many women characters who might fall into Miller's category of *ditzy*, or what might be described as the chick-lit persona. Take this exchange from *Fame Fatale*: '"It's Amber from Ace PR." These PR women, Belinda thought with professional weariness, were always called bloody Amber.' (Holden, 2002, p.77).

Top Spin (*New You Survival Guide*) and Blues (*Saint*) are middle ranking public relations agencies; Brandon Communications (*Shopaholic*) is bigger and undoubtedly slick. 'Head honcho' Luke Brandon, 32, has 'such a scary reputation [...] Everyone talks all the time about what a genius he is [...] He started Brandon Communications from nothing, and now it is the biggest financial PR company in London. A few months ago he was listed in some newspapers as one of the cleverest entrepreneurs of his generation. It was said that his IQ was phenomenally high and he had a photographic memory' (Kinsella, 2009, p.24).

Miller's framing also includes *Obsequious* (will do anything necessary to please their bosses; they have no principles but are guided by anything they think will satisfy them), *Cynical, Manipulative, Money-minded, Isolated, Accomplished* and *Unfulfilled*. Miller (1999) goes on to identify major themes that include the moral life of public relations practitioners and their effectiveness: 'Although practitioners are presented as despicable in many ways, they are at least good at their jobs [...] only rarely were they ineffective.' But she has to add: 'However, effectiveness should not be considered a sign of respect. Quite often, the least ethical practitioners are the most effective' (1999, pp.15–16).

But they can be successful. In *The New You Survival Kit* (2002) the archly named Jo Smiley is described as a highly paid 'professional pleaser', skilled in ensuring the comfort of potentially useful VIPs, who has 'learnt in her years in public relations that the best way to camouflage any moment of inadequacy was to inject it with a gentle stream of meaningless agreement.' In *Powder: An Everyday Story of Rock 'n' Roll Folk* by Kevin Sampson (2000), Hannah Brown, one of Purvert PR's up and coming press officers, is also a professional pleaser, whose popularity with bands owes something to her good drug contacts.

Sometimes public relations is glamorous, as suggested by the offices of Merchant & Taylor – the world's largest public relations firm, in *The Swimmer* – situated next to the Square de Meeûs in Brussels: 'Lavish offices. Hot chicks from all over the world in slim suits and high heels. Refrigerators stocked with free soda and beer. Espresso machines instead of filtered coffee. To go from the gray, dirty sidewalks of Brussels into the cool and softly lit glass and wood office building of Merchant & Taylor, with its silent elevators and overall whisper noise-level, was heaven' (Zander, 2014, Kindle location 303).

It is not always so glamorous. *Fame Fatale*'s Grace Armiger works in Hatto & Hatto's public relations department, '[i]f, that is, such a grand term could be applied to the small, shabby room set aside for the purposes of book publicity. Grace had tried, but the A4 sheet of paper on which she had written "Publicity Dept" had peeled away from its Blu-Tack many months ago and now hung, abashed and curling, from the back of the door ... the only facilities being the chilly lavatory on the next half-landing' (Holden, 2002, p.52).

The case of Agatha Raisin

Neither glamorous, aspirational, or a threat to society, many of the tropes inherent in the fictional portrayal of public relations coalesce in the form of PR-turned-amateur-sleuth Agatha Raisin.

Raisin is the creation of Scottish journalist turned highly prolific author Marion Chesney, who writes as M.C. Beaton. By 2015 Beaton was the most borrowed author from UK libraries, and had sold more than 15 million books (Christie, 2015). The Raisin series began with *Agatha Raisin and the Quiche of Death*, published in 1992, with number 27 in the series, *Agatha Raisin: Pushing Up Daisies,* published in 2016. There is a television version, aired on the UK channel Sky 1, starring Ashley Jensen, and the character was also played by Penelope Keith in a BBC Radio 4 dramatization. It seems fair to conclude that a significant number of people's view of public relations has been shaped in part by exposure to Raisin. In many ways she is not a great advert for the discipline:

> It helps in Public Relations to have a certain amount of charm and Agatha had none. She got results by being a sort of one-woman soft cop/hard cop combination: alternatively bullying and wheedling on behalf of her clients. Journalists often gave space to her clients just to get rid of her.
>
> She was also an expert at emotional blackmail and anyone unwise enough to accept a present or a free lunch from Agatha was pursued shamelessly until they paid her back in kind.
>
> *(Beaton, 2004, Kindle location 77)*

Readers know that realism is not vital to the Raisin novels – Agatha lives in a sleepy Cotswold village with a staggeringly high body count and her detective work is far from forensic – but Beaton's characterization must in part be coloured by her work as crime reporter in gritty Glasgow and as a successful author she must have been handled by many PRs and publicists (Anonymous, 2017).

In the stand-alone short story *Agatha Raisin's First Case*, we meet her as a 26-year-old secretary who has escaped the Birmingham slums and is in London working for bullying Jill Butterfrick, head of Butterfrick Personal Relations, for poor pay and long hours.

Agatha quickly gathers that practically all the clients are 'friends of Daddy', and guesses that the inefficient Jill would otherwise have no clients: 'Jill hasn't a clue. She takes me along as a dogsbody when she is entertaining journalists. I keep a private file on them all. I know their weaknesses. I know how to apply pressure (Beaton, 2015, Kindle location 115).

As Agatha worked around the clock, 'the sensitive girl she had once been became buried under a hard shell'. We learn that journalists, 'particularly those from the glossy magazines, had never come across a PR like Agatha before' (Beaton, 2015, Kindle location 487).

Like many fictional PRs she was adept at ferreting out a journalist's weak spots, then playing on them 'ruthlessly'; ruthlessness is a word not much mentioned in the official discourse, but is generally seen to be a business essential. Raisin is undoubtedly ruthless. Take this from *Agatha Raisin's First Case:*

> "Jerry Rothmore of the Sketch is your biggest critic," said Agatha. "I happen to know he is cheating on his wife. Jill had gone to powder her nose one day when we were having lunch with him. He went on as if I didn't exist. Phoning someone called Cynthia and talking sex."
>
> *(Beaton, 2015, Kindle location 119)*

Mentioning this to Rothmore results in him writing 'something nice' about a beleaguered client.

By the time of *Agatha Raisin and the Quiche of Death* (Beaton, 2004), Agatha is aged 53, with plain brown hair, a plain square face and a stocky figure. She has just sold Raisin Promotions. We learn that 'Agatha had never trained herself to make social chit-chat. She was only used to selling a product or asking people all about themselves to soften them up so that she could eventually sell that product' (1992, Kindle location 414). As is usual with Raisin, public relations is about publicity and boosting sales, more in keeping with the pragmatic framings of Morris and Goldsworthy, than the loftier conceptions of Heath.

Occasionally, there is a glimpse of self-realization: 'Agatha had only been used to three lines of conversation: either ordering her staff about, pressuring the media for publicity, or being oily to clients. A faint idea was stirring somewhere in her brain that Agatha Raisin was not a very lovable person' (1992, Kindle location 482).

In *Agatha Raisin and the Walkers of Dembley* (Beaton, 2009) she is dining Daily Bugle journalist Ross Andrews, on behalf of a wannabe pop star, Jeff Loon. Loon is a 'weedy, acne-pitted youth with a mouth like a sewer' but '[i]t was necessary then

120 Philip Young

to give him a new image as the darling of middle England, the kind that the mums and dads adored' (Kindle location 66).

Agatha is aware of the contradictions in this process but gets angry when the journalist simultaneously calls out the deception while being very happy to accept a free lunch:

> Over the brandies, Agatha wearily got down to business. She described Jeff Loon as a nice boy, "too nice for the pop world", who was devoted to his mother and two brothers [...] She handed over photographs and press handouts.
>
> "This is a load of shit, you know," said Ross, smiling at her blearily. "I mean, I checked up on this Jeff Loon and he's got a record, and I mean criminal record. He's been found guilty on two counts of actual bodily harm and he's also been done for taking drugs, so why are you peddling this crap about him being a mother's boy?"
>
> The pleasant middle-aged woman [...] disappeared and a hard-featured woman with eyes like gimlets faced him. "And you cut the crap, sweetie," growled Agatha. "You know damn well why you were invited here [...] If you had no intention of writing anything even half decent, then you shouldn't have come, you greedy pig."
>
> *(2009, Kindle location 117)*

The detachment of the public relations role and assumed supremacy of client interests emerges when Raisin comments: 'Oh, it's not on for PRs to complain.' Tellingly, it prefaces a threat: '"but hear this! I'm going to break the mould. Your editor is going to hear all your stories, verbatim" [...] She fished under the napkin [...] and held up a small but serviceable tape recorder' (2009, Kindle location 117).

Raisin appears to turn the tables by using a technique associated with investigative journalism, but in fact the recorder just happened to be in her handbag and she had not used it. Nonetheless, the journalist's reaction is laced with a gendered perspective that feels very dated: 'Ross Andrews swore under his breath. Public relations! He hoped never to meet anyone like Agatha Raisin again. He felt quite tearful. Oh, for the days when women were women!' (2009, Kindle location 134).

So the picture that emerges, at least from the early Raisin novels, is of public relations concerned with promotion and battling with despised reporters. Glimpses of Agatha's character are perhaps less expected in a middle-aged women – driven, short on scruples, a little insecure, lacking in glamour, cunning rather than strategic.

Conclusions

In *PR – A Persuasive Industry* (2008) Morris and Goldsworthy use representations of PR in popular culture as a driver for an opening chapter they title *The Allure of PR*. Whereas Miller suggests the picture that emerges is often 'embarrassing', Morris

Public relations in fiction **121**

and Goldsworthy's readings lead them to the view that 'PR is perhaps the ultimate postmodern industry. No-one knows what it really is, but it sounds interesting' (2008, p.13).

Just as public relations influences culture, it is also the case that culture holds up a mirror and reflects an image of public relations. And, as those who spend much time gazing into mirrors discover, the reflected image can be distorted and is often embarrassing.

Although the picture of public relations practice as revealed by fictional writing is clearly incomplete, lacking in structure, lacking in objectivity, sometimes wilfully hostile, and often happy to revel in lazy stereotypes, this chapter has attempted to suggest that it is nonetheless of value.

As Gary says in *The Last Punter*, 'I'm just a street sweeper whose job just got worse. A thousand dogs have crapped on my pavement and I don't know whether to try to clean it up or mask the smell' (Cole, 2015, Kindle location 2940).

But redemption is possible, at the least in the world of *Under the Sun*: 'She had changed. She realised it was Rupert. He'd caused her to grow up. She wasn't going to sell crap anymore. She wasn't going to lie anymore. To punters, to herself. You had to believe to sell. And she'd simply stopped believing. She was going to start an ethical PR company. She had a name: The Whole Truth' (Edmunds, 2013, Kindle location 7123).

Bibliography

Anonymous (2017) 'M.C. Beaton'. Available at: http://www.mcbeaton.com/uk/author/marionchesney. Accessed July 2, 2017.

Beaton, M.C. (2004) *Agatha Raisin and the Quiche of Death*. London: Robinson, Kindle edition.

Beaton, M.C. (2009) *Agatha Raisin and the Walkers of Dembley*. London: Robinson, Kindle edition.

Beaton, M.C. (2015) *Agatha Raisin's First Case*. London: Constable, Kindle edition.

Bedford, M. (1998) *Exit, Orange and Red*. London: Black Swan.

Buckley, C., (2012) *Boomsday*. London: Corsair, Kindle edition.

Burne James, S. (2015) 'Hack turned council PR man pens racy novel – about hack turned council PR man', *PR Week*, September 2, 2015. Available at: http://www.prweek.com/article/1362257/hack-turned-council-pr-man-pens-racy-novel-hack-turned-council-pr-man. Accessed July 2, 2017.

Burt, T. (2012) *Dark Art: The Changing Face of Public Relations*. London: Elliott & Thompson, Kindle edition.

Chartered Institute of Public Relations. (2017) *State of the Profession*. Available at: https://www.cipr.co.uk/sites/default/files/10911_State%20of%20PR%202017_f1.pdf. Accessed July 2, 2017.

Christie, J. (2015) 'Author MC Beaton on her new Hamish Macbeth books', *The Scotsman*. Available at: http://www.scotsman.com/lifestyle/culture/books/author-mc-beaton-on-her-new-hamish-macbeth-books-1-3675865. Accessed July 2, 2017.

Cole, G. (2015) *The Last Punter: Sex, Scandal, Intrigue, Politics and Death*. CreateSpace Independent Publishing Platform.

Coombs, W.T. (2007) *Protecting Organization Reputations During a Crisis: The Development and Application of Situational Crisis Communication Theory*. Corporate Reputation Review, 10(3), pp.163–176.

Edmunds, N. (2013) *Under the Sun*. Amazon Australia Services, Inc., Kindle edition.

Grunig, J. (1992) *Excellence in Public Relations and Communication Management*. London: Routledge.

Glynn, A. (2011) *Bloodland*. London: Faber & Faber, Kindle edition.

Hanington, P. (2016) *A Dying Breed*. Two Roads, Kindle edition.

Holden, W. (2002) *Fame Fatale*. London: Headline.

Huq, R. (2013) *Making Sense of Suburbia through Popular Culture*. London: Bloomsbury.

Kelly, R.T. (2008) *The Crusaders*. London: Faber & Faber.

Kinsella, S. (2009) *Confessions of a Shopaholic*. London: Black Swan.

Michie, D. (1998) *The Invisible Persuaders*. London: Bantam.

Michie, D. (2000) *Conflict of Interest*. London: Little, Brown.

Miller, K.S. (1999) 'Public relations in film and fiction: 1930 to 1995', *Journal of Public Relations Research*, 11(1): 3–28.

Morgan Jones, C. (2012) *An Agent of Deceit*. London: Pan Macmillan.

Morris, T. and Goldsworthy, S. (2008) *PR – A Persuasive Industry*. New York: Palgrave Macmillan.

Nothhaft, C., Nothhaft, H., von Platen, S. and Young, P. (2013) *Public Relations: Rules, Gamesmanship and the Professional Project – Why Academics Must Confront the Realities of Practice*. Paper presented to BledCom conference, Slovenia. Available at: http://www.bledcom.com/sites/default/files/BledCom_Zbornik2013_web_low-1%5Bsmallpdf.com%5D.pdf.

Sampson, K. (2000) *Powder*. London: Vintage.

Sayle, M. (2008) *A Crooked Sixpence*. Brighton, UK: Revel Barker.

Shea, M. (1988) *Influence: How to Make the System Work for You – A Handbook for the Modern Machiavelli*. London: Century.

Shea, M. (1995) *Spin Doctor*. London: HarperCollins.

Thebo, M. (2002) *The Saint Who Loved Me*. London: Allison & Busby.

Waterhouse, K. (1976) *Billy Liar on the Moon*. London: Book Club Associates.

Waugh, D. (2002) *The New You Survival Kit*. London: HarperCollins.

Young, P. (2013) 'Representing PR: Images, identities and innovations'. Paper presented to Barcelona PR Meeting #3, Spain.

Zander, J. (2014) *The Swimmer*. London: Head of Zeus, Kindle edition.

10

SOCIAL MEDIA AND THE RISE OF VISUAL RHETORIC

Implications for public relations theory and practice

Ganga S. Dhanesh

The distinctive characteristics of the Internet and the rapid growth of social media have enabled a social world where images and imagery-based narratives travel freely across linguistic, national and cultural borders, leading to the creation of nouveau global publics acclimatized to a culture of visual rhetoric. Clancy and Clancy (2016) argue that precisely due to its ability to transcend borders and due to its increasingly important role in contemporary global discourses, the *image* occupies a privileged position that can enable it to dislocate or disrupt rationalist or logic-based paradigms.

Evidence of the greater impact of images and narratives on persuasion/decision-making, compared to logic and rationalist argumentation, has been mounting (Quick *et al.*, 2015; Rhodes, 2015). The powerful effect of images, narratives and imagery-based narratives has been attributed in part to their ability to trigger emotions and heuristic information processing (Dixon, 2016; Goodall *et al.*, 2013; Kim and Cameron, 2011). Examples abound in recent history, particularly with the victory of the Brexit campaign in the UK and of Donald Trump in the United States wherein complex issues of immigration and public health were reduced to half-truths and delivered as emotional soundbites rather than as rational arguments.

What do these macrocultural and communication trends imply for public relations theory and practice?

Although public relations scholarship has attempted to address the ideas behind these trends in the rhetorical approach to public relations (Heath and Frandsen, 2008; Heath, Toth and Waymer, 2009), symmetrical and relational approaches continue to dominate public relations theorizing. These theories of the communicative practices of organizations that contribute to relationships between organizations and their publics and to the broader democratic system typically privilege ideas of equality, based on rationalist paradigms.

124 Ganga S. Dhanesh

This chapter argues that considering the rise of the image and a powerful imagery-led visual culture among globally dispersed publics, there is a pressing need to revisit the rhetorical approach in public relations, an approach that is probably well suited to the rise of visually conditioned publics.

Literature review

Social media and visual rhetoric

Social media have unleashed a tidal wave of the visual. It is estimated that, on average, 760 photographs are uploaded to Instagram, 67,737 YouTube videos are viewed and 7,475 tweets are sent every second (Internet Live Stats, 2016). Over 150 million people use Snapchat every day to watch stories from friends and see events from around the world, with over 10 billion videos watched per day (Snapchat, 2017). Facebook has reported a shift toward visual content on the networking site, especially with video. Since June 2014, Facebook has averaged more than one billion video views every day (Facebook, 2015). A report from Cisco (2016) has predicted that globally, three trillion minutes, equivalent to five million years, of video content will cross the Internet each month in 2020. That translates to one million minutes of video streamed or downloaded every second and that globally, Internet video traffic will account for 82 per cent of all consumer Internet traffic in 2020, up from 68 per cent in 2015.

The emergence of digital communication technologies and the rapid increase in social media platforms that increasingly foreground imagery over text have made the role of visuals in communication ever more prominent (French, 2014; Seo, 2014; Seo and Ebrahim, 2016). Users, individuals and organizations opt for 'easy-to-digest' content and share attention-grabbing images. Photo albums, pictures and videos generate far more likes and reactions from publics than content without images. Infographics have also become a popular communication tool in this age of rapid information consumption (Seo, 2014; Seo and Ebrahim, 2016). Further, images enhance the perceived credibility of the source and the message. Tweets from those who use their photos as profile pictures were rated as more credible (Morris, Counts, Roseway, Hoff and Schwarz, 2012).

Through social media, organizations can share their messages with target audiences directly, bypassing traditional media gatekeepers and infomediaries (Doerr, 2017; Seo and Ebrahim, 2016). Individuals also create, edit, upload and share content leading to a phenomenal rise in user generated content, especially, still and moving image content across a range of different social media platforms such as Pinterest, Twitter and Facebook, thus participating in the production and reproduction of visual culture in ways previously unfathomable (French, 2014).

Snapchat and Instagram, with their mostly visual affordances that also allow brief verbal expression as captions and messages; Twitter with its 140-character message bites; Facebook with its posts, status updates and live streams; and YouTube with its videos that can be commented on, all enable the social construction of

Social media and the rise of visual rhetoric **125**

a communication system that is increasingly more visual than verbal. These communication platforms enable the networked transmission of messages using powerful images and brief language bites. Words and phrases such as 'immigrant', 'our country' and 'our jobs' and their accompanying visuals hold the capacity to trigger emotional heuristics and resultant biases. Social media enable the circulation of non-curated, non-objective, partisan viewpoints often narrowly casted through stories, images and anecdotes, despite issues with source credibility and confirmation bias. These images travel freely across linguistic, national and cultural borders.

Doerr's (2017) work examining European far-right activists' use of cartoon images poking fun at immigrants to construct a shared ethno-nationalist bond of solidarity across linguistic and national borders is a case in point. Doerr traces how an anti-immigrant poster, created by the Swiss People's Party as part of its 'black sheep' campaign, depicting immigrants as the black sheep in Swiss society who must be kicked out, was translated and shared in Italy and Germany. Far-right sympathizers in these countries, inspired by the Swiss People's Party campaign, created their own 'black sheep' cartoons in which a racist bond of transnational solidarity was emphasized using images caricaturing immigrants as Europe's *other*. The poster was initially disseminated online via blogs and social networks in Switzerland. The image not only crossed linguistic and national borders through online networks, but was also picked up by mainstream media, and finally affected public and policy agendas. After the initial black sheep poster campaign, the 2010 Swiss People's Party referendum to deport 'foreign criminals' was passed by over 50 per cent of Swiss voters (Richardson and Colombo, 2014).

Similarly, Clancy and Clancy (2016) examined the high levels of opposition faced by genetically modified (GM) foods in the United States and in Europe and attributed it to the success of the visual campaign against GM organisms. Opponents of GM foods were successful in refuting rationalist arguments about the safety of GM foods by employing memetic images such as Frankenfoods that could travel freely across linguistic and cultural borders. These enthymematic images could undermine the scientific narratives without engaging in rationalist argumentation.

Further, studies examining visual propaganda over social media on the conflicts in the Middle East have found that social media played a significant role in the ongoing conflict in Syria (Seo and Ebrahim, 2016) and Israel (Seo, 2014) and that images were particularly salient in these conflict situations, as political actors and publics preferred content that was easy to understand and share.

Although a socio-cultural phenomenon of tsunamic proportions, much more theory-based empirical research on social media and visual rhetoric needs to be done (French, 2014; Seo and Ebrahim, 2016). As a starting point, Adami and Jewitt (2016), in a special issue on social media and the visual published in the journal *Visual Communication*, noted four themes in the articles in the special issue that sum up the latest research on social media and visual research: (1) emerging genres and practices: social media platforms make accessible to a large number of people the ability to create and share multimodal artefacts that include the creation of new communicative genres that fulfil varied social functions; (2) identity construction:

126 Ganga S. Dhanesh

social media provide spaces for individuals and organizations to express and create their identities through visuals shared online; (3) everyday public/private vernacular practices: individuals share visuals of private everyday activities thus making the private public; and (4) transmedia circulation, appropriation and control: images and visual artefacts can travel seamlessly over online networks making them amenable to being 'assembled, bricolaged, edited, manipulated and reused' (p.266). This feature of the malleability of images highlights issues of appropriation, ownership and authorship in social media.

These themes relating to identity construction and issues of transmedia appropriation, control and credibility are also important concerns in public relations theory and practice. However, in the field of public relations, although research on social media has been burgeoning, there has hardly been any focus on examining: the visual; the contexts that influence the creation, interpretation, transformation and transmission of imagery-laden messages; the processes of co-creation and sharing of visually heavy content; issues of source credibility and confirmation bias; and the effects of a visual culture on publics and organizations. A good starting point for public relations scholars to engage with these important topics would be to turn to the area of visual studies and visual communication.

Visual research: Scope of the field and key concepts

Although the academic study of the visual has been on the rise since the 1970s, the field itself has been fragmented, straddling multiple disciplines ranging from art history to philosophy, from sociology to anthropology, from psychology to neuroscience (Mitchell, 2002; Muller, 2007). Further, multiple terms such as visual studies, visual culture and visual communication refer to the study of the visual. Questioning whether visual studies is 'an emergent discipline, a passing moment of interdisciplinary turbulence, a research topic, a field or subfield of cultural studies, media studies, rhetoric and communication, art history, or aesthetics', Mitchell (2002, p.66) offered a useful distinction between visual studies and visual culture, positing that visual studies is the study of visual culture.

To Mitchell (2002), the domain of visual studies encompasses art history and aesthetics, scientific and technical imaging, film, television, and digital media, as well as philosophical inquiries into the epistemology of vision, semiotic studies of images and visual signs, psychoanalytic investigation of the scopic drive, phenomenological, physiological and cognitive studies of the visual process, sociological studies of spectatorship and display, visual anthropology, physical optics and animal vision (p.66). Visual culture encompasses not just the study of the visual/image based in semiotics and an understanding of the meanings of images but also the study of the historical, institutional and archival contexts that enable and constrain meaning and of the subject/viewer who is at the centre of viewing, interpreting and meaning making (Evans and Hall, 1999).

Mapping visual studies in the field of communication, Barnhurst, Vari and Rodriguez (2004) noted that after emerging from its traditional home in the arts in the late 1950s and working its way through photography and film studies, sociology and anthropology, visual studies entered the field of mass communication in the 1970s, with mainstream journals in communication publishing articles in visual studies in the 1990s. Summing up a review of the literature on visual studies in communication, Barnhurst *et al.* (2004) identified three major strains of thought: visual rhetoric, visual pragmatics and visual semantics. Visual rhetoric, 'the actual image rhetors generate when they use visual symbols for the purpose of communicating' (Foss, 2005, p.143), which considers images as key tools of persuasion, was identified as the most widely used approach to visual studies in communication. Studies on visual pragmatics consider visual practices related to the production of images and sense-making activities during audience reception. On the other hand, studies that adopt a visual semantic approach examine the visual as text and attempt to analyse the grammar, syntax or logic that organizes meanings. However, most of the visual research presented at conferences of the International Communication Association employed a visual rhetoric approach, arguing that visual imagery influences ideas, ways of living and pictures of the world, across varying audience demographics.

Noting that words such as 'image' might have different meanings in different languages, Muller (2007) identified seven different dictionary meanings of the term 'image' in the English language: 'A visible representation of something'; the 'picture or counterpart of an object produced by reflection or refraction', (and here they distinguish 'real images' from 'virtual images'); a 'natural resemblance'; a 'representation in the mind of something not perceived at the moment through the senses'; a 'metaphor or a simile'; the 'optical replica of a scene produced by a television camera'; and an 'apparition' (p.11). Muller notes that most of these definitions are immaterial in their meaning, indicating that *image* describes immaterial images. Indeed, the word *image* could be linked to the root *imitari*, thus leading to one of the fundamental debates in visual studies: can a representation or a copy produce true systems of signs? Barthes (1964, in Evans and Hall, 1999, p.33) sums up the scholarly response to this question stating, 'There are those who think that the image is an extremely rudimentary system in comparison with language and those who think that signification cannot exhaust the image's ineffable richness.' However, to Hall (1999) the image 'stands at the centre of visual culture, and its capacity to function as a sign or text which constitutes and produces meaning' (p.309).

Although Muller (2007) suggested that the term 'picture' denotes a material image, mostly a picture on the wall, a painting or a work of graphic art, in 'The Pictorial Turn Mitchell (1994) posits that the picture is 'a complex interplay between visuality, apparatus, institutions, discourse, bodies and figurality' (p.16). In such a comprehensive definition, the status of the term *picture* is elevated beyond that of the material and instead indicates a complex set of practices which enable the image and its capacity to convey meaning. Unpacking each of these terms, Evans and Hall (1999) explain that *visuality* refers to the visual register in which the image and visual meaning operate; *apparatus* refers to the means/media by which images are produced or distributed; *institutions* refer to the organized social relations of image-making and circulation; *bodies* refer to the image's privileged subjects as well as the viewer/spectator/observer, who is necessary to make meaning possible, and whose conduct images regulate; *figurality* refers to the image's privileged position in relation to 'figuring' out the world to viewers in pictorial form.

Definitions of key terms related to the visual lead to another fundamental debate in the field of visual studies. Can any media be regarded as purely visual, uncontaminated by any other sensory mode? Most of our experience of media is a mix of texts, images and sounds, rather than pure states of any one mode. 'Today, at the level of mass communications, it appears that the linguistic message is indeed present in every image: as title, caption, accompanying press article, film dialogue, comic strip balloon' (Barthes, 1964, in Evans and Hall, 1999, p.37). Benjamin (1972), writing in the context of the rise of the German National Socialists and their use of various mass media to advance their cause, highlighted the increasing inter-dependency of word and image and called for a citizenry equipped with a critical facility with verbal and visual communication (in Evans and Hall, 1999, p.7). Muller (2007) drew an interesting distinction between verbal and visual communication, arguing that while verbal communication is argument-based, visual communication is association-based.

Although the verbal and the visual coexist, modern times in Western societies are said to be increasingly visual. Jay (1993) employed the term *ocularcentrism* to describe the centrality of the visual to contemporary Western life. To Debord (1983), the world has transformed into a *society of the spectacle* and Virilio (1994) contends that new visualizing technologies have created *the vision machine* in which we are all caught. Although Mirzoeff (1998) proclaimed that 'the postmodern is a visual culture' (p.4), in postmodernity the relation between seeing and knowing has been broken because we interact increasingly with fully constructed visual experiences. Referring to the phenomenon as *simulacrum*, Baudrillard (1988) argued that in postmodern times it was not possible to distinguish between the real and the unreal. Images had become decoupled from any definite relation to a real world. Consequently, we live in a scopic regime predominated by simulations or *simulacra*.

However, casting this *pictorial turn* or *visual turn* in modern Western societies as a myth, Mitchell (2002) argued that the rise of the visual is not unique to modern times or Western societies. 'If visual culture is to mean anything, it has to be generalized as the study of all the social practices of human visuality, and not confined to modernity or the West. To live in any culture whatsoever is to live in a visual culture, except perhaps for those rare instances of societies of the blind, which for that very reason deserve special attention in any theory of visual culture' (Mitchell, 2002, p.94).

However, the rapid advance of new digital technologies, specifically of social media, has certainly speeded up the process of an increasingly image-saturated world, wherein the visual is central to the cultural construction of social life (Muller, 2007; Wise and Koskela, 2016). How does the rise of the visual, propelled by the rise of social media, affect influence, persuasion and mutual understanding, goals key to the practice and theory of public relations?

Visual communication and persuasion

Research findings have been confirming the greater impact of images and narratives on persuasion/decision-making, compared to logic and rationalist argumentation (Quick *et al.*, 2015; Rhodes, 2015). Research on visual communication across fields such as political communication (Kroon, 2010; Lobinger and Brantner, 2015;Schill, 2012), health communication (Reifegerste and Rossmann, 2017), and environment/climate change/sustainability communication (Atkinson *et al.*, 2016; Hansen and Machin, 2013; Lazard and Atkinson, 2015; Peeples, 2013; Rebich-Hespanha and Rice, 2016;Venture *et al.*, 2017) have offered increasing evidence for the persuasive impact of visual communication.

Multiple reasons have been advanced for the effectiveness of visuals in the age of social media. One reason could be users' preference for content that is simple and easy to understand (Flam and Doerr, 2015; Rose, 2012; Seo, 2014). Another reason could be the ability of visuals to transcend linguistic, national and cultural barriers. Research on transnational political communication in the European Union has shown that language poses a barrier for citizens communicating online across different countries (Doerr, 2010; Doerr and Mattoni, 2014). However, visual and digital media facilitate connections among diverse political actors across multilingual communication channels (Doerr, 2017; Fahmy, 2005; Seo, 2014).

For example, analysing the electoral success of the Swiss People's Party based on their anti-immigrant online black sheep campaign, Richardson and Colombo (2014) attributed the outcome to 'a popular, generally understood visual language which works perfectly in political communication, due to its visual simplification' (p.489). Because the posters were more visual than verbal, they communicated their basic messages instantly, crossing national, linguistic and cultural borders. Indeed, Doerr (2017) found that when the black sheep posters were re-produced in Italy and Germany, the textual content had new and varying country-specific information. On the other hand, the visuals translated well across borders and did not require much change or editing. This campaign provides a perfect example of how political actors use visual communication to overcome the barriers of verbal political communication across national borders, spreading their controversial propagandistic messages across international audiences (Doerr, 2017).

Examining why offensive images can easily transcend linguistic and national boundaries, Flam and Doerr (2015) argued it could be because images are carried through the emotional reactions they create. Visual imagery draws its persuasive power from its ability to trigger emotions necessary for persuasion and hence visuals have been an important aspect of propaganda research (Brantner *et al.*, 2011; Fahmy *et al.*, 2014; Rose, 2012).

This powerful ability of images and imagery-based narratives to trigger emotions has been explained using theories such as the heuristic-systematic model of information processing (Dixon, 2016; Goodall *et al.*, 2013; Kim and Cameron, 2011). Most of the extant research on the effect of persuasive communication on attitudes and behavioural intentions has focused mainly on the underlying *cognitive*

130 Ganga S. Dhanesh

processes (Gross, 2008). However, scholars have begun to draw on the role of *affect* in communication studies (e.g., Druckman and McDermott, 2008; Gross and D'Ambrosio, 2004; Nabi, 2003). A substantial body of research in the field of judgement and decision-making has revealed that people's judgements and decisions across a range of issues are influenced not only by rationalist thoughts and argumentation but also by the feelings and emotions they experience at the time of decision-making (Kahneman and Tversky, 1984; Mosier and Fischer, 2010).

This body of work suggests that human decision-making is influenced by both emotional, experiential systems (referred to as System 1), which are based on fast thinking or intuition, and more rational systems (referred to as System 2), which are based on slow and deliberate thinking (Kahneman, 2011). Although in many situations, rational, systematic thinking is very important, decision-making based on affect or emotion offers a shortcut to deal with complex, uncertain situations (Schwarz and Clore, 1988).

The heuristic-systematic model of persuasion proposes two separate cognitive processes to persuasion (Chaiken, 1980). When people engage in systematic processing, they judge the validity of a message by examining all applicable information, especially persuasive arguments, and by comparing this information to other knowledge they may have about the issue discussed in the message. On the other hand, heuristic processing is based on simple, pre-specified rules of thumb or heuristics where individual evaluation of messages is driven by effort minimization and information sufficiency (Chaiken *et al.*, 1989). Less rational effort in evaluating messages compared to more argument-based message evaluation enables more emotional and affective outcomes.

If we are living in an increasingly visual society, hyperconnected through transnational online social networks, and if visuals exert strong persuasive powers through emotions, and the heuristics and biases they trigger, then what do these macro-cultural and communication trends imply for public relations theory and practice?

Visual trends and the rhetorical approach to public relations

This chapter argues that although public relations scholarship has attempted to encapsulate some of these ideas related to visual communication in the rhetorical approach to public relations, public relations theorizing continues to be dominated by theoretical approaches that privilege ideas of symmetry and equality based on rationalist paradigms. Considering the rise of the image and a powerful imagery-led visual culture among globally dispersed publics, this chapter revisits the rhetorical approach in public relations as a more theoretically appropriate lens to examine visual culture.

The rhetorical tradition in public relations, as though in a counter impulse to the dominance of the functionalist streams of theorizing exemplified by Excellence theory and Relationship Management theory, articulates a space for public relations within the realms of messaging and shared meaning making that could potentially lead to a fully functioning society (Heath, 2001). Drawn from the ancient writings of Aristotle and Isocrates and from modern scholars of rhetoric such as Burke and

Perelman, the rhetorical approach in public relations rests on a few basic tenets that appear well suited to the study of visual meaning making.

First, is the idea that rhetoric is required in a context of differing opinions; when there is choice, when matters are unsettled, when opinions are divided and inconclusive. These are situations wherein inheres the potential for influence, described as the rhetorical situation (Ihlen, 2011) that deals with rhetorical problems (Heath, 2009). Whether it is the transnational flow of people stirring emotions across populations from Europe to Australia, or whether it is climate change and the role of human beings in environmental vulnerability, or whether it is suspicion and distrust of GM organisms, ferments in the world create extraordinary and tumultuous contexts that create perfect rhetorical situations. Such situations call for rhetoric from the involved organizations and publics, the masterful articulation of meanings and counter meanings, thesis and antithesis that need to be debated and resolved in the public sphere.

Second, the rhetorical approach clearly places public relations practitioners within the spaces of message and meaning making (Heath, 2009). Meanings emerge from debate and dialogue, from statement and counter-statement, from an ensuing dialectical process where the truth claims of thesis and antithesis are pitted against each other until the resolution rises above the differences of the statement and counter-statement. Rhetoric is inherently a dialogic process, a contest among multiple voices. Herein lies an important aspect that distinguishes rhetoric from propaganda: the veracity of its statements. Rhetoric aims to construct arguments based on facts, thus creating enlightened choices. Rhetorical theory emphasizes the role fact and truth play in shaping the knowledge, attitudes and behaviours of publics. Messages based on facts are substantiated by three major kinds of proofs: ethos, logos and pathos. The character (ethos) and hence credibility of the rhetor and the rational (logos) and emotional (pathos) appeals used ensure the effectiveness of the messages. Each rhetorical presentation involves invention (how to present the case), structure (how to structure the message), substance (the actual content of the message), delivery and mastery. Rhetors are also ideally expected to address both the positive and the negative, thus encouraging enlightened choice.

However, the recent ferments in the world mentioned earlier and the corresponding rhetorical situations they create have demonstrated slippage into the realm of propaganda where the truthfulness of claims made in arguments are suspect. Yet, the arguments are successful in the outcomes they are intended to create, in part due to the emotions, and simple heuristics and biases, they trigger almost automatically. A case in point would be the Brexit campaign on the UK's continued membership of the European Union. The 'Leave' side had adopted messages whose veracity was called into question after the campaign had succeeded. Similarly, in the case of the Donald Trump presidential campaign in the United States, the truthfulness of several claims had been questioned. Indeed, following Brexit and the United States presidential election, the phrase *post-truth*, defined as an adjective relating to circumstances in which 'objective facts are less influential in shaping

132 Ganga S. Dhanesh

public opinion than emotional appeals' has been declared as 'word of the year' by Oxford Dictionaries (BBC, 2016).

Third, in the rhetorical approach data are meaningless until interpreted; and interpretation depends on contexts. Rhetorical theory in public relations draws on Burke's (1968) concept of terministic screens wherein words are posited to serve as terministic screens. Even though people might be exposed to the same message, their understanding of the message is dependent on their interpretation of that experience. Each terministic screen is a perspective, subject to several rhetorical influences. Heath (2009) argues that rhetoric and public relations work to 'create, change, abandon, and enact various perspectives, the shared terministic screens that allow for cooperation and competition as well as the forming and enacting of choices' (p.40).

Finally, and perhaps most importantly, for rhetoric to be effective it must be in sync with the thoughts and vocabulary of its intended publics. If talking the language of the audience is a prerequisite for organizational rhetoric to achieve the intended outcomes, and if audiences are increasingly turning to the visual in a social media-saturated world, there is a pressing need for organizations to draw on the powers of the visual and engage in a *conversation of images* (Clancy and Clancy, 2016) with key publics. Such a rhetorical move must be embedded in an understanding of the effects of organizational rhetoric on relationships between organizations and their publics; of its contribution to the creation of a vibrant public sphere and democratic processes; and of its ability to silence, and to create ambiguity and privilege.

Implications for public relations theory and practice

Given the scale-shifting cultural changes happening in society triggered by the increasing influence of images and imagery-based narratives that flow through transnational electronic social networks, it is high time that we turned to theoretical frameworks that help us to understand imagery-laden narratives, and the emotions, heuristics and biases they trigger, because the image 'stands at the centre of visual culture, and its capacity to function as a sign or text which constitutes and produces meaning' (Hall, 1999, p.309).

Rhetorical theory seems well suited to understand visual messaging and storytelling, through which organizations can reach out to, and build relationships with, global publics conditioned to the visual. As Valentini (2015) noted, social media have emerged as an important area of research for public relations scholars as a platform where the rhetorical and relational traditions of public relations can be reconciled. While rhetoric examines the intricacies of content creation, relational theory makes the connection between the messaging and the relationships between publics and organizations. However, research on social media use by and for organizations has revealed that organizations are primarily engaging in broadcast communication strategies instead of leveraging the potential of social media to build relationships through messaging and storytelling. Further, public relations scholarship that examines organizational rhetoric seems to be primarily focused on analysing verbal rhetoric, and not visual.

Based on a review of the field of visual research and emerging work on social media and visual rhetoric, this chapter proposes the following as key questions for future public relations scholarship:

1. What are some of the political, economic, activist, cultural, technological and media contexts that influence the creation, interpretation, transformation and transmission of imagery-laden messages across electronic social networks? How do these contexts affect the practice of public relations in different countries?
2. How do issues of transmedia appropriation, control and credibility affect the production, reception, transformation and reproduction of imagery-laden messages online? How do these issues affect organizational identity construction online?
3. What are some of the meaning making strategies of visual rhetoric employed by organizational rhetors to build relationships with key publics? What are some of the visual rhetorical strategies employed by publics as they edit, transform and reuse organizational messages?
4. How does organizational visual imagery influence publics' knowledge of an issue, their opinions and attitudes towards it and perhaps even their material and communicative behaviour? How does organizational visual imagery affect the cognitive, emotional, communicative and behavioural engagement with specific issues and organizations?
5. How can rhetorical theory with its emphasis on truth and veracity of message claims deal with the strong re-emergence of visual propagandistic communication in socio-political discourse?
6. How can engaging in visual rhetoric contribute to the creation of a vibrant public sphere and democratic processes? What are the various ways in which organizational visual rhetoric can silence, create ambiguity and privilege?
7. How do emotions, heuristics and biases mediate the effect of organizational visual rhetoric on attitudes, opinions, behaviour, engagement and relationships?

Attempting to find answers to some of these questions could offer public relations practitioners theory-based empirical insights that could enable them to create rhetorical narratives that can be effective not only in terms of visual and verbal messaging but also in the final persuasive, relationship-building outcomes organizations aim for. It will also contribute to public relations theorizing that is more in sync with the messy realities and complexities of a social world increasingly enamoured with visual rhetoric.

Bibliography

Adami, E. and Jewitt, C. (2016) 'Special issue: Social media and the visual', *Visual Communication*, 15(3), pp.263–270.

Atkinson, L., Takahashi, B. and Katz-Kimchi, M. (2016) 'Climate and sustainability communication campaigns', *International Journal of Communication*, 10, pp.4,731–4,735.

134 Ganga S. Dhanesh

BBC.com (2016) '"Post-truth" declared word of the year by Oxford Dictionaries. Available at: http://www.bbc.com/news/uk-37995600 [Accessed 14 April 2017].

Barnhurst, K.G.,Vari, M. and Rodriguez, I. (2004) 'Mapping visual studies in communication', *Journal of Communication*, 54(4), pp.616–644.

Baudrillard, J. (1988) *Selected Writings*. Edited by M. Poster. Cambridge, UK: Polity Press.

Brantner, C., Lobinger, K. and Wetzstein, I. (2011) 'Effects of visual framing on emotional responses and evaluations of news stories about the Gaza conflict 2009', *Journalism and Mass Communication Quarterly*, 88, pp.523–540.

Chaiken, S. (1980) 'Heuristic versus systematic information processing and the use of source versus message cues in persuasion', *Journal of Personality and Social Psychology*, 39, pp.752–756.

Chaiken, S., Liberman, A. and Eagly, A.H. (1989) 'Heuristic and systematic information processing within and beyond the persuasion context'. In J.S. Uleman, and J.A. Bargh (eds.), *Unintended Thought*. New York: Guilford Press, pp.212–252.

Cisco. (2016) White paper: Cisco VNI Forecast and Methodology, 2015–2020. Available at: http://www.cisco.com/c/en/us/solutions/collateral/service-provider/visual-networking-index-vni/complete-white-paper-c11-481360.html [Accessed 12 April 2017].

Clancy, K.A. and Clancy, B. (2016) 'Growing monstrous organisms: The construction of anti-GMO visual rhetoric through digital media', *Critical Studies in Media Communication*, 33(3), pp.279–292.

Debord, G. (1983) *Society of the Spectacle*. Detroit, MI: Black and Red.

Dixon, G.N. (2016) Negative affect as a mechanism of exemplification effects: An experiment on two-sided risk argument recall and risk perception. *Communication Research*, 43(2), pp.1–24.

Doerr, N. (2010) 'Politicizing precarity, producing visual dialogues on migration: Transnational public spaces in social movements'. *Forum for Qualitative Social Research*, 11(2). Retrieved from http://www.qualitative-research.net/index.php/fqs/article/view/1485/3000#gcit [Accessed 26 June 2017].

Doerr, N. (2017) 'Bridging language barriers, bonding against immigrants: A visual case study of transnational network publics created by far-right activists in Europe', *Discourse and Society*, 28(1), pp.3–23.

Doerr, N. and Mattoni, A. (2014) 'Public spaces and alternative media networks in Europe: The case of the euro mayday parade against precarity', In R. Werenskjold, K. Fahlenbrach and E. Sivertsen (ed.), *The Revolution Will Not Be Televised? Media and Protest Movements* (pp.387–402). New York/Oxford, UK: Berghahn Books.

Druckman, J.N. and McDermott, R. (2008) 'Emotion and the framing of risky choice', *Political Behavior*, 30(3), pp.297–321.

Evans, J. and Hall, S. (1999) *Visual Culture: The Reader*. London: Sage Publications Ltd.

Facebook.com, (2015) *What the shift to video means for creators*. [Blog] Facebook media. Available at: https://media.fb.com/2015/01/07/what-the-shift-to-video-means-for-creators/ [Accessed 14 April 2017].

Fahmy, S. (2005) 'Photojournalists' and photo editors' attitudes and perceptions: The visual coverage of 9/11 and the Afghan war'. *Visual Communication Quarterly*, 12(3–4), pp.146–163.

Fahmy, S., Bock, M.A. and Wanta, W. (2014) *Visual Communication Theory and Research: A Mass Communication Perspective*. New York: Palgrave Macmillan.

Flam, H. and Doerr, N. (2015) 'Visuals analysis and emotion'. In J. Kleres (ed.), *Handbook of Methods of Exploring Emotions*. London: Routledge, pp.229–239.

Foss, S.K. (2005) 'Theory of visual rhetoric'. In K. Smith, S. Moriarty, G. Barbatsis and K. Kenney (eds.), *Handbook of Visual Communication: Theory, Methods and Media*. Mahwah, NJ: Lawrence Erlbaum Associates, pp.141–152.

French, L. (2014) 'Researching social media and visual culture'. In K. Woodfield (ed.), *Social Media in Social Research: Blogs on Blurring the Boundaries*. National Centre for Social Research.

Goodall, C.E., Slater, M.D. and Myers, T.A. (2013) 'Fear and anger responses to local news coverage of alcohol-related crimes, accidents, and injuries: Explaining news effects on policy support using a representative sample of messages and people', *Journal of Communication*, 63(2), pp.373–392.

Gross, K. (2008) 'Framing persuasive appeals: Episodic and thematic framing, emotional response, and policy opinion', *Political Psychology*, 29(2), pp.169–192.

Gross, K. and D'Ambrosio, L. (2004) 'Framing emotional response'. *Political Psychology*, 25(1), pp.1–29.

Hall, S. (1999) 'Introduction'. In J. Evans and S. Hall (eds.), *Visual Culture: The Reader* (pp.309–314). London: Sage Publications Ltd.

Hansen, A. and Machin, D. (2013) 'Researching visual environmental communication', *Environmental Communication*, 7(2), pp.151–168.

Heath, R.L. (2001) 'The rhetorical enactment rationale for public relations: The good organization communicating well'. In R.L. Heath (ed.), *Handbook of Public Relations* (pp.31–50). Thousand Oaks, CA: Sage Publications Inc.

Heath, R.L. (2009) 'The rhetorical tradition: Wrangle in the marketplace'. In R.L. Heath, E.L. Toth and D. Waymer (eds.), *Rhetorical and Critical Approaches to Public Relations* II (pp.17–47). New York: Routledge.

Heath, R.L. and Frandsen, F. (2008) 'Rhetorical perspective and public relations: Meaning matters'. In A. Zerfass, B., van Ruler and K. Sriramesh (eds.), *Public Relations Research: European and International Perspectives and Innovations* (pp.349–364). Netherlands: VS Verlag fur Sozialwissenschaften.

Heath, R.L., Toth, E.L. and Waymer, D. (eds.) (2009) *Rhetorical and Critical Approaches to Public Relations* II. New York: Routledge.

Ihlen, Ø. (2011) 'On barnyard scrambles: Towards a rhetoric of public relations', *Management Communication Quarterly*, 25(3), pp.423–441.

Internet live stats.com, (2016) *Internet live stats 1 second*. Available at: http://www.internetlivestats.com/one-second/ [Accessed 14 April 2017].

Jay, M. (1993) *Downcast Eyes: The Denigration of Vision in Twentieth-Century French Thought*. Berkeley: University of California Press.

Kahneman, D. (2011) *Thinking, Fast and Slow*. New York: Farrar, Straus and Giroux.

Kahneman, D. and Tversky, A. (1984) 'Choices, values, and frames', *American Psychologist*, 39(4), pp.341–350.

Kim, H.J. and Cameron, G.T. (2011) 'Emotions matter in crisis: The role of anger and sadness in the publics' response to crisis news framing and corporate crisis response', *Communication Research*, 38(6), pp.826–855.

Kroon, L.A. (2010) 'The fragility of visuals: How politicians manage their mediated visibility in the press', *Journal of Language and Politics*, 9(2), pp.219–236.

Lazard, A. and Atkinson, L. (2015) 'Putting environmental infographics center stage: The role of visuals at the elaboration likelihood model's critical point of persuasion', *Science Communication*, 37(1), pp.6–33.

Lobinger, K. and Brantner, C. (2015) 'Likable, funny or ridiculous? A Q-sort study on audience perceptions of visual portrayals of politicians', *Visual Communication*, 14(1), pp.15–40.

Mitchell, W.J.T. (1994) *Picture Theory*. Chicago, IL: University of Chicago Press.

Mitchell, W.J.T. (2002) 'Showing seeing: A critique of visual culture'. In N. Mirzoeff (ed.), *The Visual Culture Reader*, 2 edition (pp.86–101). New York: Routledge.

Mirzoeff, N. (1998) 'What is visual culture?' In N. Mirzoeff (ed.), *The Visual Culture Reader* (pp.3–13). London: Routledge.

Morris, M.R., Counts, S., Roseway, A., Hoff, A. and Schwarz, J. (2012) 'Tweeting is believing? Understanding microblog credibility perceptions'. In: Proceedings of CSCW 2012. Available at: https://www.microsoft.com/en-us/research/publication/tweeting-is-believing-understanding-microblog-credibility-perceptions/ [Accessed 14 April 2017].

Mosier, K.L. and Fischer, U. (2010) 'The role of affect in naturalistic decision making', *Journal of Cognitive Engineering and Decision Making*, 4(3), pp.240–255.

Muller, M.G. (2007) 'What is visual communication? Past and future of an emerging field of communication research', *Studies in Communication Sciences*, 7(2), pp.7–34.

Nabi, R.L. (2003) 'Exploring the framing effects of emotion: Do discrete emotions differentially influence information accessibility, information seeking, and policy preference?', *Communication Research*, 30(2), pp.224–247.

Peeples, J. (2013) 'Imaging toxins', *Environmental Communication*, 7(2), pp.191–210.

Quick, B.L., Kam, J.A., Morgan, S.E., Liberona, C.A.M. and Smith, R.A. (2015) 'Prospect theory, discrete emotions, and freedom threats: An extension of psychological reactance theory', *Journal of Communication*, 65(1), pp.40–61.

Rebich-Hespanha, S. and Rice, R.E. (2016) 'Dominant visual frames in climate change news stories: Implications for formative evaluation in climate change campaigns', *International Journal of Communication*, 10, pp.4,830–4,862.

Reifegerste, D. and Rossmann, C. (2017) 'Promoting physical activity with group pictures: Affiliation-based visual communication for high-risk populations', *Health Communication*, 32(2), pp.161–168.

Rhodes, N. (2015) 'Fear-appeal messages: Message processing and affective attitudes', *Communication Research*, 1–24. Online first. DOI: 10.1177/0093650214565916.

Richardson, J.E. and Colombo, M. (2014) 'Race and immigration in far- and extreme-right European political leaflets'. In C. Hart and P. Cap (eds.), *Contemporary Critical Discourse Studies*. London: Bloomsbury Academic.

Rose, G. (2012) *Visual Methodologies*. London: Sage.

Schill, D. (2012) 'The visual image and the political image: A review of visual communication research in the field of political communication', *Review of Communication*, 12(2), pp.118–142.

Schwarz, N. and Clore, G.L. (1988) 'Mood as information: 20 years later', *Psychological Inquiry*, 14(3/4), pp.296–303.

Seo, H. (2014) 'Visual propaganda in the age of social media: An empirical analysis of twitter images during the 2012 Israeli–Hamas conflict', *Visual Communication Quarterly*, 21(3), pp.150–161.

Seo, H. and Ebrahim, H. (2016) 'Visual propaganda on Facebook: A comparative analysis of Syrian conflicts', *Media, War and Conflict*, 9(3), pp.227–251.

Snapchat.com, (2017) 'Advertising on Snapchat'. Available at: https://www.snapchat.com/ads [Accessed 14 April 2017].

Valentini, C. (2015) 'Is using social media "good" for the public relations profession? A critical reflection', *Public Relations Review*, 41(2), pp.170–177.

Venture, V., Frisio, D.G., Ferrazzi, G. and Siletti, E. (2017) 'How scary! An analysis of visual communication concerning genetically modified organisms in Italy', *Public Understanding of Science*, 26(5), pp. 547–563.

Virilio, P. (1994) *The Vision Machine*. London: British Film Institute.

Wise, J.M. and Koskela, H. (2016) *New Visualities, New Technologies: The New Ecstasy of Communication*. New York: Routledge.

11

FROM PROPAGANDA TO PUBLIC DIPLOMACY

The Chinese context

Chun-Ju Flora Hung-Baesecke and Minghua Xu

Ever since the Chinese government launched the public diplomacy campaigns of the Chinese Dream, followed by One Belt, One Road, public and private sectors in China have all joined forces in promoting China's soft power and image at home and overseas. As the most recent part of this effort in March 2017, responding to the government's call for promoting China's image by telling stories about the country, China International Publishing Group, the Department of Higher Education of the Ministry of Education and Huazhong University of Science and Technology jointly launched a nationwide competition for creatively communicating Chinese stories, supported by Public Relations Society of China. The purpose of this competition is to create and foster a positive image of China in the global community.

Modern public relations in China began after President Deng Xiaoping initiated the economic reform that opened the country to the Western world in 1978. Since then, the development of public relations has seen various stages, leading up to the current level of maturity. The 2013 annual survey by China International Public Relations Association (CIPRA) showed that the total revenue of public relations in China had reached RMB 30 billion in 2012, with an annual growth rate of 16.5 per cent. Both global and local firms are established among the top 25 players in China's PR industry. With a full range of services, such as digital communication, consumer relations, investor relations and crisis communication, the contributions offered by public relations are much sought after by organizations in China (CIPRA, 2013).

Since the modern concept of public relations was introduced to China in the 1990s, there have been numerous studies on different topics of public relations in the country; professional development (Li *et al.*, 2012), Chinese guanxi and public relations (Huang, 2000), organization-public relationships (Hung, 2005), multinational corporations' lobbying in China (Chen, 2007), social networking sites and public engagement in China (Men and Tsai, 2013), corporate social responsibility (CSR) in China (Wang and Chaudhri, 2009), and crisis communication (Lyu, 2012).

While public relations flourished in the private sector, the government had not immediately embraced the possibilities. In recent years, though, the political narratives from the Chinese government and the Chinese Communist Party (CCP) have begun to make a difference, with, for example, the promotion of 'Chinese Dream[1]' and 'One Belt, One Road' to the international community. Studies on China (e.g. Barr, 2012; Ding, 2011) and public diplomacy (e.g. Wang, 2008; Cull, 2008) have begun to explore issues relating to China's image in the international community. However, even though the government has been viewed as the most important stakeholder for organizations in China, there is not much development in research on the government's influence in public relations practices and China's image building.

People-to-people diplomacy, or public diplomacy, has been regarded as the practice and activity of conducting propaganda or communication between representatives of sovereign states or regions. The term 'public diplomacy', coined by American political scholar Edmund Gullion, then dean of the Fletcher School of Law and Diplomacy at Tufts University, involves the influence of public attitudes on the formation and execution of foreign policies (Cull and Nicholas, 2006). Public diplomacy traditionally represents actions of governments to influence overseas publics (Wang, 2006). To a country, public diplomacy serves as a powerful tool when it comes to promoting government policies or strategies. Employing such strategies, nevertheless, can establish government and individuals' mutual trust in the international community, so as to shape a country's image. Chinese international politics scholars have been considering 'self-construction of a national image' in the world to be the primary goal for China's public diplomacy activities (Tan, 2012).

Nye (2004) contended that a country can assert its influence, and get other countries to want the outcomes it wants by means of its soft power – its culture, political values and foreign policies, instead of simply relying on hard power such as using military coercion. Furthermore Servaes (2016) considered that a nation's image at home and overseas is viewed as a nation's intangible asset. This rationale also helps explain how the government political narratives affect public relations practices in China.

In this chapter, we will start by discussing the background of the political ideologies under different leaders in China, how the ideologies affected public relations development and how public relations can join the mission of promoting China's soft power and the country's image.

Political ideology in China and the influence on public relations development

Ideologies 'map the political and social world for us. We simply cannot do without them because we cannot act without making sense of the worlds we inhabit' (Freeden, 2003, p.2). Political ideology is directed by what the political forces need to develop a suitable intellectual narrative for justifying their power and authority in certain essential areas of a society's political life.

The recent history of China is characterized by a long period of national humiliation – from the Opium Wars (1839–1842) to the end of the Sino-Japanese War in 1945 (Kaufman, 2010), called the 'Century of Humiliation'. Many Chinese perceive this to be a time when the country was attacked and exploited by foreign imperialists. Instead of emphasizing the glorious Chinese civilization throughout the country's history, Callahan (2004) noted that this part of history, a period of defeat and humiliation, has become a central element in Chinese nationalism. With this unique emphasis, Kaufman contended that 'the Century of Humiliation is part of a narrative of loss and redemption that legitimizes the PRC's political system, crediting the CCP with pulling China out of this nadir and into a globally prominent position' (p.3). Because of this background, from Mao's modernity to Deng Xiaoping's pragmatic approach of formulating socialism with Chinese characteristics, to Jiang Zemin's 'embracing the productive forces of society' (Brown, 2012, p.56), to Hu's developing a Confucian-based concept of 'harmonious society' (Wang, 2014, p.7) and fighting against inequality (Brown, 2012), and, in recent years, Xi Jinping's 'Chinese Dream' and 'One Belt, One Road', the different generations of ideologies all have emphasized the 'nation's rejuvenation' and what China has achieved since the Chinese Communist Party took power in 1949.

Since modern public relations was introduced to China, the growth of public relations has been strongly linked with the country's economic development (Hung-Baesecke and Chen, 2014). Following Deng's political ideology on deeply engaging with marketization in China, Jiang Zemin's ideology focused on 'the development trends of advanced productive forces, the orientations of an advanced culture, [and] the fundamental interests of the overwhelming majority of the people of China' (Brown, 2012, p.56). Within this period, more multinational corporations entered the market in China, among them multinational public relations firms seeking to expand their business operations in China (Hung-Baesecke and Chen, 2014). The ideology of national rejuvenation in this period was continuously encouraging market activities and enhancing the standard of living in China.

During Hu Jintao's administration, the political ideology and the per-capita GDP in China had reached the category of a middle-income country, and the situation of inequality of wealth distribution was becoming more evident. Hu's narrative shifted to the concerns on human development, the environment and human relations (Ferdinand, 2016). It was at this stage that we began to see more discussions on CSR among academics and industry practitioners.

When Xi started his administration, the ideology of the Chinese Dream shifted the nation's development focus to reach out to the world and to demonstrate that China has become one of the major powers in the world. In the following section, we will discuss China's public diplomacy development.

China's public diplomacy

Nye (2004) considered that the impact of public diplomacy on a nation's image lies in a country's soft power, its ability to influence indirectly by developing a certain climate in public opinion forums which can affect diplomatic decisions, rather than relying solely on political elites. Scholars (e.g. Altinay, 2011; Servaes, 2012) posited that, for nations with different cultural-socio-political systems, motivating exchanges in culture, education and business, as well as mutual understanding and respect for each country's differences could be the best approach for influencing public opinion. In other words, a country's soft power could only be reached by employing public diplomacy (Nye, 2008).

Until recently, China's soft power was considered relatively weak compared to that of the United States. Under Mao's ruling, the public diplomacy approach was highly personalized and was full of overbearing language and communist propaganda, separating the country from the international community (Wang and Chang, 2003). During Deng Xiaoping's administration in the 1980s, the public diplomacy ideology was adopted from Confucius' thinking, 'Tao Guang Yan Hui' (Deng, 1990), meaning one should have a clear understanding of his or her situation, be low profile and wait for the right moment to act. This was also the moment when China opened the door to the West and started adopting a market economy in a socialist society. Therefore, 'Tao Guang Yan Hui' explains the social context in which China was learning from a different economic system and, with a humble attitude, would develop and grow into the powerful economy in the world it now is, beginning from its originally isolated position (Yang *et al.*, 2012).

Jacques (2012) identified three reasons why China had little soft power in the international community: first, China was considered a relatively poor developing country; second, China does not have a multi-party democracy; and third, China did not have the appeal other Western countries enjoy, such as cultural capital and national brands. However, during Hu Jintao's administration, the political stability and the constant economic growth that resulted in China becoming one of the major global economic powers, the country began to reach out to the world. By developing a more nuanced strategy that encompassed cultural diplomacy, hosting international exhibitions and events, using international radio broadcasting, and establishing Confucius Institutes[2] around the world, the Chinese government began conveying the message that China had turned into a leading power while also supporting other parts of the world (Kurlantzick, 2007). China's mission for a global public diplomacy campaign was to 'boost its soft power to create and maintain economic ties, foster good relations with international organizations, encourage understanding, and improve its image abroad' (Yang *et al.*, p.652).

The country's image and soft power are deemed essential for China. This can be understood in the context of China's long struggle to overcome the 'Century of Humiliation' after the Opium Wars in an effort to rejuvenate the country. Cultivating a positive nation image in a public diplomacy campaign domestically and internationally means that people from other countries and other parts of the world will make more positive and more favourable judgements about this country and the events it has hosted (Kunczik, 1997; Scott, 2015). Media reports and personal experiences, such as visiting a country or developing friendships with people

From other cultures, serve as a solid foundation for building positive images of a nation (Yang *et al.*, 2012).

Historically, the Chinese government's understanding of public diplomacy has been limited. This misunderstanding of public diplomacy led people in China to view this concept as equivalent to 'external propaganda', meaning the emphasis on China's achievements and the enhancement of the country's image overseas (Wang, 2008). For example, Guo and Yang (n.d.) contended that government public relations should serve as a solid foundation for a country's soft power development. These two scholars indicated that China's external propaganda comprises advocating of nations' peaceful development, a harmonious world, mutually beneficial relationships with other countries, and a new civilization of diversity.

Domestically, Guo and Yang (n.d.) posited that the government would establish a stable environment by getting support from the public on government policies, and by active public participation in the country's social power development. In addition, by engaging 'authentic, precise, and timely communication with publics, the government has developed a positive environment for developing [the country's] soft power' (p.5). But, as we now know, public diplomacy is more than bold statements and slogans. A campaign on public diplomacy should also have a focus on the actual developments of a nation.

It was not until 2007 that the Chinese government began a serious debate on public diplomacy and soft power. For example, in 2007, the White Paper on Chinese Foreign Affairs highlights the importance of soft power. In addition, at the 17th Congress of the Communist Party of China, the party encouraged China to enhance culture as part of the nation's soft power for preserving people's basic cultural rights (Hu, 2007). Chien (2007) indicated the constraints and problems of developing China's soft power by pinpointing the lack of solid theoretical foundation for soft power development, the insufficient cultural products for soft power and lack of overseas communication. He also proposed an approach to overcoming these constraints, including the integration of public relations research with the research of soft power in political science, development of a cultural industry as a strategic move for a nation's soft power, expanding the communication power by utilizing two-way communication, turning propaganda into consensus-building communication, fading out the emphasis on political ideology, partnering with international mainstream media for the dissemination of objective information and hosting large scale international events and exhibitions such as the 2008 Beijing Olympic Games and the 2010 Shanghai World Expo.

Public relations research on public diplomacy in China

Chien's (2007) view provided a valid direction for China's soft power development. Scholars (e.g. Chang and Lin, 2014; Lee and Lin, 2017; Yang *et al.*, 2012) have employed public relations and media theories in researching public diplomacy development in China. Yang *et al.* (2012) used relationship management and image building theories from semantic network analysis for understanding Chinese public diplomacy efforts during the Libyan crisis. Their findings concluded that the image building theory still dominated public diplomacy research for China, inasmuch as how people around the world perceive the image of China has been deemed essential. In addition, their research also reflected Scott's (2015) point on China's public diplomacy rhetoric by which China positioned itself as a 'responsible Great Power' (p.252) because, when the communist party media, *People's Daily*, reported on the Libyan issue, it skilfully positioned China as a responsible international community member in actively seeking peaceful solutions, in contrast to the US and NATO's military actions. Furthermore, their research showed that, when using relationship management theory in public diplomacy, it is important to understand relationships in a multi-polar world, instead of the traditional view of the dyadic relationship between an organization and its publics. This is necessary because of the interdependence of group relationships.

In reflecting Chien's (2007) view on partnering with mainstream media for promoting China's public diplomacy effort, X. Chen, O. Chen and N. Chen (2012) found that, even though in China the government was still dominating as the primary information source for newspapers in terms of government and political news, non-mainstream news sources such as bloggers and citizen journalisms had emerged. Furthermore, public relations practitioners have become not only one of the major news sources but also selective in interacting with the media. The implications for public relations practices in promoting China's soft power are: first, it is essential for government public relations officials to work with major media overseas to effectively promote China's developments abroad; second, with the rise of digital and social media, government public relations officials should monitor the discussions on issues relevant to China in the digital world; third, and at the same time, they should engage and collaborate with the bloggers and active social/digital media users who serve as opinion leaders for spreading positive information and influencing public perceptions on China.

Chang and Lin (2014) pinpointed that the information dissemination approach taken by the Chinese government has evolved from propaganda to public diplomacy since 1950. In their research, they concluded that international propaganda activities are plausibly affecting how people perceive other nations; however, there was no strong correlation between the effect of international propaganda on the actual positive attitudes and behaviours from people in the international community.

The discussions above provide information on the current public diplomacy practices in China. We will now focus on two major initiatives the Chinese government has launched to exemplify the influence of political ideologies in China on public diplomacy, and the role public relations can play in the process.

The Chinese Dream

The current president Xi Jinping's administration has taken to widely promote the Chinese Dream, but it was during the second half of Hu Jintao's leadership that the idea of the Chinese Dream began (Ferdinand, 2016). For example, China was still under Hu Jintao's administration when the country hosted the 2008 Olympic Games, which were considered an important platform for China to showcase to the world that the CCP had 'completed the liberation of China from imperialism and had built a "rich and powerful, democratic, civilized, socialist-modernizing China"' (p.943). The same holds true for the world event of the 2010 Shanghai Expo.

Since Xi Jinping took to power, he has emphasized the Chinese Dream in his speeches at home and on visits abroad. Wang (2014) considered the Chinese Dream to be essential to Xi's administration and China's international relations policy. In his talk in 2012, Xi explained the meaning of the Chinese Dream, 'to realize the great rejuvenation of the Chinese nation is the greatest dream for the Chinese nation in modern history' (Xi, Pledges, 2012). The nation's rejuvenation rhetoric has been a staple for generations of leaders in China because of what is referred to as the 'Century of Humiliation'. With the narrative of the Chinese Dream, China intends to show to its people and the world that it has risen from the past, and that the realization of the Chinese Dream will lead to improving life in every aspect. This campaign could be seen as yet another round of the Chinese government's patriotic education campaign. However, the Chinese Dream is considered more appealing than the previous political rhetoric because of China's current economic status (Wang, 2014). Instead of focusing on the historical trauma and humiliation the country endured, the Chinese Dream highlights the glory and hope of the country.

However, unlike the American Dream, which highlighted individual achievements, the WPP study (2014) showed a unique perception of the Chinese Dream among the Chinese public. For many Chinese people, the so-called Chinese Dream combined both personal and national aspects. About two-thirds of Chinese people surveyed considered that the 'Chinese dream is the dream of the country' and the 'Chinese dream is the dream of the Chinese' (p.13). Promoted by the government and widely discussed on social media, Chinese people did feel motivated by the vision of the Chinese Dream. Extending the concept of the Chinese Dream to branding, the Chinese considered that 'Brand China' refers to the reputation of products and services made in China. Moreover, realizing the Chinese Dream meant that Chinese people wished to transform the meaning of 'Made in China' to 'Created in China' (p.13). Another insight from the Chinese Dream for brands – domestic and international – is the commitment to social responsibility. In addition to respecting the environment, considering labour conditions and ensuring product quality and safety, people expected the brands to participate in 'building a prosperous society and not simply [being] beneficiaries of that prosperity. Consumers will reward brands engaged in the realization of the Chinese Dream' (p.19). Further research also showed the pragmatic Chinese mindset on how corporations should contribute to society. The Chinese public, when compared to the American public, are less cynical about the motivations of corporations' CSR initiatives. They showed a more welcoming attitude to corporations that fulfil their responsibilities in resolving social issues, while at the same time gaining benefits for the corporations (Hung-Baesecke *et al.*, 2017).

In the 2013 Conference of the Chinese Public Relations Association (CPRA), the President of CPRA emphasized the mission of public relations professionals in China to promote the Chinese Dream. To achieve this, promoting the Chinese characteristics of socialism and communicating the Chinese Dream are the basic responsibility of public relations professionals (CPRA, 2013). With this aim, in order to rejuvenate the nation and promote the Chinese Dream in the international community, public relations professionals should communicate the Chinese Dream with easily understood and accepted language so as to enhance the new image of China. In addition, public relations professionals should develop creative communication channels and platforms for more interactions between China and the international community, between the government and the people, and between online and offline communications.

One Belt, One Road

'One Belt, One Road' is the short form of what is known as the Silk Road Economic Belt, and the 21st Century Maritime Silk Road policy initiatives. 'One Belt, One Road' is a Chinese national strategy and framework that was originally designed to establish an 'economic corridor' connecting primarily countries in Asia and Europe. It was first unveiled by Chinese President Xi Jinping at Nazarbayev University on 7 September 2013, as part of his official visit to Kazakhstan (SCIO, 2016).

Since the announcement of these initiatives, enormous changes have occurred in different areas, including new opportunities and new development patterns in economic cooperation, international trade, domestic policies, foreign affairs and cultural diplomacy. As a set of nation-designed strategies aimed at maintaining China's connection to global society, 'One Belt, One Road' has an immediate bearing on China's national image. It also provides unprecedented opportunities for promoting China to the world. Undoubtedly, great changes have taken place in China's public diplomacy due to the 'One Belt, One Road' initiative. Chinese academia has identified it as a new form of foreign policy in the new era (Ai, 2014). With increasing exposure and movement to the outside world, the 'One Belt, One Road' initiative is seen as encouraging Chinese people to engage in more cultural communication, and to enhance their understanding of the international community.

The formal application of the 'One Belt, One Road' initiative in 2016 was considered a major milestone in China's new pattern of public diplomacy, from a historical perspective (Huang, 2015). Seen as a landmark, this resourceful and seminal strategy demonstrates a prominent shift from 'The world feeds China' to 'China contributes to the world'. This shift refers to the change from the old times when the policy-making process relied on Western standards and rules to the new era where China has begun to develop global rules and to pay more attention to a more comprehensive multilateral diplomacy (Wang and Lv, 2015). This public diplomacy policy not only shows that China increasingly evaluates and considers international geopolitics, but also demonstrates the country's autonomy in developing international partnerships.

The implementation of the 'One Belt, One Road' policy has also changed how Chinese people think of their own country's image. According to Sun (2016), the Chinese people's image of China has shifted from perceptions based on Western opinions to more diverse views (Sun, 2016). Cooley's (1902) theory of 'the Looking Glass Self' states that one's perception develops within, and is expressed through human interaction. With the tremendous change inside and outside the country brought about by 'One Belt, One Road', the self-perception sources for Chinese people become more complex, as do the patterns of changes in this self-perception. The 'looking glass' Chinese people use to reflect the country's own image has thus been greatly enriched by the activities of 'One Belt, One Road'.

The School of Communication in Huazhong University of Science and Technology conducted a study in 2015 and 2016 on how Chinese think of themselves through others' viewpoints as influenced by the 'One Belt, One Road' policy. The research findings show that Chinese self-perception of its own national image has become increasingly positive since the launch of 'One Belt One Road'. The research also found that Chinese people are more positive than before in their acceptance of the four values of 'One Belt, One Road' – that is, the rise of national values, political strategy values, values of development ideas and international values of cultural exchange. The research also found that this new pattern of China's diplomacy has given Chinese people more access to information from the outside world than before and allowed them to receive information about international perspectives on China's national image.

Contributions of public relations to promoting the 'One Belt, One Road' project

Following the government's focus on the policy of 'One Belt, One Road' since 2015, the CPRA has carried out a series of cultural communication activities which include programmes such as 'Overview of One Belt, One Road', 'Peak Aesthetics', 'The Power of Image: Returning to the Silk Road', 'Sino-US Dialogues', 'Sino-Europe Strategic Cultural Communication Dialogue', etc. These activities followed the guiding philosophy of 'Culture First and Public Relations Lead' to enhance the promotion of Chinese culture and to realize the innovative elements of the campaign. CPRA also illustrated the past, the present and the future of 'One Belt, One Road' by cooperating with international mainstream media in telling Chinese stories to the world (CPRA, 2015).

China International Communication Centre, affiliated with the State Council Information Office of the People's Republic of China, has collaborated with other media organizations in launching an international 'One Belt, One Road' documentary platform in Quanzhou, Fujian Province in October 2016. To mark this special platform, the documentary 'Maritime Silk Road' was the initial broadcast in some of the major 'One Belt, One Road' countries, such as Turkey, Myanmar and Thailand. This international broadcast platform is intended to broadcast documentaries for promoting and enhancing understanding of Chinese culture and history, as well as major achievements in the 'One Belt, One Road' countries, using multimedia technology (CRI, 2016).

Moreover, Weber Shandwick China was commissioned to provide consultancy services for the 2022 Beijing Winter Olympics and has designed a series of international communication strategies with the theme 'athlete-centred, sustainable and economical'. Weber Shandwick China will organize, operate and maintain the social media platforms, including Facebook, Twitter, YouTube, Instagram and Vine, for the 2022 Beijing Winter Olympics. Weber Shandwick China considers these Winter Olympics an important part of the Chinese Dream and the nation's image, so they will endeavour to promote China's winter sports programme communication and Zhangjiakou City (host city) image with Chinese characteristics and the theme of the games. Incidentally, Zhangjiakou City is one of the major cities on the Silk Road. Weber Shandwick China will also work with different organizations' social media platforms, influential journalists and opinion leaders on effectively promoting the games (17PR, 2016).

Another example of how public relations became involved in implementing government-driven policies can be found in the food and beverage sector. Since 2013, Blue Focus Digital Shanghai, one of the major public relations firms in China, has served China's prestigious liquor brand, Kweichow Moutai. After a couple of years of service by Blue Focus, Kweichow Moutai has established a successful image in brand innovation, integrated marketing and digital marketing, and has become a leading Chinese corporation (CIPRA, 2017). In 2016, Blue Focus conducted market research for Kweichow Moutai in the liquor market in nine countries. The aim was to assist Kweichow Moutai in complying with China's policy of establishing the Chinese Dream, to enter the global market. Moreover, by launching a large branding promotion activity in Hamburg, Germany (one of the targeted countries for the 'One Belt, One Road' policy), Kweichow Moutai has become the first liquor company to carry out the nation's policy of promoting China's soft power (Xinhua, 2016).

For public relations, 'One Belt, One Road' has brought a new opportunity and a new mission to help brand China's image, to boost Chinese people's confidence, to enhance cultural understanding and to promote mutual appreciation among different civilizations. The following is what we think public relations can continue to contribute to 'One Belt, One Road'.

The Belt and Road Initiative seeks mutual benefit for all parties involved. Naturally, such changes do not happen overnight. The relationship between countries is in part based on the affection shared between people in these countries. The affection in turn depends on mutual understanding and cultural acceptance. For public relations, it is imperative to facilitate dialogues between people in these countries. By utilizing interpersonal and intercultural communication, as well as relationship management theory, public relations can help advocate tolerance towards differences among civilizations, seeking mutual benefits, and enhancing the respect of different developmental approaches pursued by different countries.

Moreover, public relations can serve as a 'cultural interpreter' as suggested by Grunig, Grunig, Sriramesh, Huang and Lyra (1995), to help understand and interpret different cultural behaviours and mindsets, transforming and introducing complex cultural meanings and behaviours by introducing them in the form of storytelling for easy understanding of people from different cultural backgrounds, and for helping Chinese people to accept diverse perspectives.

Conclusion

In this chapter we discussed how Chinese political ideologies influenced government propaganda and public diplomacy development. We also discussed at great length public diplomacy policies in China, promoting China's soft power to the world, and the respective studies on the Chinese Dream and 'One Belt, One Road'.

The Chinese government is the most important stakeholder for organizations in China and also for public relations professionals. The political ideologies in China have affected how public relations is practiced and developed. In the private and business environments in China, engaging with stakeholders and consumers by facilitating two-way dialogues has been well understood. Conversely, in the public diplomacy practices for expanding China's international influence, promoting soft power and establishing a positive image, one-way mediated communication still appears to be the norm, whether it is on using party media to convey a message to the international and domestic audience or utilizing the tactic of storytelling for enhancing the understanding of Chinese society.

Signitzer and Coombs (1992) posited that public relations and public diplomacy shared similar goals and methodologies. Lee and Lin (2017) argued that, if public diplomacy is practised in an old-school fashion as one-way communication, it will not convince the audience and will thus weaken a country's soft power. Scholars such as Fitzpatrick (2007), Gilboa (2008), Pamment (2014) and Yang *et al.* (2012) implicitly proposed the principles of relationship management, co-existence, listening and mutual interdependence for public diplomacy practices in this interconnected world. Public relations practices in public diplomacy should also go beyond journalistic middlemen and communicate directly, via social media or special events, helping the government engage in authentic dialogues so as to build consensus, reach mutual understanding, demonstrate the country's soft power and contribute to a harmonious international community.

Notes

1   Scholars use either 'Chinese Dream' or 'China Dream' in this narrative from the Chinese government. In this chapter, we will use 'Chinese Dream'.
2   Cull (2008) considered public diplomacy includes the practices of listening, advocacy, cultural diplomacy, exchange diplomacy and international broadcasting. Confucius Institutes are the central project of cultural diplomacy for the Chinese government (Hartig, 2012). Yang (2010) contended that, for the Chinese government, culture and cultural exchanges are a significant element of the country's foreign policy. The first

Confucius Institute was set up in 2004 in Seoul. Cited in Hartig (2012), the purpose of the Confucius Institute is to 'develop and facilitate teaching of the Chinese language overseas and promote educational and cultural exchange and cooperation between China and other international communities' (p.58). At the end of 2010, there were 322 Confucius Institutes in 96 countries and regions (Hartig, 2012).

Bibliography

17PR (2016) *PR & Communication: Beijing's Bid for the 2022 Winter Olympic Games.* Available at: http://www.17pr.com/news/detail/149601.html [Accessed 15 April 2017].

Ai, P. (2014) *'One Belt and One Road', New Diplomacy and Public Diplomacy* (一带一路",新外交与公共外交), Available at: http://www.china.com.cn/opinion/think/2014-12/04/content_34229073.htm [Accessed 7 March 2017].

Altinay, H. (2011) *Global Civics, Responsibilities and Rights in an Interdependent World.* Washington, DC: The Brookings Institution Press.

Barr, M. (2012). 'National branding as nation building: China's image campaign', *East Asian: An International Quarterly*, 29, pp.81–94.

Brown, K. (2012) 'The Communist party of China and ideology', *China: An International Journal*, 10(2), pp.52–68.

Callahan, W.A. (2004). 'National insecurities: Humiliation, salvation, and Chinese nationalism', *Alternatives,* 29, pp. 199–218.

Chang, T.-K. and Lin, F. (2014). From propaganda to public diplomacy: Assessing China's international practice and its image, 1950–2009. *Public Relations Review,* 40(3), pp. 450–458.

Chen, X., Chen, O. and Chen, N. (2012). How public relations functions as news sources in China. *Public Relations Review,* 38, pp. 697–703.

Chen, Y.R. (2007) 'The strategic management of government affairs in China: How multinational corporations in China interact with the Chinese government', *Journal of Public Relations Research*, 19, pp.283–306.

Chien, H. (2007). 'The current problems and strategies for China's soft power development', *External Communication*, 4, pp.44–46.

CIPRA (2013). The 2012 survey on the public relations industry in China. Beijing: China International Public Relations Association, China [in Chinese].

CIPRA (2017). *Blue Focus Digital Gains Two Great PR Awards for MOUTAI Publicity Work, Based on the Wine Industry.* Available at: http://www.cipra.org.cn/templates/T_Second/Index.aspx?nodeid=45&page=ContentPage&categoryid=0&contentid=1217 [Accessed 15 April 2017].

Cooley, C.H. (1902) *Human Nature and the Social Order.* New York: Scribner.

CPRA (2015) *Philosophy of Visible: One Belt, One Road with National Strategic Communications and Important PR Brand.* Sohu June, 2015. Available at: http://mt.sohu.com/20150615/n415021832.shtml [Accessed 15 April 2017].

CRI Online (2016) 'One Belt, One Road', Documentary Media of International Communication Platform Launched. CRI Online, October, 2016. Available at: http://news.cri.cn/2016-10-11/d28a4718-563c-8957-e51b-f9623323cfa6.html [Accessed 15 April 2017].

Cull, N. (2006) *Public Diplomacy Before Gullion: The Evolution of a Phrase.* University of Southern California: USC Public Diplomacy.

Cull, N. (2008) 'The public diplomacy of the modern Olympic Games and China's soft power strategy'. In M.E. Price and D. Dayan (eds.) *Owning the Beijing Olympics. Narratives of the New China* (pp.117–144). Ann Arbor, MI: University of Michigan Press.

Ding, S. (2011) 'Branding a rising China: An analysis of Beijing's national image management in the age of China's rise', *Journal of Asian and African Studies*, 46(3), pp.292–306.

Ferdinand, P. (2016). 'Westward ho – the China dream and "One Belt, One Road"': Chinese foreign policy under Xi Jinping'. *International Affairs*, 92(4), pp.941–957.

Fitzpatrick, K.R. (2007). 'Advancing the new public diplomacy: A public relations perspective', *The Hague Journal of Diplomacy*, 2(3), pp.187–211.

Freeden, M. (2003). *Ideology: A Very Short Introduction*. Oxford, UK: Oxford University Press.

Gilboa, E. (2008). 'Searching for a theory of public diplomacy', *The Annals of the American Academy of Political and Social Science*, 616(1), pp.55–77.

Guo, J. and Yang, C. (n.d.). 'Analyzing the interaction mechanism on China's soft power and government public relationship (GPR)', *Online Chinese Scientific Paper*. Available at: www.paper.edu.cn, 1–7 [Accessed 16 March 2017].

Grunig, J.E., Grunig, L.A., Sriramesh, K., Huang, Y.H. and Lyra, A. (1995) 'Models of public relations in an international setting', *Journal of Public Relations Research*, 7, pp.163–186.

Hartig, F. (2012). 'Confucius Institutes and the rise of China', *Journal of Chinese Political Science*, 17(1), pp.53–76.

Hu, J. (2007). 'Hold high the great banner of socialism with Chinese characteristics and strive for new victories in building a moderately prosperous society in all respects', Report to the Seventeenth National Congress of the Communist Party of China, 15 October. Available at: http://www.chinadaily.com.cn/china/2007-10/25/content_6225977.htm [Accessed 14 March 2017].

Huang, J. (2015) '"One Belt, One Road" and the Change of China's Diplomacy Pattern ("一带一路"与中国外交转型)', *Social Outlook* (社会观察), 2015(6), pp.22–24.

Huang, Y.H. (2000) 'The personal influence model and gao guanxi in Taiwan Chinese Public Relations', *Public Relations Review*, 26(2), pp.219–236.

Hung, C.J.F. (2005) 'Exploring types of organization-public relationships and their implications on relationship management in public relations', *Journal of Public Relations Research*, 17(4), pp.393–426.

Hung-Baesecke, C.J.F. and Chen, Y.R. (2014) 'China: A profession shaped by the social, political, and economic evolutions'. In T. Watson (ed.), *National Perspectives in the Development of Public Relations: Other Voices* (pp.20–33). London: Palgrave Pivot.

Hung-Baesecke, C.J.F., Stacks, D., Coombs, T., Chen, Y.R.R. and Boyd, B. (2017, March) 'From corporate social responsibility to creating shared value: A comparison study from the communication perspective in the US and China'. Paper to be presented at the 20th International Public Relations Research Conference, Orlando, USA.

Jacques, M. (2012) *When China Rules the World: The End of the Western World and the Birth of a New Global Order*. London: Penguin Books.

Kaufman, A.A. (2010) 'The "Century of Humiliation", then and now: Chinese perceptions of the international order', *PACIFIC FOCUS*, 25(1), pp.1–33.

Kurlantzick, J. (2007). *Charm Offensive: How China's Soft Power Is Transforming the World*. New Haven, CT: Yale University Press.

Lee, S.T., and Lin, J. (2017) 'An integrated approach to public diplomacy and public relations: A five-year analysis of the information subsidies of the United States, China, and Singapore', *International Journal of Strategic Communication*, 11, pp.1–17.

Li, C., Cropp, F., Sims, W. and Jin, Y. (2012) 'Perceived professional standards and roles of public relations in China: Through the lens of Chinese public relations practitioners', *Public Relations Review*, 38(5), pp.704–710. DOI: 10.1016/j.pubrev.2012.05.001.

Lyu, J. C. (2012). 'A comparative study of crisis communication strategies between mainland China and Taiwan: The melamine tainted milk powder crisis in the Chinese context',

Public Relations Review. http://dx.dio.org/10.1016/j.pubrev.2012.07.003 [Accessed 14 March 2017].

Men, L.R. and Tsai, W.H.S. (2013) 'Beyond liking or following: Understanding public engagement on social networking sites in China', *Public Relations Review*, 39(1), pp.13–22. DOI: 10.1016/j.pubrev.2012.09.013.

Nye, J.S. (2004) *Soft Power: The Means to Success in International Relations.* New York: Public Affairs.

Nye, J.S. (2008) 'Public diplomacy and soft power', *Annals of the American Academy of Political and Social Science*, 616(1), p.95.

Pamment, J. (2014) 'Articulating influence: Toward a research agenda for interpreting the evaluation of soft power, public diplomacy and nation brands', *Public Relations Review*, 40(1), pp.50–59. DOI: 10.1016/j.pubrev.2013.11.019.

SCIO (2016) The State Council Information Office of PRC. Available at: http://www.scio.gov. cn/32621/32629/32754/Document/1490044/1490044.htm [Accessed 20 March 2017].

Scott, D. (2015) 'China's public diplomacy rhetoric, 1990–2012: Pragmatic image-crafting', *Diplomacy & Statecraft*, 26, pp.249–265.

Servaes, J. (2012). 'Soft power and public diplomacy: The new frontier for public relations and international communication between the US and China', *Public Relations Review*, 38, pp.643–651.

Servaes, J. (2016) 'The Chinese dream shattered between hard and soft power?', *Media, Culture & Society*, 38(3), pp.437–449.

Signitzer, B.H. and Coombs, T. (1992) 'Public relations and public diplomacy: Conceptual convergences', *Public Relations Review*, 18(2), pp.137–147.

Sun, X. (2016) '"One Belt, One Road" and reshaping the diplomacy pattern of great peripheral diplomacy ("一带一路"与大周边外交格局的重塑)', *Journal of Yunnan Social Sciences (云南社会科学)*, 3, pp.1–6.

Tan, Y. (2012) 'Constructing China's national image in public diplomacy: by the example of China's national image advertising video (公共外交中的国家形象建构——以中国国家形象宣传片为例)', *Contemporary International Relations* (现代国际关系), 3, pp.54–60.

Wang, J. (2006). Managing national reputation and international relations in the global era: Public diplomacy revisited. *Public Relations Review,* 32(2), 91–96.

Wang, J. and Chang, T. (2003) 'Strategic public diplomacy and local press: How a high-profile head-of-state visit was covered in America's heartland', *Public Relations Review*, 30, pp.11–24.

Wang, J. and Chaudhri, V. (2009) 'Corporate social responsibility engagement and communication by Chinese companies', *Public Relations Review*, 35(3), pp.247–250.

Wang, Y. (2008). 'Public diplomacy and the rise of Chinese soft power', *Annals of the American Academy*, 616, pp.257–273.

Wang, Y. and Lv, N. (2015) 'Popular issue and critical thinking: Conversation between "One Belt, One Road" and China's diplomacy (热话题与冷思考——关于"一带一路"与中国外交的对话)', *Contemporary World and Socialism* (当代世界与社会主义), 4, pp.4–12.

Wang, Z. (2014) 'The Chinese Dream: Concept and context', *Journal of Chinese Political Science*, 19(1), pp.1–13.

WPP (2014) 'New study explores the Chinese Dream and what it means for business'. Available at: http://www.wpp.com/wpp/press/2014/feb/24/new-study-explores-the-chinese-dream-and-what-it-means-for-business/ [Accessed 7 December 2016].

Xinhua (2012) 'Xi Pledges "Great renewal of Chinese nation"'. Available at: http://news.xinhuanet.com/english/china/2012-11/29/c_132008231.htm [Accessed 20 February 2017].

Xinhua (2016) *Chinese MOUTAI Wine Landed in Germany by "One Road, One Belt" Trip*. Available at: http://www.gz.xinhuanet.com/2016-12/07/c_1120073339.htm [Accessed 16 April 2017].

Yang, A., Klyueva, A. and Taylor, M. (2012) 'Beyond a dyadic approach to public diplomacy: Understanding relationships in a multipolar world', *Public Relations Review*, 38, pp.952–994.

Yang, R. (2010) 'Soft power and higher education: An examination of China's Confucius Institutes', *Globalisation, Societies, and Education*, 8(2), pp.235–245.

12

INFLUENCES OF POSTCOLONIALISM OVER THE UNDERSTANDING AND EVOLUTION OF PUBLIC RELATIONS IN LATIN AMERICA

Juan-Carlos Molleda, Ana María Suárez Monsalve, Andréia Silveira Athaydes, Gabriel Sadi, Elim Hernández and Ricardo Valencia

Introduction

In the contemporary field of public relations, some developed countries have had an absolute primacy in the production of specialized literature. This might have been possible due to the linguistic advantages of what is broadly considered the international language for business: English. It has not been merely by chance that authors of Anglo-Saxon countries – with a predominance of authors from the United States and United Kingdom, in that order – have been the most productive in terms of research and publication, which 'gives public relations the [majority] nature of an Anglo-Saxon endeavor' (Xifra, 2003, p.94), a state of affairs that is not necessarily sensitive to the idiosyncrasy of Latin American practitioners.

In this context, and starting in the 1970s, the theoretical analysis of public relations starts showing an inspiration clearly based on the functionalist and systemic approach. This perspective is centred on the way public relations can contribute to organizations and their environments as integrated subsystems through the maintenance of an equilibrium or consensus with the ultimate goal of comprehension and mutual benefit (Sadi, 2013). This does not consider some concerns present in the Latin American public relations perspective regarding the social roles of the practice and its practitioners (Molleda, 2001).

In crafting this chapter on the interplay between postcolonialism and Latin American public relations practice, most sources have been precisely contributions produced in developed countries, which represents a factor that exemplifies the colonialist influence of the body of knowledge. Little is known in the world about the contributions of Latin America to postcolonial theory. Then, to write about the influence of postcolonialism on the understanding and evolution of public relations in Latin America, we have had to resort to a Eurocentric look at this concept. However, it has been necessary to think about the concept from Latin American theorists to understand, from our own contributions and logic, the authentic influences in our profession.

The chapter has been divided into three parts. The first section presents a brief description of what constitutes Latin America and the regional authors who have contributed to the postcolonial perspective. The second section explores the application of the postcolonial framework to the field of public relations and also includes an overview of the practice's evolution in the region. Finally, the third part documents the postcolonial approach by examining regional practices of agencies in six Latin American countries: Argentina, Brazil, Colombia, El Salvador, Mexico and Venezuela. This is accomplished through the examination of public sources and the official websites of five public relations and/or communication management agencies in each selected country.

Latin America and postcolonial theory

Latin America is a subcontinent that includes a group of countries and dependencies in the American continent where Romance languages are predominant and a combination of English, French, Dutch and indigenous languages represent a small proportion (The Indigenous Languages, n.d.). The term originated in nineteenth century France as *Amérique latine* to consider French-speaking territories in the Americas (i.e., Haiti, French Guiana, Martinique, Guadeloupe, Saint Martin and Saint Barthélemy) along with the larger group of countries where Spanish and Portuguese languages prevailed. It is therefore broader than the terms Ibero-America or Hispanic America – though it usually excludes French Canada and modern French Louisiana.

Latin America is a region that gained its independence, mostly from Spain and Portugal, at the beginning of the nineteenth century and consists of 19 sovereign states and several territories and dependencies that cover an area that stretches from the northern border of Mexico to the southern tip of South America, including the Caribbean. It has an area of approximately 19,197,000 sq km (7,412,000 sq miles), almost 13 per cent of the Earth's land surface area. As of 2015, its population was estimated to be more than 626 million.

Origin of postcolonial theory

Postcolonial theory emerged in the context of the decolonization of countries in Africa and Asia after the Second World War, especially after the breaking up of the British Empire (Mishra and Hodge, 1991). The setting of postcolonial theory in this geographical region and historical period has not prevented it from shedding light on many phenomena in Latin America.

To explain postcolonial theory from a Latin American perspective, Castro-Gómez (2005) argued that Latin American cultural studies have been divided into four groups in recent years during the transition from the twentieth to the twenty-first centuries: studies on cultural practices and policies; cultural criticism (deconstructivist or neo-Frankfurtian); subaltern studies; and, finally, postcolonial studies. In this last group, the line is drawn by Walter Mignolo and the group of 'modernity/coloniality', including Edgardo Lander, Aníbal Quijano, Enrique Dussel, Catherine Walsh, Javier Sanjinés, Fernando Coronil, Ramón Grosfoguel, Freya Schiwy, Nelson Maldonado and Santiago Castro-Gómez himself. This group of intellectuals has advanced the configuration of postcolonial theory from a Latin American approach, since, as they affirmed, postcolonial Anglo-Saxon theory is not enough to make visible the specifics about modernity/coloniality on the subcontinent.

According to their discussions, this group of theorists explained how Marxist social theory constructed the problem of colonialism from an additive perspective to modernity, not from a constitutive view of it. Karl Marx and Frederick Engels in *The Communist Manifesto* explained the bourgeoisie as a social class, emerging as the elite who could transform all social relations. Because of this transformation of the instruments and relations of production, men are 'forced to consider serenely their conditions of existence and their reciprocal relations' (Marx and Engels, cited in Castro-Gómez, 2005, p.13).

From a Eurocentric perspective, the colonial expansion of the empires served as support for modernity, through the consolidation of capitalism. This perception began to change with the rise of postcolonial studies at the end of the last century because they considered that the cognitive and symbolic dimension of coloniality contributed to the creation of epistemological paradigms and social relations of domination. Intellectuals such as 'Said, Bhabha, Spivak, Prakash, Chatterjee, Guha and Chakrabarty, [...] began to show that colonialism is not only an economic and political phenomenon but has an epistemic dimension linked to the birth of the human sciences, both in the center and in the periphery' (Castro-Gómez, 2005, p.19). Through the human sciences, an imaginary was created to legitimize imperial power and to consolidate epistemological paradigms on colonizers and those who were colonized. The ideological representation of the discourse would include the dominators and the dominated.

To understand modern epistemology, Walter Mignolo (2005) introduced the relationship between two moments in the historical trajectory of the modern colonial world. He established the connection between two historical facts to say that it is necessary to understand imperialism in the geopolitical logic of knowledge. These two historical facts that he took as examples are: in the fifteenth century, the arrival in Granada, Spain of the soldiers of Cardinal Cisneros and the consequent burning of books containing knowledge in Arabic; and in the twentieth century, the destruction of the World Trade Center in New York City, United States.

The relationship between these two events in the current state of globalization from/in Africa, Asia or Latin America, is presented in the reformulation of imperialism, capitalism and racism from the experience of these from a phenomenological

Latin American PR: Postcolonial influences **155**

perspective (the perspective of the man/woman in the colonial history of colonized peoples). Thus, Mignolo (2005) proposed to use the economic geopolitical model to reflect on the geopolitics of knowledge because 'just as it is difficult today to think economic models ignoring capitalism, it is also difficult to think epistemic models ignoring the framework in which modern epistemology (The Euro-Western modernity) accustomed us to think the world' (Mignolo, cited in Castro-Gómez, 2005, p.11).

For Mignolo, there are three intellectual positions on the matter. On the one hand, there are intellectuals who think that globalization, although not perfect, is beneficial because there are more winners than losers. On the other hand, the intellectuals are demanding reforms of global capitalism given the excesses it causes. This group includes intellectuals of the so-called 'third world' who assume globalization and seek possible ways of development for those regions of the world that have not benefitted from capitalism. A third group of intellectuals hold the extreme critique that capitalism accounts for new forms of global colonialism.

Postcolonial theory and public relations

For Curtin and Gaither (2012), post-coloniality represents, at our current juncture, a label that includes countries in varying stages of development that have been 'partially built and defined by colonial powers that left a legacy of inequality that continues today under the banner of globalization' (p.309). As a response to the binary distinction between dominant forces of the West, led by the United States, versus the resistance of countries in the global South, Curtin and Gaither (2012) proposed a vision in which public relations is observed as a continuum of economic and cultural practices. Consequently, they assess public relations as a fluid terrain for hybridity in which governments, corporations and civil society influence each other, and have conceived the practice of public relations as a circuit in which five moments interact repeatedly. These moments are: representation, production, consumption, identity and regulation. This circuit of culture in public relations has been inspired by a critical perspective that attempts to make sense of the interaction between cultural and economic processes (Du Gay *et al.*, 2013).

Postcolonial theory has several similarities with critical theory, and the extended areas of knowledge that are implied in it. Dozier and Lauzen (2000) and L'Etang (2011), for instance, call for understanding public relations as a discipline where academic fields, such as anthropology and sociology, interact with the systematic examination of their practice. In Dozier and Lauzen's (2000) view, critical theory is a catalyst and stimulant that allows public relations research to see whose interests are served by our work. Meanwhile, Mickey (2003) proposed a critical view of public relations, based on an approach to cultural studies as a vehicle for examining the profession from critical theory. It considers that actions, messages and exchanges promoted by the practice of public relations are social actions. 'Every practice in culture, defined here as social action, needs to be open to critical inquiry, because it is a construction by actors who stand to gain some of the practice', Mickey stated (2003, p.5).

In these critical perspectives, power is the central feature (Berger, 2005) and has facilitated the emergence of a 'socio-cultural turn', with public relations representing a locus of transactions that produce social and cultural meanings (Edwards and Hodges, 2011). According to these authors, in this space, public relations has a 'fluid articulation of structural and agentic elements of society' (p.4). In Dozier and Lauzen (2000), Edward and Hodges (2011) and L'Etang and Pieczka (2006), among others, public relations seems to challenge what has been called the functional model, which situates the organization, especially the corporate entity, at the center of academic research (Grunig, 1992). This has been framed in some efforts to separate public relations from the realm of corporate communications, initiating an intense debate in the field (Johnston, 2016) and possibly promoting a paradigmatic indefinition, epistemologically speaking (Sadi, 2016).

As a natural consequence, the disengagement of public relations from simply observing the dynamics between corporations and clients, to the examination of how power in society conditions its practice, has facilitated the emergence of a postcolonial approach. Munshi (2013) defined postcolonialism as a 'way of theorizing challenges and resistance to dominant, often Western theoretical and methodological perspectives' (p.2). Munshi (2013) also explained that post-colonial public relations uncovers the impact of global capitals in the profession and how those corporate forces are tied to the 'neocolonial agendas of global corporations' (p.2). In Dutta's (2016) opinion, a postcolonial critique of public relations is in essence geopolitical and questions the 'interplays' of culture and power, which are based on 'colonial relationships of exploitation and oppression' (p.248). He asserted that the dominant drive of global public relations is the reproduction of US imperialism, a force that runs under the logic of a neoliberal political economy. In his view, public relations is at the 'heart of new colonialism through the construction of new relations, narratives and images' (p.248).

In a more nuanced perspective, Munshi and Kurian (2015) conceived the possibility of an alternative for the practice of public relations. This alternative gives space to the voices of vulnerable communities. Understanding public relations as an act of resistance can be traced back by the initiative of campaigns against climate change or those in favour of Palestinian self-determination. By proposing a vision that understands public relations beyond the boundaries of government and corporations, Munshi and Kurian (2015) believed public relations can be transformed into an instrument that offers a voice to the voiceless. The similarities with some key aspects of the approach known as the Latin American School of Public Relations are evident (Molleda, 2001).

Public relations in Latin America

In 1914, with the establishment of the first public relations department in the Canadian company São Paulo Tramway Light and Power, Brazil began the institutionalization of the professional practice in Latin America (Ferrari and França, 2011). In 1936, public relations emerged as an administrative function in the transnational oil corporation Royal Dutch Shell in Venezuela, primarily as a government relations function (Merchán-López, 1993). In 1940, the first department was created at 'Shell de Venezuela' and was led by Ernesto Branch, assistant to the president.

Despite these far-reaching antecedents, the emergence of the first systematic professional practices in the region was in the 1950s, when some US multinational companies decided to replicate successful strategies that were being developed in their headquarters, and gave the responsibility of heading those departments to US expatriate practitioners (Ferrari and França, 2011). So it is relevant to state that the formal and consistent practice of public relations in Latin America has a history of about 60 or 70 years.

Another landmark in the history of public relations in the region is the participation of one of their global founders, Edward Bernays, in the propaganda campaign against the government of the leftist Guatemalan president, Jacobo Arbenz, in the 1950s. Bernays had already led, within the Committee on Public Information, the Latin News Service in the late 1910s (Streeter, 2000; Kurtz-Phelan, 2002). In 1952, Arbenz's land reforms enraged wealthy landowners, including the US firm, the United Fruit Company (Streeter, 2000). As an employee of the United Fruit Company, Bernays designed and executed a campaign that framed Arbenz as a 'communist' in the US media (Streeter, 2000; Kurtz-Phelan, 2002; Tye, 2002). Through his work with US-based journalists, Bernays was able to shape US public opinion against the government of Arbenz (Tye, 2002). Under the threat of an imminent military coup, Arbenz resigned in June 1954, and shortly afterwards Bernays helped to build the image of the new military government of Carlos Castillo Armas (Tye, 2002).

The creation of the first professional associations in Latin American countries happened in the 1950s, as well as the foundation some years later, in 1960, of a continental federation named the Inter-American Public Relations Federation (FIARP), which in 1985 changed its name to the Inter-American Public Relations Confederation (CONFIARP). Some countries, like Argentina, Colombia, Brazil and Venezuela, started to formalize education in the field quickly. Beginning in 1964, advertising and public relations sequences or majors were offered in social communication bachelor programmes at the Central University of Venezuela and University of Zulia (Maracaibo), and the communication sciences' bachelors at Catholic University Andrés Bello (Merchán-López, 1993). Also in 1964, the Universidad Argentina de la Empresa (UADE) offered the first public relations undergraduate programme, followed months later by the Colombian Pontifical Javeriana University. Meanwhile, in 1967, Brazil enacted law 5377, which allowed universities to offer public relations undergraduate programmes; the first was offered by Universidade de Sao Paulo in 1967. Three years later, a professional body named the Federal Council of Public Relations Professionals (CONFERP) was created to enforce the legislation.

The International Center for Higher Studies of Communication in Latin America (CIESPAL) contributed to the discussion by promoting social communication with an emphasis on 'alternative media' within community groups. CIESPAL was created in 1959, during the 10th United Nations Educational Scientific and Cultural

Organization Conference, in Paris, coinciding with the emergence of communication as a scientific discipline. The critical perspective of the Latin American school of communication began to be built in a more sustained way. Since then, CIESPAL has contributed with approaches on institutional communication and the connection of human, social and organizational relations to respond to the needs of Latin American people. Thus, the book *Institutional Communication, Social Approach to Public Relations* (Muriel and Rota, 1985) was a guiding text of this Latin American perspective.

In these academic terms, Argentina and Brazil have the largest number of universities offering specific public relations undergraduate programmes (Álvarez Nobell *et al.*, 2016; Ferrari, 2011). In Colombia there are three programmes in public relations and organizational communication, but only one has national and international accreditation for its academic quality, the Communication and Corporate Relations programme of the University of Medellín (SNIES, 2016). Meanwhile, most countries have fewer programmes on offer and there is even one country, Uruguay, that has none. Beyond this, the regional disciplinary research shows low levels of development in comparison to the reality of other developed regions (United States, Western European countries, Australia and New Zealand).

Public relations in Mexico has also played an important role in the country's economic development since Pre-Columbian times, but it was in 1945 when the first professional public relations exercise in Mexico took place. In that year, Federico Sánchez Fogarty, pioneer and promoter of public relations in the country, inaugurated the first agency dedicated to public relations called *Agencia Mexicana de Relaciones Públicas,* which translates to Mexican Public Relations Agency (Garcia Turincio, 2012).

Contrary to what is believed, it was in 1945 and not in 1949 when Sánchez Fogarty founded the Mexican Public Relations Agency, the first of its kind in the nation. This fact was documented in the fifth publication of the Mexican Institute of Public Relations where Sánchez Fogarty's speech can be found and which occurred at the 'First National Meeting of Public Relations' in Mexico City from 29 to 31 July 1965. This information is relevant since it locates the creation of the agency at the same time as World War II was happening, the cusp of international propaganda (Garcia Turincio, 2012).

Later, in 1947, the *Comité de Relaciones Públicas de la Confederación de Cámaras Industriales* (CONCAMIN) was founded during the presidency of Pedro A. Chapa. But it was in 1948, with Guillermo Guajardo Davis at the head of CONCAMIN, that the committee headed by Sánchez Fogarty created the project 'Principles of Social Action', which would be the basis of the Confederation's communication for about ten years (Garcia Turincio, 2012).

In 1960, the Inter-American Public Relations Federation (*Federación Interamericana de Asociaciones de Relaciones Públicas* – FIARP) was founded in Mexico City on 26 September, a date that was later proclaimed the 'Interamerican Day of Public Relations'. It was Sánchez Fogarty who founded this federation and who served as its first president (Garcia Turincio, 2012).

Nowadays, the Mexican Association of Public Relations Agencies (PRORP *Asociación Mexicana de Profesionales en Relaciones Públicas*, A.C.) is the organization that brings together all the professionals dedicated to the discipline of Public Relations in Mexico. It was founded in 1996 with the objective of overseeing the principles and values that govern public relations professionals in the nation.

According to Ferrari and França (2011), the process of consolidation of the profession in the region is associated with political, economic, social and cultural factors. The evolution of the activity occurred in a Latin American framework, characterized by its deep structural transformation and social, economic and political instability that highlighted, above all, the second half of the twentieth century. The intensification of the industrialization process, economic growth and internal migration to large urban centers contributed to the acceleration of this evolution. Therefore, the practice of public relations remained limited for much of that time, and it is not possible to talk about an important and consistent impact of the practice on the development of Latin American societies.

Ferrari and França (2011) stated that the contribution of public relations in the development of Latin American countries was characterized by the following elements: a) shortage of specific studies about the public relations theoretical conceptualization on the subcontinent; b) an initial scientific production limited or not publicized among the regional countries; c) low specialized regional academic production; and d) the consumption of foreign knowledge and practices without debate from the academy and market. For Watson (2014), however, 'from the 1980s onwards, PR practices, professionalization and education began to thrive across the region' (p.3), in parallel with the democratization of the political systems.

In previous studies, the social role of practitioners and their participation in Latin American socio-economic, political and cultural contexts has been evaluated (Moreno *et al.*, 2006; Molleda and Suárez, 2005) and allows us to infer some social sensitivity of the Latin American practitioner and a closeness to the interest that the social role of the profession has awakened in some German authors in the 1980s and 1990s (Sadi, 2014).

Latin American public relations teaching is clearly oriented by American and Spanish bibliographies. The training that the practitioner receives in Latin American countries is much more operative and instrumental than analytical and this influences their role in organizations. In most countries, professionalization and market participation are at a low level with respect to the promotion of financial contribution, as well as the generation of space for discussion on the national reality as a function of the social role (Moreno *et al.*, 2012). Although US public relations theory is used in Latin American education, it does not materialize in the action of the professionals because the context of action is different (Suárez, 2012).

In the 1990s, the profession started to be more strategic and less tactical, ensuring its presence within organizations from the viewpoint that it is an essential activity for the growth of business and for the establishment of more durable relations between organizations and their stakeholders (Ferrari and França, 2011). In that context, due to the liberalization of the economy that happened, public relations agencies – mostly US based – began to grow as companies of services and to settle in the diverse regional markets, fostering the practice to become a crucial element for the positioning of organizations in a global context.

In the 2000s, the interactions between Salvadoran public relations companies, advertising firms and international communication conglomerates became a central feature of the market of strategic communications in that country (Delgado Platero, 2007). In Colombia, meanwhile, the advancement of the field of public relations research seeks the articulation of theoretical and practical training, taking as a compass the role of this discipline in contemporary Colombian society, research oriented to specific aspects of the relations between companies, their publics and stakeholders, and the international corporations and their local roots in the globalized world (Botero *et al.*, 2014, p.319). This last quote could be extrapolated to apply to the Latin American region as a whole.

In professional terms, the practice seems to have arrived at a point of maturation in some of the most important countries like Argentina, Brazil, Colombia, Peru, Chile and Mexico, with strong national associations that foster the evolution of public relations and their practitioners. Moreover, Molleda (2000) stated that public relations officers in Latin America 'have considerable potential to become active agents of social and political transformation in a society which is demanding more participation in national development and democracy' (p.513). In this sense, two of the most important roles of public relations practitioners in the region are to labour in favour of an organization's social responsibility and their involvement with the well-being of local communities (Molleda and Ferguson, 2004).

However, low salaries are still an issue. It is assumed that the 'highest paid professionals working in Latin American public companies listed (47.1 percent above \$30,000 per year) are communication managers with over ten years of experience, a master's or doctorate title and men. Chile is the country where a higher percentage of professionals (45.6 percent) reach the highest salaries' (Moreno *et al.*, 2015, p.69).

For Watson (2014), in most Latin American countries, colonial heritage and the unifying factor of the Spanish language has helped the exchange of ideas in the practice of public relations: 'However, the practical basis of PR did not come of the former colonial powers, but of the United States which, according to its Monroe Doctrine, devotes Latin America to its sphere of influence' (p.2).

On the development of public relations agencies in Colombia, Botero, Jiménez and Botero (2014) pointed to the direct influence of US-based multinationals in the development of industry in the country. According to the authors, 'most consulting agencies operate from the field of organizational communication' (Botero *et al.*, 2014, p.69). Colombian researchers claim that the industry is growing, in particular the mining and hydrocarbons sectors, as well as the technology and innovation sectors, which have begun commissioning public relations activities, as a result of the Colombia-US Free Trade Agreement signed on 15 May 2012.

Summarizing, for Watson (2014), 'it is notable when the sheer geographical size of Latin America is considered, how all-pervasive the U.S. influence has been on the introduction of modern PR', influence that remains in the regional environment (p.2).

Foreign-based public relations agencies in Latin America

Globalization, through regional trade agreements, has been a positive factor in the growth of public relations practice and particularly if we refer to the consultancy industry. A small group of holding companies (WPP, Omnicom and Interpublic as the most important ones) currently dominate the global market, with networks that are integrated by the most relevant players all over the world.

The selected methodology for our analysis has been the examination of the public documents and websites of the top five public relations agencies in each of the chosen countries, in terms of gross annual income and number of people hired. The study of each market led us to describe the relevant characteristics of the selected countries' cultures, social stratifications, politics and economics.

In almost all these countries, bar Venezuela, at least three and in some cases four of the top five agencies are direct branches of US and UK companies (e.g. Edelman, Ketchum, Porter Novelli, Burson-Marsteller, Weber Shandwick (UK) or FleishmanHillard) and/or have a strategic alliance with American or British communication holdings (Omnicom or WPP, respectively, as stated above). Another multinational agency from Spain, Llorente & Cuenca, has a leading presence with strong branches in markets like Argentina and Colombia.

Meanwhile, in Venezuela, only one in five of the country's top agencies is affiliated with a global communication conglomerate. This may be the result of a severe economic and political crisis. In addition, the leadership of domestic agencies, two with regional reach, may have resulted from the transfer of know-how from multinational oil corporations that arrived in Venezuela in the 1910s.

That being said, the most important services in a diversified environment are generally provided for entities that have signed global contracts with multinational agencies (such as some of those mentioned above). Oil and gas, infrastructure, IT companies and governmental organizations lead the contracting of diverse public relations practices, mainly media relations, crisis communications and event planning.

The influence of US-based public relations agencies throughout the world is inescapable for Mexico. According to the 2016 Holmes Report Top 10 Global PR Agency Ranking (Holmes Report, 2016), Edelman consolidates its position as the world's biggest public relations firm, and correspondingly Mexico City houses this agency, since it is the capital of the nation and is considered the country's hub for business, politics and culture. Following Edelman, Weber Shandwick, UK (2015), the second biggest public relations firm, announced its expansion with the opening of an office in Mexico City to have a stronger presence in Latin America.

Fleishman Hillard, third on the list, also has a presence in Mexico City, operating locally and in Latin American markets to serve many of Mexico's and the world's leading companies. Though situated in 16th place last year, Porter Novelli, is another American public relations firm that has presence in Mexico, and in 2015 the Holmes Report named it the 'Mexico Agency of the Year'. Lastly, being a 100%

Mexican corporation, Zimat Consultores is considered the number one public relations agency in the nation. Since 1984, Zimat Consultores has had a history of success and leadership in Mexico, which has made them the number one according to the 2016 Annual Ranking of Public Relations Agencies conducted by the Research Department of Merca 2.0 magazine in Mexico (*Ranking de Agencias*, 2016).

Conclusion

This chapter introduces the intersection between postcolonial theory and public relations practice in Latin America, especially through the production of an indigenous body of knowledge and, as an illustration, the dominance of foreign-based public relations agencies. We made a special effort to include authors from the subcontinent who have contributed to this theoretical perspective.

The arrival and evolution of public relations as a modern practice in the hands of foreign-based multinational corporations has influenced the practice and field of study up to the present. The majority of the top agencies in selected Latin American countries (i.e., Argentina, Brazil, Colombia, El Salvador, Mexico and Venezuela) are based in the United States and United Kingdom. The exception to this trend is Venezuela, where political, economic and social challenges have forced multinational agencies out of the country or have limited them to a few multinational clients.

According to the theoretical framework used in this chapter, it is expected that the top multinational agencies in the region conduct their operations from a functionalistic and systematic perspective. Future research could delve into the different practices of domestic and multinational agencies. Most importantly, we could use the postcolonial perspective to document practices and areas of study that are more responsive to Latin American markets and communities.

Bibliography

Álvarez Nobell, A., Sadi, G. and Méndez, V. (2016) 'La institucionalización de la investigación en comunicación institucional y relaciones públicas en la Argentina'. In Mateos, C. and Herrero, J. (coord.) *La pantalla insomne* (2nd updated edition). La Laguna, Spain: Cuadernos Artesanos de Comunicación 103.

Berger, B. (2005) 'Power over, power with, and power to relations: Critical reflections on public relations, the dominant coalition, and activism. *Journal of Public Relations Research*, 17(1), pp.5–28.

Botero, L., Jiménez, M.A. and Botero, N. (2014) 'Colombia'. In: Watson, T. (2014) *National Perspectives on the Development of Public Relations. Other Voices*. London: Palgrave Macmillan.

Castro-Gómez, S. (2005) *La postcolonialidad explicado a los niños*. Popayán, Colombia: Editorial Universidad del Cauca e Instituto Pensar, Universidad Javeriana.

Curtin, P. and Gaither, T. (2012) *Globalization and Public Relations in Postcolonial Nations*. Amherst, NY: Cambria Press.

Delgado Platero, A. (2007) *La Práctica de las Relaciones Públicas en El Salvador entre 1996–2006*. San Salvador, El Salvador: Universidad Don Bosco.

Dozier, D. and Lauzen, M. (2000) 'Liberating the intellectual domain from the practice: Public relations, activism, and the role of the scholar', *Journal of Public Relations Research*, 12(1), pp.3–22.

Du Gay, P., Hall, S., Janes, L., Koed Madsen, A., Mackay, H. and Negus, K. (2013) *Doing Cultural Studies: The story of the Sony Walkman*. London: SAGE.

Dutta, M. (2016). 'A postcolonial critique of public relations'. In J. L'Etang, D. McKie, N. Snow and J. Xifra. (2016). *The Routledge Handbook of Critical Public Relations*. Abingdon, Basingstoke, UK: Routledge.

Edwards, L. and Hodges, C. (2011) *Public Relations, Society and Culture. Theoretical and Empirical Exploration*. Abingdon, UK: Routledge.

Ferrari, M.A. (2011) 'Historia y trayectoria de las Relaciones Públicas en Brasil', *Revista Internacional de Relaciones Públicas*, 1(1), pp.29–68.

Ferrari, M.A. and França, F. (2011) *Relaciones públicas. Naturaleza, función y gestión de las organizaciones contemporáneas*. Buenos Aires, Argentina: La Crujía.

Garcia Turincio, E. (2012) 'Un Precursor de las Relaciones Públicas: Federico Sánchez Fogarty en México', *Revista Mexicana de Comunicación*, 24(132), pp.35–41.

Grunig, J. (ed.) (1992) *Excellence in Public Relations and Communications Management*. Mahwah, NJ: Lawrence Erlbaum Associates.

Holmes Report Top 10 Global PR Agency Ranking (2016) Holmes Report Website. Available at: http://www.holmesreport.com/ranking-and-data/global-communications-report/2016-pr-agency-rankings/top-10 [Accessed 15 April 2017].

Johnston, J. (2016) 'Public relations, the postcolonial *other* issue of asylum seekers'. In L'Etang, D. McKie, N. Snow and J. Xifra. (2016) *The Routledge Handbook of Critical Public Relations*. Abingdon, UK: Routledge.

Kurtz-Phelan, D. (2002) 'Big Fruit'. *The New York Times*. Available at: http://www.nytimes.com/2008/03/02/books/review/Kurtz-Phelan-t.html [Accessed 15 April 2017].

L'Etang, J. (2011) 'Imagining public relations anthropology'. In: Edwards, L. and Hodges, C. *Public Relations, Society and Culture. Theoretical and Empirical Exploration*. Abingdon, Basingstoke, UK: Routledge.

L'Etang, J. and Pieczka, M. (eds.) (2006) *Public Relations. Critical Debates and Contemporary Practice*. London: Lawrence Erlbaum Associates.

Merchán-López, J. (1993) *Manual de teorías y técnicas magistrales de las relaciones públicas (3ra edición) [Manual of Theories and Master Techniques of Public Relations, 3rd edition]*. Caracas, Venezuela: Fundación Amigos de I.U.D.E.R.P.

Mickey, T. (2003). *Deconstructing Public Relations. Public Relations Criticism*. London: Lawrence Erlbaum Associates.

Mishra, V., and Hodge, B. (1991). 'What is post (-) colonialism?'. *Textual Practice*, 5(3), pp.399–414.

Molleda, J.C. (2000). 'International Paradigms: the Latin American School of Public Relations'. *Journalism Studies*, 2(4), pp.513–530.

Molleda, J.C. and Ferguson, M. (2004) 'Public relations roles in Brazil: Hierarchy eclipses gender differences', *Journal of Public Relations Research*, 16(4), pp.327–351.

Molleda, J.C., Moreno, Á., Athaydes, A. and Suárez, A.M. (2012) 'Macroencuesta latinoamericana de comunicación y relaciones públicas'. *Revista Organicom*, 7(13), pp.118–141.

Molleda, J.C. and Suárez, A.M. (2005) 'Challenges in Colombia for public relations professionals: A qualitative assessment of the economic and political environments', *Public Relations Review*, 31(1), pp.21–29.

Moreno, A., Molleda, J.C., Athaydes, A. and Suárez, A.M. (2015) *Latin America Communication Monitor 2015. Excelencia en comunicación estratégica, trabajo en la era digital, social media y profesionalización. Resultados de una encuesta en 18 países* [Latin America Communication Monitor 2015. Excellence in strategic communication, work in digital era, social media and professionalisation. Results of a survey in 18 countries]. Brussels: EUPRERA.

Moreno, A., Molleda, J.C. and Suárez, A.M. (2006) 'Comunicación estratégica y relaciones públicas en entornos socioeconómicos y políticos en transición: Estudio contextual comparativo en Colombia, México y Venezuela'. *Razón y Palabra*, 51.

Mignolo, W. (2005) 'Colonialidad global, capitalismo y hegemonía epistémica'. In Donato, R. (2005) *Culturas Imperiales, experiencia y representación en América, Asia, África*. Rosario, Argentina: Beatriz Viterbo Editora.

Munshi, D. (2013) 'Postcolonialism theory and public relations'. In Heath, R. (ed.) (2013) *Encyclopedia of Public Relations*. Thousand Oaks, CA: SAGE.

Munshi, D. and Kurian, P. (2015) 'Imagining organizational communication as sustainable citizenship'. *Management Communication Quarterly*, 29(1), pp.153–159.

Muriel, M. and Rota, G. (1985) *Comunicación Institucional, enfoque social de las Relaciones Públicas*. Quito, Ecuador: CIESPAL.

Ranking de Agencias (2016) Merca20 website. Available at: https://www.merca20.com/ranking-de-agencias-de-relaciones-publicas-2016-constructores-de-reputacion/ [Accessed 15 April 2017].

Sistema Nacional de Información de la Educación Superior, SNIES. Ministerio de Educación de Colombia (2016) Available at: http://snies.mineducacion.gov.co/consultasnies/programa# [Accessed 15 April 2017].

Sadi, G. (2013). Algunos aportes del pensamiento crítico en relaciones públicas. *Dircom*, 100, 23–28.

Sadi, G. (2014) 'En torno al objeto de estudio y las implicancias sociales de las relaciones públicas', *Revista Organicom*, 11(21), pp.31–44.

Sadi, G. (2016) 'Nuevas fronteras teóricas de las relaciones públicas'. In *Reflexiones y Desafíos de las Relaciones Públicas*. Santiago, Chile: Universidad del Pacífico.

Streeter, S.M. (2000) 'Interpreting the 1954 US intervention in Guatemala: Realist, revisionist, and postrevisionist perspectives', *The History Teacher*, 34(1), pp.61–74.

Suárez Monsalve, A.M. (2012) 'Pensar la integración latinoamericana: también desde la comunicación organizacional y las relaciones públicas', *Revista Organicom*, 8(14), pp.29–48.

The Indigenous Languages of Latin America. (n.d.) Website of the Archive of the Indigenous Languages of Latin America (AILLA). Available at: http://www.ailla.utexas.org/site/lg_about.html [Accessed 15 April 2017].

Tye, L. (2002) *The Father of Spin: Edward L. Bernays and the Birth of Public Relations*. Basingstoke, UK: Palgrave Macmillan.

Watson, T. (ed.) (2014) *Latin American and Caribbean Perspectives on the Development of Public Relations. Other Voices*. Basingstoke, UK: Palgrave Macmillan.

Weber Shandwick (2015) Available at: https://www.webershandwick.com/news/article/weber-shandwick-opens-office-in-mexico-city-expands-fast-growing-latin-amer [Accessed 15 April 2017].

Xifra, J. (2003) *Teoría y estructura de las relaciones públicas*. Madrid, Spain: McGraw-Hill.

13

FANNING THE FLAMES OF DISCONTENT

Public relations as a radical activity

Øyvind Ihlen

Public relations and public relations research have often been accused of being in the service of powerful interests and of privileging the functional objectives of organizational elites. So how can public relations be a *radical activity* and what does this even mean? The adjective 'radical' has several different definitions. It can, for instance, designate that which makes a break with what is 'usual or traditional; [the radical is] progressive, unorthodox, or innovative in outlook, conception, design, etc.' (Oxford English Dictionary, 2017). In the political realm, radical can mean that which is 'advocating thorough or far-reaching political or social reform' (Oxford English Dictionary, 2017). Within public relations, several scholars have indeed advocated for far-reaching reform over the years, both of academia and the practice (e.g., L'Etang *et al.*, 2015; McKie and Munshi, 2007; Moloney, 2000, 2006). In terms of the former, it has been argued that scholarship should not be too tightly linked to professional organizations or the social institution it studies, as this leads to a loss of perspective or a preoccupation with only one perspective (Demetrious, 2015; Dozier and Lauzen, 2000). It has also been argued that the public's 'public relations literacy' should be enhanced as a first line of defence against manipulative practice. Practitioners, for their part, are urged to engage in practices to increase communicative equality and secure a voice for the less privileged (Moloney, 2000, 2006). One vision that has been put forward sees the practitioner as an activist within the organization. Practitioners should 'always question the nature of their own institutions and strive to improve them and make them more just' (Holtzhausen, 2012, p.234). The sharing of power between organizations and their stakeholders should be the goal for public relations embracing an activist role (Berger, 2005). Several similar ideas are found in the literature and can be said to represent perspectives on public relations as a radical activity. This chapter charts such efforts and discusses *three versions of what public relations as a radical activity might be*.

166 Øyvind Ihlen

The chapter is structured in three main parts: the first part discusses what can be deemed radical tendencies in public relations scholarship, defined as that which makes a break with the traditional paradigm and calls for reforming theory and/ or practice; the second part very briefly discusses perspectives drawing on critical theory, touching on the definition, the aims and the methods of approaches relying on this tradition; the third part pursues a topic mentioned in part two, namely that public relations deals with power issues and should not only embrace consensus, but also conflict. In political theory, calls have been issued to see conflict as the constituting element of the political (Mouffe, 2005). The last part of the chapter then discusses the implications this perspective has for public relations. Ultimately, all these versions of public relations as a radical activity are united in discontent at some social and/or academic level.

Radical as breaking with the functionalist tradition

As already pointed out, public relations as a practice has largely developed in the service of large organizations or corporations. It is also widely accepted that public relations as an academic discipline has roots in managerial, functionalist and often quantitative approaches seeking to assist organizations reach their objectives with the help of communication. A long-standing definition of the practice states that: 'Public relations is the management function that establishes and maintains mutually beneficial relationships between an organization and the publics on whom its success or failure depends' (Broom and Sha, 2012, p.5). Whether mutually beneficial relationships develop is an empirical question. In many respects, public relations seems to be put to use for self-interested corporate purposes with a goal 'to achieve or resist change by persuasively advancing and potentially privileging particular meanings and actions' (Leitch and Motion, 2010, p.103). Public relations in this sense is communication that helps to strengthen the power base of those that are already powerful, which in turn has obvious implications for democracy that cause dissatisfaction and the call for a radical break.

'Radical PR' was discussed as a moniker at a research seminar at the University of Stirling in 2008. The group was described as being united in dissatisfaction with functionalist approaches and as harbouring a wish to consider the social impacts of the practice (L'Etang, 2009). The call to liberate the intellectual domain from the practice (Dozier and Lauzen, 2000) bears repeating to this day. Still, good strides have been made since critical pioneer Jacquie L'Etang had her work rejected on the grounds of it being 'too radical' (L'Etang and Pieczka, 1996, p.xi). It might be said that a turn occurred in the field during the late 1990s and in the 2000s, when critical scholarship became 'well established' (Edwards, 2015, p.22). Today, there is a range of research on how public relations works in, for and with organizations and society (e.g., Bardhan and Weaver, 2011; Edwards, 2014; Edwards and Hodges, 2011; Heath *et al.*, 2009; Ihlen *et al.*, Fredriksson, 2009; L'Etang *et al.*, 2015; L'Etang and Pieczka, 2006; McKie and Munshi, 2007). These publications draw on many different theory strands, including sociology, postmodernism, cultural theory, anthropology, rhetoric, critical theory and communication studies. In other words, this scholarship can be said to form a more or less radical shift from the functionalist paradigm. It does not put forward idealistic conceptions of what public relations is, but instead is united in the view that 'public relations should be studied as a social activity in its own right and that it must be understood in relation to its societal context' (Ihlen and Verhoeven, 2012, p.159). By implication, this also entails studying the negative consequences of public relations – a 'warts and all-perspective' (p.161). Despite decades of discussion of public relations ethics, unethical practice has certainly not been rooted out and this is not something that can or should be swept under the carpet.

The competing perspectives mentioned above were long described as *peripheral visions* (McKie and Munshi, 2005) or perspectives from *the margins* (Moffitt, 2005). With the advent of a new journal like *Public Relations Inquiry* (2012), as well as a book series and a handbook (L'Etang *et al.*, 2015) published by what is probably the world's largest academic publisher within the humanities and social sciences, it is harder to claim such an outsider role. The mentioned research perspectives can no longer be called radical in the sense that they are not unusual or non-traditional. There is also, however, within this research body critical theoretical approaches that can claim to be radical in the *political* sense, advocating far-reaching reform.

Radical as building on critical theory and perspectives

Much criticism has been directed at public relations, not least through exposés of work conducted for such interests as tobacco, asbestos and big oil (Miller and Dinan, 2008; Rampton and Stauber, 2001). Many of the publications belonging to this strand of research condemn public relations more or less wholesale, ignoring how public relations is an inevitable practice for organizations today. While the 'broad brush' criticism can be faulted, this strand of research clearly is very valuable as a form of power criticism pointing to transgressions of public relations and the implications of these. While there is much to be gained from criticism of unethical public relations practice in general, the *systemic* criticism brings in a needed political perspective.

Public relations as a radical activity can also be understood as public relations research that builds on critical theory and perspectives and ideas from this tradition. Critical theory as espoused by the Frankfurt school emphasizes how scholars should expose oppression in society through criticism of ideology and instrumental thinking (Deetz, 2005; Geuss, 1981; Hohendahl and Fisher, 2001). The goal of the critical theorist is to forward emancipation through increased reflection. Critical credos focus on helping to expose domination and increase reflexivity, and as such assist in creating 'freedom from' and 'freedom to' (McKerrow, 2001, p.619). A main point is that discourse is not solely oppressive, but that it holds a productive potential for critique of freedom and formulation of 'possibilities for future action' (McKerrow, 1989, p.92). Examples of such practice include, for instance, analyses of how the notion of 'the free market' has been used to oppose tax on tobacco

168 Øyvind Ihlen

and thus to sideline health issues (Cheney *et al.*, 2004). Similarly, Conrad (2011) has argued that public relations and organizational communication have helped perpetuate crucial ideas or myths, for instance concerning how the free market is to the benefit of everyone in society. Pointing to how such myths are constructed and promoted with the help of communication is thus a crucial task for radical public relations that draws on critical theory and critical perspectives.

Different visions of critical public relations have been formulated, such as 'reconfiguring' public relations and developing 'the field away from insularity and in the direction of environmental improvement, inclusive egalitarianism and sustainable enterprise' (McKie and Munshi, 2007, p.145). In other words, it is argued that public relations should take on board principles of sustainability and work for the good of the whole of society. Similarly, other researchers have proclaimed that there is a need to 'reclaim participative democracy' (Motion and Leitch, 2015). A success criterion would be whether 'the democratic, deliberative and decision-making roles of civil society' have been opened up or closed down as a consequence of public relations activity (Motion and Leitch, 2015, p.148). Attempts to block alternative viewpoints from being presented publicly, for instance by threatening legal action, would be a type of practice promoting the opposite perspective.

An ideal has been introduced that public relations should safeguard 'a radical democracy that ensures equality for all, respect for cultural plurality and requires confrontational intolerance of injustice' (Holtzhausen, 2012, p.239). For others, the basic question concerns how scholars can 'retain our desire to change the way the world is' (Edwards, 2015, p.24). The need for social change is emphasized (Demetrious, 2013), as is the need for public relations to truly engage with the public interest (Johnston, 2016). Scholars should, for instance, challenge 'the hegemonic assumptions in public relations around gender' and race (Daymon and Demetrious, 2013, p.3; Waymer and Heath, 2015). In line with the tradition of critical theory, several public relations scholars have pointed to a need to call out manipulative and oppressive practice (Trujillo and Toth, 1987) and to deconstruct or reveal configurations of knowledge within the field to enhance human freedom (Moloney and McKie, 2015; Pieczka, 2015). To put it differently, an important question to pursue is whether public relations 'advance[s] the hegemonic power of particular groups' (Motion and Weaver, 2005, p.50).

Some scholars have called for a shift from criticizing from the outside to actually engaging and collaborating with practitioners or joining activist groups (Dutta, 2009; Motion and Leitch, 2015). Similarly, some posit that public relations should represent the unrepresented (Munshi and Kurian, 2015). Of late, activist research seeking social change has also been conducted on social issues, such as alcohol abuse (Pieczka and Wood, 2013). These are obviously examples of putting the strategies and tools of public relations to work for non-corporate, 'good' causes. Thus, these are illustrations of how public relations in itself is not a good or bad thing, but can be put to use for good and bad purposes.

In sum, one version of public relations as a radical activity builds on critical theory that forwards goals of emancipation through reflexivity, and as such addresses issues of power and equality. In a general sense, radical public relations scholarship thus deals with and promotes social change of some sort or another, questioning orthodoxies in society.

Radical as embracing conflict

A radical break with the functionalist tradition and a view that draws on critical theory would also see public relations not as a practice to dissolve conflict, but as a way of furthering particular interests (Ihlen, 2007). In, for instance, political conflicts, relationship building and dialogue will obviously be important, but they cannot be the only tools as political values are at stake. Positioning of the organization *against* others or the values of others might be a necessity. While public relations theory values consensus and/or concurrence, this happens at the expense of the antagonistic dimension that is essential to the political. Here, an *agonistic* approach (Mouffe, 2000/2005, 2005) might offer a way forward for public relations as suggested by some public relations scholars (Davidson, 2016; Ramsey, 2015). This approach suggests ethical ways of approaching, and indeed, embracing conflict.

An agonistic approach can build on the work of Mouffe (2000/2005, 2005, 2013). In her political philosophy society is seen as 'the product of a series of practices whose aim is to establish order in a context of contingency' (Mouffe, 2013, p.2). The institutions, practices and discourses of democracy that are seeking to establish such hegemonic order she labels *politics*. She then draws a distinction between politics and *the political*. The latter term refers to a certain characteristic or dimension of society, namely the antagonistic dimension that society cannot escape. Mouffe argues against liberalist or rationalist versions of democratic theory that see rational debate as being able to forge a universal and inclusive consensus. Such viewpoints negate the antagonistic dimension and that fact that the hegemonic order it installs is necessarily an expression of power relations. Some viewpoints are excluded; you cannot achieve harmony as there will always be division and power. When 'the inescapable moment of decision' arrives, the limit of any rational consensus is demonstrated by remaining antagonistic (Mouffe, 2013, p.3). As such, conflict, difference, social division and emotions are constitutive for society. Indeed, identity necessitates difference, so there will always be an 'us and them' dimension. The danger for democracy, however, lies in how this dimension develops into a friend/enemy dimension.

Rather than ignoring, suppressing or condemning conflict, one should focus on how to turn the struggle between enemies into a struggle between adversaries. Conflict is not something that should be avoided, but conflicts should have less of an antagonistic form and more of an agonistic one. Struggles and emotions are indeed part of a vibrant democracy (Mouffe, 2013). The challenge is to reach conflictual consensus about certain democratic values and how these should be implemented. An example she mentions is the adherence to democratic values already mentioned in the previous section, for instance 'liberty' and 'equality'. Society needs democratic designs that uphold such values, but lets people debate how their interpretations of

170 Øyvind Ihlen

these values should become hegemonic. The very legitimacy of this right to fight for a particular interpretation should not be questioned. Recognizing the legitimacy of those holding opposite views is thus central, but so is the ability to forward dissent (Davidson, 2016; Mouffe, 2005; Ramsey, 2015). In this, passion as a driving force also needs to be recognized, both as something that creates engagement and contributes to identification. For Mouffe (2013), however, it is crucial that passions should be sublimated 'by mobilizing them towards democratic designs, by creating collective forms of identification around democratic objectives' (Mouffe, 2013, p.9). In other words, passions should be used for good democratic purposes.

Building on an agonistic approach, Davidson (2016) urges public relations to:

> [E]levate contest above neutral deliberation, instil a regard for opponents, an even stronger regard for disadvantaged publics who lack communication resources, and abhorrence of permanent winners and openness to new issues and challenges. It would also entail fostering of public space that welcome emotional, passionate engagement, a commitment to make power transparent and an end to the illusory assumption that policy issues are somehow neutral or technical matters awaiting communicative solution, but are always choices between conflicting alternatives.
>
> *(p.160)*

Here then, public relations practitioners are presented with some specific suggestions for how to embrace conflict in an ethical way and how to change from an antagonistic mindset to an agonistic one. Still, this version of a radical practice and also other versions calling for change seem to have high hopes for practitioners and their autonomy (Moloney and McKie, 2015). The discussion within the literature on dialogue and corporate social responsibility might be useful here. Both dialogue attempts and corporate social responsibility actions will be somewhat limited by the goal-driven rationality of organizations (Ihlen *et al.*, 2011; Theunissen and Wan Noordin, 2012). Corporations, for instance, have a very limited perspective on the world given their fundamental profit motive that typically reduces society, people and the environment to a means to this end. Thus, the 'evangelic' activist practitioner might not always fare well in organizational life, good intentions aside. There are some systemic limits to what can be accomplished, even when embracing an agonistic mindset.

Conclusion

Radical public relations might be on the verge of becoming an oxymoron if the requirement is that it must be something *new*. In the political sense, however, as critical public relations, it has more potency by calling attention to issues of power and equality. Mainstream public relations theories often seem to suggest that they have the ability to dissolve conflicts. Implicit or explicit in these theories is the perspective that conflicts are costly and should be avoided. To avoid conflict, organizations need to conduct proper 'communicative groundwork' through listening and, if needed, adjusting to stakeholders' perspectives and needs. In this chapter, however, it its advocated that radical public relations must also embrace conflict. Such a perspective, however, should not be read as an invitation to pursue one's own interests at all costs, since 'conflict is good'. Thinking along with Mouffe (2005, 2013) and scholars who have applied her work (Davidson, 2016; Ramsey, 2015), radical public relations can be said to support certain democratic values. Simultaneously, conflict over interpretation and implementation of these values is not only seen as legitimate, but as fundamental to society and the political. Public relations practice that assists in framing an alternative as 'the only legitimate one', on the other hand, would contribute to antagonistic conflict. As a radical academic activity, public relations is called upon to shine a light on such practice. Radical public relations thus works in the critical tradition that expresses discontent with the present social order.

Bibliography

Bardhan, N. and Weaver, C.K. (eds.) (2011) *Public Relations in Global Cultural Contexts: Multi-Paradigmatic Perspectives*. London: Routledge.

Berger, B.K. (2005) 'Power over, power with, and power to relations: Critical reflections on public relations, the dominant coalition, and activism', *Journal of Public Relations Research*, 17(1), pp.5–28.

Broom, G.M. and Sha, B.-L. (2012) *Cutlip and Center's Effective Public Relations* (11th ed.). Upper Saddle River, NJ: Prentice Hall.

Cheney, G., Christensen, L.T., Conrad, C. and Lair, D.J. (2004) 'Corporate rhetoric as organizational discourse'. In D. Grant, C. Hardy, C. Oswick and L.L. Putnam (eds.), *The Sage Handbook of Organizational Discourse* (pp.79–103). London: Sage.

Conrad, C. (2011). *Organizational Rhetoric: Strategies of Resistance and Domination*. Cambridge, UK: Polity.

Davidson, S. (2016). 'Public relations theory: An agonistic critique of the turns to dialogue and symmetry', *Public Relations Inquiry*, 5(2), pp.145–167. DOI: 10.1177/2046147x16649007.

Daymon, C. and Demetrious, K. (eds.) (2013) *Gender and Public Relations: Critical Perspectives on Voice, Image and Identity*. London: Routledge.

Deetz, S.A. (2005) 'Critical theory'. In S. May and D.K. Mumby (eds.), *Engaging Organizational Communication Theory & Research: Multiple Perspectives* (pp.85–111). London: Sage.

Demetrious, K. (2013) *Public Relations, Activism, and Social Change: Speaking Up*. New York: Routledge.

Demetrious, K. (2015). 'Sanitising or reforming PR? Exploring "trust" and the emergence of critical public relations'. In J. L'Etang, D. McKie, N. Snow and J. Xifra (eds.), *Routledge Handbook of Critical Public Relations* (pp.101–116). London: Routledge.

Dozier, D.M. and Lauzen, M.M. (2000) 'Liberating the intellectual domain from the practice: Public relations, activism, and the role of the scholar'. *Journal of Public Relations Research*, 12(1), pp.3–22.

Dutta, M.J. (2009) 'On Spivak: Theorizing resistance: Applying Gayatri Chakravorty Spivak in public relations'. In Ø. Ihlen, B. van Ruler and M. Fredriksson (eds.), *Public Relations and Social Theory: Key Figures and Concepts* (pp.278–300). New York: Routledge.

Edwards, L. (2014) *Power, Diversity and Public Relations*. New York: Routledge.

172 Øyvind Ihlen

Edwards, L. (2015) 'An historical overview of the emergence of critical thinking in PR'. In J. L'Etang, D. McKie, N. Snow and J. Xifra (eds.), *Routledge Handbook of Critical Public Relations* (pp.16–27). London: Routledge.

Edwards, L. and Hodges, C.E.M. (eds.) (2011) *Public Relations, Society & Culture: Theoretical and Empirical Explorations*. London: Routledge.

Geuss, R. (1981) *The Idea of a Critical Theory: Habermas & the Frankfurt School*. Cambridge, MA: Cambridge University Press.

Heath, R.L., Toth, E.L. and Waymer, D. (eds.) (2009) *Rhetorical and Critical Approaches to Public Relations* II. New York: Routledge.

Hohendahl, P.-U. and Fisher, J. (eds.) (2001) *Critical Theory: Current State and Future Prospects*. New York: Berghahn.

Holtzhausen, D.R. (2012) *Public Relations as Activism: Postmodern Approaches to Theory & Practice*. New York: Routledge.

Ihlen, Ø. (2007). 'Building on Bourdieu: A sociological grasp of public relations', *Public Relations Review*, 33(3), pp.269–274.

Ihlen, Ø., Bartlett, J. and May, S. (2011). Conclusions and take away points. In Ø. Ihlen, J. Bartlett and S. May (Eds.), *Handbook of communication and corporate social responsibility* (pp. 550-571). Oxford, UK: Wiley Blackwell.

Ihlen, Ø., van Ruler, B. and Fredriksson, M. (eds.) (2009) *Public Relations and Social Theory: Key Figures and Concepts*. New York: Routledge.

Ihlen, Ø. and Verhoeven, P. (2012) 'A public relations identity for the 2010s', *Public Relations Inquiry*, 1(2), pp.159–176.

Johnston, J. (2016). *Public Relations and the Public Interest*. New York: Routledge.

L'Etang, J., McKie, D., Snow, N. and Xifra, J. (eds.) (2015) *Routledge Handbook of Critical Public Relations*. London: Routledge.

L'Etang, J. and Pieczka, M. (eds.) (1996) *Critical Perspectives in Public Relations*. London: International Thomson Business Press.

L'Etang, J. and Pieczka, M. (eds.) (2006) *Public Relations: Critical Debates and Contemporary Practice*. Mahwah, NJ: Lawrence Erlbaum.

L'Etang, J. (2009) 'Radical PR: Catalyst for change or an aporia', *Ethical Space*, 6(2), pp.13–18.

Leitch, S. and Motion, J. (2010) 'Publics and public relations: Effective change'. In R.L. Heath (ed.), *The SAGE Handbook of Public Relations* (pp.99–110). Thousand Oaks, CA: Sage.

McKerrow, R.E. (1989) 'Critical rhetoric: Theory and praxis', *Communication Monographs*, 56(2), pp. 91–111. DOI: 10.1080/03637758909390253.

McKerrow, R.E. (2001) 'Critical rhetoric'. In T.O. Sloane (ed.), *Encyclopedia of Rhetoric* (pp.619–622). New York: Oxford University Press.

McKie, D. and Munshi, D. (2005) 'Tracking trends: Peripheral visions and public relations', *Public Relations Review*, 31(4), pp.453–457. DOI: 10.1016/j.pubrev.2005.08.001.

McKie, D. and Munshi, D. (2007) *Reconfiguring Public Relations: Ecology, Equity and Enterprise*. New York: Routledge.

Miller, D. and Dinan, W. (2008). *A Century of Spin: How Public Relations Became the Cutting Edge of Corporate Power*. London: Pluto Press.

Moffitt, M.A. (2005) 'Comments on special issue public relations from the margins', *Journal of Public Relations Research*, 17(1), pp.3–4. DOI: 10.1207/s1532754xjprr1701_2.

Moloney, K. (2000) *Rethinking Public Relations: The Spin and the Substance*. London: Routledge.

Moloney, K. (2006). *Rethinking Public Relations: PR Propaganda and Democracy* (2nd ed.). London: Routledge.

Moloney, K. and McKie, D. (2015) 'Changes to be encouraged: Radical turns in PR theorisation and small-step evolutions in PR practice'. In J. L'Etang, D. McKie, N. Snow and J. Xifra (eds.), *Routledge Handbook of Critical Public Relations* (pp.151–161). London: Routledge.

Motion, J. and Leitch, S. (2015) 'Critical discourse analysis: a search for meaning and power'. In J. L'Etang, D. McKie, N. Snow and J. Xifra (eds.), *Routledge Handbook of Critical Public Relations* (pp.142–150). London: Routledge.

Motion, J. and Weaver, C.K. (2005) 'A discourse perspective for critical public relations research: Life sciences network and the battle for truth', *Journal of Public Relations Research*, 17(1), pp.49–67.

Mouffe, C. (2000/2005) *The Democratic Paradox*. London:Verso.

Mouffe, C. (2005) *On the Political*. London: Routledge.

Mouffe, C. (2013). *Agonistics:Thinking the World Politically*. London:Verso.

Munshi, D. and Kurian, P. (2015) 'Public relations and sustainable citizenship: Towards the goal of representing the unrepresented'. In J. L'Etang, D. McKie, N. Snow and J. Xifra (eds.), *Routledge Handbook of Critical Public Relations* (pp.405–414). London: Routledge.

Oxford English Dictionary (2017) *Radical*. Available at: http://www.oed.com/view/Entry/1 57251?rskey=mLy41Y&result=1 - eidetic [Accessed 15 February 2017].

Pieczka, M. (2015) 'Dialogue and critical public relations'. In J. L'Etang, D. McKie, N. Snow and J. Xifra (eds.), *Routledge Handbook of Critical Public Relations* (pp.76–89). London: Routledge.

Pieczka, M. and Wood, E. (2013) 'Action research and public relations: Dialogue, peer learning, and the issue of alcohol', *Public Relations Inquiry*, 2(2), pp.161–181. DOI: 10.1177/2046147x13485955.

Rampton, S. and Stauber, J. (2001) *Trust Us, We're Experts! How Industry Manipulates Science and Gambles with Your Future*. New York: Jeremy P.Tarcher/Putnam.

Ramsey, P. (2015) 'The public sphere and PR: Deliberative democracy and agonistic pluralism'. In J. L'Etang, D. McKie, N. Snow and J. Xifra (eds.), *Routledge Handbook of Critical Public Relations* (pp.65–75). London: Routledge.

Theunissen, P. and Wan Noordin, W.N. (2012) 'Revisiting the concept "dialogue" in public relations', *Public Relations Review*, 38(1), pp.5–13. DOI:10.1016/j.pubrev.2011.09.006.

Trujillo, N. and Toth, E.L. (1987) 'Organizational perspectives for public relations research and practice', *Management Communication Quarterly*, 1(2), pp.199–231.

Waymer, D. and Heath, R.L. (2015) 'Critical race and public relations: The case of environmental racism and risk bearer agency'. In J. L'Etang, D. McKie, N. Snow and J. Xifra (eds.), *Routledge Handbook of Critical Public Relations* (pp.289–302). London: Routledge.

14

SUBVERSION PRACTICES

From coercion to attraction

Sergei A. Samoilenko

In 1967, Rudi Dutschke, the leader of the German student movement the 68er-Bewegung, called for a long march against cultural hegemony to change the bourgeois West Germany. His 'long march through the institutions of power' (Dalton, 1987) illustrates a call for subversion, which is understood as an attempt to transform the established social order and its structures of power, authority and hierarchy when the values and principles of a system in place are deliberately contradicted or reversed (Blackstock, 1964).

Conventionally, subversion is understood as part of psychological warfare when it is mainly seen as an external attempt aimed at disintegration of political and social institutions of the state. However, the concept of subversion is convoluted and it defies an easy definition due to the variety of forms and contexts in which it takes place. Subversion has been closely associated with practices of *propaganda* and *agitation* which seem to have fallen out of favour in contemporary communication research, mainly due to a rise of value-driven and socially responsible approaches to the practice of public relations.

However, subversion practices offer valuable insights for public relations. Acting as discourse engineers, public relations specialists are often seen as primary actors in power/knowledge contests (Motion and Leitch, 1996, 2009), as they influence the public's perception of sociocultural and political issues through framing strategies. By analysing the social environment, public relations experts select strategies to either conserve or subvert certain types of capital intended to benefit dominant actors. Such 'games of strategy' (Foucault, 1997) help various social actors achieve hegemonic status by integrating their ideas and agendas into the public discourse and making them socially acceptable. For example, public relations played a major role in the shift from a Keynesian to a neoliberal economic hegemony and in the accompanying ideological shift in Western societies during the last decades of the twentieth century (Hall and Jacques, 1989, as cited in Motion and Leitch, 2009). As

Subversion practices **175**

primary negotiators of power relations and hegemonic narratives, public relations helps organizations attain competitive advantage or even dominance in contested social and cultural environments by acquiring desired types of capital (Ihlen, 2009). That also includes competing for access to the media and for symbolic dominance in the media arena.

Naturally, the discussion of subversion leads to further examination of related concepts including *power struggle, resistance, social change,* etc. to name a few. From this perspective, this chapter argues that many modern-day grassroots campaigns contesting power distribution in their societies also provide valuable insights for public relations practitioners in terms of new forms of participatory citizen engagement. In this chapter, I will first propose a theoretical rationale explaining the basis of subversion practices. Then, the three most common approaches to subversion will be addressed. Next, I will discuss social media as new subversion tools for social change including new forms of grassroots campaigns. Finally, this chapter will provide public relations practitioners with insights from subversion practices on how to advocate for their new role as voluntary change agents.

Theoretical rationale for subversion

All human action can be conceived 'as being embedded in power structures' (Williams, 2011, p.89). Power is a process that consists of both exertion and resistance. The operation of power referred to by Foucault (1997) as 'games of strategy' represents a set of goal-oriented procedures. In this regard, power is not a destination, but a continuous process since it is always negotiated and contested by various actors.

The social world is represented through individual and collective struggles that 'seek to impose the legitimate definition of reality' (Bourdieu, 1990, p.141). In this world, players compete for resources, status and over the so-called rules of the social game that govern field relations. *Social field* refers to a network of relationships between the orientations and position held and protected by social actors. Various actors constantly engage in relationships with each other as they try to accumulate, conserve or convert different types of resources. The relations within Bourdieu's fields are hierarchical, as the main source of power for dominant groups is their accumulated capital. In other words, the possession of the capital legitimizes their power over dominated groups, as they have the resources and ability to control their territory within the field. This capital may come in various forms. For example, economic capital is represented by money and property; cultural capital is understood in terms of qualifications, skills, education; and symbolic capital comes in forms such as honour, status and prestige (Ihlen, 2009). Through a *habitus*, or a structuring mechanism that generates strategies for social actors, all members of the field who possess more of this capital share similar interests in preserving the value of their capital and resisting attempts at its subversion (Bourdieu and Wacquant, 1992; Ihlen, 2009). A side occupying powerful positions in society is interested in protecting the status quo and thus 'exerts its definitions of reality on others' (William, 2011, p.89). The conservation strategies used by the elites include

176 Sergei A. Samoilenko

preventing new participants from entering the field and promoting the values of dominant culture to the rest of the society. By contrast, other field members with deficient capital are more inclined towards subversion strategies challenging this status quo (Bourdieu, 1991).

In the political field, actors struggle for the acquisition of political capital or administrative control over public powers such as law, army, finances, etc. This competition involves mobilization of supporters around issues and the creation of competing political products by players with 'antagonistic visions about what constitutes legitimate political authority' (Saeed, 2012, p.193). Symbolic capital defined as 'a reputation for competence and an image of respectability and honorability' (Bourdieu, 1984, p.291) legitimizes power relations. The struggle to gain media access and media attention is one of the central efforts as the media has been regarded in contemporary society as an important symbol processing institution (Ihlen, 2009, p.69). The logic of the political field entails that even authoritarian leaders routinely engage in symbolic struggles to acquire political capital or maintain their political legitimacy.

Power may be exerted though totalitarian control, force or more subtly through *hegemony*. It refers primarily to the ability of the dominant classes to exercise social and cultural leadership (Gramsci, 1971). Specifically, hegemony does not operate by forcing subordinate classes against their conscious will, but rather by integrating them into the dominant culture. From this perspective, power and authority are merely understood abstractions created by language and symbolic means of production and embodied in technological objects (Williams, 2011; Winner, 1989). For Foucault (1980) discourses are governed by rules that constitute 'systems of thought' that determine the nature of discourses and the characteristics of institutions. 'The exercise of power perpetually creates knowledge and, conversely, knowledge induces effects of power' (p.52). In this relationship, *propaganda of integration* (Ellul, 1973) and advertising can be used to promote certain meanings and activities representing the hegemonic views. Various knowledge managers, such as intellectuals, media and public relations professionals, shape public opinion through relevant narratives to be congruent with the ideas of the dominant group. For example, power institutions, such as the state, the school, the church, the media and the family, are the cultural agencies and producers of knowledge and meanings for the dominant class. The games of strategy led by elite groups are intended to achieve hegemonic status through legitimizing their discourse to a point that it becomes perceived as everyday common sense.

According to Hall, Hobson, Lowe and Willis (1980), the 'structure of discourse' becomes a critical one because the different areas of social life are hierarchically organized into *dominant/preferred meanings*. Dominant meanings are institutionalized through legal and normative documents and applied according to ideological order forming a pattern of 'preferred readings'. Clearly, those in high-status positions in society will have better chances of promoting their definitions of opinions about controversial topics because of their access to more accurate and specialized information as compared with other society members (Hall, *et al.*, 1978, pp.53–81).

This observation supports the Marxist notion that the dominance of the ruling class is not only possible because of its ownership and control of the means of material production, but also due to its control of the means of 'mental production' (Marx and Engels, 1964). As a result of this structured preference to the opinions of the media elite, these powerful spokespeople become 'the primary definers of topics' (p.58). Naturally, the close ties and relations with the power institutions force the media to play a crucial role in reproducing the definitions of those who 'have privileged access' (p.59). In other words, the media stand in a position of structured subordination to these primary definers who advocate for the interests of the powerful.

Naturally, the constant conflicts of interest between classes producing new forms of knowledge ensure that hegemony can never be absolute. Gramsci (1971) argues that hegemony begins to come apart when the dominant class starts resorting to coercive measures indicating a crisis of authority. Deutsch (1973) also makes an important point that frequent use of negative and coercive strategies leads to alienation and resistance from patterns. If the ruling class is no longer 'leading' but only 'dominant' through coercive force alone, this means that the 'masses have become detached from their traditional ideologies, and no longer believe what they used to believe previously, etc.' (Gramsci, 1971, pp. 275–276). Thus, the abuse of power 'may lead to immediate compliance but will not produce commitment' (Canary and Lakey, 2013, p.116) nor will they produce any meaningful or lasting changes. Subsequently, resistance to the status quo becomes manifested in different acts of subversion, as discussed below. Various subversion practices are best understood in terms of the three most common approaches that will be addressed next.

Subversion as psychological warfare

In psychological warfare, subversion mainly refers to a series of activities intended to overthrow established authority in a country (Kitson, 1971). Historically, this kind of subversion relies on 'the use of information or information technology … to achieve or promote specific objectives over a specific adversary or adversaries' (O'Leary, 2006, p. 252), as well as *propaganda* and *agitation* practices. Young and Launer (1988) define propaganda as discourse attempting 'to conceal evidence and subvert rational processes' (p.272).

In his 'Power Through Subversion', Laurence W. Beilenson explores the ideological legacy of Vladimir Lenin and argues for the use of propaganda–agitation subversion against communist states 'with supplies and arms added where feasible and warranted by the development situation' (Beilenson, 1972, p.21). A future President Reagan's advisor also claims that subversive activities, or activities to undermine the established social order or significant political group, can be used in legal forms of freedom of speech. In this case, subversive propaganda by action, such as the press, an assembly or a political strike, is not intended to benefit social groups, such as the union or workers, 'but intended instead against the government' (p.viii). Furthermore, a criticism of a government is required 'to help a projected overthrow become subversive without regard to whether it is right or wrong' (p.v).

178 Sergei A. Samoilenko

For example, public diplomacy can be part of strategic psychological operations and employ various subversive techniques. Lord (2008) ascribes the peaceful ending of the Cold War to the cumulative impact of Western broadcasting, such as *Voice of America, Radio Free Europe* or *Radio Liberty*, and other public diplomacy programmes targeting the Eastern Bloc. Their programmes countering Soviet propaganda and promoting Western culture and lifestyle were popular not only among ordinary people but even among the very functionaries of the communist system.

Generally speaking, subversion practices in psychological/information warfare can be broken down into internal and external subversion. The actions of *internal subversion* are primarily used as a tool of power by the state within a country. State subversion may use both *agitation* and *integration* propaganda (Ellul, 1973) for a rapid transformation of society. For instance, to support a colossal subversion project needed for building a new communist state, the Soviet authorities used agitation about a new political course and integration strategies for the total moulding of a new Soviet citizen within a new ideology in the 1920s and 1930s. Lasswell (1927) and Ellul (1973) agree that the content of propaganda had to be pervasive in all aspects of the citizen's life. Thus, subversive propaganda must be total and exclude 'contradiction and discussion' (Ellul, p.11).

Subversive propaganda of agitation is also the easiest way to obtain short-term political gains, as it allows one to employ the most simple and violent sentiments through the most elementary means. Woolf (1953, p.313) points out that 'the cult of hatred and xenophobia is the cheapest and surest method of obtaining from the masses the ignorant and savage patriotism which puts the blame for every political folly or social misfortune upon the foreigner.' During state-run ideological campaigns, hatred often becomes one of the most common and useful sentiments, as 'attributing one's misfortunes and sins to "another," who must be killed in order to assure the disappearance of those misfortunes and sins' (Ellul, 1973, p.73). Thus, an adversary must be portrayed as embodying the exact opposite of what is valued in the society (e.g. evil and immoral), or depicted as subhuman or inhuman (Johnson-Cartee and Copeland, 2004).

External subversion refers to actions taken by another country in cooperation with those inside the subverted country and can be used as a tool of statecraft. Using culture to bring about change in a political system through integration of political action can be a tool of strategic subversion in the arsenal of political warfare discussed above. The effects of these cultural subversive activities are revealed over time. They target educational institutions, mass media and various forms of art, as compared to overt subversive techniques, such as street protests or other forms of civil unrest. In addition, cultural diplomacy as *soft power subversion* has been historically used for triggering political change in foreign countries. Helena Finn, a senior State Department cultural affairs practitioner, states that cultural diplomacy consists of 'efforts to improve cultural understanding' and 'winning foreigners' voluntary allegiance to the American project...' (Finn, 2003, pp.15–20). During the Cold War, US cultural diplomacy took the form of 'cultural promotion' and 'cultural offensives' (Lenczowski, 2008) designed to compete with similar campaigns by the Soviets 'to demonstrate their spiritual superiority, to claim the high ground of 'progress' […] in each and every event of what might be styled the Cultural Olympics' (Caute, 2003, p.3). The intended results of these activities are often to discredit the ideas of the ruling class and create polarization within the intended society (Lenczowski, 2008). In situations where the government is not being a good steward in protecting the values of society, the use of cultural tools can be used as a reminder of these values, as well as a medium to challenge the government's legitimacy (Kapferer, 2008). Naturally, in some countries like Iran, the state responds with preventive measures to any signs of cultural influence that appear to be subversive.

Certainly, to challenge an existing power structure, the ideas of subversive communicators must be seen by the public as an acceptable alternative to the status quo. Therefore, subversive organizations and groups frequently undertake political activities other than overtly violent activities. They can infiltrate political parties, labour unions, community groups, and charitable organizations to gain public credibility and obtain money and other resources. Rosenau (2007) identifies three main categories of external subversion: (a) establishing front groups, penetrating and manipulating existing political parties; (b) infiltrating the armed forces, the police, other institutions of the state and important non-government organizations; and (c) generating civil unrest through demonstrations, strikes, and boycotts. As Blackstock (1964) points out, the ruling and political elites are the ultimate targets of subversion because they control the physical instruments of state power. Infiltrating these institutions is important, because as they are already perceived as legitimate in the eyes of the people, and they provide a perfect platform for introducing subversive ideas to the public discourse. Through agents of influence, such as professional journalists or prominent public figures, some subversive agendas become instrumentalized and circulated in the media to influence public opinion.

During the Cold War, active measures or actions of political warfare conducted by the Soviet security services included the establishment and support of international front organizations (e.g. the World Peace Council); foreign communist, socialist and opposition parties; wars of national liberation in the Third World; and underground, revolutionary, insurgency groups. For example, the World Peace Council was established on the orders of the Communist Party of the USSR in the late 1940s and for over 40 years carried out campaigns against Western military action.

On the other hand, COINTELPRO projects run by the United States Federal Bureau of Investigation (FBI) focused on monitoring, discrediting and disrupting domestic political organizations considered subversive. These organizations included anti-Vietnam War organizers, activists of the Civil Rights Movement or Black Power movement, and many others (Jeffreys-Jones, 2007).

Subversive activities are often associated with destabilization, sedition or incitement of discontent towards the authorities. Sedition may include any commotion that is not aimed at open violence against the laws. Civil unrest, however, may be used to provoke the government into a violent response. If the government is unable to deal with the unrest, it may lead to the erosion of state power, which is

180 Sergei A. Samoilenko

directly related to the people's lack of trust in the state to maintain law and order. In turn, the public begins to question whether new leadership is needed. In his analysis of subversion tactics of radical populists in underground St. Petersburg in nineteenth-century Russia, Ely (2016) argues that urban-based campaigns of 'disorganization' used very effective forms of organization, including street smarts and fellow travellers, disguise, urban navigation, conspiracy apartments, etc. The use of these techniques enabled the populists to carry out effective strikes, scattered armed conflicts with the police and jailbreaks, which added to their legitimacy as a powerful force. Eventually, these subversive actions lead to planned destabilization of the autocratic rule and the rise of the revolutionary movement in Russia.

At the same time, subversion campaigns can be disguised under various forms of *white propaganda* (Jowett and O'Donnell, 2014), especially when information comes from trusted sources and tends to be accurate. It may involve multiple grassroots initiatives or social cause movements. The use of satire and personal ridicule in mass media is a particularly important subversion technique aiming at shaping international public perception in order to mobilize support for the act and to condemn the target government and its actions. Political comedy can reinforce negative stereotypes first appearing in news accounts, while desensitizing the public to such critique and thereby making it easier for a new agenda to become acceptable (Lichter *et al.,* 2015). For example, during the Ukrainian crisis of 2014–15, State Department Spokeswoman Jennifer Psaki was repeatedly denigrated by the Russian media, including the international television channel RT, and portrayed as a 'dumb American'. Multiple viral flashmobs and numerous examples of Internet folk art ridiculing her started to use Psaki's name as shorthand for a rating of stupidity.

Another distinctive use of subversion in psychological warfare is the use of disinformation (or *dezinformatsiya*, in Soviet KGB terminology). According to Jowett and O'Donnell (2014), disinformation is usually made up of news stories deliberately designed to weaken adversaries, which are planted in newspapers by journalists usually operating in a foreign country. The propagandist may create a deflective source or use a front group presented as independent to disseminate information in the form of a factoid or negative information. Disinformation can also be disseminated using *astroturfing* techniques or the practice of artificially creating the impression of widespread public support for a policy or cause, where little or no support in fact exists (Bailey and Samoilenko, 2017; Samoilenko, 2014). For example, the United States Central Command (Centcom), which oversees US armed operations in the Middle East and Central Asia, has awarded contracts to companies to develop persona management software that will allow its military personnel to secretly propagate pro-American propaganda on social media sites via fake online personas (Fielding and Cobain 2011).

Since the early 1990s, the Internet has become the most potent force for the spreading of disinformation and rumours. Some national governments are alleged to employ hidden paid posters to troll online discussion forums with pro-government views. Recent research has revealed the work of infamous pro-Kremlin Internet botnets flooding Western news websites and forums with rumours and bunk criticizing the Russian opposition and praising the Russian government (Chen, 2015). The Chinese state employs an army of paid online commentators (dubbed the 'fifty-cent army' after the amount they are supposedly paid per post) to spread pro-regime propaganda on online forums (Han, 2015).

In the age of Twiplomacy (http://twiplomacy.com/) the viral spread of disinformation in a form of alternative opinions and fake news is becoming more common. That is exactly what happened in December 2016 when fake news stories triggered a tense Twitter exchange between the Pakistan and Israel defence ministries (Goldman, 2016). The story posted by AWD News, alleged that the former Israeli Defense Minister threatened to 'destroy them [Pakistan] with a nuclear attack' if the country sent fighters to Syria. Social media has made it easier for subversive actors to plant disinformation in the media, as social media users continue circulating fake news even when they recognize that it causes confusion about current issues and events (Barthel *et al.* 2016). The impact of made-up news is enormous, as it not only sows public confusion, but also largely contributes to cynicism towards key institutions (Balmas, 2014).

Subversion as cultural resistance

In cultural studies subversion is mainly discussed in terms of resistance to hegemony. This struggle can be understood as a response to inequalities or an inability to fit into the system, which results in finding other alternatives to mainstream values and achieving a new status (Willis, 1977). Subversion, in this sense, becomes 'exploring alternative trajectories [...] an act of everyday resistance against consciously created limitations and unquestioned assumptions' (Petersen, 2014, pp.50–51). Leach and Wilson (2014a) specifically address subversion in the sense of 'thwarting hegemony of form, of overturning structures of authority implicit in the process of design and manufacture' (p. 5). The practices of rapture of everyday experiences can be traced back to Dada, a movement conceived during the time of the First World War in response to 'dehumanization associated with industrial mass production' and the 'waste of mechanized warfare' (Lievrouw, 2011, p.31). The Dadaists utilized techniques of abstraction and photo-montage of random text and photographs to demonstrate the absurdity of war and popular culture, and interrupted public events with cultural provocations.

In the 1950s and 1960s the Situationists (or the Situationist International), an international organization of European avant-garde artists and intellectuals, followed the Dadaists in their practice of contradicting institutionalized knowledge. Specifically, they were interested in empowering individuals to construct alternative life scenarios to the everyday spectacle created by the dominant economic system and reproduced in media, education and politics. A popular technique used by Situationist artists, *detournement*, focused on subverting the original meanings of images and other fragmentary materials of bourgeois culture into new ideas (Lievrouw, 2011).

182 Sergei A. Samoilenko

'Subversion of purpose, principle or design to some extent entails a movement against a prior state of affairs' (Leach and Wilson, 2014b, p.237). The collapse of the Soviet Union, for example, was associated with multiple attempts in cultural practices to establish the necessary break between past and present and achieve the state of mind that allowed people to accept the separation from the past. This included the revival of interest in the official symbols of communist ideology and in post-socialist artistic work, such as Soviet Nonconformist Art, Russian postmodernism, and Socialist Art (SotsArt). Various artists, including Komar and Melamid, Dmitri Prigov, combined elements of Socialist Realism and Western Pop Art to ridicule and desacralize the ideological symbols associated with the socialist past and to deprive them of their prior meaning and power. Thus, parting with the past with laughter followed Bakhtin's concept of *carnivalization*, which is an act of act of rebellion against authority: 'The carnivalesque principle abolishes hierarchies, levels social classes, and creates another life free from conventional rules and restrictions' (Stam, 1989, p.86).

Acts of nonconformity to established rules are determined by the degree of deviation from the accepted norm of conduct and subsequent public reaction to them. Hollander and Einwohner (2004, p.545) identify *overt resistance* that is visible and recognized by both targets and observers, which includes collective acts such as social movements and individual acts of refusal. Williams (2011) offers a theory of sub-cultural youth resistance in terms of three dimensions. *Macro-oriented* resistance, represented by members of environmental, social justice and animal-rights movements, is manifested by public protests and mostly described by social movement scholars (Martin, 2002). The *meso-level* represents the behaviour coming from small groups, organizations and social networks, which are held together though social linkages within and among networks of people. For example, the relationship between state and society is very typical in the Russian rhetorical tradition and is best illustrated by the common Russian saying, 'assistance to drowning persons is in the hands of those persons themselves.' This is actually a parody of Karl Marx's famous words often quoted by Soviet propaganda: '[T]he emancipation of the working classes must be conquered by the working classes themselves' (Marx, 1867). In a way, this proactive and vigilant behaviour could be explained by a distrust of the ability of government institutions, banks and law enforcement organs to perform their duties. This readiness for mobilization could be viewed as a sign of non-violent opposition 'between us and them,' when citizens often realize that they cannot rely on anyone but themselves and feel justified in resorting to various forms of non-compliant behaviour.

Finally, the *micro-dimension* represents different forms of resistance as an individual rational choice and behaviour in particular situations. These acts of resistance can be placed along a continuum from passive to active. The passive forms of resistance are rather symbolic and demonstrated in everyday opposition to everyday culture. For example, a skinhead's Doc Marten work boots, jeans and suspenders represented a desire to recreate and normalize the traditional working-class community that was deteriorating around him (Clarke, 1976 as cited in Williams, 2011).

According to Hollander and Einwohner (2004), *covert resistance* is intentional yet goes unnoticed – and thus, unpunished – by its targets, but is still recognized as resistance by culturally aware observers. Covert individual resistance may not be influential on a macro-level, but it can potentially lead to increased social awareness that could be reproduced on a larger scale in a form of sabotage.

As mentioned above, non-conformity can be expressed in subversive forms by 'appropriating mainstream cultural materials and reorganizing their meanings' (Williams, 2011, p. 93). Conventionally, humour and satire have been used as a universal response to the power of the state. In this case, being subversive refers to 'questioning, poking fun at, and undermining the established order in general' (Melin, 2009). Satire and ridicule are the most potent forms of subversion for artists and comics (e.g., Charlie Chaplin), and can take the shape of films, television, books and even political street protests.

In June 2017, Russian radical street-art group Voina ('War', in Russian), which included future Pussy Riot members, painted a giant 65-metre-long phallus on the surface of the Liteyny drawbridge leading to the Bolshoy Dom, the headquarters of the Federal Security Service in St. Petersburg, just in time for it to be raised in mocking glory in full view of the citizens of St. Petersburg over the town's FSB (ex-KGB) headquarters. Entitled 'Dick Captured by the FSB', it remained in raised position for hours (Plutser-Sarno, 2010). The performance was intended to highlight their opposition to security measures planned by the FSB for the 2010 International Economic Forum in St. Petersburg.

Another technique of cultural subversion, *subvertising*, grew out of the Situationist practice of *détournement*. Subverting refers to the practice of making spoofs or parodies of corporate and political advertisements (Barley, 2001) often by the alteration of an existing image in a satirical manner. For example, in 1972, the logo of Richard Nixon's re-election campaign posters was subvertised with two x's in Nixon's name (as in the Exxon logo) to suggest that the Republican Party was owned by corporations. A *subvertisement* can also be referred to as a meme hack and can be a part of social hacking or *culture jamming*. This technique is used by many anti-consumerist activists fighting against social conformity and mainstream media culture to create cognitive dissonance among the public. In 2001, Jonah Peretti, a co-founder of *The Huffington Post*, challenged Nike with a request to print 'sweatshop' on custom order shoes. After the email went viral online, it made its way quickly into mass media news raising questions about expensive shoes made by child sweatshop labour. Today's various forms of remediation trace back to the Dada movement supporting Marshall McLuhan's 'axiom about old media becoming the content of the new' (Lievrouw, 2011, p.217). For example, *remix culture* has become an essential element in cultural subversion, constantly rewriting media and producing new versions. 'Through the remix we can take apart and break down popular culture, and through sampling rearrange traditional narratives' (Campbell, 2009). Remediation comes to life through repackaging and reframing of established meanings and traditional narratives. For example, the yellow ribbon goes back to the US Civil War as a symbol of hope that loved ones would return home safe. During the first Gulf War

184 Sergei A. Samoilenko

the meaning of the yellow ribbon began to shift to an association with the phrase 'support our troops' which subtly implied that if you support the troops, you can't criticize the war. According to Reinsborough and Canning (2010), this powerful control meme was used to attack the peace movement then and in the lead-up to the 2003 invasion by framing invasion opponents as unpatriotic. In response, creative activist Andrew Boyd helped launch an alternative narrative by merging the yellow ribbon with the peace symbol to reframe the control meme to show that being anti-war is also pro-troops.

Subversion as technological modernization

Development communication refers to the notion that mass media can create a public 'atmosphere favourable to change, which is assumed indispensable for modernizing traditional societies through technological advancement and economic growth' (Beltrán, 1993). At the same time, Lerner (1958) argues about the consequences of exposure to information and communication technologies (ICT) that can permanently change people in other societies for better or for worse. According to Schiller (1969), 'if free trade is the mechanism by which a powerful economy penetrates and dominates a weaker one, the "free flow of information" ... is the channel thorough which different life styles and value systems can be imposed on poor and vulnerable societies' (pp.8–9). These are not neutral media, but rather quality and results from a conscious design process, or 'things with attitude' as suggested by Attfield (2000). These things are 'created with a specific end in view – whether to fulfill a particular task, to make a statement, to objectify moral values ..., to exercise social control or flaunt political power' (Attfield, 2000, p.12). By triggering public political participation and encouraging practices of knowledge production, new technologies bring new practices and offer new epistemologies that can potentially bring subversion to new contexts.

During the Cold War decades, the information warfare between the US and the Soviet Union used the modernization paradigm to win over the Third World countries. On 20 January 1949, President Truman added a 'fourth point' to his State of the Union address on the US Cold War strategy, suggesting that the world turn to help developing countries and thereby win those countries to the US side of the conflict. For example, *Voice of America* (VOA), created by the United States government to confront the propaganda of the Axis powers, especially Germany and Japan, continued its work during the Cold War to support white propaganda narratives created by the intelligence services. The propaganda efforts to 'win hearts and minds' involved the same people who worked during World War II in psychological warfare (McAnany, 2012; Simpson, 1994). The proclamation of a need to help developing countries modernize set an ideological agenda for subsequent decades (Rist, 1997).

This paramount paradigm of modernization became dominant mainly due to the technological and political power of advanced nations aimed at capturing new economic and ideological markets. For example, the US commercial media companies began to build broadcast subsidiaries in Latin American for radio and television and later to build markets for export of media content to the rest of the world. The Soviet Union, on the other hand, offered its own ideological-strategic approach targeting intellectuals to replace the dogma of the church with Marxism. According to Miller (1989), in 1982, Latin Americans could tune in to Soviet radio broadcasting for 105 hours per week and at least seventeen Soviet journals were translated and distributed in Latin America.

Despite the clear benefits of technological advancement, both Western and Soviet modernization supporting unified knowledge were in fact subversive, as they often undermined indigenous practices by overwriting local knowledge. Inayatullah (1967) points out that modernization theory is more than Westernization, which promotes copying another culture at the expense of its own traditional values. While some people became integral parts of modernization, others, like indigenous knowledge holders, were excluded or forced to participate on new, dictated terms. For example, Schramm, Nelson and Betham (1981) conducted a study in American Samoa on the effect of using educational television. This experiment was a failure in many ways as they found that educational television did not help bring the government closer to the local people, and simply became 'a means of adult entertainment' (p.190). As McAnany (2012) concludes, television was assumed to be the best solution without any real examination of the cultural context to identify the most critical issues in Samoa. In the Soviet case, the forced modernization of some parts of its territory, such as Far North or Central Asia, pushed indigenous populations to adapt to what was seen as modernity, such as general literacy and free public healthcare, but also more cultural, 'colonial' features such as linguistic Russification, and the denial of traditional values such as, for instance, shamanistic beliefs and traditional pharmacopeia for Far North native peoples (Slezkin, 1996).

Economic and technological modernization is symbiotic with the issues of dependency created by modernizing elites in other societies. Many US government agencies were criticized by various scholars for creating development dependency, promoting political ideologies, or contributing to local government corruption in distributing the aid. Frank (1969) argues that the aid from advanced capitalist countries 'did the exact opposite of aiding recipient countries; it instead created dependency and underdevelopment' (p. 69). Other scholars (Escobar, 1995; Rist, 1997) claim that the very notion of development aid is ideological and inevitably reflects the needs and incentives of the donors, not the recipients. According to Dutta (2006), democracy promotion initiatives are often circulated in aid efforts supported by organizations such as the United States Agency for International Development (USAID) that actually seek to create pro-US public opinion in the targeted communities in the name of the development and create spaces of support for neoliberal policies.

Clearly, the imposition of new technological practices disseminating and integrating new norms and values, may be perceived by local populations as a threat to their group identity. The societal dilemma is based on the notion that if the members of the group cannot externalize their identity or pass it on to future generations, their identity ceases to exist (Roe, 2005, p.43). Thus, indigenous people

186 Sergei A. Samoilenko

themselves resist separation from their local knowledge and traditions (Takeshita, 2001) and often resort to securitization practices. Members of ethno-national groups may demand their political elites protect their national symbols, culture and language. These measures are aimed at strengthening their group identity, and thus, defending it from external influences.

The participatory communication approach has defined people's participation as an essential component of meaningful social development in the age of techno-logical innovation (McAnany, 2012). There are several Latin American visionaries who became the true source of inspiration for the participatory paradigm. For example, a Brazilian Catholic pedagogue, Paulo Freire, proposed a 'pedagogy of the oppressed' (Freire, 1970) for self-discovery through free dialogue and 'conscientiza-tion'. Antonio Pasquali (1963) was an early critic of the mass media that accedes to the needs of dominant classes. Frank Gerace, an American working in Bolivia and Peru, was the first to suggest a model of 'horizontal communication'. Finally, the Chilean journalist Fernando Reyes Matta proposed a participatory model for 'alternative communication' which resulted in rural cassette forums in Uruguay and mediated distance education in Mexico, Peru and Ecuador (Beltrán, 1993). In the 1950s and 1960s, Bolivian mining workers' unions established several radio stations through contributions from their measly salaries. 'The mineworkers wanted their own radio station because the traditional media in the city rarely or never carried reports about them' (Vierecke, 2014). Radio Catavi became the first trade union broadcaster to go on air in 1949 followed by many other stations helping Bolivian workers exchange information with other miners elsewhere and organizing union resistance against the authoritarian government. In recent years, these bottom-up approaches have been significantly altered by the Internet and new mobile tech-nologies offering new models of production and collaboration.

New media as subversion tools for social change

The participatory paradigm (Gerace, 1973) has delineated a bottom-up approach for most contemporary grassroots campaigns from the ground up, aimed at improv-ing local conditions by putting pressure on legislators or government officials, or changing the entire system from below. Lievrouw (2011, pp.23–26) classifies con-temporary alternative and activist new media into five basic genres. In addition to the previously discussed 'culture jamming,' these include *alternative computing, partici-patory journalism, mediated mobilization* and *commons knowledge.* 'Alternative comput-ing' combines technical expertise with explicit ethical commitments for personal amusement or criminal purposes. It is represented by *hacktivism*, aimed at expos-ing institutional or corporate wrongdoing. 'Participatory journalism' (i.e. *citizen journalism*) offers alternative narratives to mainstream news and opinion. Through blogging and investigative reporting, it covers issues that are normally sidelined by the mainstream media. *Mediated mobilization* refers to organizing protests, rallies and flashmobs through social networking sites. And finally, 'commons knowledge' involves creating and organizing new knowledge through wikis, tagging and other tools of online collaboration. The *folksonomic* methods of peer production challenge and question institutionally sanctioned expertise.

These new models of civic engagement allow ordinary citizens to become agents of persuasion and engage their personal networks for various social and political causes. Most citizens now use their inner circles as trust filters to evaluate political information. Increased media attention to the political agendas of independent bloggers and advocacy groups has given ordinary citizens more prominence in national debates (Samoilenko, 2014). In 2012, various organizations, including Tumblr, Reddit, Twitter and Fight for the Future, organized a protest against the proposed Stop Online Piracy Act (SOPA). This action involved 115,000 websites, with Wikipedia going dark for 24 hours, causing three million people to email the US Congress to express their opposition to the bill. As a result, congressional leaders shelved the proposed legislation until they could find a better solution to online piracy and protection of intellectual property.

New forms of free cooperation increase when networked individuals create *communities of concern* around crowdsourced platforms that emerge as bottom-up grassroots initiatives. In the past decade, *crowdsourcing* has been used to organize protests, report on poor government performance, track aid flows or even find mayoral candidates. In societies with increased government control over political participation and traditional media, social media can be viewed as a balancing force to the traditional media. For example, the *networked framing* (Meraz and Papacharissi, 2013) challenges existing theories of agenda setting and traditional framing in the news. A crowdsourcing mapping platform *Ushahidi* was used by the first generation of Russian online activists for crisis communication about wildfires in an environment in which traditional media has been mostly controlled by the state. 'The struggle begins when we see a clash of frames, and it is based on ability to gather alternative data, or contradict data that was provided by government' (Machleder and Asmolov, 2011). Through networked platforms, Russian citizens were able to self-organize around a special issue, coordinate collective actions, and challenge government narratives by creating their own online tools for surveillance and data gathering.

Smartphones and mobile technology help activists to access their social networks on the go. What is now being called *hashtag politics* (Meisel, 2012), has changed the political landscape, giving grassroots activists from both political parties a new way to share their views and gain followers. Like a frame, a hashtag organizes and amplifies public conversations. The role of the organizer practicing hashtag politics is to organize the conversation around a topic hashtag and then curate the conversation to draw more supporters (Samoilenko, 2014). Tanya Kappo (@ Nehiyawskwew) and her followers started the '#idlenomore' hashtag in support for the event Idle No More to address the Canadian First Nations people's objections to a government agenda to impose legislation on aboriginal people without their consent. The hashtag went viral after her followers started tweeting about other indigenous issues. Soon National Chief Shawn Atleo and others called for a march to Parliament, which drew serious media attention. Interestingly, political attitudes and skills acquired online are responsible for the construction of *choreography of*

188 Sergei A. Samoilenko

assembly (Gerbaudo, 2012), which can later translate into real-life street protests and social movements.

The discussion of subversion from three different perspectives helps us better understand the complexity of this phenomenon and the importance of historical, social and cultural contexts defining the scope and boundaries of subversion practices. Additionally, understanding shifting power relations between traditional institutions, individuals and their online communities provides important insights into the qualities of massive, internationally connected groups and movements and the consequences of their subversive potential. Finally, I will discuss a few implications from the history of subversion campaigns for public relations practitioners.

Subversion lessons for public relations specialists

Traditionally, public relations research dealt with the management aspects of communication and Western experience. It often showed little interest in discussing the position of individual actors or understanding why their voices were rarely heard in public and often silenced (Yannas, 2005). This dominant view supports the management aspect of public relations, as represented by *Excellence Study* (Grunig, 1992), *Relationship Management* (Ledingham and Bruning, 1998), and *Issues Management* (Heath, 2002). These public relations perspectives primarily ascribe to a positivist epistemology and aim to producing instrumental knowledge to control and solve systemic problems. In other words, they speak on behalf of government authorities and corporations as the agents of 'globalization from above' and offer public relations practitioners very little incentive 'to give voice to the powerless and marginalized' (Yannas, 2005). Even when analyzing global development practices, Quarry and Ramirez (2009) express doubts about the ability of large institutions to promote real social change without creating development dependency and exerting ideological influence.

Lately, the idea of culture as a series of autonomous and closed systems of meaning and practices has become less relevant, mainly due to the increased complexity of the new globalized world and increased user-generated production. In today's fast-paced world, cultures are not fixed, but are constantly contested and transformed by online communities. Likewise, cultural practices and identities are no longer dependent on their place or origin; they are constantly reproduced in new forms, places, and meanings. Connected citizens and communities are now more empowered than ever before to challenge traditional knowledge structures and push forward their own communication agendas. While it is often inconvenient for governments and corporations to accept those metamorphoses, they are now forced to change to keep up with the fluidity and flexibility of contemporary cultures.

Moreover, it has become critical for public relations practitioners to not only to observe modern transformations, but actively participate in constantly emerging new online communities to understand culture, social norms, and needs. The idea is that public relations is not used to exploit, but rather to assimilate within these communities and become a valuable resource to their members. The naturalistic inquiry, such as digital ethnography, thus becomes particularly useful for studying and analysing the sociology and dynamics of global social networks. By 'going native,' public relations practitioners become part of online communities and start identifying with them. The quality of such integration will be dependent on the degree of involvement with the public and the earned credibility of public relations specialists.

For most political institutions and corporations, social change now is not solely an organizational strategy, but the norm to be inevitably pursued. With technology changing rapidly, these structures simply must be able to respond to challenges and innovate. As every organization seeks improvement over time, change is usually assumed to be a positive adjustment or transformation for the better (Phalpher, 1999). One way for public relations practitioners to integrate the logic of subversion into their strategic planning is to become synergetic with the community of interest and learn to feel its collective pulse. Public relations practitioners should learn how to recognize the symptoms of public fatigue of conventional forms, ideas, and systemic practices, and should suggest a new course of action when it is urgently needed. Thus, public relations should seize opportunities to become voluntary agents of change in their communities.

Clearly, public relations should work in the greatest interest of society, rather than the narrow interest of their organizations. Unlike subversion practices that simply seek to bring down the existing social order and overwrite local knowledge, public relations for positive development should aim at providing sustainability by creating shared values for multiple players in the social field and finding solutions to their problems. While social movements and their outcomes are often short-lived and unpredictable, deliberate development efforts create more sustainable social change (McAnany, 2012). By creating opportunities for alternative communication, public relations strategists should expand people's access to, and participation in, grassroots activities for positive transformation. Active participation in the lives of physical and virtual networks and contribution to the welfare of communities will further determine the success of their operations.

Bibliography

Attfield, J. (2000) *Wild Things: The Material Culture of Everyday Life*. Oxford, UK: Berg.

Bailey, A. and Samoilenko, S. (2017). 'Astroturfing'. In A.V. Ledeneva and International Board (eds.), *The Global Encyclopaedia of Informality*. London: UCL University Press. Retrieved from http://in-formality.com/wiki/index.php?title=Astroturfing.

Balmas, M. (2014) 'When fake news becomes real: Combined exposure to multiple news sources and political attitudes of inefficacy, alienation, and cynicism', *Communication Research*, 41(3), pp.430–454.

Barley, A. (2001, May 21) 'Battle of the image', *New Statesman*. Retrieved 28 July, 2017 from: http://www.newstatesman.com/node/153475.

Barthel, M., Mitchell, A. and Holcomb, J. (2016) Many Americans believe fake news is sowing confusion. *Pew Research Center*. Retrieved 28 July, 2017 from http://www.journalism. org/2016/12/15/many-americans-believe-fake-news-is-sowing-confusion/.

Beilenson, L.W. (1972) *Power through Subversion*. Washington, D.C.: Public Affairs Press.

Beltrán, L.R. (1993) 'Communication for development in Latin America: A forty year's appraisal'. In D. Nostbakken and C. Morrow (eds.), *Cultural Expression in the Global Village* (pp.9–31). Penang, Malaysia: Southbound Publishers.

Blackstock, P.W. (1964) *The Strategy of Subversion: Manipulating the Politics of Other Nations*. Chicago, IL: Quadrangle Books.

Bourdieu, P. (1984) *Distinction: A Social Critique of the Judgement of Taste*. London: Routledge.

Bourdieu, P. (1990) *The Logic of Practice*. Cambridge, UK: Polity.

Bourdieu, P. (1991) *Language and Symbolic Power*. Cambridge, UK: Polity.

Bourdieu, P. and Wacquant, L.J.D. (1992) *An Invitation to Reflexive Sociology*. Chicago, IL: University of Chicago Press.

Campbell, L. (2009) *Dotmocracy: Crowdsourcing, Mashups, and Social Change*. Retrieved 28 July, 2017 from http://www.experientia.com/blog/dotmocracy-crowdsourcing-mashups-and-social-change-ebook/.

Canary, D.J. and Lakey, S.G. (2013) *Strategic Conflict: Research-Based Principles for Managing Interpersonal Conflicts*. London: Taylor & Francis.

Cardoso, F.H and Faletto, E. (1979) *Dependency and Development in Latin America*. Berkeley and Los Angeles, CA: University of California Press.

Caute, D. (2003) *The Dancer Defects: The Struggle for Cultural Supremacy During the Cold War*. Oxford, UK: Oxford University Press.

Chen, A. (2015, June 2) 'The agency', *The New York Times*. Retrieved 28 July, 2017 from http://www.nytimes.com/2015/06/07/magazine/the-agency.html?

Clarke, J. (1976) 'The skinheads and the magical recovery of community'. In S. Hall and T. Jefferson (eds.), *Resistance through Rituals* (pp.99–102). London: Routledge.

Dalton, R. (1987) 'Generational change in elite political beliefs: The growth of ideological polarization', *The Journal of Politics*, 49(4), pp.976–97.

Deutsch, M. (1973) *The Resolution of Conflict*. New Haven, CT: Yale University Press.

Dutta, M. (2006) 'Theoretical approaches to entertainment education', *Health Communication*, 20, pp.221–231.

Ellul, J. (1973) *Propaganda: The Formation of Men's Attitudes*. New York: Random House.

Ely, C. (2016) *Underground Petersburg. Radical Populism, Urban Space, and the Tactics of Subversion in Reform-Era Russia*. DeKalb, IL: Northern Illinois University Press.

Escobar, A. (1995) *Encountering Development: The Making and the Unmaking of the Third World*. Princeton, NJ: Princeton University Press.

Fielding, N. and Cobain, I. (2011, March 17) 'Revealed: US spy operation that manipulates social media'. *The Guardian*. Retrieved 28 July, 2017 from https://www.theguardian.com/technology/2011/mar/17/us-spy-operation-social-networks.

Finn, H.K. (2003) The case for cultural diplomacy. *Foreign Affairs*, 82(6), 15–20.

Foucault, M. (1980) *Power/Knowledge: Selected Interviews and Other Writings 1972–1977*. New York: Pantheon.

Foucault, M. (1997) 'The ethics of the concern for the self as a practice of freedom'. In P. Rabinow (ed.), *Michel Foucault: Ethics, Subjectivity and Truth* (pp.281–301). New York: New York University Press.

Freire, P. (1970) *Pedagogy of the Oppressed*. New York: Seabury Press.

Gerace, F. (1973) *Comunicación Horizontal (Horizontal communication)*. Lima, Peru: Librería Studium.

Gerbaudo, P. (2012) *Tweets and the Streets: Social Media and Contemporary Activism*. London: Pluto Press.

Gramsci, A. (1971) 'Introduction'. In Q. Hoare and G.N. Smith (eds.), *Selections from the Prison Notebooks* (pp.xvii–xcvi). New York: International Publishers.

Grunig, J.E. (1992) 'Excellence in public relations and communication management'. Hillsdale, NJ: Lawrence Erlbaum.

Goldman, R. (2016, December 24) 'Reading fake news, Pakistani Minister directs nuclear threat at Israel', *The New York Times.* Retrieved 28 July, 2017 from https://www.nytimes.com/2016/12/24/world/asia/pakistan-israel-khawaja-asif-fake-news-nuclear.html?_r=0.

Hall, S., Critcher, C., Jefferson, T., Clarke, J. and Roberts, B. (1978) *Policing the Crisis: Mugging, the State, and Law and Order.* London: Macmillan.

Hall, S., Hobson, D., Lowe, A. and Willis, P. (1980) *Culture, Media, Language.* London: Hutchinsen.

Hall, S. and Jacques, M. (1989) *New Times: The Changing Face of Politics in the 1990s.* London: Lawrence & Wishart.

Han, R. (2015) 'Manufacturing consent in cyberspace: China's "Fifty-Cent Army"', *Journal of Current Chinese Affairs,* 44(2), pp.105–34.

Heath, R.L. (2002) 'Issues management: Its past, present and future', *Journal of Public Affairs,* 2(2), pp.209–214.

Hollander, J.A. and Einwohner, R.L. (2004) 'Conceptualizing resistance', *Sociological Forum,* 19(4), pp.533–554.

Ihlen, Ø. (2009) 'On Pierre Bourdieu: Public relations in field struggles'. In Ø. Ihlen, B. van Ruler and M. Fredriksson (eds.), *Public Relations and Social Theory: Key Figures and Concepts* (pp.71–91). New York: Routledge.

Jeffreys-Jones, R. (2007) *The FBI: A History.* New Haven, CT: Yale University Press.

Johnson-Cartee, K.S. and Copeland, G.A. (2004) *Strategic Political Communication: Rethinking Social Influence, Persuasion, and Propaganda.* Lanham, MD: Rowman & Littlefield Publishers.

Jowett, G.S., and O'Donnell, V. (2014) *Propaganda and Persuasion.* Thousand Oaks, CA: Sage.

Inayatullah, C. (1967) 'Toward a non-Western model of development'. In D. Lerner and W. Schramm (eds.), *Communication and Change in Developing Countries.* Honolulu, HI: East–West Center Press.

Kapferer, J. (2008) 'The state and the arts: Articulating power and subversion'. New York: Berghahn Books.

Kitson, F. (1971) *Low Intensity Operations: Subversion, Insurgency and Peacekeeping.* London: Faber and Faber Limited.

Lasswell, H. (1927) *Propaganda Techniques in the World War.* New York: Knopf.

Leach, J. and Wilson, L. (2014a) 'Anthropology, cross-cultural encounter, and the politics of design'. In J. Leach and L. Wilson (eds). *Subversion, Conversion, Development. Cross-Cultural Knowledge Exchange and the Politics of Design* (pp. 1–18). Cambridge, MA: MIT Press.

Leach, J. and Wilson, L. (2014b) 'Subversion, conversion, development: Imaginaries, knowledge forms, and the uses of ICTs'. In J. Leach and L. Wilson (eds.), *Subversion, Conversion, Development. Cross-Cultural Knowledge Exchange and the Politics of Design* (pp.231–244). Cambridge, MA: MIT Press.

Ledingham, J.A. and Bruning, S.D. (1998) 'Relationship management and public relations: Dimensions of an Organization-Public Relationship", in *Public Relations Review,* 24(1), pp.55–65.

Lenczowski, J. (2008) 'Cultural diplomacy, political influence & integrated strategy'. In J. Lievrouw, L.A. (2011) *Alternative and Activist New Media.* Cambridge, UK: Polity Press.

Lerner, D. (1958) *The Passing of Traditional Society: Modernizing the Middle East.* New York: Free Press.

Lichter, S.R., Baumgartner, J.C. and Morris, J.C. (2015) *Politics Is a Joke! How TV Comedians Are Remaking Political Life.* Boulder, CO: Westview.

Lievrouw, L.A. (2011) *Alternative and Activist New Media.* Cambridge, UK: Polity Press.

Lord, C. (2008) 'Public diplomacy and soft power'. In J. Michael Waller (ed.), *Strategic Influence: Public Diplomacy, Counterpropaganda, and Political Warfare* (pp.61–73). Washington, D.C.: The Institute of World Politics Press.

McAnany, E.G. (2012) *Saving the World: A Brief History of Communication for Development and Social Change*. Chicago, IL: University of Illinois Press.

Machleder, J. and Asmolov, G. (2011) *Social Change and the Russian Network Society: Redefining Development Priorities in New Information Environments*. Retrieved 28 July, 2017 from Internews Website: https://www.internews.org/sites/default/files/resources/Internews_Research_RussiaNetworkSociety1.pdf.

Martin, G. (2002) 'Conceptualizing cultural politics in subcultural and social movement studies', *Social Movement Studies*, 1(1), pp.73–88.

Marx, K. (1867) *Rules and Administrative Regulations of the International Workingmen's Association*. Retrieved 28 July, 2017 from: http://www.marxists.org/archive/marx/iwma/documents/1867/rules.htm.

Marx, K. and Engels, F. (1964) *The German Ideology*. Moscow: Progress Publishers.

Melin, E. (2009, April 14) *Top 10 Subversive Comedies*. Retrieved 28 July, 2017 from http://www.scene-stealers.com/top-10s/top-10-subversive-comedies/.

Meisel, D. (2012) 'Hashtag politics'. In A. Boyd (ed.), *Beautiful Trouble: A Toolbox for Revolution*. New York: OR Books.

Meraz, S. and Papacharissi, Z. (2013) 'Networked gatekeeping and networked framing on #Egypt', *The International Journal of Press/Politics*, 18(2), pp.138–166.

Miller, N. (1989) *Soviet Relations with Latin America 1959–1987*. Cambridge, UK: Cambridge University Press.

Motion, J. and Leitch, S. (1996) 'A discursive perspective from New Zealand: Another world view', *Public Relations Review*, 22(3), pp.297–309.

Motion, J. and Leitch, S. (2009) 'On Foucault: A tool for public relations'. In Ø. Ihlen, B. van Ruler and M. Fredriksson (eds.), *Public Relations and Social Theory: Key Figures and Concepts* (pp.83–102). New York: Routledge.

O'Leary, M. (2006) *The Dictionary of Homeland Security and Defense*. Lincoln, NE: iUniverse.

Pasquali, A. (1963) *Comunicación y cultura de masas [Communication and mass culture]*. Caracas, Venezuela: Monte Avila Editores.

Petersen, G. (2014) 'Freifunk: When technology and politics assemble into subversion'. In J. Leach and L. Wilson (eds.), *Subversion, Conversion, Development. Cross-Cultural Knowledge Exchange and the Politics of Design* (pp.39–56). Cambridge, MA: MIT Press.

Phalpher, R. (1999) 'Sustaining organizational change', *Engineering Digest*, 23, pp.3–4. London: Zed.

Plutser-Sarno, A. (2010, June 22) 'Towering penis graffiti startles St. Petersburg residents'. *France 24*. Retrieved 28 July, 2017 from http://observers.france24.com/en/20100622-giant-penis-towers-over-st-petersburg-skyline-russia-liteiny-bridge-art-voina.

Quarry, W. and Ramírez, R. (2009) *Communication for Another Development: Listening before Telling*. London: Zed.

Reinsborough, P. and Canning, D. (2010) *Re: Imagining Change: How to Use Story-Based Strategy to Win Campaigns, Build Movements, and Change the World*. Oakland, CA: PM Press.

Rist, G. (1997) *A History of Development: From Western Origins to Global Faith*. London: Zed.

Roe, P. (2005) *Ethnic Violence and the Societal Security Dilemma*. London and New York: Routledge.

Rosenau, W. (2007) *Subversion and Insurgency: RAND Counterinsurgency Study*. Paper 2. Occasional Papers. Santa Monica, CA: RAND Corporation.

Saeed, S. (2012) Political fields and religious movements: The exclusion of the Ahmadiyya community in Pakistan. *Political Power and Social Theory*, 23, pp. 189–223.

Samoilenko, S. (2014) 'Campaigns, grassroots'. In K. Harvey (ed.), *Encyclopedia of Social Media and Politics*, 1, pp.189–193). Thousand Oaks, CA: SAGE Publications, Inc.

Schiller, H. (1969) *Mass Communication and American Empire*. Boston: Beacon Press.

Schramm, W., Nelson, L.M. and Betham, M.T. (1981) *Bold Experiment: The Story of Educational Television in American Samoa*. Stanford, CA: Stanford University Press.

Simpson, C. (1994) *Science of Coercion: Communication Research and Psychological Warfare, 1945–1960*. New York: Oxford University Press.

Slezkin, Y. (1996) *Arctic Mirrors: Russia and the Small Peoples of the North*. Ithaca, NY: Cornell University Press.

Stam, R. (1989) *Subversive Pleasures: Bakhtin, Cultural Criticism and Film*. Baltimore, MD: The Johns Hopkins University Press.

Takeshita, C. (2001) 'Bioprospecting and its discontents: Indigenous resistances as legitimate politics', *Alternatives: Global, Local, Political*, 26(3), pp.259–282.

Vierecke, L. (2014, December 29) *Village Voices*. Retrieved 28 July, 2017 from https://www.dandc.eu/en/article/why-community-radios-matter-so-much-indigenous-people-bolivia.

Williams, J.P. (2011) *Subcultural Theory: Traditions and Concepts*. Cambridge, UK: Polity Press.

Willis, P.E. (1977) *Learning to Labor: How Working-Class Kids Get Working-Class Jobs*. New York: Columbia University Press.

Winner, L. (1989) *The Whale and the Reactor: A Search for Limits in the Age of High Technology*. Chicago, IL: University of Chicago Press.

Woolf, L. (1953) *Principia Politica*. London: Hogarth.

Yannas, P. (2005) *PR Theory and Education in the Age of Globalization*. Presented at 'Public Communication and Globalization: Education in the Value of Democracy' conference; Sofia, Bulgaria.

Young, M.J. and Launer, M.K. (1988) *Flights of Fancy, Flight of Doom: KAL 007 and Soviet-American Rhetoric*. Lanham, MD: United Press of America, Inc.

15

ANALYSING TERRORIST USE OF PUBLIC RELATIONS

ISIS and Al Qaeda

Greg Simons

A symbiotic relationship existing between the mass media and terrorism has been noted by observers for some time (Wilkinson, 1997). Mass media can consciously or unwittingly promote terrorism through its emphasis on projecting fear and an uncertain future to media consumers (Altheide, 2007). Other similarities to other means and tools of communication have been noted too. Although it may seem strange to include public relations and terrorism in the same context, there is some logic in doing so. 'Both promote ideas and events, symbolic and otherwise, designed to generate media coverage. Both share the need to create a drama to tell a story in an often hostile and unsympathetic world. [...] Both, in sum, share the common objectives of commanding attention, delivering a message, and influencing opinion' (Rada, 1985, 26). It has been said that publicity is the oxygen of terrorism.

One of the factors that motivates terrorists to engage in communication is to try and offset their weaker tangible military strength by affecting audience perception and opinion of their power (Bockstette, 2009). Is it feasible to apply the lens of public relations to the communication strategy and practice of such terrorist organisations as Islamic State and al Qaeda in order to inform the logic of the messaging? Al Qaeda and ISIS have both been selected from a rather broad market of different terrorist organizations and brands as they both maintain a high-profile brand and reputation, and their expertise in communication is well recognized too. As such, they are the organizations in which it is most likely to find evidence of public relations practice.

Public relations is best understood within a political or business environment, but it is increasingly being applied to armed conflict. The bridge from public relations to terrorism can be found in the political aspects of the natural aims and goals of terrorists. It has been noted that terrorism can be best understood through 'its discursive elements of identity, identification, power and narrative advocacy statements on theme and variation' (Heath and Waymer, 2014, p.227). Bearing this in mind, acts of terrorism have been described as being 'disasters created for public relations, realistically calculated and managed interventions, strategically guided by a new but increasingly influential fundamentalist realpolitik' (Richards, 2004, p.172).

This chapter shall begin by initially outlining some key definitions that are used, such as public relations and terrorism, both of which are widely interpreted and controversial terms. With the definitions clarified, the next step is to explore the communication value of acts of terrorism. The links between public relations and terrorism will be analysed by a literature review, and in particular the words and deeds of al Qaeda and Islamic State will be examined with public relations as a lens.

What is public relations?

Kevin Maloney (2006, p.15) states that 'public relations is such a pervasive activity in our society today that it is impossible for a citizen or consumer to avoid.' The implication is that public relations is 'everywhere' in our day to day lives. It shapes our perceptions, opinions and relationships. The term 'public relations' is very widely understood, as is the practice. In research, it has been shown that there are a multitude of definitions; a study of definitions from 1900–1976 demonstrated that there were 472 definitions in existence (Butterick, 2011, p.6). This research gives a hint of the complexity in defining public relations. Public relations can also be seen and understood from a multitude of different angles and perspectives, operating with varied means of communication (TV, radio, social media … etc.), various theoretical lenses and practical applications, which is witnessed in the diversity and range of the discipline in the chapters contained within this edited volume.

For the sake of reducing some of the complexity, some of the crossover and similarities shall be explored. Attention will be given to the more operational aspects of communication. Public relations is also defined as 'the management of mutually influential relationships within a web of stakeholder and organisational relationships' (Coombs and Holladay, 2010, p.3). Others view it 'in basic descriptive functional terms [as involving] the communication and exchange of ideas either in response to, or to facilitate change' (L'Etang, 2011, p.18). Historically speaking, there are different logics for the emergence of public relations as a social institution – functionalist, institutional and cultural (Vos, 2011). Public relations is shaped and informed by the cultural specifics of the human environment in which it is located (Sriramesh and Verčič, 2012). In the chapter on public relations in fiction, Philip Young states that public relations is central to the processes of promotional culture (Young, 2018). He adds that 'public relations and promotional culture are inherent in the creation of popular culture.' The direct relevance of this to the subject of this chapter will be explained further on.

However, public relations should not be disconnected from the real world in terms of its practice and goals. A central argument of Maloney (2005, p.551) is 'that in societies that are market orientated, capitalist, liberal democracies, PR is about giving "voice" to organisations and groups holding different values, behaving differently, and promoting different interests […].' Perhaps a taboo question could

196 Greg Simons

be are illiberal and undemocratic entities able to use public relations in a liberal, open and democratic environment with some prospect of success? Ihlen and van Ruler note that 'public relations is often studied from a managerial, instrumental perspective or a psychological, behavioural perspective. To understand the role of public relations in building trust or mistrust and to develop – or destroy – a licence to operate, it needs also to be studied as a social phenomenon' (2007, p.243). This has led some in public relations research to bring Bourdieu (1992) into their research in order to understand the meaning of social attributes through understanding the context of the relationships in which they are relevant, stressing that 'these relationships exist within fields, where members of a particular group practice according to unconscious rules and norms informed by habitus' (Edwards, 2006, p.229). In doing so, the structures and systems of domination and symbolic power that define relations in wider society are exposed.

Those systems and structures of power and domination in turn create other systems and structures that challenge them in order to bring about change. In the chapter on public relations as a radical activity (Ihlen, 2018), the author rightly questions the assumption that this is the sole preserve of the powerful groups in society to ensure their continued dominance. It is suggested that public relations can also be used as a means to call attention to issues of power and inequality. Therefore, the effect is to perform a function that calls into question the interpretation and legitimacy of certain values. An as yet under-researched aspect is how gender interprets public relations. For example, "critical feminist public relations research is both 'critical' (in terms of power relations) and 'political', by speaking about and to the lived experience rather than a theoretical ideal" (Daymon and Demetrious 2014, p.10). It is about being able to overcome structural obstacles and barriers to achieve transformative changes in society. This has implications for the future direction of communications. It has been noted that 'communicators will act as change consultants and project managers. Communication will become more project and topic related' (Zerfass *et al.* 2016, p.49). This concerns an organization's ability to manage relationships and communications in order to bring about change, sometimes in an environment that is hostile or adverse to change or transformation.

This is the basis for forming functional relationships between the messenger and the target publics. The communication often uses an emotional basis in order to persuade the target audience. There is a strong emotional and symbolic component to public relations, but it 'must be rooted in actions to be effective' (Coombs and Holladay, 2010, p.8). From a rather clinical and uncomplicated perspective:

> Public relations is the management function that establishes and maintains mutually beneficial relationships between an organisation and the publics on whom its success or failure depends.
>
> *(Cutlip et al., 2000, p.6)*

It is about managing relationships by managing communications with a target audience in order to attain organizational goals and objectives. Even if there is at times a great sense of optimism and hope in the 'miracles' that can be achieved through public relations, there are various factors that need to be taken in to account. L'Etang argues against the dangers of getting too caught up in definitions: 'I can also see others dangers of being caught like a fly in amber in endless paradigms and want to escape again – to explore public relations practice [...]' (2005, p.524). One of the goals of the public relations industry is to get informational products in to mass media content, and from here the possibility of influencing the frame and perception on public issues, events and processes (Hallahan, 1999). In order to influence perception and opinion in the selected target publics, careful attention to and management of information flows is necessary.

As noted by L'Etang, public relations can be used as a means to facilitate and bring about change in society, however, in the current state of international politics, the state-level of organization does not possess a monopoly on this function/ability. There are an increasing number of non-state actors seeking to bring about some sort of change in society, and the methods they can employ may involve the use of oppositional values and norms to the incumbent system and elite.

Historically, military theoreticians, such as Carl von Clausewitz and Sun Tzu, have considered war to be politics waged by another means. This has more recently been recognized in relation to terrorism too: 'terrorism, like war, is a form of political struggle' (Stout, 2009, p.876). The current level of technology and developments in the contemporary world further facilitate this kind of physical armed conflict (kinetic) with its twin of a war of ideas (non-kinetic) (Waller, 2007). Castells has made note of the dual uses of public relations, publicity and marketing: 'if credibility, trust, and character become critical issues in deciding the political outcome, the destruction of credibility and character assassination become the most potent political weapons' (2007, p.243). Dhanesh (2018) engages in the issue of the effect of technology, the Internet and social media as an effective tool of public relations. It is noted that the emotional logic inducing effects of these media has the ability to overcome rational logic (especially with the use of images – pictures and video), which creates a situation where faulty logic can prevail and affect decision-making processes. This can bring about the perception of a crisis of the political and/or social legitimacy of one party, and the offering of an alternative and legitimate political and social vision.

Defining terrorism and terrorism as a form of communication

The definition of terrorism is an extremely problematic question and a very highly politicized issue; consequently, there is very little consensus on a common understanding and characterization (Nacos, 2007; Moeller, 2009; Tuman, 2010; Freedman and Thussu, 2012). In defining the term, some take the approach of identifying the tactics and goals of terrorism:

- Terrorism deliberately targets civilians.
- The victims and the intended audience of a terrorist act are not the same.

198 Greg Simons

- The psychological impact of a terrorist act is intended to be greater than the physical damage caused. The goal of terrorism is to send a message, not defeat the enemy

(Moeller, 2009, p.18)

This approach reveals that terrorism, as it is used by the weaker actor in an asymmetric conflict, tends to employ military operations as a means to support their information operations. An underlying reason for this state of being is that the communication aspect is a force multiplier, possibly projecting a greater kinetic ability than what is actually possessed. As war is a deeply political affair, where politics determines the outcome of wars (Payne, 2005), perception and opinion of processes and events are the key to increasing the chances of a successful realization of the political aims and goals.

Wilkinson has identified five notable features of an act of terrorism: (1) it is premeditated and intended to create a climate of extreme fear; (2) it is directed at a wider audience than the immediate victims; (3) it involves attacks on random or symbolic targets (including civilians); (4) it is considered by the target society as being extra-normal (i.e. violates norms in regulating disputes, protest and dissent); and (5) a key aim is to influence the political behaviour of governments, communities or specific social groups (Wilkinson, 1997, p.51). Terrorist groups seek to create a demand for change and to offer themselves as an alternative vision of a political and/or social order, and this is done through increasing the perceptions of risk, uncertainty and fear in a society (Picard, 1989; Kydd and Walter, 2006; Heath and Waymer, 2014). Words and deeds are used to create these effects in order to shape the environment of perception. 'Over time, terrorist enactments create and augment moments of uncertainty, risk, and identity formation. These enactments not only address key themes but also competing identities and identifications' (Heath and Waymer, 2014, p.240). The social and political environment and context in which terrorism and terrorists are physically located is an important part of the equation to consider and should not be neglected. Dingley noted that:

Terrorism is fundamentally a social activity directed at political ends and springs from its contemporary social environment, which invariably comes down to economics and its relationship with the social and cultural. Terrorism is a product of its environs, just like any other socio-political phenomenon and must be understood as such.

(2010, pp.110–111)

An apparent connection emerges from this quote, which is terrorism is intended to bring about some sort catalyst of change in a given society. The relevance and links between terrorism and public relations are somewhat contingent on whether there is a focus on the tangible aspects of terrorism or the intangible ones. Research, at times, plays down the role and significance of the communicational aspects of terrorism (Surette *et al.*, 2009). Other researchers attempt to consider an act of terrorism beyond the lens of law and security, to view this as an act of political communication (albeit with the use of violence) (Nacos, 2007; Tuman, 2010).

Viewing terrorism as a form of communication, rather than merely a criminal act, draws one's attention to the potential of the act as a form of publicity.

When terrorists commit or threaten to commit an act of violence against a target, they are working towards a set of very media-dependent objectives: (1) to draw the attention and awareness of various audiences and thereby set in motion a conditioning of their targets to fear; (2) to gain recognition of their motives and to provoke audiences to explore the question as to why the terrorists hate and attack them; (3) to gain the respect and sympathy of those in whose name and interests they claim to act; (4) to develop a quasi-legitimate status and to garner the same or similar media treatment that legitimate political actors receive (Nacos, 2007, p.20). Therefore, there are specific cultural and political roots that link terrorists' media of choice and the content and style of the messages. 'Audience' ('target', in the case of terrorists) reception is also an important and complex factor to consider too.

> [that] lay people do indeed draw upon and construct interpretative repertoires, cultural frames, public narratives, and metaphors as lenses through which to construct their understandings of terrorism suggests that when elites effectively frame public appeals in terms of certain public narratives and cultural frames [...] they are tapping into a potentially powerful set of culturally embedded interpretative frames which lay people readily access and employ in their daily talk and text.
>
> *(Jackson and Hall, 2016, p.305)*

Terrorism is very much linked to the politics of perception. This concerns not only actual and real facts and events, but more the perception of those things; it influences the opinion and reaction of the audiences to terrorists and terrorism. The theatre of perception plays into assumptions of legitimacy and illegitimacy, and competing visions of values and norms for society. Terrorism is a means to an end, which is creating the opportunity and ability to overcome powerful systemic structures in order to transform society; therefore there is an emphasis placed on the current and a projected lived experience and not a theoretical ideal. As such, there is some relevance to the feminist understanding of public relations.

Terrorism and public relations

How do public relations and armed conflict interact and connect? As early as the mid-1980s, an academic noted that 'modern terrorism and public relations share a symbiotic, if different relationship, with the mass media [...] Both share the objectives of commanding attention, delivering a message, and influencing opinion' (Rada, 1985, p.26). Terrorism is, on a theoretical level, intended to bring about some sort of social impact in a targeted society. But this creates a problem with the ability to observe and measure the effect. 'However, social impact is not directly observable so we consider information in media as a proxy' (Prieto-Rodríguez *et al.*, 2009, p.813). Thus, the influencing of the nature and quality of the content of mass media is considered a vital communication strategy. Public relations has certainly been

200 Greg Simons

used in armed conflicts, but tends to raise questions concerning social responsibility and/or unethical practice (Fisher, 2009). However, the exercise of examining the role of public relations in terrorist organisations' words and deeds does come with a certain risk of muddying the clarity and distinctions between them.

An act of terrorism has been likened, on occasion, to a theatre that is designed to attract attention and, ultimately, publicity in order to bring political value to the action (Tsfati and Weimann, 2002). There are some similarities with the practice of public relations that emerge, demonstrating that there is also a certain value to be attained through looking at the links too. Some preliminary groundwork needs to be laid, which can be found in stressing the differences.

Public communications need to be differentiated in two ways, firstly in terms of the distinction between spectacular and participatory types of public sphere, and secondly in terms of the distinction between values-based and power-based modes of address (Richards, 2004, p.169).

The terrorist organizations' 'interactive' communications are a power-based mode of address to target publics to develop a negative political relationship, which utilize the rhetorical tool of pathos (namely fear and the avoidance of a negative consequence) to realize their political goals and tasks. Therefore, a distinct link needs to occur between the deed and the word. 'Terrorist groups as organisations use public relations strategically to enhance the groups' ability (or highlight their inability) to create and use social capital to forward their mission and role in society' (Heath and Waymer, 2014, pp.241–242). To look at the role of public relations from Young's reference to promotional culture (2018), terrorist groups are using this lens in order to promote their vision of norms and values, which inform the relationships with the structures and systems of symbolic power and domination that exist in a given society. To bring this about requires the subversion of an existing structure and system in order to promote an alternative. Within the feminist perspective of public relations, it involves a struggle to overcome the dominant and powerful structures and systems in order to 'transform' society. Sergei Samoilenko's chapter on subversion (2018) also contains aspects of relevance for this present chapter. In particular, where public relations serves a purpose to subvert a dominant political and social order and structures of power in order to transform that society and bring about change. He notes the role of information communication technologies, where social media is a useful tool for realizing the act of subversion.

As such, the pros and cons of the daily lived experience need to be communicated in a way and manner that resonates with the target groups. How does this look at the practical level involving case studies? Two terrorist organizations have been chosen, both of which have developed a strong reputation for effectively communicating with multiple target audiences – al Qaeda and the Islamic State.

Al Qaeda

The terrorist group al Qaeda employed a very deliberate and high-profile strategy to generate interest among media outlets to carry their information products, which

Analysing terrorist use of public relations **201**

was intended to influence discourse and attitudes on certain topics (Lynch, 2006; Ciovacco, 2009). When it comes to analysing the political and cultural context of al Qaeda, which is used to inform their deeds and words, their world view and motivations are an important starting point. 'Al Qaeda's world-view is a hybridization of two (overlapping) components – one is a hostility to US global hegemony, which they share with many other third world political movements; the other is a uniquely Muslim fundamentalist opposition to western cultural hegemony' (Louw, 2003, p.213). These are the central ideas that inform the communications and the actions of the organization.

A series of key, politically symbolic statements need to be clear and communicate the vision and goals to different target audiences; these were often in an emotional, value and norm-laden form. They need to capture the mind and imagination of those publics in order to resonate with them. One of those statements was the idea of an *Islamic utopia* – to create the perception of an ideal Islamic political and social space. This is an important myth as it has embedded notions of belonging, identity and exclusiveness (Payne, 2009, pp.111–112). Another statement of 'reality' was *victimhood and being attacked* – the idea that the vision of the ideal Islamic homeland was being thwarted by Westerners (aka *Crusaders*) and corrupt Muslim leaders (Payne, 2009, p.112). A third statement of 'reality' was a 'logical' culmination of the previous two – *Jihad is the only just response* (Payne, 2009, p.112). It is framed within a religious justification, but the root of it is to bring about a physical counteraction to a perceived injustice. It is a call to action through the communication of an alternate desired reality. There are two other distinct communicated realities – *terrorism as a legitimate tactic in Jihad* and the *glory of martyrdom* (Payne, 2009, pp.113–114). These tactics are justified on the basis of serving the greater good – to realize the ideal Islamic homeland and to fight oppressive enemies. The result is a diametrically opposed set of values and realities, which are communicated but require the persuasion of an audience in order to be physically realized. It is the offering of an alternative identity, a sense of belonging and purpose, which requires the message receivers to be emotionally engaged and in a committed relationship with the message sender.

The group used spectacular and very newsworthy large-scale events to attract media attention and publicity. Although al Qaeda had been in existence for some time and active in committing acts of terrorism, their fame or infamy was sealed with the iconic 11 September 2001 attacks (aka 9/11) on the United States mainland. This highly symbolic political act (of little to no military value) was beamed to worldwide audiences. The terror group was successful in communicating to at least three target publics simultaneously – the US public, al Qaeda's own constituency and to Muslims in general (Louw, 2003, p.215). This multiple audience and meaning facet has been noted by others too. The 9/11 attacks showed that 'public opinion is galvanised in a number of positive ways: in admiration of bin Laden, in pride at the attacks and the scale of their theatrical ambition, in the excitement at the possibility to which they symbolically gesture of destroying American power, in satisfaction at the revenge taken for the felt injustice in Palestine or elsewhere, and

202 Greg Simons

so on' (Richards, 2004, p.171). These are all emotional factors that can be used to motivate, agitate and prime those audiences, even for different ends.

Al Qaeda's communications – both word and deed – align and are mutually reinforcing. This has been noted by observers of their communication strategy, which does separate them from some earlier terrorist organizations.

> This is not a nihilist terrorism directed solely towards an audience of divine nature. Its actions follow strategic objectives that are repeatedly reiterated in communiqués. At the same time, they make sure that this terrorism can be imitated by others that share the same ideology and used to gain sympathy, support, and volunteers to fight the Jihad.
>
> *(Torres et al., 2006, p.418)*

As seen from the above quote, the deeds were used to reinforce the words of al Qaeda in the form of a mutually reinforcing set of tangible and intangible factors based around a value and norm laden concept that opposed an existing political and social order. The legitimacy and strength of the organization rested, to some extent, on being able to undermine the legitimacy and reputation of their opponent (Simons, 2016, pp.5–6). Communications are intended to affect the relative intangible strengths of al Qaeda and their opponents, especially with regards to belief in the system and the will to fight.

Al Qaeda managed its brand and reputation as a terrorist organization with a strategy not too far removed (differences appear in the specific manner of words and deeds) from a business or political organization. It had a publicly recognizable brand, which was visualized through a concrete organizational logo; it attempted to ensure that words and deeds were aligned; it segmented its target audiences and communicated accordingly. Al Qaeda differentiated itself from other 'competition' in the marketplace of terrorist organizations, with iconic acts of terrorism, a heavy reliance on the ethos of its leader Osama bin Laden, and its attempt to create a franchised social movement based upon its organizational vision and goals.

Al Qaeda's public relations efforts are aimed at subverting their opponent's power and authority by attacking their source of legitimacy. The attraction to the group is in part owing to a fatigue or sense of injustice or anger at the status quo system and structures of power and dominance. Often, it can be those small everyday things in life that can be a catalyst, such as the lack of belief in a functioning justice system administered by the government in Kabul, which makes the lure of the courts run by the Taliban and other such groups seem attractive. Al Qaeda once made a direct appeal to African Americans, asking them why they fought for a country and a system that denied them their basic rights and freedoms, a logical implication being that they could enjoy equality under the al Qaeda system of rules and norms, which they cannot enjoy under the current system. They have been effective communicators, assisted greatly by advances in new Information Communication Technologies to deliver emotionally resonant messages to their target groups.

Islamic State

Both al Qaeda and the Islamic State have been characterized as representing existential threats to the symbolic centres of Western culture and values (Kagan *et al.*, 2016). In some regards, Islamic State (ISIS) has been seen as the successor to the most recognized terrorist organization in the world, replacing al Qaeda in the global marketplace of terrorist organizations (Byman, 2015; Chastain, 2015). Al Qaeda some years earlier gained additional publicity when many terrorist attacks were attributed to the terrorist organization by the mass media, government and military officials, which had the effect of boosting the organization's reputation and making its brand more widely recognized. This precedent has been repeated again with ISIS, which is blamed for many terrorist attacks, which in turn enhances and projects the brand and reputation of the organization with the connection of deed and word (even if this connection did not exist in reality). The effect of this attribution is to create and sustain an organizational myth, which is kept alive and perpetuated by the target audiences (Burke, 2015). In order to understand these organizations' communication strategies and approach, there is a need to understand what ISIS rhetorically stands for in terms of values and goals.

According to the Media Operative manual, ISIS has three main information principles: (1) present an alternative narrative, a comprehensive offer of existence; (2) counter the 'intellectual invasion' conducted by mainstream news media; (3) launch propaganda 'projectiles' against their opponents (Winter, 2017). As with al Qaeda, ISIS positions itself as being in opposition to corrupt ideals and practices in favour of building a utopian Islamic society. But they maintain a much more rigid control of their brand and reputation. ISIS explains its position as being a defensive posture that is intended to right historical injustices and to work towards the construction of an idealised state – the caliphate. There are both positive and negative aspects to the political relationships that they intend to form with different publics.

The negative relationship is formed against the 'internal' (namely what they see as corrupt and/or impure governments) and the external enemies (those that support the internal enemy and hold views and/or policies that contradict ISIS aims and goals). Other negative relationships and motivations involve senses of 'empowering' those otherwise powerless people to 'right' perceived injustices (political, religious, social etc.). The positive relationships involve those recruited to help build the utopian Islamic state, which gives a sense of purpose and belonging to people that may not experience those feelings in the Western world. Thus, in word and deed, ISIS wants to project itself as standing for creating an ideal and pure Islamic society, and as opposing different injustices (Simons, 2016; Simons and Sillanpaa, 2016). How did ISIS package its informational product in order to attract publicity?

Where al Qaeda gained media publicity and public notoriety by enacting large-scale acts of terrorism as public spectacles (such as 9/11), ISIS gained their notoriety through a much smaller-scale, but personal level, of media-ready infotainment with different gruesome methods of executing people, and by enforcing a very strict and conservative lifestyle. The group has been very successful at self-promoting communications, which centre on its reputation and brand. The group varies its communication style and content according to the nature of the target group. Videos featuring more gore and blood are used to target groups and areas of the Middle East, but these are edited to present a more cleaned up and refined version to the Western world (Sarno, 2016). Some commentators have noted the apparent contradictions of how they communicate with the organizational goals.

ISIS is a group that has learned to promote itself using well-planned marketing and public relations. They have learned to present themselves using very sophisticated public relations approaches and methods. While their cause may not be acceptable to us, they use it in the way that increases their brand with their target market and public relations specialists can learn from their tactics. ISIS may want to re-emerge in the world in a less enlightened time, and they are doing it with the full force and power of the digital age (ibid.).

ISIS' communication strategy is intended to bring about the organizational goals of social and political change within a defined area of the Middle East and Mediterranean; it is the intangible means intended to bring about a tangible goal. As with al Qaeda, ISIS have their own in-built media and communication department that turns out a steady flow of informational product, ready to be transmitted and communicated. A great deal of effort is made to ingrain symbolic meaning in their media products, which are intended to have a significant psychological impact to inspire and mobilize their target audience (Greenberg, 2014). The success of ISIS rests on a number of different factors: the existence of discontent and/or isolated individuals and groups to connect with via their message of belonging and a sense of purpose, or a thirst for revenge for perceived or actual injustices; they also need to be successful on the physical battlefield as this makes the group more appealing than fighting for what may appear to be a losing cause.

ISIS has been effective in getting their message across by the strategy of communicating the faults and the injustices of the day to day living experience in enemy societies. The intention is to demonize the socially constructed enemy figure and to inspire followers, supporters and recruits. They also project their particular vision of a utopian society based on a new set of rules and values to give their sympathizers and members something to aspire to. These messages (in picture and video format) have a significant emotional effect on the target audiences. One observer stated that 'ISIS is winning the war on social media with effective branding, information distribution, and agenda-setting' (Alexander, 2017). In terms of expressing daily living experience, ISIS makes considerable use of video material, which appears on social media. These videos vary greatly in nature and content, the most famous being the beheadings (and other gruesome deaths), which can be intended to instil fear in the enemy, but also to offer an outlet for those potential recruits and supporters to indulge in satisfying some sense of 'justice' for a real or perceived injustice committed by their enemy. Battle scenes are also part of the offering, but there are others that project the building of a new utopian society and in doing so attempt to attract citizens and workers to build the new state. A very deliberate approach is followed. 'The Islamic State brand must be implicitly positive, an offer of an attractive lifestyle as well as an outright rejection of the status quo' (Winter, 2017).

Conclusion

Whether or not terrorist groups use public relations is a somewhat controversial and perhaps even a taboo question. This perhaps relates to an emotional reaction to the intent and possible consequences of the communication. Therefore, a greater level of psychological comfort may be experienced by dismissing the communication as being propaganda and not public relations. This is because propaganda is believed to be what the 'other' does and not what 'we' do.

The question posed at the beginning of this chapter was: is it feasible to apply the lens of public relations to the communication strategy and practice of such terrorist organizations as ISIS and al Qaeda in order to inform an understanding of the logic of their messaging? Following from the critical feminist perspective on public relations, terrorist communications are both critical and political in nature. It should also be recognized that their communications are distinctly project and topic related in nature. Within the context of this chapter, public relations is defined as being a strategic management process that establishes and maintains reciprocal relationships between an organization and its publics, which is critical for the success of that organization. This involves the imparting of information to the public, an attempt at persuasion to modify the behaviour and opinion of those publics, and to integrate attitudes and actions within the target public in trying to facilitate some sort of social and/or political change in a given society. In order to enact these aspects, publicity is needed to provoke mass media to broadcast a set of messages to the target publics. In the case of the terrorist organizations that were analysed, an obstructive marketing approach was undertaken, by offering their ideas, values and norms as a viable set of alternatives to the tangibly more powerful governments and social systems that they seek to overthrow. The information approach was intended to serve as a force and strength multiplier in this asymmetric struggle.

The feminist perspective on public relations informs the terrorists' use of it quite well, especially in terms of the critical approach. This is related to the issue of breaking the dominance of a structure and/or system by altering the perception of the existing power relations in a particular society. It is attempted by breaking the unconscious rules and norms that occupy a particular habitus, by eroding the perception of trust and bonds that exist between the powerful and powerless. With the erosion of this relationship it can be possible to challenge the powerful, eventually overcoming structural obstacles and barriers to transformation (if successful). Public relations potentially offers an avenue for even illiberal and undemocratic entities to have their voice heard. This will resonate if it strikes the right note at the right time, appealing to emotional sentiment in an audience.

Al Qaeda and ISIS position themselves as offering an alternative social and political reality to Western-led globalism, which is centred around an emotionally-based set of values and norms that appeal to higher human needs (as understood in Maslow's Hierarchy of Needs). Military operations play a subordinate role to information operations as they are symbolic acts that are intended to generate publicity. This is the means by which such organizations attempt to project their influence via the resulting discussions in a target society and to influence perception and opinion by shaping the information flows.

Reputation and brand are extremely important to terrorist organisations, such as al Qaeda and ISIS, as a 'good' (i.e. notorious) association inspires additional funding, support, active participation and greater publicity among those with a favourable view. It creates additional fear and recognition among the enemy publics. Communication tends to be managed at a strategic level in the organization and is a force multiplier, which requires dialogic communication with target audiences in order to have the opportunity to realize any desired or planned tangible result. The communication is rooted in words and deeds that are used by the likes of al Qaeda and ISIS to persuade the target groups that their private interests and the organizational interests coincide and a mutually 'beneficial' political relationship can be formed on this basis. In other words, these are the basic functions of public relations, albeit with a very sinister purpose.

Bibliography

Alexander, A. (2017) 'How to fight ISIS online: Why the Islamic State is winning on social media', *Foreign Affairs*. Available at: https://www.foreignaffairs.com/articles/middle-east/2017-04-07/how-fight-isis-online?cid=int-lea&pgtype=hpg, 7 April 2017 [Accessed 8 April 2017].

Altheide, D.L. (2007) 'The mass media and terrorism', *Discourse and Communication*, 1(3), pp.287–308.

Bockstette, C. (2009) 'Taliban and Jihadist terrorist use of strategic communication', *Connections: The Quarterly Journal*, 8(3), pp.1–24.

Bourdieu, P. (1992) *The Field of Cultural Production: Essays in Art and Literature*. Cambridge, UK: Polity Press.

Butterick, K. (2011) *Introducing Public Relations: Theory and Practice*. London: Sage.

Burke, J. (2015) 'There is no silver bullet': ISIS, Al Qaeda and the myths of terrorism', *The Guardian*. Available at: https://www.theguardian.com/world/2015/aug/19/isis-al-qaida-myths-terrorism-war-mistakes-9-11, 19 August 2015 [Accessed 19 November 2016].

Byman, D.L., (2015) 'Testimony – Comparing al Qaeda and ISIS: Different goals, different targets', *Brookings Institute*. Available at: https://www.brookings.edu/testimonies/comparing-al-qaeda-and-isis-different-goals-different-targets/, 29 April 2015 [Accessed 19 November 2016].

Castells, M. (2007) 'Communication, power and counter-power in the network society', *International Journal of Communication*, 1, pp.238–266.

Chastain, M. (2015) 'Report: Terror attacks rise, ISIS replaces al-Qaeda as top terrorists', *Breitbart News*. Available at: http://www.breitbart.com/national-security/2015/06/21/report-terror-attacks-rise-isis-replaces-al-qaeda-as-top-terrorists/, 21 June 2015 [Accessed 19 November 2016].

Ciovacco, C.J. (2009) 'The contours of al Qaeda's media strategy', *Studies in Conflict & Terrorism*, 32(10), pp.853–875.

Coombs, W.T. and Holladay, S.J. (2010) *PR Strategy and Application: Managing Influence*. Chichester, UK: Wiley-Blackwell.

Cutlip, S.M., Center, A.H. and Broom, G.M. (2000) *Effective Public Relations*, 8th ed. Upper Saddle River, NJ: Prentice Hall.

Daymon, C. and Demetrious, K. (eds.) (2014) *Gender and Public Relations: Critical Perspectives on Voice, Image and Identity*. London: Routledge.

Dhanesh, G. (2018) 'Social media and the rise of visual rhetoric: Implications for public relations theory and practice'. In Bridgen, E. and Verčič, D. *Experiencing Public Relations: International Voices*. Oxon, UK: Routledge.

Dingley, J. (2010) *Terrorism and the Politics of Social Change: A Durkheimian Analysis*. Farnham, UK: Ashgate.

Edwards, L. (2006) 'Rethinking power in public relations', *Public Relations Review*, 32, pp.229–231.

Fisher, J.R. (2009) 'Public relations and war: Socially responsible or unethical', *Journal of International Business Disciplines*, 4(1), November, pp.54–67.

Freedman, D. and Thussu, D.K. (eds.) (2012) *Media and Terrorism: Global Perspectives*. London: Sage.

Greenberg, H.R. (2014) 'On ISIS, its uniform, and its public relations campaign', *Psychiatric Times*. Available at: http://www.psychiatrictimes.com/blogs/isis-its-uniform-and-its-public-relations-campaign, 29 September 2014 [Accessed 19 November 2016].

Hallahan, K. (1999) 'Seven models of framing: Implications for public relations', *Journal of Public Relations Research*, 11(3), pp.205–242.

Heath, R.L. and Waymer, D. (2014) 'Terrorism: Social capital, social construction, and constructive society', *Public Relations Inquiry*, 3(2), pp.227–244.

Ihlen, Ø. (2018) 'Fanning the flames of discontent: Public relations as a radical activity'. In Bridgen, E. and Verčič, D. (2018) *Experiencing Public Relations: International Voices*. Oxon, UK: Routledge.

Ihlen, Ø. and van Ruler, B. (2007) 'How public relations works: Theoretical roots and public relations perspectives', *Public Relations Review*, 33, pp.243–248.

Jackson, R. and Hall, G. (2016) 'Talking about terrorism: A study of vernacular discourse', *Politics*, 36(3), pp.292–307.

Kagan, F.W., Kagan, K., Cafarella, J., Gambhir, H. and Zimmerman, K. (2016) 'US grand strategy: Destroying ISIS and al Qaeda, report one', *Al Qaeda and ISIS: Existential Threats to the US and Europe, The Institute for the Study of War*. Washington, DC, January.

Kydd, A.H. and Walter, B.F. (2006) 'The strategies of terrorism', *International Security*, 31(1), Summer, pp.49–80.

L'Etang, J. (2011) *Public Relations: Concepts, Practice and Critique*. London: Sage.

L'Etang, J. (2005) 'Critical public relations: Some reflections', *Public Relations Review*, 31, pp.521–526.

Louw, P.E. (2003) 'The "war against terrorism": A public relations challenge for the Pentagon', *Gazette: The International Journal for Communication Studies*, 65(3), pp.211–230.

Lynch, M. (2006) 'Al-Qaeda's media strategies', *The National Interest*, 83, Spring, pp.50–56.

Maloney, K. (2006) *Rethinking Public Relations: PR Propaganda and Democracy*. New York: Routledge.

Maloney, K. (2005) 'Trust and public relations: Center and edge', *Public Relations Review*, 31, pp.550–55.

Moeller, S.D. (2009) *Packaging Terrorism: Co-opting the News for Politics and Profit*. Chichester, UK: Wiley-Blackwell.

Nacos, B.L. (2007) *Mass Mediated Terrorism: The Central Role of the Media in Terrorism and Counterterrorism*. Lanham, MD: Rowman and Littlefield.

Payne, K. (2009) 'Winning the battle of ideas: Propaganda, ideology, and terror', *Studies in Conflict and Terrorism*, 32(2), pp.109–128.

Payne, K. (2005) 'The media as an instrument of war', *Parameters*, Spring, pp.81–93.

Picard, R.G. (1989) 'Press relations of terrorist organisations', *Public Relations Review*, 15(4), Winter, pp.12–23.

Prieto-Rodríguez, J., Rodríguez, J.G., Salas, R. and Suarez-Pandiello, J. (2009) 'Quantifying fear: The social impact of terrorism', *Journal of Policy Modelling*, 31, pp.803–817.

Rada, S.E. (1985) 'Trans-national terrorism as public relations?', *Public Relations Review*, 11(3), Autumn, pp.26–33.

Richards, B. (2004) 'Terrorism and public relations', *Public Relations Review*, 30, pp.169–176.

Samoilenko, S. (2018) 'Subversion practices: From coercion to attraction'. In Bridgen, E. and Verčič, D. (2018) *Experiencing Public Relations: International Voices.* Oxon, UK: Routledge.

Sarno, A. (2016) 'What we can learn about successful PR from ISIS', *Everything PR*, http://everything-pr.com/isis-public-relations/82906/, 25 July 2016 [Accessed 19 November 2016].

Simons, G. and Sillanpaa, A. (2016) 'The Kremlin and DAESH information activities', NATO Stratcom Centre of Excellence, Riga, October.

Simons, G. (2016) 'Islamic extremism and the war for hearts and minds', *Global Affairs*, 2(1), pp.91–99.

Sriramesh, K. and Verčič, D. (eds.) (2012) *Culture and Public Relations: Links and Implications.* New York: Routledge.

Stout, M. (2009) 'In search of Salafi Jihadist strategic thought: Mining the words of the terrorists', *Studies in Conflict & Terrorism*, 32(10), pp. 876–892.

Surette, R., Hansen, K. and Noble, G. (2009) 'Measuring media oriented terrorism', *Journal of Criminal Justice*, 37, pp.360–370.

Tsfati, Y. and Weimann, G. (2002) 'Www.terrorism.com: Terror on the Internet', *Studies in Conflict and Terrorism*, 25(5), pp.317–332.

Torres, M.R., Jordán, J. and Horsburgh, N. (2006) 'Analysis and evolution of the global Jihadist movement of propaganda', *Terrorism and Political Violence*, 18(3), pp.399–421.

Tuman, J.S. (2010) *Communicating Terror: The Rhetorical Dimensions of Terrorism*, 2nd ed. Thousand Oaks, CA: Sage.

Vos, T.P. (2011) 'Explaining the origins of public relations: Logics of historical explanation', *Journal of Public Relations Research*, 23(2), pp. 119–140.

Waller, J.M. (2007) *Fighting the War of Ideas Like a Real War.* Washington, DC: The Institute of World Politics Press.

Wilkinson, P. (1997) 'The media and terrorism: A reassessment', *Terrorism and Political Violence*, 9(2), pp.51–64.

Winter, C. (2017) 'What I learned from reading the Islamic State's propaganda instruction manual', *Lawfare*. Available at: https://lawfareblog.com/what-i-learned-reading-islamic-states-propaganda-instruction-manual, 2 April 2017 [Accessed 8 April 2017].

Young, P. (2018) 'Public relations in fiction'. In Bridgen, E. and Verčič, D. (2018) *Experiencing Public Relations: International Voices.* Oxon, UK: Routledge.

Zerfass, A., Verčič, D. and Wiesenberg, M. (2016) 'Managing CEO communication and positioning: A cross-national study among corporate communication leaders', *Journal of Communication Management*, 20(1), pp.37–55.

16

EPILOGUE: HOW PEOPLE EXPERIENCE PUBLIC RELATIONS

Applying Martin Buber's phenomenology to 'PR tree'

Jordi Xifra

Experiencing public relations means experiencing *something*. Experiencing is a phenomenon related to something and refers to a philosophical question (that of otherness) that directly connects with a long rationalist tradition represented by many of the most eminent philosophers and social thinkers in history: Aristotle, Plato, Descartes, Spinoza, Kant, Hobbes, Fichte, Hegel, Nietzsche, Husserl, Bergson, Buber, Girard, Levinas and Merleau-Ponty, among others.

Experiencing, according to the *Merriam-Webster* dictionary, has two main meanings: (1) direct observation of or participation in events as a basis of knowledge and; (2) the fact or state of having been affected by or gained knowledge through direct observation or participation ('Experience', n.d.). Hence, we wander through the realm of relationships with others. Therefore, experiencing public relations is a meta-relational phenomenon. This book is a good example of this phenomenon, since each chapter presents a way of experiencing public relations, from the point of view of content and approach, and from a theoretical and practical point of view.

In spite of the multiplicity of philosophers and thinkers who have dealt with otherness, there is one whose proposal and approach to the subject seems to me very adequate when it comes to critically summarizing the contents of the chapters of this book. He is one of the contemporary thinkers who, in a most original way, has dealt with the subject of relations with others: Martin Buber, who, in his celebrated book *I and Thou* (1923/1958)[1], offers the famous example of the different ways of approaching our relationship with a tree. Thus, the purpose of this epilogue is to assess what has been said in the pages that precede it, following the same approach that Buber made through his example of the ways of relating to a tree.

Martin Buber's *I and Thou* has long been acclaimed as a classic of modern thought. Many prominent writers have acknowledged its influence on their work;

210 Jordi Xifra

students of intellectual history consider it a landmark; and the generation born after the Second World War considers Buber one of its prophets (Barzilai, 1998). Buber's main proposition is that we may address existence in two ways: (1) that of the 'I' towards an 'It' and towards an object that is separate in itself, which we either use or experience; and (2) that of the 'I' towards 'Thou', in which we move into existence in a relationship without bounds.

One of the major themes of *I and Thou* is that human life finds its meaningfulness in relationships. All of our relationships, Buber contends, bring us ultimately into relationship with God, who is the Eternal Thou. Experiencing public relations is related to a new religion, the academic one. Working and researching in the field of public relations is a form of survival in the jungle of social sciences, in which public relations is not the best recognized discipline. From this standpoint, notwithstanding Buber's philosophy of otherness, his religious approach fits very well with my intended approach and it is the main reason for choosing his thinking instead of other central thinkers that I had in mind before starting to write this epilogue, in particular Baruch Spinoza and Henri Bergson.

According to Buber, relationships in the world can exist in three spheres, namely: life with *nature*, life with *fellow beings* and life with *spiritual beings*. Buber's invitation is to have an 'I-Thou' relationship, in all these spheres of relationships. In this world of the 'I-Thou' relationship, every 'I' encounters the 'Thou'. The 'I-It' relationship is not a relationship, rather it is only an experience. When I contemplate a tree I get to know the tree but it remains as an object of experience. Buber says that the inner longing to 'relate with' is present at all stages of life. In 'I-It' relationships the other part of the relationship – for Buber a person, but in our metaphorical application of his phenomenology, the other part is public relations – is characterized by specifics like colour, physical structure and similar things, hence the other person no longer remains to be 'Thou'. The other individual is looked at only as an object. Let's look at it in Buber's words:

> I contemplate a tree.
>
> I can accept it as a picture: a rigid pillar in a flood of light, or splashes of green traversed by the gentleness of the blue silver ground.
>
> I can feel it as movement: the flowing veins around the sturdy, striving core, the sucking of the roots, the breathing of the leaves, the infinite commerce with earth and air – and the growing itself in its darkness.
>
> I can assign it to a species and observe it as an instance, with an eye to its construction and its way of life.
>
> I can overcome its uniqueness and form so rigorously that I recognize it only as an expression of the law – those laws according to which a constant opposition of forces is continually adjusted, or those laws according to which the elements mix and separate.
>
> I can dissolve it into a number, into a pure relation between numbers, and eternalize it.
>
> Throughout all of this the tree remains my object and has its place and its time span, its kind and condition.

But it can also happen, if will and grace are joined, that as I contemplate the tree I am drawn into a relation, and the tree ceases to be an It. The power of exclusiveness has seized me.

This does not require me to forego any of the modes of contemplation. There is nothing that I must not see in order to see, and there is no knowledge that I must forget. Rather is everything, picture and movement, species and instance, law and number included and inseparably fused.

Whatever belongs to the tree is included: its form and its mechanics, its colors and its chemistry, its conversation with the elements and its conversation with the stars – all this in its entirety.

The tree is no impression, no play of my imagination, no aspect of a mood; it confronts me bodily and has to deal with me as I must deal with it – only differently.

One should not try to dilute the meaning of the relation: relation is reciprocity.

Does the tree then have consciousness, similar to our own? I have no experience of that. But thinking that you have brought this off in your own case, must you again divide the indivisible? What I encounter is neither the soul of a tree nor a dryad, but the tree itself.

(Buber, 1923/1958, p. 14–15)

Can we apply the example of the tree to public relations and build a 'public relations tree'? What would happen if we did the same exercise that Buber did with the tree, replacing it with public relations? The first thing we should do is look at public relations. That is easy, because it is what the authors of the chapters that shape this book have done. Now, how have they contemplated it? As a tree? As if it were Buber's tree? With the same approaches as Buber? Or with others of their own? A lot of questions for an epilogue.

Firstly, we can say that the chapters of this book show that public relations, like Buber's tree, can be contemplated, since approaching public relations is to contemplate it, although sometimes without respecting the proper distance. When we approach public relations we can do it in different ways, as Buber does with his tree. Thus, following his example it is evident that the idea of 'picture' is perfectly valid for our purposes. In fact, the chapters authored by Bridgen, Fitch and Young[2] deal with the image of public relations. Although the idea of 'picture' works for the tree, the equivalent for public relations is the image it has. In fact, the relationships between people and groups imply an experience and this experience turns into a mental representation, or image.

Even if some chapters deal with the representations of public relations in terms of image – although we can affirm that every chapter is a particular image of its (co)author because experiencing is not possible without a prior representation of the object with which we want to experiment – Rensburg's chapter has a special signification with regard to the metaphor of the public relations tree. Indeed, the title of the chapter includes the term 'anatomy', and anatomy represents the human

212 Jordi Xifra

body as a tree. Furthermore, Rensburg uses the botanical metaphor of ramification to articulate her discourse about South-African spokespersons. From this standpoint, Rensburg's chapter offers one of the most accurate descriptions of a public relations function, according with Buberian phenomenology. Nevertheless, the rest of the chapters also fit well into the metaphor of tree.

Concerning Buber's picture of the tree as a movement, a first question emerges: can we approach public relations as a movement? Edwards (2012) demonstrated this recently. Indeed, for this critical scholar, we can approach public relations as a 'flow of purposive communication produced on behalf of individuals, formally constituted and informally constituted groups, through their continuous transactions with other social entities' (p.21), because:

> The notion of flow captures the dynamic nature of PR and reinforces its temporal and spatial dimensions. It also captures the notion that the people who participate in the flow are implicated in the direction it takes. That direction is not necessarily visible to those whose acts create it, but it forms and shapes their practice nonetheless.
>
> *(p.22)*

Although the idea of public relations as a flow has not been developed beyond the reference to Edwards, Willis' chapter offers a very good example of this idea. When he relates his former experience as practitioner, he is explaining the story of someone who participated in the kind of flow described by Edwards. However, much remains to be done to develop an idea that fits perfectly with the Buberian principles of public relations contemplation.

On the other hand, can we assign public relations to a species? One of my first papers on the field was entitled 'Undergraduate public relations education in Spain: Endangered species?' (2007).

The idea of an endangered species was a metaphor, but if we look at what Buber says, the concept of species can be applied less metaphorically to public relations. Our thinker justifies the approach as a species because the tree can be observed 'as an instance, with an eye to its construction and its way of life' (p.14). That is, it is an element within a system. The system of observation of postmodernity par excellence is the audio-visual system through which the popular culture is built.

Young's chapter deals with the link between popular culture and public relations. As this scholar points out (following the ideas of Rupa Huq), the concept of public relations is also the fruit of the popular imagination, and this is the fundamental point of this link. In other words, public relations can be experienced through mediation not only of the mass media, but through their discourses, fictional or otherwise. The fiction products – or using the terminology of Nothhaft, fictitious scenarios – that are part of popular culture are a media species (which is not endangered). Therefore, when Young states that 'PR is what people think it is, and that what they think it is comes, in part, from their interactions with popular culture' (Young, 2018) he is

Martin Buber's phenomenology and 'PR tree' **213**

talking about a specific kind of public relations: the one that lives in the habitat of popular culture.

This kind of public relations species has a particular language and a singular discourse that characterizes it. Few studies have been concerned with investigating how public relations and their practice have been both constructed and interpreted visually. For this reason, it is necessary to celebrate the inclusion of a chapter such as the Fitch one, about how public relations are experienced in *Babylon* (a TV drama produced by British broadcaster Channel 4). Fitch shows how visual representations of public relations help to understand how practices and practitioners are both constructed and interpreted in popular culture, and also how visual culture constructs and interprets these practices and professionals. It is about this same rhetoric that Dhanesh speaks in her chapter on the rise of visual rhetoric in social media.

Coming back to Buber's example, it would be more intriguing to approach public relations as a law – 'those laws according to which a constant opposition of forces is continually adjusted, or those laws according to which the elements mix and separate' (Buber, 1923/1958, p.14). This description reminds me of the well-known theory of the boundary-spanning function of public relations professionals, who work in continuous tension with the environment and with the need to adjust the needs of their organization to the environmental requirements. But this is not the correct meaning of Buber's thought to apply to our discipline. The idea is another, which in this book is discussed in the chapter by Hung-Baesecke and Xu. In fact, public relations has often survived intellectually by feeding on its interdisciplinarity. All interdisciplinary knowledge implies an opposition of intellectual forces under permanent adjustment. The intersection between public relations and international relations has one of its manifestations in the public diplomacy function. But public diplomacy is not always analysed from a communicational and relational perspective. Public diplomacy analyses that come from international relations ignore its public relations dimension: they separate public relations from public diplomacy. In contrast, Hung-Baesecke and Xu's chapter shows how international relations and public relations share elements and functions, as the term *relations* which they share suggests – we often forget that sharing words means, at least, some (theoretical and practical) connections.

The public relations body of knowledge – by the way, why is the term 'body of knowledge' no longer used in our field, when it was a concept widely used in the last twenty years of the last century? Do we no longer experience public relations as a body of knowledge? Or has the body degraded? – has been constructed in an interdisciplinary way, but in reference to major disciplines such as psychology and, above all, ethics.

Nonetheless, one of the major problems of public relations experimentation has been its alignment with those forms of communication that are considered unethical. Williams' and Bridgen's chapters contribute to this reflection.

May we dissolve public relations into a number, into a pure relationship between numbers, and externalize it? What a hard question to answer! However, the

214 Jordi Xifra

mathematics of public relations is not only possible, but should be possible. Indeed, the macro-research project led by James Grunig in search of excellence, and published under the title *Excellence in Public Relations and Communication Management* (Grunig, 1992) – incidentally, can excellence theory be approached as a public relations paradigm extinct species? I think so – closes with a last chapter with which practically nobody has been occupied and that is surely the most important contribution, not only in theoretical but also practical terms, of the whole investigation. In that chapter, his author, William P. Ehling, proposed an econometric model for evaluating public relations in a tangible (and economic) way. I have always considered Ehling's (1992) contribution to be the most important one in the research on excellence, since it gave answers to crucial questions that arise in professional practice. To be able to economically quantify the results and to know the cost/benefit (economic) relation of a public relations campaign is still a pending task that has not been paid enough attention by public relations scholars, maybe because it involves mathematical knowledge, a common obstacle in some fields of the social sciences.

In this book we don't find contributions to financially quantifying the outcomes of public relations campaigns, but Jelen-Sanchez has shown that academia is still far from the practice. There are many research interests and lines, but there is not a concern for those who can contribute to improving the perception of public relations. And this pending task is very necessary because organizations are the first to have to experience public relations as a useful and effective function for their economic results. Can we reduce reputation benefits to economic terms? For this is econometrics. But because econometrics specialists do not experience public relations and the public relations scholars do not experience econometrics, the situation is perpetuated and organizations can only experience advertising as an economically tangible function that more easily helps – not better – their success as economic subjects.

Neither economics nor mathematics is part of the periphery of public relations that Willis explores in his chapter. In Willis' words: 'as a research community we lack a rounded appreciation of the organizational environments in which PR practice takes place. Developing this type of understanding has yet to be a significant driver of research in the field and arrests our development towards becoming a fully functioning academic community.' The question is if public relations should be experienced accordingly with the importance of its contribution to organizational management.

In his chapter, Nothhaft refers to an investigation in which he and other colleagues argued that the logical structure of public relations was gamesmanship, that is, the 'attempt to win one game by playing another' (Howe, 2004, p.124). As Nothhaft argues, the game played is winning favour for one's good and rational arguments in public 'debate', but public relations practitioners attempt to win it by influencing what is debated how, in which emotional context, in which affective frame. This is a way of recapturing the main origins of the critique of Grunig's dominant paradigm through the application of the (mathematical) theory of games (Murphy, 1991). Murphy's application of game theory to public relations was the first attempt to mathematize the field.

Martin Buber's phenomenology and 'PR tree'   **215**

Although the chapter co-authored by Molleda, Suárez, Athaydes, Sadi, Hernández and Valencia is far from the idea of mathematizing public relations, it is no longer an approximation that has a lot to do with the idea of turning public relations into a numerical relationship, where behind the term Latin America are hidden the idiosyncrasies of each country. In fact, approaches to public relations since globalization tend to result in general conclusions that often forget the local characteristics. From this perspective, Sriramesh and Verčič (2003) present an interesting way to combine the local with the global. This seminal research is precisely like a tree, because it represents the international tree of public relations, where from a common trunk of principles, budgets and contextual frameworks emerge the branches of each country that feed and grow with the sap from the trunk.

At this point, it is therefore appropriate to ask, always following Buber, whether, as with the tree, despite these different approaches, public relations can remain an object of experimentation, if it continues occupying a place in space and in time and whether it preserves its nature and constitution. There is no mystery, and the answer is affirmative, as the chapters in this book demonstrate.

As Buber (1923/1958) stated, 'The tree is no impression, no play of my imagination, no aspect of a mood; it confronts me bodily and has to deal with me as I must deal with it – only differently. One should not try to dilute the meaning of the relation: relation is reciprocity' (p.15).

This statement directly affects the influence of the scholar on his object of study. The chapters of this book are also the result of the relationship that their authors and co-authors maintain with their object of study. At the same time, they are also proof that public relations is not a discipline anchored in time and space; it has to evolve and grow, like any tree or plant. That is why experiencing public relations is no longer immersed in a network of mutually beneficial relationships between organizations and their publics. Those scholars that just believe that public relations is the management of mutually beneficial relationships between organizations and their publics are – or should be – the really endangered species. Nowadays, experiencing public relations is also an act of radicalism and provocation; it is an act of intersubjectivity, in which the results of research depend not only on the data obtained objectively, but on how the researcher has been affected by this object of study and his relationship with it. This is demonstrated by the chapters by Bridgen, Ihlen, Samoilenko and Simons, which contribute to experiencing another way of experiencing public relations. Work about terrorism (Simons), subversion (Samoilenko), crap (Bridgen) or public relations as radical activity (Ihlen), are new and different forms of experimentation. These chapters are radical and critical forms of experiencing public relations, which are contrasted with other more classic but no less interesting forms.

However, I am not able to end this epilogue without highlighting a fact that has always surprised me. It seems as if some of the contributors to this book have experienced *PR* and not *public relations*. Years ago, British scholar Sam Black (1989) complained that it was a mistake to use the acronym PR instead of 'public relations'. I have always thought he was right. Indeed, using the PR acronym doesn't contribute

216 Jordi Xifra

to solving the identity problems of the discipline. However, eminent scholars still prefer to use PR. What are the reasons for this? Perhaps there is a future research opportunity on the role of sociolinguistics in public relations, but I hope that in the future the tree of PR will end up being the tree of public relations, because in the experimentation of otherness there is also the social recognition observed by Spinoza and Hegel. But this is another story that could be part of another book project – or not; it depends on how you, the reader, experience this last idea of the epilogue.

Notes

1 *I and Thou* was first published in 1923 and was often translated from German to English. The first translation was made by Ronald G. Smith and was published in 1937.
2 In order to lighten the reading of this epilogue, I will make the references to the chapters of the book just with the name of the author(s).

Bibliography

Barzilai, D. (1998) 'Homo dialogicus: Martin Huber's existential phenomenology of the human', *The Journal of Jewish Thought and Philosophy*, 8, pp.53–66.

Black, S. (1989) *Introduction to Public Relations*. London: Modino Press.

Buber, M. (1923/1958). *I and Thou*. London: Continuum.

Edwards, L. (2012). 'Defining the "object" of public relations research: A new starting point'. *Public Relations Inquiry*, 1(1), pp.7–30.

Ehling, W.P. (1992) 'Estimating the value of public relations and communication to an organization'. In J.E. Grunig (ed.), *Excellence in Public Relations and Communication Management* (pp. 617–638). Hillsdale, NJ: Lawrence Erlbaum Associates.

Experience (n.d.). In *Merriam Webster Online*. Available at https://www.merriam-webster.com/dictionary/experience [Accessed 11 April 2017].

Grunig, J.E. (ed.) (1992) *Excellence in Public Relations and Communication Management*. Hillsdale, NJ: Lawrence Erlbaum Associates.

Howe, L. (2004) 'Gamesmanship', *Journal of the Philosophy of Sport*, 31(2), pp.212–225.

Murphy, P. (1991) 'The limits of symmetry: A game theory approach to symmetric and asymmetric public relations', *Public Relations Research Annual*, 3, pp.115–131.

Sriramesh, K., Verčič, D. (2003) *The Global Public Relations Handbook: Theory, Research, and Practice*. Mahwah, NJ: Lawrence Erlbaum.

Xifra, J. (2007) 'Undergraduate public relations education in Spain: Endangered species?', *Public Relations Review*, 33(2), pp.206–213.

INDEX

9/11, 134, 154, 201, 203
21st Century Maritime Silk Road. *See* One
   Belt, One Road

Adami, E. 125
Agatha Raisin and the Quiche of Death
   (Beaton) 113–14, 118, 119
Agatha Raisin and the Walkers of Dembley
   (Beaton) 119–20
Agatha Raisin: Pushing Up Daisies (Beaton)
   118
Agatha Raisin's First Case (Beaton) 119
Agencia Mexicana de Relaciones Públicas 158
agitation practices 177, 178
agonistic approach 169–70
al Qaeda 200–2, 205–6
Alaimo, K. 85
Aldridge, M. 72
American culture 31, 102
American Dream 143
An Agent of Deceit (Morgan Jones) 108
Anthony, S. 96
apparatuses, fact-producing 28, 33, 35,
   36, 127
Arbenz, J. 157
Argentina 158, 160
Armas, C.C. 157
Armstrong, J. 97
Ashcraft, K.L. 74
Ashforth, B. 68–9, 70, 74
Ashra, N. 52, 58
astroturfing techniques 180
Asunta, L. 52, 58

Athaydes, A. 152–62, 215
Atleo, S. 186
Attfield, J. 184
AWD News 181

Babylon (Bain and Armstrong) 97–103
backstage of public relations 1, 2–3, 61, 78
Bain, P. 45
Bain, S. 97
Barnhurst, K.G. 126–7
Barthes 127
Baudrillard, J. 128
Beaton, M.C. 113–14, 118–20
Bedford, M. 113
Beilenson, L.W. 177
Benjamin 128
Bentham, M.T. 185
Bernays, E. 28, 31, 157
Billy Liar on the Moon (Waterhouse) 112,
   113, 117
bin Laden, O. 201, 202
Black, S. 215–16
black sheep campaign 125, 129
Blackstock, P.W. 179
Bloodland (Glynn) 108
Blue Focus Digital Shanghai 146
Blyton, P. 46
bodies (images) 127–8
Bolivia 186
Bolton, S.C. 70
Boomsday (Buckley) 108, 111, 115–16
Boorstin, D. 31, 95, 102
Botero, L. 160

218 Index

Botero, N. 160
Bourdieu, P. 54, 57, 58, 175, 196
Boyd, A. 184
brainstorming 44–6
Branch, E. 157
Brazil 156–7, 158, 160
Brexit 131
Bridgen, E. 1–5, 211, 213, 215
British fiction. *See* fiction
Broom, G.M. 86
Buber, M. 209–16
Buckley, C. 108, 111
Burke, K. 132
Burt, T. 108–9
Butler, N. 46

Callaghan, W.A. 139
Canning, D. 184
capital 175–6
carnivalization 182
case studies research: overview 19, 106;
    PR Week 68–78; practitioners 59–63;
    terrorism 200–4
Castells, M. 197
Castro-Gómez, S. 154
CCP (Chinese Communist Party) 137,
    139, 141
Centcom (United States Central
    Command) 180
centres of calculation 27, 35
'Century of Humiliation' 139, 140, 143
CEOs (Chief Executive Officers) 84
Chaiken, S. 85
Chen, N. 142
Chen, O. 142
Chen, X. 142
Chesney, M. 118. *See also* Beaton, M.C.
Chia, R. 40, 43, 44, 47
Chien, H. 141
Chile 160, 186
China: Chinese Dream campaign 137,
    138, 139, 142–4, 146, 147n1; One
    Belt, One Road campaign 137, 138,
    139, 144–7; political ideologies 138–9;
    public diplomacy 138, 139–41; public
    relations studies 137–8, 141–2, 213; use
    of Internet 181
China International Communication
    Centre 145
China International Publishing Group 137
Chinese Dream 137, 138, 139, 142–4, 146,
    147n1
Chiume, E. M. 89
choreography of assembly 186–7

CIESPAL (International Center for Higher
    Studies of Communication in Latin
    America) 157–8
CIPR (Chartered Institute of Public
    Relations) 52, 68, 72, 76, 78, 106, 117
CIPRA (China International Public
    Relations Association) 137
Cisco 124
civil servants 84–5
civil unrest 179–80. *See also* subversion
Clancy, B. 123, 125
Clancy, K.A. 123, 125
Clifford, M. 71, 74–5, 76–7
Code of Athens 29–30, 35
COINTELPRO projects 179
Colbert, S. 31
Cold War 178–9, 184
Cole, G. 109, 116
Colley, H. 54
Collinson, D. 46
Colombia 158, 160
Colombo, M. 129
Colorado Coal Strike 29
commons knowledge 186–7
communication: challenges 82; crisis 7,
    16–17; digital 7, 17, 90, 124, 128, 142;
    management 196–7; power based 200;
    public relations as 2, 4, 36, 39–40; studies
    9–10; terrorist acts as 198–9; visual 129–
    30. *See also* corporate communications;
    media; spokespeople
The Communist Manifesto (Marx and Engels)
    154
communities of concern 186
complexity perspectives 43–5, 47–8
CONFERP (Federal Council of Public
    Relations Professionals) 157
Confessions of a Shopaholic (Kinsella) 112,
    115, 117
CONFIARP (Inter-American Public
    Relations Confederation) 157
conflict. *See also* subversion; embracing
    169–71; public relations in armed 97–8,
    194–5, 197–8, 199–200
Conflict of Interest (Michie) 109, 115
Confucius 140
Confucius Institutes 140, 147–8n2
Conrad, C. 168
conservation strategies 175–6
constructivist approach 9, 60, 68, 105–6
content analysis research 7–8, 11, 13–20
Cooley, C.H. 145
Coombs, T. 147
Coombs, W.T. 72, 109–10

Cornelissen, J. 33–4
Coronil, F. 154
Corporate Communication (Cornelissen) 33–4
corporate communications 36, 58, 156. *See also* public relations; spokespeople
corporations 161–2, 166, 170
Coulson, A. 71, 74–5
covert resistance 183
CPRA (Chinese Public Relations Association) 144, 145
crisis communication 7, 16–17
critical discourse analysis 70–8
critical feminist public relations 196, 199, 200, 205
critical scholarship: concerns 10; development 8, 12, 14, 17; disagreements with functionalist 14; European focus 19
critical theory: and postcolonial theory 155–6; and radical public relations 167–71
critical/cultural paradigms 9
A Crooked Sixpence (Sayle) 110
Cross, P. 75
Crouch, C. 31
crowdsourcing 186
Crusaders (Kelly) 111–12
CSR (corporate social responsibility) 16, 143, 170
Cull, N. 147–8n2
cultural resistance 181–4
culture jamming 183, 186
Curtin, P.A. 8, 12, 155
Cutlip 33

Dadaists 181, 183
Dark Art (Burt) 108–9
Davidson, S. 170
Davis, A. 32–3
Davis, D.S. 72
Daymon, C. 59
Debord, G. 31, 87, 128
Declaration of Principles (Lee) 28–9, 35, 37n
Delphi study 13
Department of Higher Education, Ministry of Education (China) 137
DeSanto, B. 33
détournement 181, 183
Deutsch, M. 177
development aid 185
Dhanesh, G. 96, 123–33, 197, 213
digital communication 7, 17, 90, 124, 128, 142. *See also* media
Dingley, J. 198
dirty work. *See also PR Week*; categories 66–8; defining 66; research 68–9

disinformation 30–1, 81, 180–1
DiStaso, M.W. 11
Doerr, N. 129
Doorley, J. 33
Dozier, D. 155, 156
Dühring, L. 9
Dussel, E. 154
Dutschke, R. 174
Dutta, M. 156, 185
A Dying Breed (Hanington) 111

Ecuador 186
Edelman (public relations firm) 161
Edmunds, N. 108
Edwards, L. 7, 8, 17, 156, 212
Effective Public Relations (Cutlip) 33
Ehling, W.P. 214
Einwohner, R.L. 182, 183
El Salvador 160
Ellul, J. 178
eloquence 82–3
Ely, C. 180
Emerson, R.M. 76
emotional taint 70. *See also PR Week*
emotional-intelligence model (of professionalism) 51–2, 57–8
"Empire of Illusion: The end of literacy and the triumph of spectacle" (Hedges) 31
Engels, F. 154, 177
Enlightenment ideals 30–1
epistemologies 11, 17, 18, 154, 184, 188
ethics: as concern 73, 105, 167; need for research 17; presented in fiction 101–2, 108–9, 113–14; in textbooks 33–5
ethnocentrism 9, 14–15, 22n3
ethnography 12, 19, 20, 52, 53, 58, 59, 105, 189
ethos 131
EUPRERA (European Public Relations Education and Researach Association) 2
European scholarship 9, 13, 14, 19, 52
Evans, J. 128
Evetts, J. 56, 61, 62
Excellence in Public Relations and Communication Management (Grunig) 214
Excellence study 8, 9, 16, 106, 130, 188, 214
Excellence Study (Grunig) 188
Exit, Orange and Red (Bedford) 113
experiments research 19, 22n5
Exploring Public Relations (Gregory) 34–5
external subversion practices 178–81

Facebook 124–5
fact-producing apparatuses 28, 33, 35, 36, 127
facts/factuality. *See also* truth; Ivy Lee

220 Index

on 28–9; and public relations 28–36; textbook handling of term 32–5
Fairclough, N. 41
fake news 30–1, 81, 180–1
Falconi, T.M. 2
Fame Fatale (Holden) 110, 112, 117, 118
Faranda, W. 84
Faulconbridge, J. 56
FBI (Federal Bureau of Investigation) 179
Federal Council of Public Relations Professionals (CONFERP) 157
feminist perspective: as alternative 7, 196; in fiction 98–9; and terrorism 196, 199, 200, 205
Ferrari, M.A. 159
FIARP (Inter-American Public Relations Federation) 157
fiction: Agatha Raison case 118–20; *Babylon* 97–103; defining public relations 110–11; emotions 109–10; journalism perspective 112–14; as lens to view public relations 106–7, 121; public relations dark side 115–16; public relations practitioners 109, 112–13; public relations themes 113–14; stereotyping 116–18, 120; tactics 109
figurality 128
Finn, H. 178
Fitch, K. 95–103, 211, 213
Fitzpatrick, K.R. 147
Flam, H. 129
Flanagan, T. 90
Fleishman Hillard (public relations firm) 161
focus groups 11, 19
folksonomic methods 185–6
Foucault, M. 53–4, 176
França, F. 159
Frank 185
Frankfurt school 167
Freidson, E. 55, 56, 62
Friedman, A. 54
Friere, P. 186
frontstage of public relations 1, 2–3, 4, 78
functional approach. *See also* Excellence study; breaking with 21–2, 166–7, 169; critique of 7; in Latin America 152, 156–7, 162; traditional 6, 7, 8, 10, 14, 17
functionalist approach. *See* functional approach
funding of research 12–13, 21

game theory 214
games of strategy 174, 175, 176
gamesmanship 36

Gans, H.J. 73
Garcia, H.F. 33
Garvey, Liz (fictional) 98–102
Gerace, F. 186
German National Socialists 128
Germany 129
Gilboa, E. 147
global public relations. *See* international public relations
globalization 154–5, 161–2, 188
Glynn, Alan 108
GM (genetically modified) foods 125, 131
Goffman, E. 1, 56, 60–1, 63n1
Goldsworthy, S. 34, 35, 107, 116–17, 120–1
Gramsci, A. 177
Gregory, A. 34–5, 36
Grosfoguel, R. 154
Grunig, J.E. 8, 9, 86, 147, 188, 214
Grunig, L.A. 86, 147
Grunigian/functionalist scholars 14
Guatemala 157
Guéry, F. 54
Gullion, E. 138
Guo, J. 141

hacktivism 186
Haidt, J. 31
Hall, S. 127, 128, 176
Hallahan, K. 29
Hanington, Peter 111
Hansen, A. 72
hard power 137, 138
Hartig, F. 147–8n2
hashtag politics 186
Heath, R.L. 10, 132
Hedges, C. 31
hegemony: defining 176; opposition to Western 201; in power institutions 176–7; subversion as resistance 181–2
Hernández, E. 152–62, 215
Hess, A. 52
Hess, S. 86
heuristic-systematic model (persuasion) 130
Hillgrove, R. 75
Hitchcock, D. 48
Hobson, D. 176
Hodges, C.E.M. 7, 156
Hoedemaekers, C. 46
Holden, W. 110, 112
Holladay, S.J. 72
Hollander, J.A. 182, 183
Holloway, I. 59
Hoy, P. 32
Huang, Y.H. 147

Huazhong University of Science and Technology 137, 145
Hughes, E. 66, 67
humour 44–7
Hung-Baesecke, C. 137–48, 213
Huq, R. 105, 212

I and Thou (Buber) 209–10
Iannucci, A. 97
Idle No More 186
Ihlen, Ø. 10–11, 58, 165–71, 196, 215
I'm Alan Partridge 44–5
image 127–8. *See also* visual communication
The Image: A Guide to Pseudo-Events in America (Boorstin) 31
impression management 1, 60–1, 90, 180
Inayatullah, C. 185
Influence: How to Make the System Work for You (Shea) 109
Instagram 98–9, 124
Institutional Communication, Social Approach to Public Relations (Muriel and Rota) 158
institutions: defining 127
Inter-American Public Relations Confederation (CONFIARP) 157
interdisciplinarity 9, 21, 126, 213
internal subversion practices 178
international public relations 8, 15, 17, 137–8, 213. *See also* China
Internet 123, 124, 180–1, 186
interpretive research method 11, 19, 58
interview research method 13, 19, 52
introspective studies 7, 11, 13, 16
The Invisible Persuaders (Michie) 109
IPR (Institute of Public Relations) 52
Islamic State (ISIS) 203–4, 205–6
Israel 125, 181
Issues Management (Heath) 188
Italy 129

Jacques, M. 140
Jay, M. 128
JCM *(Journal of Communication Management)* 13, 18, *19*
Jelen-Sanchez, A. 6–22, 12, 13, 214
Jensen, A. 118
Jewitt, C. 125
Jiménez, M.A. 160
Jiménez de Cisneros 154
Jinping, X. 139, 142–3, 144
Jintao, H. 139, 140, 142–3
John Lewis 75
Johnston, J. 98
Joseph, P. 99
journalism 29, 30, 35, 186

journalists: in fiction 112, 115; in *PR Week* 72–3, 74–5, 76–8; as spokespersons 83, 89; for trade publications 72–3
Jowett, G.S. 180
JPRR *(Journal of Public Relations Research)* 8, 13, 18, *19*

Kahneman, D. 31
Kappo, T. 186
Kauffman, A.A. 139
Keith, P. 118
Kelly, J. 113
Kelly, R. 111–12
Khumalo, B. 90
Kinsella, S. 112
Kinsky, E. 99, 100
Kipping, M. 52
Klyueva, A. 147
Kreiner, G. 68–9, 70, 74
Kuhn, T.S. 8–9, 14
Kurian, P. 156
Kweichow Moutai 146

Lander, E. 154
Larson, M.S. 54
Larsson, S. 109
Lasswell, H. 178
The Last Punter (Cole) 109, 116, 121
Latin America: cultural studies 154–5; defining 153; foreign broadcasting in 184–5; foreign-based PR agencies in 161–2; public relations history 156–60
Latin American School of Public Opinion 156
Latour, B. 27, 35
Launer, M.K. 177
Lauzen, M. 155, 156
Leach, J. 181
Ledingham, J.A. 188
Lee, I. 28–9
Lee, M. 85, 86
Lee, S.T. 147
Lenin, V. 177
Lerner, D. 184
L'Etang, J. 52, 55, 96, 155, 156, 166, 197
Lewis, J.P. 90
Lievrouw 186
Lin, J. 147
Lippmann, W. 29, 31, 36
Lloyd, J. 29
logos 131
Lord, C. 178
Lowe, A. 176
Lunn, E. 75
Lyra, A. 147

222 Index

Macdonald, K.M. 54
macro-oriented resistance 182
Maharaj, M. 84, 88, 89
Maheswaran, D. 85
Maimane, M. 87–8
Majavu, A. 89
Making Sense of Suburbia Through Popular Culture (Huq) 105
Malawi 89
Maldonado, N. 154
Maloney, K. 195–6
management approach. *See* functional approach
Managing Public Relations (Moss and DeSanto) 33
Mandela, N. 87
Manheim, J.B. 33–4
Mao 139, 140
marginalized. *See* peripheral voices
Marland, A. 90
Marling, B. 98
Marx, K. 154, 177, 182
mass media. *See* media
Mastering Public Relations (Davis) 32–3
Matrat, L. 29
Matta, F. R. 186
Mbeki, T. 90
McAnany, E.G. 185
McKie, D. 7, 41
McLuhan, M. 183
McMurray, R. 69, 70
McNeil, K. 110
Meadows, C. 9–10, 22n1
Meadows, C.W. 9–10, 22n1
media. *See also* digital communication; social media; for grassroots initiatives 186–8; Internet 123, 124, 180–1, 186; terrorist use of 194, 198–200
mediatied mobilization 186
meso-level resistance 182
Mexico 158–9, 160, 161–2, 186
Michie, D. 109
Mickey, T. 155
micro-dimension resistance 182
Middle East 125
Mignolo, W. 154, 155
Miller, K.S. 98, 111, 116–17
Miller, N. 185
Millerson, G. 53, 55–6
Mirzoeff, N. 128
Mitchell, W.J.T. 126, 127, 128
mixed research approach 11, 18–19
Molleda, J.C. 152–62, 160, 215
monkey tennis 44–5, 46

moral taint 67, 70. *See also PR Week*
Morgan, G. 86
Morgan Jones, C. 108
Morris, T. 34, 35, 107, 116–17, 120–1
Moss, D. 33
Mouffe, C. 169–70, 171
Muller, M.G. 127, 128
multinational corporations 161–2
Munshi, D. 41, 156
Murphy, P. 214
Muzio, D. 56

Nelson, L.M. 185
neo-Frankfurtian 154
networked framing 186
The New You Survival Guide (Waugh) 117
Nixon, R. 183
Noon, M. 46
normative approach. *See* functional approach
Nothhaft, H. 26–36, 212, 214
Nye, J.S. 138, 139–40

obliquity 47
occupational professionalism 53, 54, 55, 56, 62
ocularcentrism 128
O'Donnell, V. 180
Olympic Games (2008) 143
One Belt, One Road 137, 138, 139, 144–7
'One Belt, One Road' documentary platform 145–6
organizations: environments 47–8; ethnography 58; focused research 8, 10, 18, 47–8; professionalism 53, 55–6, 58, 61, 62; public relations at service of 166–7, 189, 215
overt resistance 182

Pakistan 181
Pamment, J. 147
participatory journalism 186
Pasadeos, Y. 8
Pasquali, A. 186
passive non-action 43, 47, 182
pathos 131
people-to-people diplomacy. *See* public diplomacy
Peretti, J. 183
peripheral visions 167
peripheral voices 48, 49, 154, 188, 214
personality model (of professionalism) 51–2, 57–8, 63
persuasion 34, 127, 129–32, 130. *See also* propaganda

Peru 160, 186
Peston, R. 76–7
The Phantom Public (Lippmann) 31
phenomenological perspective 154–5
Phillips, M. 54
Pieczka, M. 52, 156
Pinterest 124
PIO (Public Information Officers) 86
Pitts, R.E. 85
the political 169
political appointees 84–5, 89
political ideology 138–9
politics 169, 175–6, 187
Pollner, M. 76
Pompper, D. 22n1
Porter Novelli (public relations firm) 161
positivist approach 11, 18, 188
postcolonial theory: origins/nature
    153–4, 155; and public relations 155–6;
    similaries with critical theory 155–6
post-coloniality 155
post-democracy 28, 31, 35
post-facuality. *See* post-truth
post-feminist programmes 97, 98–9
postmodern paradigms 9
post-positivism 9, 11, 19
post-truth 28, 30, 31, 35, 36, 82, 87, 101–2,
    131–2
*Powder: An Everyday Story of Rock' n' Roll
    Folk* (Sampson) 117
power 176–7. *See also* subversion
'Power Through Subversion'
    (Beilenson) 177
PR (acronym) 215–16
PR Today (Morris and Goldsworthy) 34
PR Week: critical view 72, 73–6; news
    values 72–3; overview 68, 70–2;
    rhetorical devices 73; use of journalists
    72–3, 74–5, 76–8
PR—A Persuasive Industry (Morris and
    Goldsworthy) 120–1
Presentation of Self in Everyday Life
    (Goffman) 1
Press Gazette 72
PRI *(Public Relations Inquiry)* 13, 18, *19*
profession 52–3
professionalism: defining 52–3; dynamic
    practice 55; emotional-intelligence
    model 51–2, 57–8; expertise 54–5; lived
    experience 59–63; occupational 53,
    54, 55, 56, 62; organizational 53, 55–6,
    58, 61, 62; personality 51–2, 57–8, 63;
    role of the individual 56–8; structural
    approaches 53–4; theory types 51–2

professionalization 52–3, 55
propaganda. *See also* spin; defining 177;
    external subversion practices 178–81;
    internal subversion practices 177–8;
    public relations as 76, 111, 138, 141, 142,
    147, 157–8, 205; *versus* rhetoric 131;
    white 180–1
propaganda of integration 176
PRR *(Public Relations Review)* 8, 13, 18, *19*
Psaki, J. 180
psychological warfare 177–81
public diplomacy: China's goal 138;
    Chinese Dream campaign 137, 138, 139,
    142–4, 146; coining term 138; One Belt,
    One Road campaign 137, 138, 139,
    144–7; public relations research 137–8,
    141–2, 213; strategic 178
public relations: backstage 1, 2–3, 61, 78;
    compared with Buber's tree 211–16;
    defining 1, 7, 106, 166, 195–7, 205; and
    facts 28–36; founders 28; frontstage 1,
    2–3, 4, 78; numbers who work in 2; as
    propaganda 76, 111, 138, 141, 142, 147,
    157–8, 205
public relations agencies (in Latin America)
    159, 160–2
Public Relations Consultants' Association
    (UK) 2
public relations discipline. *See also* public
    relations scholars; ethnocentricity
    9; Jelen's study methods 13; Jelen's
    study results 14–22; nature of research
    6; paradigms 9; research methods/
    approaches 11–12; status and critiques
    7–11; theories 9–10, 15–16
*Public relations in film and fiction: 1930 to
    1995* (Miller) 116
Public Relations Inquiry 167
public relations literacy 165
public relations practitioners: as agents
    of change 189; in *Babylon* 98–9; in
    the backstage 1; effect on China's
    PR 142; embracing conflict 170–1;
    in fiction 109, 112–13; gender in
    UK 117; lived experience 59–63;
    personality model preference 51–2;
    in *PR Week* 73–8; rhetorical approach
    131–3; view of 77; Willis's experience
    41–9
public relations research: methods 11–12,
    18–20; topics 10–11, 16–18; Willis on
    42–3
public relations scholars: ethnocentric focus
    8, 9, 14; expansion of research 16–17;

224 Index

pressures on 12–13, 20–1; views on discipline 14–15; on visual representation 96–7
Public Relations Society of China 137
public relations textbooks 32–5
public relations theories 9–10, 15–16, 22n4, 140, 142
publics 165, 196–7, 200, 201, 205, 215
Pussy Riot 183

qualitative research 11–12, 18, 19
quantitative research 3, 6, 11, 18–19
Quarry, W. 188
Quijano, A. 154

Raaz, O. 32
radical public relations: breaking with tradition 166–7; building on critical theory 167–9; defining 165; embracing conflict 169–71
Radio Catavi 186
Raisin, A. (fictional) 118–20
Ramirez, R. 188
Reidenbach, E. 85
Reinsborough, P. 184
relational theory 132
Relationship Management (Ledingham) 188
relationship management theory 130, 142
remix culture 183
Rensburg, R. 81–92, 211–12
Reputation Management (Doorley and Garcia) 33
research funding 12–13, 21
rhetorical approach 123–4, 130–3
Richardson, J.E. 129
ridicule 180, 183
Roberts, D. 30, 31
Rodriguez, I. 126–7
Rogers, D. 71, 73
Rosenau, W. 179
Royal Dutch Shell 156–7
Russell, D.S. 44

Sadi, G. 152–62, 215
The Saint Who Loved Me (Thebo) 113, 114, 115, 117
Saltzman, J. 98–9
Samaritans (UK charity) 67
Samoa 185
Samoilenko, S. 174–89, 200, 215
Sampson, K. 117
Sander, J. 108
Sandman, P.M. 91
Sanjinés, J. 154

São Paulo Tramway Light and Power 156
satire 44, 45–6, 107, 180, 183
Sayle, M. 110
Schiller, H. 184
Schiwy, F. 154
Schramm, W. 185
Scott, D. 142
sedition 179
Seiffert, J. 36
Seitel, F.P. 86
Servaes, J. 138
Sha, B. 86
Shanghai Expo (2010) 143
Shea, M. 109, 114–15
Signitzer, B.H. 147
Silk Road Economic Belt. *See* One Belt, One Road
simalacra 128
Simons, G. 194–206, 215
Sisco, H.F. 10
Situational Crisis Communications Theory 109–10
situational theory of publics 9, 10, 15
Situationists 181, 183
Sixsmith, M. 114–15
SMIs (Social Media Interventions) 84
Snapchat 124–5
social media: Chinese use of 142, 143, 146; effectiveness of visuals 129–30; Facebook 124–5; Instagram 98–9, 124; interventions 84; key concepts 126–8; prevalence 82, 124–5; Snapchat 124–5; and spokespersons 84, 87, 89, 91; studies 125–7; subversion via 186–8, 200, 204; visual rhetoric 124–6, 127, 130–3, 213; YouTube 124–5
Society of the Spectacle (Debord) 31, 87
socio-cultural scholarship 8, 10, 12, 14, 17
socio-cultural shift 7, 8, 14, 156
soft power 137, 138–42, 146, 147, 178. *See also* Chinese Dream; One Belt, One Road
SOPA (Stop Online Piracy Act) 187
South Africa 87–8, 212. *See also* spokespeople
Soviet Union: *carnivalization* 182; forced modernization 185; ideological approach 185; propaganda 179, 180; use of Internet 180–1; *Ushahidi* 186
spin 33, 72, 77, 91. *See also* propaganda
Spin Doctor (Shea) 109
spin doctors 84–5, 89, 115, 116
spokespeople: defining 82–3; dilemmas in South Africa 87–9; duties 83–4;

essential qualities 90–2; performance dimensions 4, 85–7; types 83–5; used in *PR Week* 72–3

Sriramesh, K. 147, 215

St. Petersburg (Russia) 180, 183

Stacks, D.W. 11

stereotypes: of female PR practitioners 98–9; film and fiction 116–17, 121; PR as shorthand for 110

Stevens, N. 84

The Stornaway Way (McNeil) 110

Strategy in Influence and Influence Campaigns (Manheim) 33–4

structural approaches (to professionalism) 53–4

Suárez, A.M. 152–62, 215

subversion: as cultural resistance 181–4; defining 174, 181; humour as 45–7; media tools for 186–8; as psychological warfare 177–81; as techological modernization 184–6; value for practitioners 188–9

subversive propaganda 177–81

subvertising 183

Sun, X. 145

survey research method 11, 19, 22, 76, 117, 137

Svensson, L.G. 51, 54–5, 56, 57

The Swimmer (Sander) 108, 115, 118

Swiss People's Party 125, 129

Switzerland 125

Syria 125

systemic approach 120–1, 152, 162, 167, 199

Taylor, M. 147

Taylor, P. 45

techological modernization 184–6

Ter Keurs, H. 88

terministic screens 132

terrorism: defining 197–9; features 198; and feminist public relations 196, 199, 200, 205; goals 197–8, 197–9; and public relations 194–5, 198–200, 205–6

terrorist groups: al Quaeda 200–2, 205–6; Islamic State 203–4, 205–6; tactics 198

Thank You For Smoking 111

Thebo, M. 113

theoretical diversity 9–10, 15–16

Thipanyane, T. 88

Thompson, E.P. 48

Thummes, K. 36

Toogood, L. 29

triangulation research 11, 19

Troester, R. 85

Truman, H. 184

truth 72–3, 88, 101–2, 103, 114, 131. *See also* post-truth; spin

Twiplomacy 181

Twitter 102, 124–5, 181

UK. *See also Babylon* (Bain and Armstrong); fiction; Brexit 131; numbers in public relations 2; public relations lived experience 58–63; television 44–5; UK-based agencies in Latin America 161–2

Ukraine 180

Under the Sun (Edmunds) 108, 114, 121

United Fruit Company 157

United States: 9/11, 134, 154, 201, 203; American culture 31, 102; American Dream 143; cultural diplomacy 178–9; numbers employed in public relations 2; presidential campaign 131; purpose of aid efforts 185; as scholarship focus 8, 9, 14–15; terrorist appeal to African Americans 202; US-based agencies in Latin America 160, 161–2

Uruguay 158

USAID (United States Agency for International Development) 185

Ushahidi 186

Valencia, R. 152–62, 215

Valentini, C. 132

Van Hoof, J.J. 88

van Linde, R. 89

van Onselen, G. 89

van Ruler, B. 51–2, 57, 196

Van Vuuren, M. 88

Vari, M. 126–7

Venezuela 156–7, 161, 162

Verčič, D. 7, 15, 195, 215

Verhoeven, J.W.M. 88

Verhoeven, P. 10–11

Virilio, P. 128

visual communication 129–30

Visual Communication 125

visual representations: of public relations (fictional) 97–103; scholarship on 4, 20, 96–7; types 95

visual rhetoric 124–6, 127, 130–3, 213

visual semantics 127

visual studies: communication trends 129–30; rhetorical approach 130–3; scope/concepts 126–8

226 Index

visuality 127
VOA *(Voice of America)* 184
Voina 183

Walsh, C. 154
Wang, Z. 143
Warburton, T.I. 85
Ward, J. 67, 69, 70
The Water Clock (Kelly) 113
Waterhouse, K. 112, 113
Watson, T. 159, 160
Waugh, D. 117
Weber Shandwick 146, 161
Wehmeier, S. 13, 32
Weick, K.E. 43
Western societies 43, 128, 140, 144, 156, 174, 201, 203, 205
white collar workers 68, 69
White Paper on Chinese Foreign Affairs 141
white propaganda 180, 184
Whitehead, A.N. 43
Wilkinson, P. 198
Williams, J.P. 182
Williams, S. 48, 51–63, 213

Willis, P. 39–49, 176, 214
Wilson, L. 181
Woolf 178
World Peace Council 179
World Trade Center 134, 154, 201, 203
WPP study 143
Wyatt, R. 71, 73, 74–5, 76

Xiaoping, D. 137, 139, 140
Xu, M. 137–48, 213

Yang, A. 141–2, 147
Yang, C. 141
yellow ribbon 183–4
Young, M.J. 177
Young, P. 105–21, 195, 200, 211, 212–13
YouTube 124–5

Zemin, Jiang 139
Zhangjiakou City (China) 146
Zille, H. 87–8
Zimat Consultores (public relations firm) 161–2
Zuma, J. 84, 88–9